Seasons of the WORD

Reflections on the Sunday Readings
with full Gospel Index

Denis McBride, C.SS.R.

A REDEMPTORIST PUBLICATION

To
JOHN D. O'LEARY
pastor, teacher, friend,
in respect and gratitude
from across the Atlantic

Published by
Redemptorist Publications

Design: Rosemarie Pink

Copyright © 1991 Redemptorist Publications
A Registered Charity Limited by guarantee.
Registered in England 3261721

First Printed   August 1991
Third Printing   November 2000

ISBN 0 85231 132 X

Printed by Estudios Gráficos Zure, Spain

Redemptorist
P U B L I C A T I O N S
Alphonsus House Chawton Hampshire GU34 3HQ
Telephone 01420 88222   Fax 01420 88805
rp@redempt.org   www.redempt.org

Contents

PREFACE

Each week, in countless places throughout the world, large numbers of Catholics gather together in a building. Like many other Christians, we turn up to do something together. The local church, the living community of faith, meets in the local church, the space dedicated to worship, to celebrate our common faith in Jesus as Lord. We turn up in hope – maybe because hope is the habit that gets us there – to take our part in the action of the Mass.

During the first part of the Mass we hear excerpts from the scriptures being read, scriptures that cover an unfolding story from Adam in the garden of Eden to Paul in captivity in Rome. Written at different times, in different cultures, for different peoples, these different readings are recognised by the universal church and welcomed by us as the word of God. We try to listen as best we can.

Sometimes the differences seems so marked, the people who inhabit the biblical landscape so alien, their concern so strange, that we are left wondering what connection there is between what we've heard and where we are in our lives. How can these strange stories of the past bear upon our present lives? Our attention spans vary; we can hold on only for so long; we can become bored easily. Our response of "Thanks be to God" at the end of some readings may be muttered more in relief than gratitude.

At other times, however, some passage may be heard as a word addressed to us, because the people introduced and the issues raised appear so close to our own struggles in life. In their pain we can see something of our own; in their halting efforts we find encouragement to carry on. At times like these we feel lucky, graced, challenged. Our hearts are warmed, our minds are fed, our sense of belonging is deepened, and we are drawn into a moral climate of conviction.

We all know that the word of God does not work automatically: it has to be worked on, opened up, wrestled with, prayed about. Sometimes, perhaps not as often as it should, the homily bridges the gap between what the readings say and where we are.

The scriptures work best when there is a moment of recognition between the revealed word of God and our ordinary lives. Our concrete experience is the point of contact between ourselves and God. God's word is not just about the action of God but about the *interaction* between who he is and who we are, between what he offers and what we bring to the experience. Although we return to the same words again and again, *we* are different; our stories have changed, however little, for better or worse. New experience and new insight can help us to understand old words anew. Just as the word of God can illuminate our experience, so our growing experience can throw light on the word of God. This is not to dismiss faith and create a god out of the stuff of experience; it is only to recognise our human limits, that we can understand and believe only from where we are.

The reflections that follow are offered as one way among many of understanding the scriptural readings. The majority were originally written to help preachers in their weekly task of preparing the homily, and were first published in eleven quarterly volumes of the *Living Word,* the homily service of Redemptorist Publications. About thirty of the pieces are published here for the first time, to cover the complete cycle of liturgical readings.

These reflections are now aimed at a wider readership, in the hope that they might be of some service to the growing number of individuals and groups who make time to study and pray the scriptures.

Behind all our efforts is our common desire to come closer to the person of Jesus of Nazareth. In the words of the first letter of John, "the Word, who is life, this is our subject." We want to deepen our faith in him and our understanding of his values, and allow the Spirit's power to make a gradual difference in our unfinished lives. My hope is that this book will play some small part in this lifelong enterprise.

Finally, I would like to express my special thanks to my confrere John Trenchard CSSR for suggesting and supporting the original venture; Redemptorist Publications for risking it; Rosemary Gallagher, my patient editor, for seeing it through; Roger Smith, a giant of equanimity, for redesigning the whole work; Rosemarie Pink for enduring seasons of typesetting; and Sr Myra Cumming SHCJ for reading and correcting the proofs.

THE SEASON OF ADVENT

At the ready

Doing nothing

One of the great American characters of the early nineteenth century was Daniel Webster, a famous lawyer and statesman. Although he ran unsuccessfully for the presidency, his speeches were celebrated for their clarity and wit. When people asked him why he worked so hard he told the story of an incident that happened when he was a child at home on a poor farm in New Hampshire. His father left him and his brother Ezekiel for the day with instructions on the work they had to do. When his father returned and saw the work undone he questioned his sons about their laziness. "What have you been doing, Ezekiel?"

"Nothing, sir," replied Ezekiel.

"Well, Daniel, what have you been doing?"

"I've been helping Ezekiel, sir."

Doing nothing may present an attractive face in childhood stories but it gets sharp treatment in the biblical writings. We are told often that we must be alert and be ready. But ready for what? At this time of the year people are trying to get ready for Christmas, for winter, for cars that won't start, and for heating bills that won't stop. Some people are preparing for exams, some are preparing for death, some are preparing for new life in their families. Life goes on in the midst of all this coming and going.

In the days of Noah everyone is busy about the normal: eating and drinking, making new relationships, holding on to old ones. But in the midst of all this normal business there is an old eccentric who is busy with his family building a boat – in spite of the fact there is nowhere in sight to sail it. In the end Noah is the one who is ready because he is alert to something others are doing nothing about: the coming catastrophe.

Being ready

We all know today that the catastrophe we face is not a flood but a nuclear war. It could be argued that the only people who are prepared for that are the military who maintain a total watch around the clock. The entire Western defence system follows the advice to be vigilant, to stay awake, to be ready. Noah built an ark to ride out the disaster of the flood. But no one can ride out a nuclear disaster: there is no place to flee; there is no shelter deep enough; there is no sanctuary from radioactive storms. But hopefully there is another way to prepare for peace other than by stockpiling more nuclear weapons: to convert to the goal of peace the enormous energies we use for war. As Lester Pearson, a former Prime Minister of Canada, said in his Nobel Prize speech: "We prepare for war like precocious giants and for peace like retarded pygmies."

In the tale of Noah we are not being advised to run out and build a boat, or buy a parachute, or construct an air-raid shelter. We are being asked to listen to the Lord so that, as Isaiah says, "he may instruct us in his ways and we may walk in his paths." Probably none of us will be here to see that blessed day that Isaiah describes. "Nation will not lift sword against nation, there will be more more training for war." From the Gospel we see that Jesus himself seemed to think that war would be a permanent feature on the human landscape and we know that history has not contradicted him. The theatre of war has always been well attended and often over-crowded. No matter who the authors are, how different their language or accent, the script is predictably the same and the outcome is sadly familiar. And the message always seems to be forgotten.

That is why we have to pay attention to the word of the Lord. As Paul says in today's second reading, "You know 'the time' has come: you must wake up now." He tells the Christians in Rome to avoid drunken orgies and wranglings and jealousies. None of this makes them alert to the *kind of time* they are living in; it just numbs their spiritual sensitivity to the world beyond their own flesh. When people are engaged full-time is satisfying their own craving they are not disposed to face reality and take responsibility for their own world.

Ready to care
So it is that Jesus talks about the *future coming* of the Son of Man to encourage people to take responsibility for the *present time*. The only way to be ready for an unpredictable event is to make the present a time of fidelity. Then there is nothing to fear. In the Gospel Jesus gives his advice before his passion: it's as if he himself is aware that he doesn't have all the time in the world. He must be ready for the time of pain ahead and he uses the present to prepare himself.

The only way to secure the future is to care about the present. We are all responsible for the world we live in; we are not passive victims of the inevitable. If we do nothing, we can hardly accuse the world of conspiring against us. Peace never comes because people are not bothered. There's nothing automatic about peace. It is not caring and not bothering that gives permission to the fanatic to blow us all up. Because we care for the world the Lord has given us we stay awake to what is happening in it, good and evil. Otherwise the last time becomes the present tense.

Waiting for the Redeemer

Waiting

A woman stands at the end of a pier, her eyes scanning the horizon as she waits for her husband's ship to come home. A father climbs a hill to the lookout, exercising his hope that his younger son will come home soon. Young parents wait with growing expectation for the birth of their child. An old man sits in a nursing home, still waiting for the day when his family will visit him. All of them wait, and that waiting tests the quality of their hope. They are powerless to bring about what they hope for; all they can do is wait.

Waiting is part of life, and there is no life without it. All of us waited to be born, waited to be nourished, waited to be loved. We learn soon enough that the fulness of life is not available to us like instant coffee. There is always more to life and to people than we can ever manage to absorb at any one time. So, we have to wait.

Advent is the time when we are reminded that we have to wait for God. We cannot grasp God, we cannot possess God, we cannot see God; we can only wait for God to let himself be known. And when we wait for God we confess our own incompleteness, we acknowledge that there is always more to God than what we know, we proclaim our hope in a God we can never *have*. When we wait for God, our waiting is a prayer: we testify to our own poverty and to his greatness.

Waiting for the Redeemer

In today's first reading we get a glimpse of the difficulty people face when their waiting for God seems to be in vain. The exiles have returned from their captivity in Babylon, spurred on by fresh hope that God will adopt them again as his people. But Jerusalem is a heap of ruins, God seems to have fallen in love with long distance, and the people can see no signs to confirm their hope. They become exhausted with waiting; they grow tired of hearing nothing from God.

The only thing the people can do to renew their hope is *to remember* what God actually did for them in the past and to hold on to their relationship with him:

> You, Lord, yourself are our Father,
> Our Redeemer is your ancient name...
> Oh that you would tear the heavens open and come down
> — at your Presence the mountains would melt.

When the people remember God as their Redeemer they bring the past into the present, and that sacred memory acts like a light in the midst of darkness. *The memory of God's love is life*; it gives the people a reason to wait; it builds up their hope. They remember to hope. That is why their memories are so precious: they make the difference between despair and hope, between death and life. What they remember keeps them awake to what is still to come: God will live up to his ancient name and be the Redeemer of his people. Because they hope, they wait. And until the Redeemer comes, the people will not give up the strenuous habit of hoping.

Jesus, the Redeemer
Their hope is not in vain, but so many people fail to recognise the Redeemer when he does come. As Christians we celebrate the name of the Redeemer, Jesus, the only name by which we are saved. He is the chosen one, the beloved Son, God's answer to the cries of a waiting, struggling people. He is the ancient name of God become flesh in our midst.

In Jesus God pursues mankind with a love that is tireless, a love that refuses to allow hate and indifference and stupidity to steal its power. The Redeemer walks the roads of Palestine seeking out the legion of the lost and the broken and the wounded. His enduring love takes the shape of outstretched arms on a cross, and it is on a tree that the Redeemer proves what a redeemer must do: empty himself for the sake of others. In Jesus God lives up to his ancient name.

The story of Jesus the Redeemer has become the sacred story of *our* Christian tradition, a memory that we are pledged to keep alive until he comes again. We are between two times: between the first coming of Jesus and his second coming on the last day. We remember the first; we wait for the second. And today's Gospel tells us how to wait: we must wait together and stay awake to the times that we live in.

And we stay alert by living the values of the Redeemer in our own place and time. The memory of Jesus becomes life for us not only in the eucharist but when we share with others the truth and the values that Jesus so readily shared with us. His memory comes alive when we bring him into the present tense; thus people can experience something of God's forgiveness and love through our graced struggle. Meantime, we wait. And we pray that the Lord will grant us peace "as we wait in joyful hope for the coming of our Saviour, Jesus Christ."

Staying awake for liberation

Outlooks

Occasionally we meet them. People who seem to breeze through life no matter what fortune or fate brings their way. Whatever the pressure of life, they seem to carry on with effortless ease. They never seem troubled by doubt or oppressed by misfortune. Somehow they don't seem particularly anxious about the state of the world, or what the future might hold. Sometimes we wonder whether they have secret inner resources which enable them to cope. In a more suspicious mood we might wonder whether they are really sleepwalking through life, unaware of what is happening around them.

On the other hand we find ourselves all too aware of the large muddle of the world and the little muddle of our own lives. There are times when the sheer scale of the world's problems and our own overwhelms us and we wonder whether we can do anything to change the future. So, why bother? In the end there is the danger that we fall sick of the palsy of despair. We are so small, our systems are so unwieldy, the world is so complex, that all our effort seems wasted. We scramble for a last picnic before the nuclear winter engulfs us all.

Or we sit in the company of the black woman from Harlem who was interviewed about her "prospects". Looking out of her slum dwelling she said: "Nothing will change here. The future happens somewhere else. Always somewhere else."

Looking beyond disaster

In today's Gospel, Luke gives us the last address of Jesus' public ministry. And Jesus is clearly fretful about the future as he paints a bleak picture of the end of the world. There is talk of nations in agony, of bewilderment, of people dying of fear, of the power which menaces the world. It is a nightmare view of total disaster which "will come down on every living man on the face of the earth".

Given that vision of ultimate collapse it is hardly surprising that, as Jesus anticipates, it might lead people to drink! Being sober and awake might not seem very attractive in the face of such catastrophe. Nightmares are bad experiences we usually wake up from, not experiences we stay awake for. Yet that is Jesus' advice: "Stay awake, praying at all times for the strength to survive all that is going to happen." But, why stay awake? What is there to stay awake for?

In Jesus' view of the future there is a far side to disaster. Jesus' forecast is liberation. After the horror story, we might take some convincing that it's not all horror. Jesus' view is that the terrible things that will happen are signs that something else is happening: the saving visit of the Son of Man at the end of time. The disaster is the end age. The good news is that out of that comes final liberation for the true disciple. It is what we pray for in the Eucharistic prayer:

we hope to share in your glory
when every tear will be wiped away.
On that day we shall see you our God as you are.

Memory and hope

Like the prophets before him, Jesus is painting a grim picture of the *future* in order to influence what is happening now. He doesn't want to paralyse people with fear but to energise them to action. The real purpose of speaking of the final day is to say something about today – that we should stay awake. And since the future is determined by those who share responsibility for shaping it – we must all stay awake to what is happening now. The future starts from where we are today.

Today's Gospel encourages us to do two things which are difficult to hold together: to be realistic about the way the world is going, and at the same time not lose hope in the future. Difficult. The danger is that we see the terror clearly, and lose reason for hoping. And given the muddle we're often in, Jesus has to convince us about a future that is really liberating. The way he does that best is through his own life from birth to resurrection.

So, Advent reminds us that we don't have to sleepwalk into the future. We have to remember the story of Jesus again, and that memory of love becomes the ground of our hope. The future holds hope only because we are convinced of God's actions in the past. That's why we retell the story again and again beginning with each Advent. We all need to be reminded of God's love. We need to check the record to assure ourselves. When we do, we see how far-reaching God's love is when we look at his Son, Jesus. Only when we keep looking at him throughout the year, can we keep reason for hoping.

Then we can measure up the challenge of the first reading: to practice honesty and integrity in the land. And to dwell in confidence.

The voice that cries from the wilderness

A wilderness voice

All four Gospels testify to an important truth: that John the Baptist stands at the beginning of the Gospel. He is the one who marks the end of the time of waiting and the beginning of the new age in Jesus. He is the last of the great prophets, the one who came after a long period when no prophet spoke to the people. The great sequence of prophetic witness had been broken off in the history of Israel and people lamented that the spirit had been silenced. God spoke only through the echo of his voice. The people had been without a messenger from God to challenge them with the word. However, in John the Baptist the people could see an end to God's silence. Through John they could hear the word of God.

John the Baptist has an unusual address: c/o the wilderness. But that is the traditional place associated with the growth of Israel's religion. It was in the desert that Israel first met God, and the story of the people's wanderings through the wilderness became the story of their growth from crisis to settlement in the promised land. In the desert the people were tested, and later, when they failed God, they were told that they would be taken back into the desert where God would speak again to their heart (Hos.2:16).

So it is appropriate that the word of God should come again to the people in the wilderness. Matthew tells us that John the Baptist preaches in the wilderness and that all the people in Judea and Jerusalem make their way to him. This is an extraordinary tribute to John's power. Why should busloads of people go into the wilderness? Hardly for a day's outing: there is nothing to see. It is a mark of John's charismatic power that he can stay in the wilderness and attract people to the place they would normally avoid. It is a portrait of Israel again hearing the word of God in the desert. John is the voice speaking in the wilderness.

John's challenge

John appears as a somewhat eccentric figure when you look at his wardrobe and his diet: he wears a garment of camel-hair with a leather belt, and his food is locusts and wild honey. It is like a portrait of early punk! This portrayal of John puts him within the prophetic tradition (cf 2 Kings 1:18).

John is conscious of his mission to call Israel to repentance and to baptise those who do repent. The people come and listen to him because they believe he speaks the authentic word of the Lord. Those who are moved by his call confess their sins and are baptised by John. The baptisms

16

take place in one of the fords in the lower Jordan where the water is low enough for the people to wade across. Thus the baptisms are public affairs. In their baptism the people make a public profession to begin to change their lives.

John calls *everyone* to change. When he sees the Pharisees and the Sadducees, the leaders of orthodox religion, he is clearly not overwhelmed by their authority but is blunt and forthright. He warns them that they will not be spared judgement because they belong to the chosen people. Having an entry in *Who's Who* which states that you have Abraham for a father is not enough for entry into the heavenly kingdom. John is profoundly unimpressed that people have an impressive pedigree or come from the right address. No one can live on borrowed fidelity. Thus good ancestors guarantee nothing.

When people trace their family tree back to Abraham, that does not absolve them from taking responsibility here and now. Family trees are no different from other trees: good roots are not enough; there must be fruits that others can see and be nourished by. Roots refer to the past; fruits speak of the health of the tree now. And for John the tree of Israel is unhealthy because the axe is already laid at the roots.

The one who is to come

John calls the whole of Israel without exception to a change of heart. If the people do not change, John says that they will be overcome by a catastrophe that will destroy Israel. The judgement of the people will not be carried out by John himself; he speaks of the one who is to come who will baptise with the Holy Spirit and with fire. John warns of fireworks ahead. He calls the attention of Israel to its infidelity; the one who is to come will be more powerful and will exercise God's authority of judgement. We recognise the one John spoke of as Jesus, someone who will continue warning of the coming destruction and calling the whole people to a change of heart.

That call is addressed to us. We hear it especially during the time of Advent when as a community we are called to a change of heart. That challenge is addressed to each of us. There are no exceptions. We are probably all aware of areas in our own lives that need to be changed and to be touched by the power of God's forgiveness. We all need to be recalled into the fidelity of our own baptism; we all need to be challenged again by the word of the Lord. We don't have to make a trek into the wilderness to hear the word of the Lord. We hear it here, in this place. Hearing it and acting on it – this is the best preparation for the one who is to come.

Fostering greatness in others

God's watchman

Today we heard the opening of the Gospel of Mark, which introduces us to the two great figures that stand at the beginning of the Christian story: Jesus and John the Baptist. All four evangelists witness to the truth that you cannot tell the story of Jesus without first speaking about John the Baptist. It is the towering figure of John that introduces the adult Jesus in all the Gospels. John worked no miracles, held no office, belonged to no religious party. Yet his importance for Jesus was unique: he stands as the only religious leader that Jesus ever sought out and spoke of with deep affection and admiration. He is described as a voice crying in the wilderness, a large presence that dominates the emptiness of the wasteland.

In his poem *St John Baptist*, Sidney Keyes catches something of the place of John in sacred history:

> I, John, not reed but root;
> Not vested priest nor saviour but a voice
> Crying daylong like a cricket in the heat,
> Demand your worship. Not for me
> But for the traveller I am calling
> From beyond Jordan and the limestone hills,
> Whose runner and rude servant I am only.
> Not man entirely but God's watchman,
> I dwell among the blistered rocks
> Awaiting the wide dawn, the wonder
> Of His first coming, and the Dove's descent.

God speaks again

John is a waiting figure, God's watchman, but his waiting is anything but passive. He does not go into the wilderness to sit in solitude and wait for the one who is to come; rather, the word of God invades his whole being, calling the people of Israel to a radical change of heart in readiness for the approach of the Lord. From the wilderness his voice has a powerful reach: it attracts a people who have grown accustomed to the silence of God, a people who are hungry to be nourished again by the word which they recognise to be God's own word.

It is worth noting that since the death of the last of the writing prophets, the voice of God had not been heard in the land. It was believed that the spirit of prophecy had been quenched and that God spoke only through "the echo of his voice". That long silence is broken when John speaks, and this is what gives John his unique authority. Through him the silence of God is ended: the spirit of prophecy is alive again as it was in the days of old. That is why, as Mark says, all Judaea and all Jerusalem make their way to John: in him the people discern the living word of God.

People respond to the revivalist preaching of John by confessing their sins to him and undergoing a baptism of repentance. To the word of God spoken through John, people give their own word to change their lives. Their change of heart is shown in their public baptism, which would have taken place at one of the fords in the river Jordan. John's baptism marks a new beginning for them, a time of personal spiritual renewal, when they would aim themselves again at a life of fidelity to God.

Fostering greatness in others

The purpose of this energetic renewal movement is to prepare for the one who is to come. And we know that "one" to be Jesus of Nazareth. Although John has his own group of disciples, he does not make himself the focus of his prophetic witness; he does not claim that *he* is the way, the truth and the life. "Someone is following me, someone who is more powerful that I am, and I am not fit to kneel down and undo the strap of his sandals." John understands his own powerful place within the larger context of God's plan and this frees him to defer to the one who will baptise with the Holy Spirit. Jesus' greatness does not diminish John's importance; John is important precisely because of who Jesus is.

John's way is a challenge to all of us: to foster the greatness in others without feeling threatened about the value of our own contribution; to be free to celebrate the importance of others because we have a sense of our own worth and value before God. John manages to do all this, and, not surprisingly, Jesus will return the compliment when he speaks about John to the crowds, telling them that there is no greater mother's son than John the Baptist.

As the relationship between John and Jesus teaches us, the generosity in recognising the goodness in others can help them call out the good that is in ourselves. When that happens, there are no losers.

Beginning to change

Insight and change

Sometimes when people point out something that is wrong with us we can see what they're saying, recognise it as true, but proceed to do nothing about it. Like the father who told his daughter, "We must have a little chat" and she responded by pointing out that the only time they ever had a "little chat" was when he wanted to lecture her on something. "And besides," she said, "why is it that you always come off looking so good?" He recognised that what she said was true, but doubted his ability to change.

We know from experience that insight doesn't necessarily lead us to change. Recognising the truth does not compel us to alter our ways. Particularly when our self-esteem is injured, the truth can have the effect of paralysing us rather than energising us to action. Sometimes the prospect of what the change would involve disheartens us. We feel it's too much; we're too long in the tooth; we're too set in our ways. Or we're not ready yet.

Most of us can recognise ourselves in St Augustine's honest reflection: "You showed me that what I said was true, and I was convinced by the truth. But my only answer was those dreary words: 'Soon, soon; presently, presently' or 'Leave me alone for a little while.' But my 'presently' came to no present, and my 'little while' lasted a long time."

None of us is born again that easily.

Imagining the best

In today's readings we hear four voices encouraging people to imagine a good future that God has in store for them. They all invite us to imagine the best and then act accordingly.

In the first reading the prophet asks the people to change their wardrobe – to throw away the dress of sorrow and distress and wrap the cloak of God's integrity around them. Things are going to look up, they should be dressed appropriately and have courage again in the future. So, too, the psalmist asks people to imagine a time when they will no longer be in bondage sowing in tears, but will return full of joy carrying a harvest of goods.

In his letter to the Philippians, Paul takes a similar line. He compliments the people for helping him in his work, tells them how much he loves them, and invites them to prepare for that day "when you will reach perfect goodness". Finally, John the Baptist in the Gospel story is travelling around the Jordan district announcing to anyone within earshot the great day to come when "all mankind shall see the salvation of God."

None of these voices assaults people with the bare truth, which could serve only to deepen their helplessness. At the heart of them all is the voice of hope which encourages people to change their ways and grow because good things will come of it. People are invited to imagine the best there is in God and in themselves and give that best the opportunity to take charge of their lives.

Encouraging change

All the readings share a marvellous insight: people begin to change when they are encouraged to see the best in themselves, not when they are asked to dwell with the worst in themselves. Simply to tell people what is wrong with them and leave it at that can be to leave them a wreck. It's like leaving the scene of an accident. And people rarely change when they are left to themselves, enclosed in their own weakness, staring at their own mistakes. That's a lonely project precisely because there is no one to care whether change takes place or not.

We all need help and encouragement to leave behind familiar ways which have become destructive. We need help in imagining ourselves differently, and imagining the good effect that will have on others. We have to take time to reflect what kind of person God wants us to be, what his plan is for us. We need faith in the future, to see the power of God working in the change. To have Paul's certainty that God will not abandon us in our halting efforts, but "that the One who began this good work in you will see that it is finished."

In all this we need each other's help and encouragement. To change we need others prodding us on: "Go! You can do it!" We need to call out the best in each other like Paul does with his converts, and rejoice with people in the changes they have made for the better. After all, Paul himself had to make big changes in his life, and it was the Philippians who gave *him* encouragement in his big change by accepting him as an apostle of the Lord.

If our community is to be constantly converted to the Lord we all have to breathe in encouragement and breathe it out. Perhaps this Advent we could exercise that encouragement in a simple, practical way. That will be a change for the better. In the words of Cardinal Newman: "To be human is to change. To be perfect is to have changed often."

The voice that questions from prison

John's view of Jesus

When we think about John the Baptist, we usually think of him as the one who went before Jesus to prepare the people for his coming. That is why we hear so much about John in Advent. We rarely think of John as someone who retained his own disciples after the beginning of Jesus' ministry, someone who continued to command a large following – not least because many people thought that he might be the Messiah (Lk. 3:15). There is no suggestion that John thought of himself as the Messiah, yet we know that twenty years after the death of Jesus there were still disciples of John – some of whom were received into the Church when they heard about the Holy Spirit for the first time (Acts 19).

In the Gospels of Mark and Luke there is no suggestion that John actually *recognised* Jesus as the Messiah. In Matthew's version of Jesus' baptism, John does recognise Jesus; but, as we hear in today's Gospel, Matthew also preserves the tradition that John had his doubts about Jesus. In last week's Gospel we heard John's voice crying from the wilderness about the one who was to come; in this week's Gospel we hear John's voice questioning from prison if Jesus is that one.

Today's Gospel opens in the dark of a dungeon. John has openly denounced Herod for divorcing his own wife and marrying his brother's wife, Herodias. King Herod, who was nervous about political unrest and anxious about his own appointment by the Romans, had John thrown into Machaerus, a fortress east of the Dead Sea. We know that John is not released from prison. From the dungeon he sends his own disciples to Jesus to find out if his life's work has its term in Jesus himself. No doubt John can see that Jesus has a special role in the kingdom; but is Jesus the one prophecy has spoken about? Is Jesus the one who is to come, or have the people to wait for someone else?

Jesus' answer to John

John is confused. Remember from last week's Gospel how John spoke of the one to come as a strict judge who would bring a fiery judgement, a dispenser of wrath from whom people would have to flee. That's John's image of the Messiah. Then he hears what Jesus is doing: he heals the sick; he blesses the gentle and the peacemakers; he tells people that they must not judge one another but indeed love their enemies; he does not require his disciples to fast – unlike the disciples of John. Jesus' Messiahship, therefore, seems a world away from that imagined by John.

When John's disciples do come, Jesus does not say to them: "of course

I am the one." He tells them to pay attention to what is happening: the afflicted are healed, the dead are raised to new life, and the good news is preached to the poor. We heard from the prophecy of Isaiah how the messianic age was portrayed as one of great healing. Jesus appeals to prophecy: *in his work these prophecies are fulfilled.* Those who meet Jesus must work out from what he does and says who he is. This is a decision in faith; Jesus cannot make it for anyone. He cannot make it for John.

When John's disciples return to their master in the dungeon, does John believe that Jesus is the Christ? Does he continue to doubt? The Gospel does not tell us because the Gospel is more interested in Jesus. John's time is over. The one for whom he prepared has come. As the Chinese proverb says: "When a finger points at the moon, only a fool keeps looking at the finger."

Jesus' view of John

What we do know is what Jesus thought of John. He compliments John in a way that he never compliments another religious leader. Not only is John a prophet, he is more than a prophet because in him prophecy begins to be fulfilled even if he himself cannot see it. Yet, Jesus says, the least in the kingdom is greater than John. What makes the least in the kingdom greater than John? The basic requirement for entering the kingdom which Jesus inaugurates is to recognise who he is. In the early church, when the Gospel is being written, the first credo was three words. Jesus is Lord. The first credo is a *recognition* of who Jesus is. The least in the kingdom can do what John cannot do: recognise who Jesus is. That is why they are greater than John.

So, Jesus moves on. He continues his ministry. When he gets questions from people, all he can do is point to what God is doing in him and stay loyal to his own vision of things. He cannot go into hiding every time someone poses a question or expresses a doubt. When people fix him with their questioning stares he has to continue his work. He has to do what he has to do. Perhaps he suspects that dungeons are not the best place for clarity. When it comes to his own time of pain he will have a few questions himself.

The question of John is our question too. Is Jesus the one for us, or are we waiting for someone else? Is his Gospel enough for us? Do we find in Jesus the true answer to our longings? Probably this Advent we have a few questions of our own.

Making way for the light

Light

In a lengthy interview a year before he died, the great sculptor Henry Moore reflected on how his early years in a Yorkshire mining village influenced his later work:

> One of the first and strongest things I recall were the slag heaps, like pyramids, like mountains, artificial mountains. There were pit heaps all over – the great waste, the unburnable rubbish. We played about in them and got very dirty. I remember our street and I can see the sun just managing to penetrate the fog, and the coal heap at the end.

His father, a miner, was very fond of baked apples for pudding, and little Henry had to go to their dank, dark cellar to fetch them. He was frightened of the dark, so he used to go down the steps sideways, always with one eye on the lighted doorway. Later when he was carving deep into his sculpture he said he always felt he wanted to find a way out, remembering that cellar.

Many of Moore's massive sculptured forms have holes in them, but for him the holes have their own significance: what appears essential is left out; the light is let in. To many people his sculptures are just puzzling, but to many others they have a massive dignity. In the mining village where he grew up there was always competition between the sun and the fog, between the daylight and the pitch black of the mines, between a small child and the enormous slag heaps. In his work the light always wins, the child comes to shape the slag heaps into human form.

The essential place of the light

Today's Gospel begins with the absence of the light: John the Baptist is a witness to speak for the light, but he is not the light in person. John is the rugged figure whose task is described by the evangelists as laying low mountains and hills, shaping a path through the wasteland. He is God's sculptor, giving shape and form to an indeterminate mass of people, insisting always on the essential place of the light. When he faces critical opposition, he points away from himself to his work in preparing for the one to come.

John keeps declaring "I am not" in order to point to the one who can say "I am". The identity of the one coming after John is unknown, but John is clear in his own mind that he is not the light. He must make way for the light, create a space for the light to shine through. And when people see the light, his own task is finished.

John the Baptist's role can be appreciated fully only when the light does come in the person of Jesus. Only then can people realise the true measure of John's worth and the unique place this enigmatic man has in the Christian tradition. It is interesting to recall that John's stature among his own people was so great that many of them came to believe that he was the messiah. Indeed when Jesus comes to ask his own followers who people think he is, the apostles tell him that some hold him to be John the Baptist come back to life. Even in the early Church, some time after the completion of Jesus' ministry, a sectarian Baptist group still holds on to the belief that John, not Jesus, is the Christ. And that is why the fourth Gospel is so emphatic about John's role: it stresses that John is a *witness* to the light.

Making way for the light

Like John, we are asked to make way for the light. None of us is the light: our role is to let the light through the chunks of solid darkness that litter our human landscape. That appears a mountainous task besides which our own abilities and commitment look so small. Who are we to compete against such large darkness?

Advent calls on us to make what contribution we can. To look first at ourselves and work quietly on the darkness that hides within us – the selfishness, the unforgiveness, and the lack of love that keep the light of good news from so many people. On the larger social issues – like justice and peace – which require the witness of a caring community, we are challenged by the Gospel to work *together*.

Like Henry Moore carving through stone until he comes to the light, we have to keep working our way towards the light that is Christ. Our work may appear fruitless or just odd to those who look at our efforts, but the space we create is significant. Holiness is the constant struggle of letting Christ be the light that shines through everything we do. So let our work puzzle people. Who cares, when the light gets through.

"What must we do then?"

Dancing among the ruins

You are shuffling along to work. It's a dreary Monday morning and Friday is too far away even to think about. Out of the drizzle she comes, and you can see from the spring in her step and the expression on her face that she is very happy. You wonder if she is an alien from another planet. She appears lit from within and her face looks as if she has rented the sun. She beams joy.

Suddenly she embraces you and kisses you on both cheeks, just for good measure. After you have disentangled yourself you say: "What have you got to smile about? It's a rotten day, half the world is hungry and the other half is at war, and you're beaming. How come?" She looks puzzled for a moment, gives you a large wink, and goes off with her joy intact. You shuffle on, wondering.

There's nothing quite so puzzling as someone else's joy when we are feeling down. Or someone else's sadness while we are feeling on top of the world. The ultimate puzzle is when people are joyful in the midst of suffering and desolation, when people dance among the ruins that surround them, refusing to be locked into an environment of despair. Like Zephaniah the prophet – calling through the slums of a defeated Jerusalem for a grand party to celebrate the real fortune of the people. Like St Paul – a prisoner in his cell awaiting his approaching death and writing letters to cheer other people up. Like John the Baptist – a wilderness voice in occupied territory announcing Good News to his own country people.

How come?

The authority of John

Zephaniah, John the Baptist and Paul all shared one belief: that the Lord was very near. God's nearness didn't act as a threat to them, but funded them with a radical source of joy that no one could steal from them – not even the executioner. Their joy in the closeness of God gave an edge to their preaching exhorting others to make ready; it gave them a vision to see the far side of disaster; it moved them to draw others into that sense of joy. None of them was enclosed in his own joy; each moved out hoping his inner joy would be catching.

The picture of John the Baptist as a man who moves in deep joy is not one you hear about very often. John is usually portrayed as a lonesome figure, with a weird wardrobe and weirder diet, who rants and raves at anyone with ears. But John was a magnetic character who intrigued people to seek him out and also follow him. People don't journey into the wilderness just to get insulted; people don't become disciples for the wardrobe and diet. In John's person people could catch something of God's way.

Which is why people ask him: "What must we do, then?" And John's answer is to challenge people's generosity and sense of fairness so that others may have reason to rejoice. Give bread to the hungry and clothes to those who have none. When the tax-collectors ask what to do, John tells them to keep to the going rate without over-taxing people in order to cream off the extra arithmetic for themselves. People are burdened enough. Be just. To the soldiers who accompany tax-collectors to protect them and give some muscle to their requests, John tells these heavies not to use their position as a weapon for their own reward. Be content with your pay and stop stealing from the poor and the weak. They extort from others making them poorer; John exhorts them to be happy in doing what is just.

John makes such a deep impression on people that word goes around that he might be the Christ. Again, that expectancy is a measure of John's effect on people. John doesn't claim to know *who* the Messiah is; all he knows is that *he* is not. That role is for someone else, someone greater and more powerful than John.

God's closeness
John the Baptist and Paul both shared a radical sense of God's nearness. Both were executed. The joy of God's closeness was a power that carried them through times of horror, so neither had to deny the difficulty of their experience. Both men faced an opposition determined to destroy them; both had a belief to encourage them beyond the reality of imprisonment and execution.

We all need a power that carries us through difficult times, that prods us on when we face the reality of our weakness and limitation. To believe in the abiding presence of a God who cares gives us a deep sense of joy in the midst of our own stops and starts. That presence always challenges our generosity and calls on our sense of justice. It keeps us on our toes. It enables us to continue living even when the calendar is crowded with dreary Mondays.

Who knows? It might even put a spring into our Advent shuffle!

The virgin will conceive

The dynasty of David

The time is the late 8th century B.C. The place is the small kingdom of Judah. The problem is whether the dynasty will survive or not. Ahaz is the king of Judah and he is afraid that his two neighbours from the north will destroy the kingdom. The king of Israel and the king of Syria have already invaded Judah but they failed to take Jerusalem or capture Ahaz; instead, they left with a number of captives and anything they could plunder. Ahaz awaits another attack and looks around for help. He decides to go to Assyria, a superpower with a highly aggressive foreign policy, and ask for help to wipe out his hostile neighbours. The great prophet Isaiah is an advisor to King Ahaz. He is strongly against what the king intends to do.

Isaiah argues that the dynasty of David is not going to be preserved through playing power politics with Assyria, but only through trust in God. The prophet gives the king a sign: "the maiden is with child and will soon give birth to a son whom she will call Immanuel, a name which means 'God-is-with-us'."

This sign is given to Ahaz to assure him that the house of David will continue with God's help: "Before the child knows how to receive the bad and choose the good, the lands whose kings are frightening you will be deserted." (7:16) Isaiah tells the king that before this child is out of the nursery the two hostile kingdoms will have lost their power. But King Ahaz refuses to accept the word of the prophet. Assyria smashes the coalition of the two kingdoms and leaves Judah untouched provided it shows its submission by regular tribute.

Jesus, son of David, Son of God

When Matthew writes his Gospel he adopts that sign to Ahaz and gives it a whole new meaning. He celebrates Jesus as the ultimate fulfilment of prophecy, the royal child of the house of David, born of a virgin, who will be God-with-us. In Jesus the dynasty of David has its most celebrated son. But the child is not only the son of David, he is also the Son of God. In the early church the understanding of Jesus as Son of God came only after the resurrection. As St Paul says in today's reading: Jesus "was proclaimed Son of God in all his power through his resurrection from the dead."

Matthew is writing some forty years after the resurrection and he is anxious to show that Jesus was Son of God at his conception. That is why the virginity of Mary is so important: it points to who Jesus really is. Although Mary is betrothed to Joseph, she is found to be with child through the Holy Spirit. Joseph, who is described as a "son of David", decides to divorce Mary because he is shocked by her pregnancy. However, the word of God tells him to take Mary into his house: when he agrees to do this he takes public responsibility for Mary and the child – thus acknowledging him as his own. When Joseph exercises the right to name the child he becomes the *legal* father. Thus it is through Joseph that Jesus becomes "son of David".

It is through the Holy Spirit that Jesus is the Son of God. Mary's virginity points to that truth. Jesus is conceived without the intervention of a human father: that makes him unique. It will also be the ground of a later accusation that Jesus is illegitimate – an accusation that some Jews critical of Christianity made in the first century, and one which can be heard in calling Jesus "son of Mary" (Mk.6:3). The charge of illegitimacy would not have any *historical* foundation unless there was something unusual about Jesus' birth. Through the reaction of Joseph, Matthew's Gospel alerts us to the gossip and scandal that could surround this birth. Who can believe that virginity and motherhood can go together?

Mary

A virgin mother has no precedent in the religious tradition. A truth that is radically new will always shock people – particularly those who limit what can be true to what they have always known to be true. Often we only give permission to truth to get through to us when it meets with our approval. We like our truths familiar and tame; we do not like them to jolt us out of the familiar into the realm of new possibility.

But the Holy Spirit which came to Mary is not tame. It is the force which made the beginning of creation. It is the force which makes the beginning of this new creation. Through its power the virgin Mary conceives and gives birth to the Son of God. In her a new creation comes to life.

There is something else radically new about Mary. She is the woman at the centre of our history. It is a woman, not a man, who brings about Jesus' real presence into the world. She can say of him "This is my body, this is my blood" in a way that no other person can say of him. Through her, his presence is known and celebrated. For he is not only the son of David and the Son of God: he is her son whom she will bring forth for the life of the world.

The choice that makes us worth it

Freedom of choice

When it comes to talents, some people seem to have an abundance: they are kind, bright, artistic, personable, sought after – as well as not having a big head! Some people strive earnestly for talents that others seem to have effortlessly. There are those who train, sweat, struggle, diet, try to say the right things, try to please, smile endlessly, and yet, for all their efforts, they seem to be overlooked.

Like the rich prince in the fairy tale who goes into serious training to win the heart of the princess. He tries every charm in his book, but she has her eyes fixed elsewhere and marries a penniless woodcutter who didn't *do* anything to win her favour. The woodcutter was chosen because of the mysterious preference of the princess's love. And the prince was left to wonder why he couldn't *earn* the love of the princess. After all, he had done all the right things.

Like our friend the bewildered prince, when we see how some people are chosen we ask: "What did they do to deserve that?" We presume that they must have done something special and we get tangled up trying to scrutinise their performance for some clue. And in all this we forget the *freedom* of the one who chose them in the first place.

God's choice of Mary

In today's Gospel we celebrate the extravagant love of God who freely chose Mary to be the mother of his beloved Son. God's choice of Mary made her "full of grace". If grace is God's gift, Mary was full of God's gifts. There's no point in asking what Mary did to deserve that: she didn't do anything to deserve it, because it was sheer gift. Nobody *deserves* gifts; nobody is *entitled to* favours. Gifts and favours reflect the generosity of the giver, not the worthiness of the receiver.

The Gospel does not begin with what Mary does; it begins with what God does through Mary. When Mary is chosen to be the mother of God's Son, God's choice of her is not a reward for dedicated work or an answer to Mary's prayer. Rather, God's choice of Mary is the result of God's freedom to choose Mary from among all women. When God chooses Mary, his choice makes her worthy, as his love has made her full of grace. This truth is reflected in the Magnificat, when Mary prays:

> My soul glorifies *the Lord*
> and my spirit rejoices in God my saviour
> because *He* has looked on the lowliness
> of his handmaid.

Yes, from this day forward,
all generations will call me blessed,
for the *Almighty* has done great things for me.

Because of God's mysterious preference, because he has freely chosen to look on Mary in such a way, because he has made her full of grace, all generations – as we today – call her blessed. For God graced Mary for a mission that was not for herself: her mission in the plan of God was to give Jesus to every generation of the human family.

Mary's response and ours
Some people suspect that because Mary was so talented by God, this makes her no longer really human. Certainly, Mary has a unique role to play in history: as the Church teaches, she "occupies a place in the Church which is the highest after Christ and closest to us". *(Lumen Gentium, 54)* Being chosen by God for such a task does not exclude Mary from the human race; God's choice of her does not free her from making *her* choice for God. Mary was asked to put her freedom, her whole person at the service of God's plan.

The difference between us and Mary is not that Mary was chosen while we are not; rather, it is that she fully responded to be chosen for her role while we remain hesitant and half-hearted about responding to what God asks of us. God has chosen *all of us*. This great truth was expressed by St Paul when he wrote: "God chose us, chose us in Christ, to be holy and spotless and to live through love in his presence". (Ephesians 1)

Like Mary, we face God's choice of us; like her, we are challenged to say yes. If we could see ourselves as the result of God's choice rather than a mobile mistake, we might be keener to say yes! God has chosen every single person here today; he has a role for each of us. He waits for our choice that puts our freedom at his service.

God's word to Mary in today's Gospel is a word of supreme value: "Rejoice, highly favoured". Perhaps we don't really believe that God favours us; maybe we have reached the stage where we don't think we are worth anything anyway. So today, let that be God's word to you: "Rejoice, highly favoured, for I have chosen you to be holy and live through live in my presence. Yes, you! Rejoice."

Promises, promises!

Delivering the goods

She says: "That's all very well for you to say, but when do I get the wedding ring?"

He says: "Soon, soon, I promise you. Just trust me, dear. Really, you'll see."

She says: "Promises, promises, promises! I've been living on those for years and they make a rotten diet. It must be the lack of vitamins, dear."

To make a promise is always to put yourself in debt; it invites another person to trust in you until you can deliver on your word. Sometimes we promise too much too quickly and we soon learn that we can't deliver the goods. As Ovid observed two thousand years ago, when it comes to promises we can all be millionaires. On the other hand, we're sometimes so doubtful of our own capacity to keep promises that we don't make any. So, we live in the absence of promise, which means that other people have to do the same.

To believe a promise is an act of trust in the person who makes it; it is to live in expectation holding fast to someone's word. And when promises are fulfilled there is a deepening of the original trust. However, if people have a distinctly wobbly track-record on keeping their word, we tend to be cautious about their sparkling new promises. We may file them under "Long Shots" and forget them: none of us wants to conspire in our own disappointment. Or when things look uncertain we may send accusing reminders, "But you promised."

Of course, in all this we know that we cannot retire completely from giving and receiving promises. Life itself comes to us as a promise, and trust has to be exercised in the midst of the real frailty within and around us. So, when it comes to God's promises we feel hopeful that at least *He* will deliver.

The Old Testament meets the New

In today's first reading the prophet Micah announces the great promise of God: that the small tribe which settled in the insignificant town of Bethlehem will one day produce the ruler of Israel. But between that promise and its fulfilment there is a long interim period of destruction, suffering and exile. When your country is overrun and you are dumped in a strange land, when your songs are unsung and your musical instruments are in storage, it's difficult to hold on to a promise, even when that is the promise of God. But it's precisely that promise that gives substance to the hope of the people, and gives a direction to their lives. At the end of the exile the remnant who still believe return to rebuild their lives in the hope that God will indeed keep his promises.

At the beginning of Luke's Gospel we are introduced to an aged, married couple who stay alive on that hope – Zechariah and Elizabeth, the parents of John the Baptist. They represent the hope that did not die, and they see it fulfilled in their son, John, who is to prepare for the one from Bethlehem. And it is the fulfilled hope of that old couple which is given to Mary as a sign: "Know this too, your kinswoman Elizabeth has, in her old age, herself conceived a son...for nothing is impossible with God."

Mary hurries to see this sign of a hope fulfilled. In the meeting of the old Elizabeth and the young Mary the Old Testament meets the New Testament, the ancient promise meets its fulfilment in two mothers – Elizabeth, the mother of the last great prophet who will go before the Lord, and Mary, the mother of the Lord himself. It is a time of good news, of great blessing; it is a time for womb-shaking rejoicing. The old promises are new events, and now is the time of their long awaited fulfilment. It's a great time!

Promise enfleshed

It is through Mary that God is seen to keep the promise announced through the prophet Micah so long ago. The promise of God will take flesh in her and be formed in the person of Jesus. In today's Gospel Mary is blessed for believing "that the promises made her by the Lord would be fulfilled." In Mary we can see that God doesn't just make promises, but keeps them. In Mary we can see someone who allows the promise of God to shape her whole life – not in a passive way, but because she says "yes" to the promise *happening* in her.

The promise has a name: Jesus. He will fulfil all that has gone before and give new meaning to all that will happen after him. He stands at the very centre of time – B.C./A.D. And he is the one who stands at the very centre of our lives.

At Christmas we celebrate the great event that Jesus is the kept promise of God. He comes to us again as gift of the Father and invites us to have the confidence to make a few promises ourselves. As Christians we are a people of promises, and God holds fast to the words of promise we have made him. As Advent closes we thank God for keeping his word to us, and ask him to help us keep our word to him and each other. As W.H. Auden wrote:

"Words are for those with promises to keep."

THE
SEASON OF
CHRISTMAS

In deep shadow, a light has shone

Christmas

High in the Andes, an Indian prince is anointed in the darkness. Then, on a large raft in the centre of a sacred lake, his naked body is plastered with gold dust by members of his tribe. They turn away so that they do not look on his face. They all wait in silence. Then the sun comes over the horizon and bathes in its light the Indian prince, gold in glory. He plunges into the lake, and the people cast jewels and sacred objects of gold into the water to sanctify the place where he swims. He is the legendary *Eldorado*, the gilded one. The ceremony is the annual ritual to the god of the sun on behalf of the people who depend on its power.

For most primitive peoples throughout history, the sun was the supreme god, surveying the world, giving it light and warmth. And in the winter, these primitive peoples would light fires in the hope that they could strengthen the failing power of the sun. By the 3rd century the sun-god was proclaimed principal patron of the Roman Empire, and December 25th was the date celebrated as the birthday of the invincible sun. This was the date of the winter solstice – on this day the sun began its return to the northern skies – and bonfires were lit to welcome back the sun after the darkness of the short days.

The feast of Christmas originated when the cult of the sun was particularly strong in Rome. The pagan festival was baptised by the church in Rome which used the same date to celebrate the birth of Christ. We do not know the date of Jesus' birth, but we do know why December 25th was chosen as the date to celebrate the birth. For us the Yule logs and candles symbolise the warmth and light of another sun: the Son of God. In the darkness of this night we celebrate the birth of the light of the world.

The light that comes as a child

Ancient religions as well as modern have always used the themes of light and darkness as a way of speaking about religious experience. Light has always been associated with goodness, knowledge and hope. Darkness has symbolised evil, ignorance and despair. In the first reading we heard the prophet Isaiah voice his hope to the people of Judah:

The people that walked in darkness
has seen a great light;
on those who live in the land of deep shadow
a light has shone.

In the Christian tradition we interpret that light to be Jesus the Christ, "the true light that enlightens all men" (Jn.1:9). Without him, we are stumbling around in the dark; without him, we can come to prefer the dark to the light. He is the only light that darkness cannot overpower.

That light comes to us not as a bolt from the sky, but as a child from his mother's womb. A child that was born in obscurity. With the birth of every child there is new life, new hope, and a new innocence which graces a world that is tired of pain and contradiction. Like any baby, Jesus as a baby does not question the way of the world, he does not speak the wisdom of God, he does not demand to be heeded. People can take him or leave him. Only later will he become a stumbling block to the Jews and a folly to the Gentiles. At the moment, there is just a child.

The child who is Christ the Lord
But this is not the birth of any child. Luke is anxious to tell us in the Gospel the true identity of *this* child. So the angels announce to the shepherds and to us the meaning of all that is happening in obscurity. Their annunciation pierces the disguise of obscurity and peals out the identity of this child: "Today in the town of David a saviour has been born to you; he is Christ the Lord."

The angels proclaim at the beginning of the Gospel what Jesus' followers came to believe only after the resurrection: that Jesus is the saviour, Christ the Lord. We believe what they proclaim. Because we believe that Christ died and rose again, we can take the light of our faith back to the manger. The light of our faith lights up the darkness of the manger so that we can see there the beginning of salvation. When we look in the manger, we see not just a child; with the eyes of faith we see the saviour of the world. When we look on the face of this child, we look on the face of Jesus Christ, the Son of God. Without our faith, we see only the face of another child.

Christmas is a great celebration of our faith in Jesus. We gather to celebrate light in the midst of darkness, we celebrate the new hope that Jesus has generated in people down the centuries. He is our light; he is our hope. When we want to know God, it is to Jesus that we turn; when we want to worship God, it is through Jesus that we hymn our praises. We too give glory to God in the highest for revealing himself to the lowly: "Through him, with him, in him, in the unity of the Holy Spirit, all honour and glory is yours, almighty Father, for ever and ever."

Old story, new hope

Hearing the old story

Each year we hear again the ancient Christmas story. Each year we retell the astonishing entrance that God made into our broken world and we are moved by God's capacity to surprise us with love. Something new had happened; something original and fresh had been revealed; nothing would ever be quite the same again. God made the choice to break the silence of ages, to give himself away in a Word. The most important Word that God has ever spoken took flesh in the womb of a young maiden, and like all flesh was born as a fragile bundle of new life.

The mystery of God was concentrated in a child; the hope of God's love was fastened on to this little one. God was choosing to visit his people – not through the dreams and words of the prophets, but in human flesh. The God who lived in the highest heavens chose another address; he decided to pitch his tent among us.

The Christmas story we hear each year is the same, but we are different. Our world is different. Our memories have grown, our hopes have been tested, our love has been called on in new ways. But no matter what changes we have undergone, what losses we have mourned, the Christmas story speaks to us again of new birth and the possibility of our own rebirth. It tells us that things can be different; it gives substance to our hope that new life is possible because of the birth of the Son of God.

The gift of life

The birth of every child is a gift of life. God's original blessing is the gift of life; in a baby we can see the blessing of God. A child who did not request life receives the gift of beginning, grows to crave for life, fight for life, struggle to preserve life. To be born is to be gifted by a God who is Life itself, and that is why reverence for human life is reverence for the God of life.

The birth of every child is a small protest against the tired view that there is nothing new under the sun, that we are condemned to a future which only repeats the stupidities of the past. And the birth of Jesus is God's protest against letting things be, abandoning people to their own devices, leaving people to fall back on the poverty of their own resources. Jesus is the help of God among us; he is the one Word on God's telegram of hope.

No one knows what any child will turn out to be. But by the time the Gospel is written, long after Jesus' mission has been completed, the Christian community can celebrate the true identity of Jesus. That is why

Luke can begin his Gospel with the celebration of the birth of *the Messiah.* Luke knows who this child has turned out to be, so there is no obscurity about the birth story. He dates back in time what the Christian community has come to recognise in the power of the Spirit: that Jesus is the Messiah, the Son of God, the gift of God's own life.

The gift that is given for us

It is difficult to imagine the celebration of Christmas without the help of Luke's Gospel. It is the artist Luke who puts us in touch with the young virgin with child, Joseph her husband, the surprised shepherds, the jubilant angels announcing the good news. We are drawn into a drama that is larger than our own; we are invited to share the mood of joy and hope; we are asked to take our own place in the dark of the manger and behold the gift of God, wrapped in swaddling clothes.

Luke's invitation, which has been extended to all believers down the centuries, reaches us again tonight: to come and worship, to see for ourselves the fragility of God, the littleness of the mighty one, the sheer tenderness of a love that is offered to all peoples.

With the birth of this child a new adventure in faith begins. A new approach to God is opened up for us, a new way of relating to each other is asked of us. Because this child becomes for all of us the Way, the Truth and the Life.

That is why we make the journey back to Bethlehem each year: to rediscover our own roots in the gift of Jesus. For us, it is a journey home. As G.K. Chesterton wrote:

> To an open house in the evening,
> home shall men come,
> to an older place than Eden,
> and a taller town than Rome.
> To the end of the way of the wandering star,
> to the things that cannot be and that are,
> to the place where God was homeless
> and all men are at home.

"There is a child born for us"

A sense of the particular

It won't come as any Christmas surprise to say that everyone here tonight was born of particular parents, in a particular place on the map, and at a particular time in history. We all have about us a sense of the particular which gives some form to our identity, and some shape to our sense of who we are. Our own roots give us a sense of belonging – belonging to a mixed bag of people, and to places that may make no impression on others but are special to us because they mark the address of childhood.

Sometimes we return to hunt for the leftovers of childhood. Old and battered toys become precious again; rediscovered hide-outs where we sheltered from an adult world and devised grim plots; faded books with our names importantly scrawled on the fly-leaf; photographs of maiden aunts who always remained vaguely forty and who have now shuffled off to God. Memories too of old scars and bumps in the night.

It's funny how when people want to ask us who we are, the question often comes: "Where are you from?" Perhaps it is because the *land* we come from offers the first clue to others of our hidden identity. They might quietly guess our age. It's as if people need to register us in place and in time before they can really grow to know us and accept us.

Perhaps the same is true of God: perhaps he must register himself in place and in time before we can grow to know him and love him.

The meaning of the Gospel

At the centre of Christianity is the great proclamation of the identity of Jesus: that he is not only the son of Mary, that he is the Son of God; that he is not only the prophet from Nazareth, that he is Christ the Lord. That proclamation was made by the early church only after the resurrection when the apostles came to see in the power of the spirit the full truth about Jesus. It was that great truth which inspired the writing of the four Gospels, which are great testimonies to the person of Jesus.

So the Gospels can take the light of the resurrection back in time to the beginnings of Jesus' life to see there *more* than obscurity but the beginnings of greatness; to see with the eyes of faith the *significance* of this child. And tonight we hear the most memorable and poetic of these testimonies from Luke: the celebration of the truth that at his birth Jesus is saviour of us all.

In his story Luke registers the birth of Jesus at a particular time in history and on a particular place on the map. The story shows that Jesus does not arrive in history as a traveller without baggage, who must choose a name, a family, a past, a whole identity for himself. He is not rootless, but is born a member of a specific tribe; he does not begin from zero, but enters an unfolding history between a yesterday and a tomorrow; he does not invent himself, but will discover himself as a unique link in a long line of faith. He is a Palestinian Jew born in the reign of Caesar Augustus and King Herod. He is in time, and therefore, in-between times.

So the birth of the saviour is located in space and time, the natural boundaries of every human life-story. To be human is always to be somewhere, never nowhere; it is always to exist some time, never no time. "Once upon a time" is fairytale time: "the reign of Augustus" is real time. Luke registers the birth of Jesus as a sign of the historical reality of the visit of God, and a witness to the fulfilment of God's plan.

In the person of Jesus God has visited the people. He has registered himself in place and in time. And that is why we celebrate tonight.

God's particulars
Tonight we celebrate the love of God for us which shows itself in the fragile bundle of the child Jesus. And we can celebrate our love of God in Jesus. Perhaps it is true to say that we can love only what we can get our arms around. To love we need a particular name, a particular face, a particular person. And we have God's particulars in Jesus. When we look at Jesus we no longer have to guess at God. And, like Mary and Joseph, we can all get our arms around the child from Bethlehem.

The Gospel invites us to take the child with us. Not to drop him back in the crib when we leave here, but to welcome into our hearts the gift of God in Jesus. In Jesus we have the sure proof that God loves us, and we all need to live in the assurance of that love. The great truth of Christmas is that no matter what happens to us, God's love is not negotiable. It is never in doubt, So, tonight let us celebrate that love which proclaims: "I have loved you with an everlasting love." And the name of that love is Jesus.

"The Word is made flesh"

Overcoming absence

When an American playwright reflected on his childhood he told the story of how his father who was a telephone engineer sometimes worked away from home. At first, his father was away only a couple of days and this happened rarely, but then his absences became more frequent and also lasted longer. Eventually, his father never returned home. The telephone engineer had fallen in love with long distance and his son had to live his life in the felt absence of his father. There was no word, no call, no contact. Just silence and absence.

It's impossible to have a relationship with someone who is always absent and always silent. Usually we overcome our separation from those we love and miss by staying in contact with them – keeping in touch through phoning or writing. And Christmas has become a traditional time for keeping alive old bonds of friendship by a word of greeting.

Of course the best way to keep alive the love of absent friends and relatives is to visit them. The visit is the traditional way of conquering distance and overcoming absence: so we talk of "going to see" someone, "showing our face", and "spending some time together". And in the giving and receiving of hospitality, in being *present* to each other again, our relationship grows and deepens.

The silence of God

If it's difficult to live with the prolonged silence of those we love, it's even more difficult to live in the silence of the God who loves us. It was a truth of ancient religion that the wisdom of God was hidden, wrapped in silence. That silence was hard to bear, and caused many people anguish of heart and mind – like the psalmist who prayed in desperation:

> O my God, I call by day and you give no reply;
> I call by night and I find no peace. (Ps.21)

But God did speak. As the second reading tells us: "At various times in the past and in different ways, God spoke to our ancestors through the prophets". Through God's spokesmen the word of God broke through the silence and called on the people to stay faithful to their commitment to him.

But who could have guessed that one day God would speak a word like Jesus? At the heart of Christianity is the belief that the most precious word God spoke became a person: the word of God became flesh in Jesus. The great silence of God is broken forever, so that we can say with St Paul: "I proclaim Jesus Christ, the revelation of a mystery kept secret for endless ages". (Rom. 16:25) In Jesus we rejoice that God is more than silence: he is Word among us.

The absence of God

Just as the silence of God was hard to bear, so was the experience of his absence. It was another truth of ancient religion that to be holy was to be separate, to be distant, to be totally other. To be God was to be invisible: nobody could see the face of God and live. So there are stories of God playing hide-and-seek, teasing his people with glimpses of himself.

True love can't rest or relax in the absence of the loved one. It never becomes accustomed to absence, but starts seeking out the presence of the loved one. Like the psalmist who prays:

My heart has said: "Seek his face."
It is your face, O Lord, that I seek;
hide not your face. (Ps.26)

It is a central belief of our faith that God did not hide his face, but revealed it in his Son, Jesus. That God did not stay separate and distant, but visited us in Jesus of Nazareth. In Jesus, the divine game of hide-and-seek is ended.

Jesus: God's presence and word

At Christmas we celebrate the consoling truth that God did not fall in love with long distance but came among us in Jesus. You cannot save anyone from long distance: you have to be there. In Jesus, God is here. Close. And it is through Jesus that we can pray to God not only "Hosanna in the highest heavens" but also "Hosanna among us". God has a new address. He has pitched his tent among us.

At Christmas we celebrate the great truth that God is not wrapped in silence, but wrapped in swaddling clothes and laid in a manger. In the infant Jesus we have the comical image of the gurgle of God breaking the silence. He is the one who will show us how close God is, who will teach us how to call God "Abba", and who will die to prove the measure of God's love for us.

For us, and for millions of people since the birth of Christ, we have a new way not just of understanding life but of living it. It is a truth of history that for twenty centuries untold numbers of people have been grasped by this child from Bethlehem, have been caught up in his message, and have had their lives profoundly changed by him. We are numbered among them today. Let us rejoice in the one who reveals the face of God to us, who is the Word of God for us.

Family of all sorts

Family wardrobe
Fashions in clothes come and go. The long and the short, the tight and the loose, make their appearance with surprising variety. Sometimes, when we look at old family photographs, we smile at the styles and cuts; sometimes we see those styles re-emerge under different disguises. St Paul speaks to us today about the essential wardrobe for every Christian: "be clothed in sincere compassion, in kindness and humility, gentleness and patience...Over all these clothes, put on love."

Whatever the fashion of the day might be, whatever the age group, Paul tells us the essential clothing for every Christian. Without love, no Christian is properly dressed. And today, as we celebrate the feast of the Holy Family, we look with gratitude to our own families and to the family of believers. The family that needs the young, the middle-aged, and the old.

The young
The young have been born into a world that is fragile and nervous about its future. They need people to nurture them, believe in them, and give them hope about their own place in the world. They might appear suspicious of authority, not least because they expect too much of it and are disappointed when it shows itself to be as weak and fractured as the rest of people.

They can respond with enormous generosity to the concrete needs of other people: when their love is called upon, they rarely disappoint. We need their idealism, their energy, their commitment, and their love. Sometimes their honesty accuses us of cover-up because they are impatient with compromise. They can see in Jesus someone whose undivided love for the poor and the afflicted shines like a light through the haziness of our own preference.

They want their voice heard in the Church. It is not the voice of experience, but Jesus himself suggested that even children have a way of getting to the heart of things that adults can miss. They don't want us to teach them to hate but lead them to the truth – a truth that protects the vulnerable and has patience with the immature. The young need help to face up to life's disappointments without losing heart. They are God's children.

The middle-aged
We need too those who are in the prime of life, the vast legion of the middle-aged. We need those who have tasted enough of life to know what is cheap and futile, to know what is good and worthwhile, and to have the commitment to live the difference. We need the selfless love of parents

who will invest the best of themselves in their families. We also need the selfless love of single people who will seek the welfare of others.

Those who have failed in their achievements and those who cannot find work have a place in our family of faith. They have a place not out of pity, but because God has a special care for those who suffer. Our community also needs those who face up to violence with the determination of peace. Those who have the generosity to listen to troubled people and help them in the long journey to healing.

Every family needs those who have the knack of bringing out the best in people while shrugging off the bitterness and resentment they meet. Those who have staying power and keep on caring even when the response is so mean and the returns are so shabby. Those whose holiness is quiet, who persevere in the faith no matter what fortune and fate bring their way. These too are the children of God.

The old
The old are an essential part of God's family. They may be young in heart and have the openness to greet the future with hope. They have the kind of wisdom which comes from experiencing the teaching which life itself brings. They can look back at their aspirations, measure their disappointments, and still claim that it is all worth the long struggle of love.

They have a faith which has outdistanced change, a change that has seen popes come and popes go, altars moved here and tabernacles moved there, churches demolished and new ones built. Sometimes they might wonder what all the fuss is about when in the midst of all the bustle their own prayer life continues undiminished.

Some are troubled by illness and afraid of dying. Some fear more the death of loneliness, and hope that they will not be excluded from the festival of life. They have time for others, even though others may have little time for them. They can enjoy the freedom to say what they think, and a humour that is free of resentment. They deserve not only respect but the Gospel affection that enables all of us to face the future. They are the elderly children of God.

Conclusion
The human family and the Christian family are graced with the young, the middle-aged, and the old. No matter what age we are, no matter what clothes we wear and styles we prefer, we should all "be clothed in sincere compassion, in kindness and humility, gentleness and patience." If we complete this wardrobe by love we will always be dressed for the kingdom. And no one can complain of our taste.

Natural attachments

Attachment
In the middle of the night a young boy wakes up in a hospital bed. He feels very frightened and very alone. He is suffering intense pain: burns cover forty percent of his body. Someone had doused him with alcohol and then had set him on fire. He starts crying out for his mother. The nurse leaves her night-post to comfort him; she holds him, hugs him, whispers to him that the pain will go away sooner than he thinks. However, nothing that the nurse does seems to lessen the boy's pain. He still cries for his mother. And the nurse is confused and angry: it was his mother who set him on fire.

The young boy's pain at being separated from his mother – even though she had inflicted such cruelty on him – was greater than the pain of his burns. That deep attachment to the mother makes separation from her the worst experience a child can undergo.

During World War II the noted child psychoanalyst Anna Freud directed three nurseries, which housed young children separated from their families. In *War and Children* she wrote:

> The war acquires comparatively little significance for children so long as it only threatens their lives, disturbs their material comfort or cuts their food rations. It becomes enormously significant the moment it breaks up family life and uproots the first emotional attachments of the child within the family group. London children, therefore, were on the whole much less upset by bombing than by evacuation to the country as a protection against it...
>
> It is a known fact that children will cling even to mothers who are continually cross and sometimes cruel to them.

Mother and child
The regular presence of parents is a constant assurance of safety for every young child. The family, no matter what its shortcomings, is the fundamental human connection. There are flaws in every human connection, but even the most fragile families tend to be more supportive to a young child than an institutional upbringing. No matter how much the institution cares, it can never replace the natural bond between mother and child. We know that the warm, intimate relationship the child has with his mother is essential for the growth of his inner life. This is not to underestimate the role of the father: it is simply to admit the truth that in most homes it is still the mother who feeds and cleans the young child, keeps him warm, comforts him in distress. Above all it is the mother who is *there* for the young child.

Parents are the first teachers of love; their attachment to their children shows them that they are worthy of love, shows them how to love. It is very hard for a child to grow up without the caring support of that attachment. And Luke shows us in today's Gospel how the parents of Jesus fulfil the requirements of their religious tradition, and how the child Jesus grows in wisdom and maturity under their care.

From the mutual love between Mary and Joseph and from their love of him, the child Jesus will be schooled in love and grow in the security of their attachment to him. To know the meaning of love, Jesus will only have to consult his experience.

That love will give him the security and the freedom which will enable him to become himself, and although he is more than Mary and Joseph can ever give him, their influence on him can never be underestimated. The time will come when Jesus – like all children – must separate himself from his family to make his own way in life; but as a child he is wholly dependent on the love that is offered from his own family. That is the glory and the limit of his humanity.

Our own family

In remembering the Holy Family, we look to our own family in gratitude for what we have received. The feast of the Holy Family we celebrate today is not an old one – it was instituted in 1921; but the Christian family has been celebrated by all who care to admit their indebtedness to it as the lively place where they were at home with God and an assortment of weird and wonderful relatives. In the Christian family we learn that God never comes alone; he is always accompanied by a legion of others who, in their own shy and halting way, show us something of his loving kindness. In the Christian family we can catch something of the God who accepts us as we are and who keeps on loving us stubbornly to the end.

None of our families is all holy; each is a mixture of all sorts of conflicts, compulsions and craziness that tests our love and forgiveness. But in the midst of all that, there is God. There is no other place to find him. It is the place where he found us.

The word grows in community

Jesus and his Jewish family

When it comes to thinking about Jesus it it easy to forget that Jesus was brought up as a pious law-abiding member of the Jewish race. The Jewish religion was his religion; his God was the God of Abraham, Isaac and Jacob; the psalms would have been his prayers; his religious education would have been the experience of his people in history as we have it in the Old Testament.

Jesus was not an alien from outer space: he did not suddenly emerge from nowhere, but emerged from within the tradition of Judaism in first-century Palestine. He did not grow up by himself in the wilderness, but grew up within a family and within a particular neighbourhood.

As the Gospel tells us today, Jesus was brought up in Nazareth by Mary and Joseph and like a good Jewish son lived under their wisdom and authority. From them he would have his first experience of being loved, of being held, of being listened to, and of being nurtured. He was a member of the extended Jewish family which, unlike our nuclear family, includes every kind of kinship no matter how remote. And like every family, the Gospel also tells us that Jesus had his share of peculiar relatives and neighbours.

In his later life, in his teachings and compassionate outreach to people, Jesus will speak the word of God in a new way. But first, as a child he is brought up to inherit that word from his own tradition, to pray it, to be at home in the customs of his own people, and to honour the great festivals – like the feast of Passover, commemorating the liberation from bondage in Egypt, and the feast of Tabernacles, commemorating the dwelling of the Jews in the wilderness. Jesus grew up living and breathing the traditions of his own Jewish people. In a word, he belonged.

Jesus and his Father

Of course when children grow up they have a way of branching out on their own. They want to be more than inheritors of a tradition; they want to make their own mark. They want to exercise not only the dog but their own initiative. Sometimes parents can feel utterly bewildered and hurt by the direction their children take in life: they cannot fathom why Mark, who has more than distinguished himself in physics at university, now wants to spend his time on the high seas catching fish. But all parents have to learn that their children are not born to be miniature reflections of themselves. Children are *other* people.

Later in his life when Jesus begins to formulate his own values and preach his own vision, he comes into open conflict with his own religious tradition. So the formula goes: "You have heard it said to you...but I say to you." Many Pharisees are deeply shocked to see Jesus breaking the law and encouraging his disciples to do the same. Why doesn't Jesus simply remain within the confines of his own religious tradition?

Jesus' neighbours refuse to believe that Jesus is anything more than the son of a local carpenter. Even Jesus' relatives come to believe that he is out of his mind when he brings home the kind of people that others are happy to leave on the junk heap. The relatives are frankly embarrassed and want to take charge of him. But Jesus takes his charge from somewhere else.

The adult Jesus has to face a conflict between two loyalties: loyalty to his Jewish family versus loyalty to his Father. Jesus is pulled in two directions – the way his family want him to go, and the way his Father wants him to go.

That conflict is *foreshadowed* in today's gospel when the young Jesus of twelve years old is seen to opt for his Father's business, rather than go the way of his family. When that option is explained to Mary and Joseph, Luke tells us that they do not understand what he is talking about. But that conflict will emerge only later in the ministry: here it is foreshadowed, and Luke softens the scene when he says that Jesus lives under the authority of Mary and Joseph and grows in wisdom and stature.

Jesus and his new family
At the centre of Jesus' family life and at the centre of his ministry is one irreplaceable person: God his Father. That relationship is for Jesus the most important of his life: ultimately, it is what gives him his direction and support and will sustain him in his passion and death. When Jesus comes to describe his own family in the Gospel it is not a relationship of blood but a relationship of fidelity to the word of God: "My mother and my brothers are those who hear the word of the God and do it."

We are all asked, like Jesus, to centre our lives on the word of God. Whether we live alone or in a family, whether we have busloads of relatives or none, we can all be a member of Jesus' new family. There is only one qualification: to hear the word of God and do it. Because Jesus extended his family, today's feast really belongs to all of us. So take a good look around at the family!

Nurturing the Word

Divine comedy

At the beginning of the Old Testament there is the story of an empty womb. Given the age count of the old couple, Abraham and Sarah, an empty womb would come as no surprise to anyone; but there is an added difficulty in the fact that Sarah has always been barren. In spite of this the old couple live in hope of having their own child. The promise of God has led them to believe it possible, and they make the promise of God their daily bread – nourishing their fond hope that one day they will be parents.

One day three visitors arrive. They are carriers of the most precious news that God is a keeper of promises and Sarah will have a child in her old age because God will visit her in a special way. The response to this long-awaited news is laughter: when Sarah hears the announcement from her hiding-place behind the door, she laughs.

There is the marvellous image of a woman, who has been a pensioner for years, with her apron in her mouth laughing through her false teeth at the idea of herself as a mother at last! Sarah can laugh at the idea of a baby being born not in the maternity ward but in the geriatric ward; she can laugh in delight at the prospect of an old, empty cradle being occupied at last.

Laughter is a good response to the fulfilment of the promise of God: that the couple will have a son not out of necessity or medical ingenuity, but because of the ability of God to do the humanly impossible. It is divine comedy: Sarah gets the joke, and she conceives and gives birth to the promise of God. Not surprisingly when her son is born he is called Isaac – which in Hebrew means 'laughter'. The promise has become flesh, and taken shape in the bundle of a baby.

There is rejoicing that God has indeed visited his people – that without him the great family of Abraham, Isaac and Jacob, could not have started. God made their beginning; for nothing is impossible to God.

New creation

At the beginning of the New Testament is the story of an empty womb. Matthew and Luke open their Gospels celebrating how God visits his people in the birth of Jesus. A young Jewish girl called Mary is chosen to be the mother of the Son of God. There is no suggestion that Mary – like Sarah – is longing and praying for a child of her own; there is no suggestion that Mary – like Sarah – is old and barren. Mary is a young virgin; but just as old age and barrenness are not barriers to the plan of God, neither is youth or virginity. For nothing is impossible with God.

In the Gospel Mary's virginity is important because it points to the truth of who her child is – "so the child will be holy and will be called Son of God." (Lk 1:35) Having a child is not *Mary's* idea; it is *God's*. As John puts it eloquently in his Gospel, Jesus is born

> not out of human stock
> or urge of the flesh
> or will of man
> but of God himself. (1:13)

Being the mother of Jesus is not something Mary can arrange for herself; it is something arranged by God. The child Jesus does not come as an answer to her longing and prayer, but comes as the new creation of God. Mary can say yes or no to God's choice of her. And today we celebrate Mary's 'yes' to being the mother of Jesus, the mother of God.

Mothering Jesus
In being the mother of Jesus Mary does the same as any mother – nurturing within her womb the great process of a little one taking shape. Another human being is formed in the mother's body, but the mother can never keep the child within her. Motherhood means not only *having* a baby, but *letting go* of the baby. Birth is not possessive: it is letting another life take its rightful place in the world. Birth is the act of painful separation – when the mother must let her child go for the first time.

And as every mother knows, giving birth is only the first of many times when mothers have to let go. Parents cannot 'have' their children all the time, for the time comes when they must foster not only their presence, but foster their going. Trust them to make their own lives in their own way.

That is something which Mary has to do – not only to nurture Jesus in his growing, but eventually let him go his way to make his appointed future. Jesus is Mary's son. He is her own, but not her own. He belongs to her, but also to many. Mary has to do what the Father did – let go of his beloved Son. And that is what Mary does: she does not anxiously clutch Jesus to herself, but gives him to us. She asks us to do what she does: share Jesus with everyone. Give him as life to others.

A God as good as his Word

Beginning with words

All of us go through life making promises to each other. Our promises vary from saying we'll meet someone at a certain time to committing ourselves to a certain person or to a way of life. Some promises are easy to keep and cost little: "Don't worry! I'll meet you at the corner shop at five o'clock." Other promises can take a whole life to keep: "To have and to hold from this day forward, for better for worse, for richer for poorer, in sickness and in health, to love and to cherish, till death us do part." When we make promises we invest *ourselves* in our words; we ask others to believe that we're as good as our word. We tell others that they can afford to hope in us.

At solemn moments of our life we use words to pledge our future. New beginnings are usually marked by words that are carefully said and publicly announced. Witnesses are usually around to take note of what is being said. It's as if the words we speak have a life of their own. As the poet Emily Dickinson wrote:

> A word is dead
> When it is said,
> Some say.
> I say it just
> Begins to live
> That day.

We hope that our words will live, but we know that there's nothing magical about them. It doesn't follow as night the day that we will do what we say. We spend a lot of time trying to catch up with our words. We often lag behind them; we fail to keep our promises; often we can't be bothered. When we fail to be as good as our word, people wonder whether our word is all that good. When we fail often, people pay little attention to what we say. And when that happens our words become like old currency that has no value. Or like "Monopoly" money – good only for games.

The Word that begins everything

In today's Gospel we hear the magnificent Prologue to John's Gospel: how in the beginning there was the Word through whom all things came to be. When John comes to speak about Jesus you notice how he goes back beyond the time of Jesus' birth and conception to the very beginning of time itself. He sees Jesus as the Word that was with God, the Word that was God. This Word was not only at the beginning; it *made* the beginning for

all creation. The Word of God worked. It wasn't just an empty word decorating the air; it was a Word that had power to make the beginning of the world.

Remember that in one of the stories of creation it tells how the world began through the word of God. "God said, 'Let there be ...' and so there was." In this story of Genesis, the story of the beginning, God is seen to make the beginning through his word. All that God has to do is to speak. When he speaks you know that something is *happening*. He speaks the world into existence. His word is creative: it always goes beyond himself to make happen what is said.

For God, to say is to do, to speak is to accomplish, to promise is to fulfil. God is always as good as his word. And John rejoices in his Gospel that this Word which made the beginning now comes into the world. The Word becomes flesh and dwells among us. The Word is not only a great power that makes all things; the Word is a person and becomes little in time and space. The Word of God has a new address. He comes among people, among his own elect, but experiences rejection. The Word is a person in search of a hearing, a human being in search of acceptance, the Son of God in search of acknowledgement. This is the great mystery we celebrate at Christmas.

He lives among us

At Christmas we celebrate the great mystery of God among us. This is very difficult to grasp: that God gave himself away in the person of Jesus, that he chose to reveal himself in the reality of the life and death of Jesus. This is a unique story in the history of religions. We believe that our main resource for understanding God is the person of his Son, Jesus. In Jesus we have everything there is to know about God.

At Christmas we celebrate the humility of God who came among us himself. We celebrate the love that waits for an answer. We know that if our words fail, the Word of God never fails. It has power still. That is why we pray before communion: "Lord, I am not worthy to receive you, but only *say the word and I shall be healed.*" We pray that God will speak his Word again in us. That just as he made the beginning through his Word, he will make a new beginning in us.

In this Eucharist we pray that the Word will grow in us; that it will influence all our own words so that we will be as good as our word. For this to be done, the Word of God and our own word will become one. And our own word will then work.

God revealed in Christ

Looking for Jesus

In her poem "A Legend from Russia", Phyliss McGinley tells the story of the old grandmother, Babushka, who is invited to meet the royal child just born in Bethlehem. The old woman is about to retire for the night "when out of the winter's rush and roar came shepherds knocking at her door." They share with her the good news that the long awaited child has now been born and beg her to come and give what help she can. Babushka is a good-hearted woman, but the warmth of her bed looks more appealing than a cold journey on a winter's night. She tells her night callers that she will go tomorrow, and when they ask her to give them some food that they can take in her stead, she again tells them, "Tomorrow".

When tomorrow dawns Babushka is as good as her promise. She prepares a basket with goods and gifts:

> A shawl for the Lady, soft as June,
> For the Child in the Crib a silver spoon,
> Rattles and toys and an ivory game.
> But the stable was empty when she came.

Babushka arrives too late to meet the royal child and share her gifts. She is angry with herself for not accepting the invitation and she begins to wander the world looking for the Christ-child. She joins the legions of wanderers down history who search for the one who will bring new hope and new meaning into their lives. In her search she finds children everywhere; she finds many children in their cradles and many mothers nursing their infants. With each child she finds, she leaves gifts in the hope that *that* child is the Christ-child. But she never knows for sure.

Those who worship; those who reject

In today's Gospel we have Matthew's story of the magi, pagan astrologers, who do indeed find the Christ-child and bring him their gifts. In writing his Gospel towards the end of the first century, Matthew is aware that Judaism has rejected Jesus as the Christ while many pagans (Gentiles) have accepted him. That situation is reflected in the story when we see King Herod and the Jewish leaders united in their rejection of Jesus, while the pagan travellers from faraway lands come to worship the child king of the Jews.

The star leads the wise men to Jerusalem where their inquiry causes confusion throughout the city. King Herod is especially nervous. He is portrayed like the Pharaoh at the time of the exodus from Egypt. The

Jewish historian Josephus tells us of the ancient legend surrounding Pharaoh: he was warned by astrologers that a liberator would be born who would lead the captive Hebrews to freedom. Pharaoh responded by ordering the massacre of newborn male children to ensure the liberator would never survive. However, the father of Moses was forewarned in a dream and Moses escaped to become the great leader of Israel.

In Matthew's Gospel, Jesus is the new Moses and the new Israel: "I have called my son out of Egypt" (2:15). King Herod is the second Pharaoh whose ruthlessness leads him to massacre innocent children – though Joseph is warned in a dream to flee with the mother and the child. The magi are seeking the king of the Jews, a title that was given to Herod by the Romans. *He* was ruler over all the Jewish territories for forty years and was merciless when his own security was threatened. Proof of that is the fact that he murdered one of his wives and two of his sons.

In the Gospel story, King Herod wants to know where this new king is. But Matthew knows that neither the ruling families of Judea nor the chief priests and the teachers of the law are interested in doing homage to Jesus. In the story of the magi, Matthew shows what Paul declares in his letter: that pagans share the promise of Christ Jesus "through the Gospel." Jesus, who was given first to the Jews as their king, is now given to all peoples. He is for all nations.

We, the seekers

When the wise men leave their gifts with the Christ-child they take away a treasure that surpasses anything they brought themselves. They take away the gift of knowing who Jesus is; they are enriched by their encounter with him; they can enrich others with the truth of their own experience. They are a summary of all those who journey in hope to Jesus and find in him their heart's desire. The wise men do not stay in Judea; they do not build a monument to mark the place of discovery. They return to their own country: faith in Jesus is not limited to any geographical boundary, but is a gift to be shared with others.

Our presence here numbers us among those who seek the face of the living God. We come here each week to celebrate our faith in Jesus as our Lord. At the end of each Eucharist we are "sent" to share with others what we have experienced here. We do not have to tramp the world like Babushka seeking the Christ-child. We find Christ here in the word and in the breaking of the bread and in the midst of the community. Let us celebrate the presence of the Lord here and enrich the lives of others with the light that has been revealed to us.

Exploring for God

The coming of the stranger

Many stories, ancient and modern, begin with the arrival of a stranger in a small town. With the coming of the outsider, the settled way of the neighbourhood is disturbed and the scene is primed for conflict. In a place where everyone knows everyone else a sudden and unannounced arrival can provoke reactions, from mild curiosity to acute fear. People's attention is engaged; questions are asked. Who is he? Why *this* place? Does this unknown traveller know something the locals do not? Is he privy to some secret knowledge? Will his presence mean danger for someone? Will the town ever be the same after he has gone?

In today's Gospel we hear Matthew's classic story of the arrival of strangers in Jerusalem. Their number is unknown – assumed to be three from the gifts they bring. They are called "magi", which is variously translated as astrologers, magicians, wise men. Whoever they are, their identity is never revealed. They know something the local people do not: that the king of the Jews has just been born in the neighbourhood of Jerusalem. The presence of the strangers, who are privy to this special knowledge, worries King Herod, the chief priests, the scribes, and the whole of Jerusalem. On hearing the news the establishment of Judaea gathers in an aristocratic huddle of discontent. The outsiders have unsettled the institution. The scene is set for conflict.

When two wisdoms collide

Matthew develops the scene with the care of a master storyteller. He ranges the wise men who follow natural means – a star – against the wise men of Judaea who are able to follow their own sign – the scriptures. It is clear from the story that the wise men of Judaea have enough information in the scriptures to discover the place where the new king will be born; but their discovery is useless, for it does not lead them to homage. They are not disposed to *act* on what has been revealed.

By contrast, the pagan strangers, after they have gone as far as they can in following the star, are willing to be instructed in a scripture that is foreign to them. They act on what has been given to them, and their journey leads them to their destination. They offer homage to the child, offer him their gifts, and then make their own way back to their country.

Matthew shows how the two wisdoms collide: the wisdom of the religious institution and the wisdom of the pagan strangers. Writing at a time when many non-Jews, Gentiles, were entering the Christian community, while many Jews had rejected the message of the Gospel,

Matthew demonstrates in the story of the magi that Jesus comes not only for the Jewish race but for the human race. In the second reading Paul proclaims the universal appeal of God's revelation in Jesus: "it means that pagans now share the same inheritance, that they are parts of the same body, and that the same promise has been made to them, in Christ Jesus, through the Gospel."

The different ways to God
The wise strangers of Matthew's Gospel are the vanguard of all Gentiles who make their own journey to God in Christ. They may have taken a route that seemed curious to a religious establishment that had so many antique maps in their possession; but God draws all sorts of different people to him by all sorts of different routes. The wandering magi were led to God more by natural wonder than dogmatic instruction, and this has made them symbols of hope for all who struggle to God by strange routes. A prayer to the magi, which Evelyn Waugh wrote for one of his fictional characters, catches something of this hope:

> You are my especial patrons, and patrons of all latecomers,
> of all who have a tedious journey to make to the truth,
> of all who are confused with knowledge and speculation,
> of all who through politeness make themselves partners in guilt,
> of all who stand in danger by reason of their talents...
>
> For his sake who did not reject your curious gifts, pray always for all the learned, the oblique, the delicate. Let them not be quite forgotten at the throne of God when the simple come into their kingdom.

In the spirit of that prayer the magi are the patrons of all those who see signposts to God that others neither see nor follow. Most of us travel to God by the routes that have been mapped out by generations of faithful Christians, but we should be hesitant to condemn those who take other roads in their search for the same God. If we are all exploring God, if we are journeying in faith and in love, then we can teach each other something new about the almighty. We may seem strange to each other, but what if the stranger is the one who has the address of God?

Finding out where Jesus is

The quest

Once upon a time, in a far off land deep in shadow, there lived two orphans who were very unhappy living in shadowland. One day they decided to leave their homeland and journey beyond the grey mountains until they could come face to face with the light that makes colours. So while the rest of the country was fast asleep in their grey beds, they packed their few belongings in a knapsack and set off on their quest to discover the light and bring it back to shadowland.

Most of the stories we remember from our own childhood are stories of quests where the hero leaves the world of the familiar and sets out for an unknown country in search of something special or someone special. Many of our great religious stories follow the same pattern – tales of people like Abraham and Moses who leave their homes for unfamiliar places and risk a legion of misfortunes in the hope that they will come to a place of peace and prosperity.

In Matthew's Gospel we have one of the most popular religious quest stories – the wise men who come from the east to seek the infant king of the Jews. It is a story which has caught the imagination of poets and artists – like T.S. Eliot in his poem, *The Journey of the Magi:*

> A cold coming we had of it,
> Just the worst time of the year
> For a journey, and such a long journey:
> The ways deep and the weather sharp,
> The very dead of winter.

Jesus for all

Matthew tells the story of how some wise men arrive in Jerusalem asking where they can find the newborn king whose star they have followed from the east. The old-born king, Herod, is not exactly delighted at the news – perhaps because he fears his own star may lose its place in the firmament in the light of the new competition. He calls together the wise men from Jerusalem, who consult the scriptures to find that a leader will emerge from Bethlehem in the land of Judah.

The wise men from the east continue their quest and come to journey's end in Bethlehem where the star halts over a house. They enter it and see the child with his mother Mary. They pay homage to the child, leave their unusual gifts of gold, frankincense and myrrh, and then quietly return to their own country without reporting to Herod.

Matthew's is the only Gospel to tell the story, and the question arises:

what does it *mean?* We sense that Matthew is telling us a wonderful truth, is revealing to us some hidden event, is trying to engage us in good news. And in the second reading today Paul tells us the meaning of the story when he writes: "God's secret plan was revealed to me and was unknown in past generations; it means that the Gentiles now share the same inheritance as the Jews, they are members of the same body, they share the same promise in Christ through the Gospel."

That is the meaning of the story of the magi! Matthew describes beautifully in a story the same truth that Paul affirms in his letter: the truth that Jesus is for all peoples. The wise men are the Gentiles, the non-Jews, like ourselves. We come from all over the world and we can find Jesus and do him homage. He is the infant king of the Jews but he is not the exclusive property of any tribe or nation: he belongs to us all, as we can all belong to him.

He is journey's end for all who seek the face of God, for all who seek for meaning and purpose in their lives. He came not only for the chosen race, but for the human race. He is for all of us.

We the seekers
In a sense the wise men are the ancestors of all of us who seek. We are all seekers: we seek for love, for acceptance, and for understanding. And we know that the journey towards wholeness and holiness is a journey without end. We do not have stars in the sky to guide us; but even the wise men had to stop being stargazers and consult the scriptures to find out where Jesus was. We don't have stars to guide us, but we do have the scriptures and each other in our journey to God.

The scriptures and the star led the wise men from the east to Bethlehem – which literally means "House of Bread". That is where our journey has taken us today, here in the house of bread.

We come here to this place as seekers hoping to find Jesus again in the word of the scripture and in the breaking of the bread. We believe that the scriptures will lead us to him again, and that we can commune with him in the breaking of the bread. In the word and in the sacrament we meet Jesus again. And we meet him in each other, in our frailty and brokenness. The Lord is present in each of us here.

We are all the hiding-place of God. Let us pray that the Lord will show himself through us to all peoples.

Funding people for change

The beginning of change

When we see people make a dramatic change in their lives we're usually curious to discover why. What makes people change the direction of their lives? Is it necessity? Are they just dissatisfied with their old way of life, or drawn to a new way of life? Why should someone give up the quiet security of village life and begin a way of life that will put him in a danger zone where secular and religious authority will be united against him? Why should Jesus leave the region of Galilee and head south on a three-day journey to see a prophet who lives in the wilderness?

In today's Gospel we have Matthew's account of Jesus' baptism – the great event that stands between the hidden life of Nazareth and the public life of the travelling ministry. Matthew tells us that Jesus heads south because he wants baptism from John. John's baptism was directed to his fellow Jews as a call to repentance to prepare the way for the promised one. In the Gospels of Mark and Luke there is no suggestion that John actually recognises Jesus to be the expected Messiah. In Matthew's Gospel, however, John is seen to recognise Jesus as one who is greater than himself – even though Matthew tells us later that John wonders in prison if Jesus is the one who is to come (11:3).

Matthew tells us that the purpose of Jesus' baptism is to *fulfil God's saving plan*. Jesus does not have to be baptised to be cleansed; rather, his baptism is seen in the Gospel as the moment when God's plan is fulfilled in Jesus. So, what's the plan that is fulfilled?

A plan fulfilled

When Jesus comes out of the water after his baptism, the heavens are opened, the Spirit of God descends on him, and a voice from heaven recognises him as "my Son, the Beloved". None of the evangelists suggests that any bystander notices these wonderful elements: it is not said that the people marvelled, or were astonished, or gave praise to God – reactions that are usually noted when miraculous happenings occur. Matthew is bringing out the *meaning* of Jesus' baptism in these elements: he is showing how Jesus, the Son of God, is the *fulfilment* of the ancient plan of God.

Part of that plan was expressed in the reading we heard from Isaiah:

Here is my servant whom I uphold,
my chosen one in whom my soul delights.

I have endowed him with my spirit
that he may bring true justice to the nations.

This word of God is seen to be fulfilled in Jesus, and Matthew actually uses this text as part of his Gospel (12:18). In the later Isaiah we hear the great prayer of the people: how God brought them through the waters, how God's spirit rested on them, the hope that God would "tear the heavens open and come down", the hope that God "our Father" would not stay silent (Is.63:7-64-11).

It is against the rich background of those ancient prophecies that Matthew tells the story of Jesus' baptism. *Now* is the time of fulfilment when the heavens *are* opened, when the Spirit of God *does* descend, and when God the Father *does* affirm his servant and son who comes out of the water. Matthew declares that *in Jesus* all the ancient hopes and longings are accomplished. Jesus is the Son of God; the Spirit of God rests on him; he will begin his ministry with the Father's authority and love.

In his account of Jesus' baptism, Matthew makes an important declaration of faith in Jesus: in him all prophecy is completed and a new age begins. The beginning of Jesus' public ministry is also the end of the long time of waiting. Jesus' baptism fulfils all the saving plan of God.

Funding others for change
The new beginnings that we make in our own lives may not mark the fulfilment of anyone's prophecy, but they probably mark the fulfilment of someone's hope. Sometimes we are so hesitant about making a new start that we end up in no man's land waiting for more weather reports. Every new beginning is a risk, and we undertake that risk sooner when we have people to underwrite our change. Sometimes we change only because we have someone who has lived out an ancient hope that our secret self can indeed grow strong and thrive. It's not a coincidence that Jesus only begins his big change when he is funded with the Father's love and support through his encounter with John the Baptist.

People are reluctant to change when they see that people are indifferent about whether they change or not. John the Baptist gave Jesus support; we know *that* because we know it was after his time with John that Jesus changed from living as an artisan in a small town to taking to the road in pursuit of his mission. John is a very important figure for Jesus: he is the only religious leader that leaves a deep impression on Jesus. And the good news is that Jesus himself is the one who underwrites our changes, who cares deeply that we do change for the better. The cross stands as the eternal proof of that.

Catching up with our baptism

A quiet emergence

During this coming year our principal guide to the story of Jesus will be the evangelist Mark. He is one of the great thinkers of early Christianity, the first Christian to put into writing his version of the story of Jesus The very early communities in the Church did not feel any need to commit the memory of Jesus to writing: they still had the apostles with them, and they all lived in expectation of the immediate return of Jesus. Preserving a written memory of Jesus, therefore, would be a waste of time – there would be nobody around to read it! This view changed, so that some thirty years after the death of Jesus there is not the same sense of urgency. Now it becomes important to assemble the traditional stories of Jesus and put them into some shape. Mark is the first to do this. It was he who invented the Gospel.

When Matthew and Luke come to write their Gospels, they begin their accounts with stories of the birth of Jesus. These are the Christmas stories, so familiar to us all. Luke has angelic choirs announcing the eternal significance of Jesus' birth; Matthew has wise men who come from a far country to waken up a sleepy Jerusalem with the news of the birth of their new king. These stories draw us into an early recognition of the greatness of Jesus.

In sharp contrast, Mark has nothing of this theological grandeur, nothing of this entrance of majesty. The earliest of the Gospel writers chooses to begin the story of Jesus not with the birth of the child but with the baptism of the adult Jesus. It is a quiet emergence from obscurity, a humble beginning. From a past that can only be guessed at, Jesus is called to a unique mission. The beginning that Jesus makes in public is the beginning that Mark makes for his Gospel.

The baptism

Jesus is not the only person who seeks out John the Baptist. Mark says that all the country of Judaea and all the people of Jerusalem journey out to the place where John is baptising in the Jordan. John's preaching has attracted people from the south to join his movement of revival. But Jesus is not from Judaea; he is not from the city of Jerusalem. He is a native of Galilee, the most northerly province of Palestine, the one least known for its religious orthodoxy. As the Pharisees tell Nicodemus: "Go into the matter, and see for yourself: prophets do not come out of Galilee." (Jn. 7:52) Galilee was renowned for the armed Zealots who hid out in the highlands, not for any prophets. However, Jesus is to change that.

So it is that the Galilean comes south. It is a measure of John's importance that Jesus makes a three-day journey south to the place in the Jordan valley where people immerse themselves in the river in response to John's call. It is unlikely that Jesus' relationship with John was confined to the moment of baptism; but it is the baptism that is the most important moment. Jesus is baptised in the company of many other people; for him, as for them, a new time begins.

The baptism marks a significant time for Jesus personally: he experiences his call to mission, he is grasped by the Spirit of God, he is recognised as the chosen servant and Son. The baptism also signals that a time of waiting has been ended – waiting for the heavens to open, the pouring out of the spirit, the new time of salvation. Jesus' new beginning is God's new beginning: through the person of Jesus God will reach out to people in a new way. Whatever Jesus does will be accomplished by the power of God's Spirit in him. That is the significance of his baptism.

Growing into our own baptism
The Spirit that empowered Jesus to make his new beginning is the same Spirit that empowered us in our baptism. Few of us can remember that moment; most of us were carried to the font, infants in the arms of our parents or godparents. Our name was given to us, our commitment was spoken for us, our future was promised to God. We spend our lives catching up with our beginning, struggling to make good the large promises made on our behalf. What started at our christening needs to be validated by our personal decisions. We have not left our baptism behind us; it faces us each day as God's expectation of us.

Our baptism is not the only time we are empowered by the Spirit. The great medieval theologian Thomas Aquinas spoke of "new sending in the Spirit", times of grace when God enlivens people in special ways for different tasks. The Spirit does not retire at our baptism; he is not shy about helping adults. We should all pray for the sending of the Spirit, particularly when we face change and important decisions. The Spirit of God is the power behind new beginnings. If we are willing to begin, he is there to grace our new venture in faith.

The public beginning

The risk of beginning

"Do you remember the first time we met?" she asks.

"Well, it's a long time ago, dear," her husband replies.

"Oh, but you must remember. You were wearing that dreadful donkey-brown suit and I was awash in ocean green."

"Really," he says.

"Yes, and you were so shy about introducing yourself, clutching nervously at your tie. And I smiled at you, and then you started to inspect the carpet. Remember? It's a good job I made the first move – otherwise there wouldn't have been any *us,* would there, dear?"

"No, I suppose not, dear."

Sometimes beginnings are not remembered because they didn't seem important at the time: it was just another wet Wednesday with nothing much happening, and no promise in the air. However, some events in our lives *become* important because we can see later that it was *then* that something started, it was when we met that particular person that our lives changed. And when we remember that time we invest a significance in it that wasn't there at the time.

Of course there are beginnings that we know are important at the time – like baptisms, marriages, and ordinations. We like to mark these beginnings as important, so we surround them with ceremony to give a sense of occasion. So the relatives are called in, photographers are hired, priests officiate, solemn words are spoken, cameras click, music is played, and there is an atmosphere of rejoicing.

But there is also a certain nervousness in the air, since no matter how big the beginning is, it is only that – a *beginning.* The participants might wonder whether they'll be able to honour all the solemn words, whether they will have the capacity to make them come true. All beginnings are risks. All beginners need help.

The baptism of Jesus

We rarely think of Jesus as a beginner, just as we rarely think of Jesus needing help. But in today's feast we celebrate those two things: Jesus makes a big beginning to his ministry, and he receives help in the power of the Holy Spirit.

All the Gospels agree that John the Baptist was very important in the life of Jesus. It is the towering, fearless figure of John that stands between the hidden life of Jesus and his public ministry. Before Jesus goes to John he is known by the local people simply as the son of a carpenter, who stays in the small town of Nazareth. After his time with John, Jesus becomes widely known as a wandering preacher with a unique prophetic mission. Clearly, something happened to Jesus while he was with John. He underwent a change that gave his life a new direction.

While he is with John, Jesus makes his big beginning. As Peter says in the second reading, "Jesus of Nazareth began in Galilee after John had been preaching baptism." John was a very important turning-point in the life of Jesus – so important that Jesus says of him later: "of all the children born of women, there is no one greater than John" (Lk.7:28). And in the fourth Gospel we are told that the first disciples of Jesus are ex-disciples of John.

In fact John was so important that some people in the first century thought that *he* was the Messiah – as Luke tells us in today's Gospel. One of the reasons they thought that was because like many people Jesus went to John to be baptised. Perhaps that is why Luke has the Baptist in prison before he tells the story of Jesus' baptism: to assure his readers of the supremacy of Jesus!

In today's Gospel we heard how after his baptism Jesus is at prayer. The opening of the heavens is a signal for the descent of the Spirit. You can see the Old Testament backdrop for this scene in Isaiah when he writes: (63:15-19)

Look down from the heavens and regard us...
Lord do not hold back, for you are our Father.
O that you would rend the heavens and come down...

Now Luke celebrates the time when God no longer holds back but rends the heavens to signal the beginning of Jesus' ministry. Jesus is anointed for his prophetic mission by the Holy Spirit, the great enabler, the one who helps people to achieve God's plan. So, Jesus is not alone when he makes his great beginning. He begins his journey in the power of the Holy Spirit and in the love of the Father. He starts out on a difficult road that will eventually lead to an appointment with death.

As we celebrate Jesus' great public beginning, we look at our own beginnings. And if some of them look a bit shabby now or half-hearted, we take consolation from the Gospel challenge to begin *again.* There probably won't be any doves or voices from heaven, but as Gospel people we make our beginnings like Jesus. We are not alone. We make them in the power of the Spirit and in the love of the Father. So, let us take courage to face our own road.

THE SEASON OF LENT

On the spiritual life

Introduction

At the beginning of Lent the Church sets before us Jesus' reflections on the three great cardinal works of the spiritual life: prayer, fasting, and almsgiving. We are invited to become involved in all three, so it is only right that we should reflect on Jesus' advice which is the word of God for us today.

Before speaking on any of the three, Jesus first gives an opening warning about practising piety in order to be seen by people, about being publicly pious while keeping a wandering eye alert on audience reaction. Jesus' position is unambiguous: he's against it. He's not against people sharing their light with others, for the point of that is to give glory to God. He's against people using religion to direct attention to themselves.

Prayer

The Jews were required to pray at set times of the day: at 9 in the morning, at noontime, and at 3 in the afternoon. Wherever they were, they were supposed to stop, stretch out their arms with hands facing heavenwards, and bow their heads. But some people would make sure that it so happened that they were on a top step or at a busy street corner on the stroke of noon, so that they could do a muscular demonstration of fidelity in public, ensuring that their prayers were loud and long. Jesus doesn't think much of posturing prayers which stop the traffic and which are calculated for home consumption, when people might confuse length with fidelity, or confuse fluency with sincerity.

The point about prayer is that it is addressed to the Father, not to those who have their tape-recorders switched on. And Jesus gives the test of true prayer: that it is an activity that goes on in the secret places of our lives, when the audience has all gone home, when the tape-recorders are off, when our doors are closed, and when our hearts are open to the Father who loves us. As one of the great rabbis put it: "God says to Israel, pray in the synagogue of your city; if you cannot, pray in your bed; if you cannot, commune with your heart and be still."

Fasting

Like prayer, fasting was an important part of the spiritual tradition and was a sign of repentance. Fasting was always linked to repentance: if it is not, it can be reduced simply to the theology of weightwatchers. Jesus criticises those who make sure that their faces look sufficiently collapsed to leave nobody in any doubt that their owners are on the job. In Palestine the two days of fasting were Monday and Thursday, which also happened to be the

market days. People could use the market-place to advertise their religious fervour. Jesus says no to this. Undertaker faces are no guarantee of authentic Christianity. Your face should look as if you have rented the sun. Again, what is important is that God knows what you do.

What are we to fast from? St John Chrysostom wrote: "I tell you it is possible to fast while not fasting. Is this a riddle? By enjoying food while having no taste for sin. That is a better kind of fasting." We are first obliged to fast from sin. There is no point in missing dinner and spending the evening demolishing our neighbour. We must starve our sins before we starve our stomachs, and that will keep fasting linked to repentance.

Almsgiving

When it comes to giving alms to the poor, Jesus thinks little of those who make sure that the trumpet sounds first, that people are paying attention before the gift is given. Jesus gives the maxim: "your left hand must not know what your right hand is doing." In the temple there was a room called the Chamber of the Silent, where people could atone for their sins by making offerings anonymously from which the poor could be helped secretly. This is the kind of giving approved by Jesus: it is quiet and it is for the benefit of the poor.

What can we give? We should share the most precious gifts we have received: love, compassion, understanding and forgiveness. That is what forgiveness is for – it is for giving. "With all his giving, he never gives himself." We are asked to give ourselves, and in that we have the marvellous example of Jesus. He gave generously of himself: he was at great pains to share with others his time, his energy, his many gifts. In the end he gave himself away and shares with us his body and blood.

Conclusion

So the Church asks us at the beginning of Lent to renew our own lives in the great spiritual works of prayer, fasting, and almsgiving, and to heed Jesus' advice in today's Gospel. Today we try to begin and we receive the ashes as a sign that we are willing to undertake the Gospel way of life. When we receive the ashes we hear again the first words of Jesus in Mark's Gospel: "Repent and be faithful to the Gospel." So, let us begin our Lent.

69

The word of God that questions us

In the beginning

To explain the present we always need to look at the past. We know that if we live our lives forwards we understand them backwards. So to discover why things have turned out the way they have, we make a journey into the past in an effort to uncover the origin of it all. All great cultures and religions have a sacred story that describes the beginning of the world. Most of these stories are a variation on a simple theme: in the beginning it was good, but then it got worse! To account for the order and disorder of their own world the ancient storytellers and writers told tales of the beginning. That is genesis, the story of the beginning.

In today's first reading we hear from the great Hebrew story of genesis how it all went wrong. At first it was blissful in the garden of Eden. Man and woman knew happiness together and no shame as they lived in harmony with nature and the animal kingdom. It was the age of innocence and of peace with God, but it did not last. In eating the forbidden fruit, Adam and Eve disobey the word of God. Their eyes testify to their new knowledge and lost innocence: ashamed of themselves and afraid of God, their first reaction is to hide parts of themselves from each other and the whole of themselves from God. Cover-up becomes the new way of relating to God and each other.

The writer of Genesis tells us a profound truth about sin and its effects. Because of sin there is dislocation everywhere; everything becomes askew; nothing is as it was planned to be. It means that we can be open neither with God nor with each other. We spend our time and energy in cover-up. We cannot face God. In the Genesis story God has to come searching for Adam and Eve. So the first question of God in the Bible is the everlasting one: "Where are you?" And if salvation is a matter of being found by God, that first question is the root of all biblical questions: "Where are you?"

The word of God

When God finds Adam and Eve he expels them from the garden into the wasteland. The first human beings are the first refugees: in the beginning there was the exile. Banished from the garden they must make do in a world where they will have to struggle for survival; a world where human relationships will be fragile; a world where fidelity to God's word will always be a challenge. Genesis tells us that sin enters the world through disobedience to the word of God. But there is a promise of salvation which leaves room for hope. As Paul tells us in the second reading: as sin entered the world through one man's disobedience, so salvation enters the world through one man's obedience. That one man is Jesus of Nazareth.

Jesus comes in the name of God. Like God in the garden of Eden, he comes to look for those who have hidden themselves from God: "I have come to seek out and to save the lost." Jesus is the one who comes seeking us out, calling our names, knocking on our doors, asking to be let in. He is the quest of God in search of a lost people.

The mission of Jesus is to save. Of all the verbs that describe what Jesus does, the verb "to save" is the most important. Saving is the verb of God. Jesus is the Saviour. But his mission to save is not free from trial. He is tempted to abandon trust in his Father and go the way of power and prestige and public display. Before his mission gets under way the Gospel shows him in the wasteland facing a series of temptations, the same temptations that Israel faced in the desert.

Jesus is seen to face temptation with the power of the word of God. He does not argue himself; he uses the word of scripture and makes fidelity to that word the mark of his mission. He lives by the word of God. He feeds on that word. Obedience to that word will take him through trial and temptation to the cross itself, the great sign of our salvation. In Jesus' obedience to the word of God we are saved.

Lent

At Easter we will celebrate the resurrection, the most important feast in the Christian calendar. Now we begin Lent as a time to ready ourselves for that great feast. We are invited to let God find us where we are. He has the same question to ask each of us: "Where are you?" During this Lent we can make time to look where we are in our lives and discover God's presence anew. We are challenged to make time to listen to his word. We are invited to let him get close to who we are and how we are.

Traditionally Lent is a time when we give up some things or take up some things. Whatever we do, it would be a good idea to allow the word of God to get close. The word comes to question who we are; it comes to support the kind of people we could be. We could make a little time – five or ten minutes each day – to let the word form us as it formed Jesus. Let it influence what we do and say. Let the word of God find us so that we can emerge from our hiding places into the peace of his presence.

Facing Satan

Facing the adversary

When political leaders are faced with financial upheaval, they often like to divert people's attention from the obvious crisis. When the emperor Nero was faced with economic collapse in Rome in A.D. 64, his chosen distraction was the burning of the city. The fire burnt for a week and destroyed half of the imperial city. Nero accused the Christians, who up to that time had been tolerated as a Jewish sect, and an era of persecution began. The followers of Jesus were thrown to the wild beasts in the arena, and the citizens of Rome were entertained by the humiliation and cruel death of their fellow human beings. People's attention was diverted from economic questions, but the bill for the diversion was paid by innocents.

The evangelist Mark wrote his Gospel for the persecuted Christians in Rome, who lived in constant fear of being thrown to the wild beasts. When Mark opens his account of the story of Jesus, he tells how Jesus is with the wild beasts in the wilderness. Jesus is the innocent one, but his innocence does not protect him from conflict, from trial, from suffering, from facing the adversary. Innocence does not dispel conflict; rather, it attracts it. Before the beginning of his ministry Jesus is seen to face trial in the wilderness, the traditional arena of Satan. Before going public, the resolve of the innocent one is put to the test.

Satan

Mark says that Jesus was tempted by Satan. The word Satan in Hebrew simply means an *adversary,* and in the Old Testament it was first used of human opponents. For example, when the Philistines were afraid that the young David would emerge as their *satan,* they simply meant their enemy (1 Sam 29:4). When King Solomon delighted that there was neither *satan* nor misfortune any more, he meant that he was at rest from his enemies (1 Kgs 5:4). The original meaning of the word Satan was anyone who was a dangerous opponent. Later the word came to mean one who pleads a case against another, an accuser of people before God, the public prosecutor of heaven. Finally it came to mean God's Adversary, a demonic spirit opposed to God.

By the time of the New Testament, Satan was understood to be the principal spirit of evil who was involved in a mighty struggle against God, a struggle that would only end in the last days of history. When Jesus comes to be baptised, the Father declares him to be his beloved Son. Now in the wasteland the Son of God meets the Adversary of God. The Son must decide whether to follow the way of the Father or the way of Satan. His new beginning is a time of change and a time of temptation. But it is also a time for clarification. It always helps to know who and what you are against. And who better than your enemy to help you clarify what you must oppose and what you must defend.

When Jesus emerges from the wilderness of temptation, he does not leave temptation forever behind him. The Adversary will appear again in the ministry – as when Jesus tells Peter: "Get behind me, Satan! Because the way you think is not God's way but man's" (Mk 9:33). Jesus has to think God's way, and he becomes the spokesman not for Satan but for the Father. When he begins preaching he tells the people that the time has come to let God rule in their lives. If this is to happen they must repent and believe the Good News. What God is doing is Good News. And the Good News is not only the message of Jesus but Jesus himself.

Facing Lent

Few of us associate the time of Lenten discipline with Good News, particularly if that means facing the adversary within and around us. At the beginning of Lent the Church always takes us into the wilderness with Jesus, to face the power that is opposed to the Gospel. The Good News is that we do this *with Jesus and in the company of his followers.*

None of us should have to face the wilderness alone; none of us should be thrown back on our own resources. We are all tempted; we all fail; we all sin. Sometimes we might wonder if there is an exit from the wilderness. All of us need to hear like Jesus the voice of the Father that recognises us as his beloved children. When we hear that voice the call to repent is the call to stay in the company of the one who loves us. The Gospel challenges us to change our minds about the way we think, change our hearts about the Gospel we ignore, and change our ways about habits of sin.

This is a lifetime's task. Jesus did not overcome Satan in the wilderness, he achieved that only in his death. Lent reminds us of our need *to begin again* facing the enemy within us. And the Good News is that when we do that we take the road that leads us to the kingdom of God.

In the desert

Hunger and doubt

At the heart of the Old Testament there is a great story of liberation: how God intervened to free his people from slavery. The people were immigrants in Egypt, used as cheap labour, and their number was kept low by the systematic killing of newborn male infants. In the story of the exodus the Jews still celebrate the momentous event of freedom from oppression and the beginning of their journey to the promised land. And in today's first reading we heard how the people always kept that good memory alive.

However, after they were freed from slavery the people of Israel had to face a new problem: the wilderness. Their new freedom meant new pain and some of them didn't think much of an escape that led them into a wilderness! Some preferred living under Pharaoh: they preferred the security that went with bondage to the pain that went with freedom. For the price of freedom was wilderness.

During their 40 years in the desert the people were tested. They were hungry and wondered if God would pay attention. They were divided in their hearts about God: they wanted to trust him, but their empty stomachs made them doubt. The promised land seemed far away and their hunger was here and now. They were told there was a purpose in their hunger: "to teach you that man does not live by bread alone but by every word that comes from the mouth of God." (Deut.6:4) The great commandment asked them to be *wholehearted* in their commitment to God.

The testing of Jesus

It is against that background of Israel's testing in the desert that the story in today's Gospel is told. Jesus is the new Israel; he has spent 40 days in the wilderness; he is hungry and is tested. And he is tested to see if he will keep the ancient law of his people: to serve God with his whole heart, with his whole soul, and with his whole might.

Jesus is tested to see if he is totally committed or not. Is he like Israel in the desert – half-hearted about God's plan? Can you be hungry and still trust God? Can you follow God with your *whole heart* even when you are aware of the vacancy inside you? The Gospel tells us that Jesus is wholehearted in his commitment and stays loyal to his Father's plan. And when he preaches Jesus sets great store by the undivided heart: "Do not set your hearts on things to eat and to drink...set your heart first on the kingdom of God and these he will give you as well." (Lk 12:29f)

Jesus is also tempted to believe that he can serve God without pain. Do a swan dive from the wing of the temple and land without a scratch! The question is: can Jesus love God with his *whole soul* even when his own life is in danger? Will Jesus risk his life for the sake of his mission or will he opt for self-preservation? Can you love God even when your life is slipping away?

Jesus' whole life answers yes to this question. He knows that loving God does not mean exemption from harm. He will teach us that we will be saved; he does not tell us that we will be safe. In the end, Jesus' own death on the cross proves that he loves more than life itself – when no angels will come to keep him from harm.

Finally, Jesus is tested about his attitude to power and wealth. To get power will he go to any lengths? Will he love God with his *whole might,* with everything he is and has? Or will he grasp for the kind of power and prestige that most people aspire to and most people admire? Will he base his kingdom on twelve shaky apostles or on the firm ground of real estate?

Jesus' whole life says no to that kind of power and authority. And he will teach his own followers to avoid that kind of power: "You know that among pagans the rulers lord it over them, and their great men make their authority felt. This is not to happen among you. No; anyone who wants to be great among you must be your servant" (Mt.20:24f). And Jesus teaches that with his whole life: he is the Servant of God.

Our testing

Jesus lives his life facing real temptations and that is a measure of his humanity. As we enter Lent we ask ourselves how we face those temptations too. When times get rough and we feel hungry and alone, do we still trust in God? When our life just seems a vast vacancy, do we still believe in the Father who loves us? Are we willing to risk our necks for the sake of the Gospel, or do we settle for guarding our own security? Do we make our authority felt so that people are degraded, or is it a real service to others?

These are not easy questions. They were not easy for Jesus. That is why we need forty days: to let these questions reach us again so that at Easter we can proclaim with an undivided heart that Jesus is the Lord of our lives.

Journey of life and death

The life journey

One of the ancient images we still use to describe life is the "journey" that we all make from the womb to the grave. The image of the journey speaks of a passage through time and places; it includes the people we have met, the kind of time we have had, and the successes and failures we have experienced on the way. Although many people aspire to the same goals in life, everyone's journey is different in its own details. We all have to make our own journey; it is life's task that no one can do for us.

With most of the journeys we make in life we know our destination and how to get there. If we are unsure, we just check the map. But our life journey is not so easy. This is because life is not only a journey, it is a *search:* we all have to discover for ourselves the paths that will lead us to what we seek. Some of the roads we take lead us to dead ends, and unless we want to pitch our tent in a dead end we move on. We learn that it is important to keep going. As Robert Louis Stevenson observed:

> To travel hopefully is a better thing than to arrive, and the true success is to labour.

Changing direction

In the course of their lives many people change direction and explore unfamiliar paths. In today's first reading we hear how something happens to Abram that dramatically changes the course of his life. He is invited to leave the world of the familiar, his country and his father's house, and find his security in the promise of God. He cannot see either the land or the family he has been promised, yet he begins this journey without maps. Living as a nomad he has no land, and with his wife Sarai barren he has no children. But he travels hopefully in the belief that one day his journey will lead to the fulfilment of God's promises.

Throughout his journeying Abram experiences setbacks and trials; but he travels on, rooted in the conviction that God's purposes are being furthered. This same conviction works in the heart of another man who changed direction in his life: Paul. As we hear from the second reading Paul is persuaded that the hardships which come from following the Gospel do indeed serve the purposes of God. Something happened to Paul which altered the whole course of his life. And even though many people were suspicious of the new direction he was following, Paul himself maintained this course until his death. In his death itself God's plan was being furthered.

To know that suffering and death can further God's plan is not easy to appreciate. Especially when that death is your own. This is something which Jesus has to face. Remember too that Jesus has changed direction in his life – a change that confused his family and neighbours when he left Nazareth to take up the work of the wondering prophet. The more Jesus shares his understanding of the reality of God and the kingdom, the more determined are the religious authorities to be rid of him.

As his ministry develops Jesus becomes increasingly aware that to carry out his Father's mission will bring him face to face with a violent death. Before he tells us the story of the transfiguration Matthew tells us how "Jesus began to make it clear to his disciples that he was destined to go to Jerusalem and suffer grievously at the hands of the elders and the chief priests and scribes, to be put to death and raised on the third day." (16:21) Matthew tells us that Jesus understands his journey to death as one which furthers the plan of God.

Confirmed by love

The Gospels tell us that Jesus did not face the knowledge of his violent death alone. That kind of knowledge can paralyse someone. What the story of the transfiguration tells us is that Jesus is enabled to make that journey to Jerusalem in the declared love of the Father. The direction which Jesus has to follow will cost him his life. In the story of the transfiguration Matthew shows us that Jesus is not just the one who is to suffer but that he is the beloved Son of God. These two go together. The suffering and the glory are evident in the one person of Jesus. In the transfiguration the name of Jesus is called in love: he is named and owned by the Father, and we are all directed to listen to him.

In our own journeys we can face difficult decisions more surely in the knowledge that we are loved and supported. When we hear our name called in love we can face our road to Jerusalem. The power of that love funds us to face the future, just as its absence makes the future a loveless landscape. In the death of Christ God demonstrated the extremes of his love. It is that love that we celebrate here. It helps us to travel hopefully. It enables us to keep on striving until we can rest at last in the love that knows our name best.

Facing the mountain of death

Holocaust

An old man and an old woman, Abraham and Sarah, stand at the beginning of Israel's faith. The arithmetic of their ages was impressive, yet they longed for a son, prayed for a son, waited for a son. When the son arrived, the ancient parents called him Isaac, which means laughter. So it was that Abraham's faith in God was rewarded. He was God's original accomplice, the first to turn his back on civilization for the sake of a promise that had no place on a map. He is hailed as the father of the Jews and the Arabs, and as our forefather in faith. He stands as a large presence at the beginning of so many journeys in faith.

The day comes when Abraham is tested by God. "Take your son," God said "your only child Isaac whom you love, and go to the land of Moriah. There you shall offer him as a burnt offering, on a mountain I will point out to you." Abraham is asked to make a burnt offering of his son. The Hebrew word used is *ola,* which means holocaust. The ultimate act of child abuse.

Abraham agrees. There is no argument, no protest, no anguished madness. A father is asked to be the executioner of his beloved son. The secret is his alone. He says nothing to Sarah, the mother of this new victim. Their future is concentrated in this child, and now Abraham is expected to put a torch to his son and future hope. He takes the road to Moriah.

The writing is spare and terse. We know nothing of the journey – whether there was any conversation between the one who was to face death and the one who was to make death – we are simply told that they arrive. The wood is arranged for the fire, the altar is built for the victim, the knife is at hand for the executioner. When Abraham seizes the knife to kill his son, he is given a new command, not to kill his son. Instead of making human sacrifice, Abraham makes an animal sacrifice of a ram that is caught in a bush nearby.

Questions

The action comes to an end, but the painful questions begin. If God needs that kind of human suffering to be God, who needs that kind of God? The theology that makes God out to be a torturer and a sadist is one that invites us to worship the executioner. If Abraham had killed his son, wouldn't his image of a loving and compassionate God go up in the flames? If Abraham emerges as totally committed to God, what worth is his commitment when it makes a victim out of the innocent? What about Isaac? Are innocents always the casualties of other people's total commitment? Some people may argue that Abraham's suffering was good for him; but as Elie Wiesel, a survivor of the Holocaust, noted:

> the idea that suffering is good for Jews is one that owes its popularity to our enemies...I have never really been able to accept the idea that inhumanity could be one more way for man to move closer to God.

But perhaps the story of Abraham and Isaac is an instruction by the writer, an argument which shows that God is *not* pleased with human sacrifice. Ritual murder and human sacrifice were common practice among the people of the region. In the story of Abraham human sacrifice *appears to be what God wants but turns out to be what God actually abolishes.* The angel stops the ritual slaughter of a human being, and an animal is sacrificed instead. Thus animal sacrifice replaces human sacrifice, just as later bread and wine will replace animal sacrifice. In that understanding some humane progress can be measured.

The Father's risk
This progress, however, seems to suffer a set back in the second reading when Paul says that "God did not spare his own Son". Moriah is followed by Golgotha, except that this time no angel turns up to halt the execution and save the innocent victim. This interpretation comes close to making God the Father out to be an executioner, someone who actually plans the cruel death of his beloved Son.

No one would accept this as tolerable of any human being. Why should we ascribe to God the kind of behaviour we find repulsive in humanity? In letting go of his Son, the Father had to let him enter fully into the human condition. (It was the devil, not the Father, who wanted Jesus to play at being God.) All parents worry about the fate of their children, and they cannot take responsibility for the variety of complex events that shape their childrens' lives. That is the risk of letting go. Parents don't plan their childrens' pain; they can only suffer with them. So it is when the Father sees his beloved Son face death on Golgotha. That event is the consequence of his Son's way of loving. The Father in his time will honour this.

On the mountain

A name called in love

Maude and Harry have been married for fifteen years and their relationship is limited to newspapers exchanged at breakfast-table and weather reports noted at dinner-table. Maude spends her days lingering over the housework because she dreads the time when she has nothing to do. Harry works long hours and says he is too tired to talk in the evenings – so they settle for drowsy boredom in front of the television. Maude never hears Harry call her by her name; only as "you". She feels like an old plant that has been left to wither quietly behind a curtain in the attic.

One day Maude's friend, Mabel, arrives and tries some advice: "Maude, take a look at yourself! You're always going around with a colony of curlers in your head and tripping over your face. You're a mobile mess, dear. What you need is a new hairdo and a new outfit – then Harry will notice you. Get some spark, dear! Tomorrow, we will go shopping."

Next day Maude spends hours at the hairdresser and at various stores. Mabel is enthusiastic about the results, but Maude feels the whole exercise is wasted effort. After their long day they return to wait for Harry. And when the key turns in the lock Maude stands up feeling foolish.

When Harry comes in, he stops; he looks at his wife and when he sees her he realises what he has done. He moves over to her, takes her in his arms, and calls her name over and over again. When that happens, Maude becomes radiant and aglow. She is transfigured – not because she has a new outfit but because this is the first time in years she has heard her name called in love.

Jesus recognised in love

In today's Gospel we hear the story of Jesus becoming radiant and aglow as he is recognised by God as "my Son, the Chosen One." Jesus has had less success in being recognised by others. Because of what Jesus *does* and *says,* people begin asking questions about who he really is. The neighbours think they know: "This is Joseph's son, surely." Others are not so sure. The disciples ask: "Who is this who commands the waves?" Most people reckon that Jesus is more than meets the eye.

Jesus also promotes the question about himself by asking: "Who do people say I am?...Who do you say I am?" These are risky questions to ask because people have a habit of getting the answers wrong! In answer to his questions Jesus is told that he is an ancient prophet come back – like Elijah – or the messiah who will have victory without suffering. Of course no one will fully know who Jesus is until after the resurrection; but, meantime, the question is important. Nobody gets the answer right and Jesus goes to the mountain to pray.

In the experience of prayer it is clear that Jesus is not Elijah. Neither is he Moses, the greatest of the ancient prophets. They appear on the scene to direct our attention to a journey Jesus must make to Jerusalem. Peter makes a suggestion that echoes down history: if in doubt, build! But the focus is not on architectural posterity, but on who Jesus is: "This is my Son, the Chosen One. Listen to him." Is it any wonder Jesus is radiant and aglow? He has an answer to his prayer. There is someone who gets his name right and that someone is his Father. The deepest part of Jesus is called forth. The Father doesn't just recognise Jesus but *recognises him in love* as his chosen one, and that transfigures Jesus. That recognition is allied to what Jesus must do: being who he is means he must take the road to Jerusalem. And when Jesus comes down the mountain that is what he does: he sets his face towards Jerusalem where he will come face to face with death.

The transfiguration enables Jesus to make the most difficult journey in his life – to take the road that leads to Calvary.

The ministry of transfiguration
Transfiguration is not a solitary event in the Gospel but one that happens over and over again. Throughout his public ministry Jesus transfigured many people – the broken, the wounded, and the wayward. He called to the deepest part of people and transfigured them by the power of God's love, the same power that transfigured Jesus himself. For Jesus that experience was getting closer to who he really was. And we all get closer to who we really are when we hear our name called in love. When that happens we become radiant, and we are enabled to face the future.

We can understand transfiguration better when we ask: what would it take to transfigure *us?* What would it take to transfigure the people we know? Who calls our name in love? Whose name do we call in love? In our Lenten journey we are asked to transfigure each other by the power of God's love in us. We are all called to the ministry of transfiguration. And like Maude and Harry we might even get a face-lift in the process!

Stories at a well

Meeting difference

When two people meet for the first time they can soon become overwhelmed by the real difference between them. The difference of sex, age, personality, background, religion, nationality etc. can all contribute to making the encounter short, sharp and hopeless. The two people might be unable to face each other honestly because the barriers between them seem insurmountable. Nothing will happen unless one of them takes the initiative to overcome the difference between them. And nothing will come of that initiative unless the other person is intrigued into responding.

A man and a woman meet at a well beyond the edge of town. They are strangers – not only because they have never met before but because they should never be meeting at all. He is a Jew who is travelling through foreign territory; she is a Samaritan who is on home ground. Their peoples have been estranged from each other for centuries, and that ancient hostility has been kept alive by each generation. According to their own traditions they should remain strangers to each other. But will *this* man and *this* woman allow that estrangement to dictate their attitudes to each other? Will they rise above the mutual hostility of their own traditions and face each other honestly?

Jesus and the woman

Of course this is not just any man; for that matter the Samaritan is not just any woman. In writing the story John is anxious to tell his readers who Jesus is: that he is the Messiah and the saviour of all peoples. But first he shows us Jesus as the weary and thirsty traveller who wants to make inroads into people's lives. No matter who they are. It is Jesus who makes the first move expressing his need for a drink from her. Thirst knows no boundaries.

The woman is taken aback that a Jew, no matter how thirsty, would bother to ask a Samaritan for a drink. Jesus expects her to be a *good* Samaritan and his expectation confuses her. He then intrigues her by suggesting that if she knew his real identity she would ask him for living water. The fact that he has no bucket worries her, but the water Jesus has to give turns into a spring inside people. Thinking that Jesus has a cure for thirst the woman calls him "sir" and now imagines she can avoid trekking to wells in the middle of nowhere.

But Jesus is not talking about making the water authorities redundant. He now focuses on the woman's track record with men. She has a thirst for meeting Mr Right, but the thirst has not been satisfied after five husbands.

And she is living with another man. Clearly this woman is familiar with disappointment in love; clearly she is still hoping to meet the right man who can fulfil her deepest needs. Now she is facing a man who is not just another man.

She knows that. She now calls Jesus "prophet". He is a man who knows who she is and yet does not leave her in a heap of pain. He doesn't call her names; he doesn't reprimand her; he merely states how things are. But she moves the conversation on to discuss the proper place to worship God. Jesus is talking about her sex life and she wants to have a seminar on liturgy! When people get too close to where we live, we all want to take a helicopter out of the conversation and move it to a painless, abstract level.

The woman as messenger

Jesus follows her cue and talks about the liturgy. But he is not too concerned about the proper address to worship God; he is more concerned that the worship of God be done in spirit and in truth. Jesus leads the conversation back to where it was. The truth. How can you worship God if you don't face the truth about yourself? What kind of cosmetic worship are we talking about that is not linked to who people are and how they are?

So Jesus tells the woman who *he* is. Jesus is reluctant to admit to his own people that he is the Christ; but he tells this outsider who he is. And in telling her who he is, he gives himself away to her. He gives her the living water – so she can go home without her buckets and jars and face her own people. She leaves him to handle his bewildered disciples while she runs off to tell the town about the man who revealed her to herself.

She does not keep her experience a secret. She turns her experience of Jesus into a message for others. Jesus has freed her to carry his message to others. Because of her the whole town come to meet Jesus. Many believe in Jesus because of her story; many more come to believe in him when they meet him for themselves.

She is a summary of how people come to understand Jesus: first as a Jew; then as a prophet; then as the Messiah; then as the Saviour of the world. She is one of the first witnesses of John's Gospel who leads others to Jesus. Her past does not hinder her from being a messenger of Good News. She has a story to tell.

At long last she has met the right man.

Disturbing the peace

Aggression

Psychologists tell us, in case we are in any doubt, that aggression is part of our make-up and plays an important part in the way we relate to others. We speak openly of nations that have aggressive foreign policies, businessmen who make aggressive deals, but we are reluctant to speak about our own aggressive attitudes and behaviour. Sometimes we cover our aggression in the language of politeness, but more often than not our real feelings leak through the strain of civility.

Perhaps our reluctance to own our own aggression is because we tend to associate aggression with the destructive variety – like the thoughtless infliction of cruelty on others. But aggression can be a constructive act. The word aggression comes from the Latin root *aggredi,* which means "to go forward, to approach, to move against". Constructive aggression means taking the initiative to support what is important; it means working in a hostile environment against the power that devalues your beliefs.

A good example of constructive aggression can be seen in the effective campaign against slavery in the United States. The abolitionists were not content just to assert their values; they moved against the authorities that protected slave-trading. They risked their lives when they confronted angry mobs, but their belief was strengthened by the fierce opposition they faced. One of the prominent leaders of the movement was William Lloyd Garrison. He wrote about the subject of slavery:

> On this subject, I do not wish to think, or speak or write, with moderation. No, No! Tell a man whose house is on fire, to give a moderate alarm; tell the mother to gradually extricate her babe from the fire; but urge me not to use moderation in a cause like the present! I am in earnest. I will not equivocate – I will not excuse – I will not retreat a single inch...The apathy of the people is enough to make every statue leap from its pedestal.

Disturbing the peace

If there had been statues in the Temple, they would probably have leapt off their pedestals when Jesus organised a riot in the Temple precincts. In the story of today's Gospel Jesus is openly aggressive. Words give way to actions; verbal opposition gives way to forceful defiance. Jesus moves into the arena of the chief priests to work against the power that devalues his beliefs. There is no politeness or subtlety about the scene. If Jesus is worried about being arrested for disturbing the peace, no one could guess that from his behaviour. His verbs are clearly aggressive: making a whip, driving the traders and cattle out of the Temple, knocking over tables of money. Where there was peace, he brings total disruption; where there was business as usual, he brings unusual hostility.

By way of explanation the evangelist John tells us that Jesus' disciples remember the words of scripture, "Zeal for your house will devour me." Jesus is consumed by zeal, by a passion that shows itself in positive aggression. The outer court of the Temple has become a market where animals can be bought for sacrifice, and where visiting pilgrims can change their money into the coinage acceptable to the Temple authorities. Jesus' command is clear: "Take all this out of here and stop turning my Father's house into a market."

After Jesus clears out the Temple, the holy place is reclaimed for the worship of God. But soon enough, as John tells us, the Temple will be replaced by a new sanctuary where people can meet God – in the person of the risen Jesus himself.

For the sake of the kingdom
The portrait of Jesus in today's Gospel is a world away from the storybook caricature of Jesus, the meek and mild figure whose harmlessness looks indistinguishable from blankness. An equal caricature is to use this passage to make Jesus into a godfather of violence, a revolutionary willing to support annihilation for the sake of the cause. Jesus did use force in the Temple; he was certainly aggressive. But he did not use force to secure a coup d'état – he was not a nationalist leader. Nor did he use aggression to gain power for himself – his kingdom could not be established by violence.

Jesus' aggression was at the service of his Father's house, for the advancement of the kingdom of God. The casualties of his aggression turned out to be displaced traders and cattle. Not dead people.

If our own aggression could be employed for the advancement of God's kingdom, perhaps God's kingdom would be a more obvious domain in today's world. But we hang back from confronting the powers that devalue our beliefs. In drawing back we continue to give permission to the traders to occupy the Temple. Sometimes disturbing the peace is the only Christian option.

Out of bondage

The God who notices

Eventually, she decides to ask her husband: "Well then, what do you think? Don't you like the dress, dear?"

Without looking up from his paper, he asks: "What dress, dear?"

"The one I've been wearing for the last three hours," she says. "Of course, you haven't noticed have you? Not our alert Harold! You used to notice every time I changed a curl, and now you wouldn't notice if my hair was tartan! *And* you've forgotten our anniversary again. The trouble with you is that you just don't notice any more, do you? It really makes me wonder."

Without looking up from his paper, Harold mumbles to himself and begins to wonder too.

When people fail to notice, or no longer have the time, we begin to wonder about the quality of their love. It's difficult to ignore people *and* claim to love them at the same time. Which makes *awareness* a very important human virtue because it is the precondition of love. We can't love people we don't even notice. Love presupposes awareness; it grows in awareness. So too, love heightens our awareness: because we care for people we pay attention to what is going on in their lives.

It is very important for our faith to believe that God actually cares enough to notice what happens to us, that his reaction to events is not: "I don't want to know." In today's first reading we have the ancient revelation of who God is. The story tells of God revealing himself to Moses, and even though Moses must hide his face from God, he hopes that God will not close his eyes from the affliction of his people. The first part of the revelation puts that fear to rest for it shows God to be a God who notices: "I have *seen* the miserable state of my people in Egypt...I am well *aware* of their suffering." God does see what is happening; therefore, there is reason to hope.

The God who is moved to care

The reason for hoping is because the God of Abraham, Isaac and Jacob is not like other gods: "they have mouths but cannot speak; they have eyes but cannot see; they have ears but cannot hear" (Ps 115). Other gods are dumb, blind and deaf to what is happening; our God, on the other hand, is capable of being reached because he is capable of being moved. He is not simply an onlooker, one who gazes but keeps his distance. That is why the all-seeing eye of God is a radically incomplete image of God: God is more than an unblinking onlooker who spends an eternity staring at people's mistakes and misfortunes. The revelation to Moses shows a God of action who is moved *to act* on what he sees: "I mean to deliver them out of the hands of the Egyptians and bring them to a land where milk and honey flows."

That revelation is central to the whole tradition of the Old Testament. God is not the unmoved mover; he is moved to act on what he sees. He cares deeply about what happens to his people, and in this instance his care takes the shape of historical liberation. He is a God who is openly against oppression; he is a God who frankly opposes what Pharaoh is doing. So Moses is chosen as a leader to give voice to God's care for his oppressed people; to give voice to God's opposition against the manufactured suffering of his people; to take the lead in organising the liberation of his own people. Moses is the care of God in motion.

The God who is always there

Through Moses we know that God sees and is moved to act on what he sees. But the question is whether God will stay awake on human suffering. Will he *keep on* caring for his people or will the day come when he will run out of mercy? Will the time ever come when God will be dismissed in the same way as some people who are past their best: "Who him? Isn't he just an old has-been now?"

The answer to that question is given in the revelation to Moses. The answer is in the name of God, "I am who I am". The very name of God affirms his fidelity and staying power. He will never be a "has-been" God for he will always be "I am". His name is an assurance of his presence: *"I'll be there"*. So there is the good news that God does not take people on and then drop them at the first sign of trouble. He does not flirt with people. Over against our infidelity his name affirms his unchanging fidelity to us.

Conclusion

As you can see, there's a lot in that revelation to Moses! We have an insight into the ministry of God: the one who pays attention, who is moved to save his people, and who stays constant in his love. In Jesus we can see those three truths written large. But what about in ourselves? How do we pay attention to people's misery? Do we act on what we see? Are we faithful to our name of Christians? To answer those questions we would have to give ourselves away like God did.

More than meets the eye

Eccentric choices

"Once upon a time there was a king who had three sons, the youngest of whom was called Simpleton and was despised and mocked for his overwhelming stupidity." By the end of the story, however, it is Simpleton who has won the hand of the princess and inherited the kingdom. In the world of the fairy tale it is usually the least likely candidate who wins in the end. The least likely candidate is often the youngest son, who is seen to be stupid compared with his elder brothers: he is innocent of their worldly wisdom and cunning. He is the psychological summary of all that is weak and third-rate, and his chances of success in life are regarded as a joke.

Yet he is the one who succeeds. And he does this – not because he follows a course on "How to succeed with nothing going for you" – but because something happens to him. He is *chosen to succeed* by those who see more in him than meets the eye. His success is not due to his native effort but to the fact that he is helped by others who have special powers.

In today's first reading we hear how the prophet Samuel is commissioned by God to choose a successor to King Saul. He is sent to Jesse of Bethlehem to anoint one of his eight sons as the future king. Samuel is impressed by the eldest son and presumes that this young man of great height will be God's choice. But no. The prophet learns: "God does not see as man sees; man looks at appearances but the Lord looks at the heart."

Jesse presents seven of his sons to the prophet; it doesn't occur to him that his youngest son might be suitable: he is only a shepherd boy. None of the seven comes up to expectation, so number eight is called in from the hills. The Lord sees in David something more than meets the eye. And the young shepherd boy is God's eccentric choice for future king.

A blind beggar becomes a theologian

In today's Gospel we have another example of God's choice, one which confuses the religious leaders of the day: a blind beggar who becomes a theologian! John's beautifully crafted story tells how a blind man comes to see the light in Jesus, both physically and spiritually. When Jesus' disciples first see the blind man they presume that his affliction is a result of sin. But Jesus sees in the blind man something else: this roadside beggar who has always inhabited a world of darkness will be the one to display the work of God and point to who Jesus really is.

When Jesus heals the blind man he returns home a new man. His surprised neighbours check their memory and some refuse to believe their eyes. They are unwilling to let this new event interfere with their fast memories – in spite of the man's protest: "I am the man." He doesn't claim any special knowledge of the one who cured him but identifies him simply as "The man called Jesus."

The Pharisees have their seminar too and are doubtful that given who Jesus is, he could produce such a sign. Unlike the healed man, the Pharisees are sure who Jesus is. But as they grow more blind, the former blind man grows in insight and now identifies Jesus as a prophet. This is not a welcome development, and the man's parents are hauled in as prospective allies in the case against Jesus. They state that their son is old enough to speak for himself. And speak for himself he does! He refuses to deny his own experience: "I only know I was blind and now I can see."

He soon realises that he will be listened to only when his testimony confirms the prejudice of his interrogators. But rather than frighten him, this knowledge frees him to develop his evaluation of Jesus as a man of God. He does this so well that he annoys his listeners who refuse to be enlightened by the likes of this simpleton. They drive him away, but Jesus seeks out this budding theologian and reveals himself to him. Now the rejected man is the only one in the community who sees Jesus as the Son of Man.

God's choice of us

Both the story of the blind man and the story of David speak to us of God's choices. Because God sees the heart he chooses differently from the way that we do. Both David and the blind man are remembered and celebrated by the Christian community because they point beyond themselves to the reality of the divine. We honour David as the one who points ultimately to the Son of David; we recall the man born blind as the one who points to the Son of Man, the light of the world.

God has elected us to display his works. In our baptism we have been chosen to point to Jesus by the witness of our Christian lives. To many people, including ourselves, we may seem an unlikely choice. But our greatness lies in the fact that we have been chosen, not in ourselves alone. Allowing God to work in us, we can keep alive the story of God's eccentric choices!

God's work of art

The doctor and God

In his novel *Dr Fischer of Geneva* Graham Greene explores two competing forces in human life, self-respect and greed. The title character is a man who has made a vocation out of treating other people with open contempt. Dr Fischer has made his millions from a toothpaste which controls the decay caused by eating too many Swiss chocolates. He surrounds himself with a group of people whom he delights in teasing and tormenting. At his famous parties he plays on his guests' greed by offering them luxurious presents if they submit themselves to his humiliations. The guests accept the insults for the sake of the gifts. In the process of winning expensive presents, they lose what self-respect they had. But they keep coming back again and again.

When asked by a guest why he has an obsession to humiliate people and then offer them gifts, Dr Fischer explains that what he is doing simply reflects what God does all the time. The doctor says of God:

> Well, the believers and sentimentalists say he is greedy for our love. I prefer to think that, judging from the world he is supposed to have made, he can only be greedy for our humiliation, and *that* greed how could he ever exhaust? It's bottomless. The world grows more and more miserable while he twists the endless screw, though he gives us presents...to alleviate the humiliations we suffer.

Dr Fischer sees himself made in the image and likeness of a God who gives presents and makes bribes in between the humiliations he inflicts on others. Perhaps that idea of God is not as rare as we would like to think: when we see how many people are crushed and disappointed by life, we all might wonder if God has a dark side to him.

The Pharisee and Jesus

In today's Gospel scene a Pharisee talks to Jesus about God. Nicodemus has arrived under cover of darkness, and he misunderstands what the Light of the world is saying to him. This gives Jesus the opportunity to clarify his meaning, so he declares: "God loved the world so much that he gave his only Son". God's supreme gift was given out of love, not out of a desire to humiliate or condemn the world. If God's basic attitude to the world was one of divine contempt or icy detachment then his gifts would indeed be torment. If God is greedy for anything it is for people's acceptance of his love. There is a divine hunger for human love – that is why God sent his only Son. So there is a human hunger for divine love – that is why God sent his Son. In the person of Jesus two hungers meet, and two hungers are satisfied.

The Gospel expresses the hope that if we really believed God loved us we would surely emerge from our elected darkness. In the dark it is difficult to see God; it is difficult to think about him. Like Dr Fischer we tend to make God into our own image and likeness. So we hug the dark and guess wildly.

Perhaps we would come into the light more readily if we believed that the light we are entering is not the light of condemnation. If some of us are afraid of the dark, all of us are afraid of the light. We are afraid of standing in a place that is overlit, exposed and defenceless. But that is a *dark* image of God. God is not waiting outside the door from the dark, ready to humiliate us with the light of truth. The purpose of the light is to enlighten, not to blind. God wants to see us in the light. After all, as the second reading tells us: "We are God's work of art, created in Christ Jesus to live the good life as from the beginning he had meant us to live it."

God's work of art

Most of us would have difficulty in imagining ourselves as God's work of art; it takes less effort to see ourselves as God's mistake – a piece of promise that on close scrutiny turns out to be nothing more than a fake. That may be our image of ourselves, as it is for many Catholics, but that is no reason for ascribing the same view to God. It is Gospel that we were created in God's love, that we are his work of art. We have to begin imagining ourselves as God sees us.

Works of art should not be left to rot away in the dark, neglected and unseen. If they have been abandoned for a long time they will need sensitive restoration to be saved and brought to life again. Lent gives us the opportunity to think again about the task of restoration and allow God to bring out the best in us. Like all restorers, God needs light to do his work. We should trust his good intentions and come out where he can see us. Who knows, we might even begin to value God's work ourselves. And if that happened, we might see more of God's art in other people.

91

Coming home

Separation anxiety

Psychologists tell us that the deepest fear of children expresses itself in separation anxiety – the fear of being abandoned by their parents. Children are afraid that the love which brought them into the world, which names them and claims them, which gives them security, will be withdrawn so that they will end up discarded and disowned, and left on the scrap heap. Separation anxiety is the fear of living in the absence of familiar love, of having no place to belong to, of being left at the lost-property office unlooked for and unclaimed.

Of course, we don't have to be geniuses to appreciate that *that* fear is not limited to children! It's part of the baggage of all of us. We all know from experience that there is no such thing as *automatic love.* It is not automatic that a father loves his son, or that a brother loves his brother, or that a daughter loves her mother. We know that when young people leave some homes their absence is not registered as loss, but greeted with relief. They are summed up as being "just a dead loss". Relatives may dismissively say: "Well, he'll be no loss to anyone." For good measure, some are told to do humanity a favour and "get lost".

Mixed family

That attitude of writing people off as lost causes is the problem in today's Gospel. The sinners come to hear Jesus, but the Pharisees and scribes come to complain that Jesus welcomes sinners and eats with them. The Pharisees want Jesus to let the sinners *stay* lost. Why bother with the likes of them? The Pharisees, whose name means "separated ones", see themselves as having no relationship with the sinners. Jesus sees both groups as children of the Father and, therefore, brothers to each other. Rather than argue the point, Jesus tells a story about a father who has two sons and who loses them both.

The younger son gets lost in a far country while the elder son gets lost staying at home. The younger son leaves home, but his journey leads him to a place of hunger, of degradation, and of possible death. He is in danger of dying far away, forgotten and forsaken. But the younger son comes to himself in a pigpen when he realises that he doesn't really belong there, but has a home to belong to. There's nothing like hunger to sharpen your sense of belonging! The prospect of regular, square meals is enough to head him in the right direction, and he makes the journey of return on a full speech and an empty stomach.

All this time his father has not accepted the loss of his son as "just one of those things". His son's being lost has not nullified their relationship: if the son has let go of his father, the father has not let go of his son. He is a father who stays on the look-out, whose eyes hunt the horizon for the return of his son, whose love educates his hope that his son will come back. And when he does see his son a long way off he is moved with pity to run and meet him. When someone comes to meet you, your journey is always shorter. The father's love takes the initiative. He meets his son with love's extravagance and rather than listening to a boring speech, he organises a good party. After all, his son is found.

The elder son is the type who stays out in the fields long after the cows have come home. When he makes his return journey, unlike his younger brother he doesn't make it to home. His father comes out a second time that day to meet a son but all he gets is another boring speech! "All these years I have slaved for you" shows how the elder brother sees fidelity as slavery. He is enslaved by his own sense of justice. He wants to maintain the estate without any obligations to his brother. He has no reach in him. In fact *he* is the "separated one" who refuses to recognise his brother as his brother, but is content for him to stay lost. Unlike his father, he cannot surprise his brother with the quality of his mercy. His hard work has made him hard-hearted. As Yeats wrote:

> Too long a sacrifice
> Can make a stone of the heart.

The best in us

When we look at ourselves we can probably see parts of each of the three characters in us. There is the part of the father in us which has a keen eye for those who are lost and a good nose for when a party is needed. There is the part of the younger son in us which wants to grab everything we can and try everything we shouldn't. And there is the part of the elder brother in us which makes other people pay for our loveless fidelity. All three characters are within us competing to shape our life. This Lent let's pray that the father in each of us will be fit and willing to run for mercy. There's a lot of people in our lives who are still a long way off.

Calling the dead to new life

Regret and healing

When someone we love dies we become acutely aware of a large absence in our life, an absence that seems to fill the world. The death of those we love brings into sharp focus their unique quality, and we often regret that we didn't make more room for them in our life. Any of us who has watched the last moments of a life knows that it can become a time of regret and reproach – when our sorrow can take the form of wishing: "If only I had..."

But we know too that the time of dying can be a time of healing. This is shown simply and movingly by Simone de Beauvoir in her small book, *A Very Easy Death,* in which she reflects on her relationship with her dying mother:

> I had grown fond of this dying woman. As we talked in the half-darkness I allayed an old unhappiness; I was renewing the dialogue that had been broken off during my adolescence and that our differences and our likenesses had never allowed us to take up again. And the early tenderness that I had thought dead for ever came to life again, since it had become possible for it to slip into simple words and actions.

Their rediscovery of each other had waited a long time, right up to the door of death; but the lateness of the hour did not lessen the power of their reconciliation. This last time together had become for both mother and daughter a time of healing, of new life. A tender relationship that was dead was brought to life again.

Calling the dead to new life

In today's Gospel we hear how the death of Lazarus leaves a large absence in the lives of those who loved him. By the time Jesus arrives Lazarus is already dead, and Martha voices her regret: if Jesus had been with them earlier, things would surely have turned out differently. But Jesus' absence is essential to the story. John tells us at the beginning of his account that *through* the death of Lazarus the Son of God will be glorified. Just as the blindness of the man in last week's Gospel served as the occasion to show *Jesus as the light,* so the death of Lazarus will serve to show *Jesus as the life.*

The evangelist John is now showing us a great truth about Jesus that he proclaimed at the beginning of his Gospel:

All that came to be had life in him
and that life was the light of men,
a light that shines in the dark,
a light that darkness could not overpower. (1:4-5)

When Jesus tells Martha that her brother will rise again, he will show her that he means now: "I am the resurrection and the Life." The darkness of the tomb is not too dark for Jesus; the death of Lazarus does not mean that it is too late for Jesus to be his life. In a loud voice Jesus calls to the dead: "Lazarus, here! Come out!"

The great miracle is that while he is dead Lazarus hears the word of Jesus and obeys it. Hearing the voice of the Son of God, Lazarus lives again. The great prophetic word of Jesus is seen to happen:

I tell you most solemnly,
the hour will come – in fact it is here already –
when the dead will hear the voice of the Son of God,
and all who hear it will live. (5:25)

When Lazarus comes forth he is still wearing the clothes of a dead man. He is still enshrouded. Jesus now addresses the community: "Unbind him; let him go free." In obeying the word of Jesus the community plays its part in helping Lazarus unwind and emerge into the light of his new life.

Our own task

The story of the raising of Lazarus proclaims the great truth that Jesus is Lord of life. He has power to call us out of our tombs – for the Christian life only begins when we, even though we are dead, hear the word of God and obey it. We know from experience that we don't have to be dead physically to be in need of being raised up. We can be dead in the midst of life – hoping for a word and a community that will put us together again.

The voice of Jesus calls us all away from making the tomb our natural habitat. It also challenges us to take responsibility for our brother who, like Lazarus, is loved by Jesus. If we see someone buried alive we are invited to do as Jesus and the community do in the Gospel: call them, and help them go free. If we do that as part of our Lenten task then resurrection at Easter won't come as too much of a surprise.

The cross: loss and gain

Loss

Life begins in loss. In the act of birth we were pushed out from the warm womb of our mother, then dragged helpless into the big world of watching adults. Disconnected from our mother, we screamed and protested as we were held upside down in the hands of a stranger who slapped us. Some welcome! Our new separateness was frightening. Even though we were returned to our mother, we inhabited a space that was different from her's. To gain a place in the new world, we first had to lose our place in the old one. The act of birth is inseparable from the pain of letting go. That was our first education.

When we think of loss we usually have in mind the loss of some loved one in death. But the experience of loss plays a larger part in our lives than we might think: we lose not only by someone's death, but by leaving and being left, by letting go and moving on, by relinquishing our false dreams. Throughout our lives we have to face a whole series of *necessary losses,* people and relationships and attachments we have to give up if we are to grow. Our gradual development is marked by renunciation, for it is only through losses that we learn to change and adapt and make new gains. No pain, no gain.

As we grow older we have to let go of our youthful good health, our perfect vision, our waistlines, our earnestness to save the world, our unreal expectations of others, our naive belief in the progress of the earth. The time comes when we have to let go of life itself, and that final act can be as painful a leavetaking as the act of birth. But in the midst of this litany of loss there can be new growth and new life. As Jesus says in today's Gospel:

> Truly, truly, I say to you, unless a grain of wheat falls into the earth and dies, it remains alone; but if it dies, it bears much fruit.

The way of the cross

Jesus' death is ahead of him. The hour has come. The pilgrims are arriving in Jerusalem for the feast of the Passover, including some Greek converts who want to see Jesus. At this Passover feast the sacrificial lamb will be Jesus himself. Now the time has come for Jesus when there is no more time. He must face the loss of freedom, the loss of friends, the loss of support, and the loss of his own life. Not surprisingly, all this loss troubles him.

The other three Gospels speak of Jesus' agony on the Mount of Olives, how Jesus anguished over his approaching death, hoping and praying that it might be the Father's will to avoid the violent consequences of the mission. In John's Gospel there is no agony scene. Jesus is troubled, but he rejects the temptation to ask the Father to save him from what is to come: "What shall I say: Father, save me from this hour? But it was for this very reason that I have come to this hour. Father, glorify your name." In this portrayal Jesus is aware that the pain and the loss cannot be avoided if the Father's name is to be glorified. There is going to be gain from the pain; there is going to be glory from the way of the cross.

For Jesus to imagine that his suffering is avoidable is a false hope that has to be relinquished. The losing of his life is a necessary loss.

The way of the cross, which appeared as a possibility at the beginning of the ministry, now presents itself as inevitable. The hour has come. His decision is to go through the humiliation and agony of the cross, and be put to death. This, as John admits, does not mean that Jesus is untroubled about what is ahead. The pain will still be acute; the loss will still be crushing. But the Father's solidarity with his Son will keep Jesus going to the end. Only that gives point to it all.

Loss and gain

Jesus' loss is our gain. His radical act of self-forgetfulness stands at the centre of the Christian story. He is the grain of wheat that died in order to bear much fruit. That is why the cross has such a position of prominence wherever Christians gather. The great loss of Jesus' life – *and the loss was great* – has become in time the ground of our hope. It points us beyond the reality of suffering to the reality of Easter.

In the midst of our own loss, however, it is difficult to imagine what good can emerge from the pain. Sometimes the pain can reduce us to silence, so that we become dumb witnesses preoccupied with our own affliction. Few of us can see any point to pain at the time – often the pain *is* the fact that it all seems pointless. The Christian community needed time to make sense of the death of Jesus, they needed help to see that their immense loss was more than a terrible accident. We too need time and help. Only then can we look back, like the Gospel does, and cherish what good has emerged from the loss.

Being freed

No one deserves mercy

The story is told of a young French soldier who deserted Napoleon's army but who, within a matter of hours, was caught by his own troops. To discourage soldiers from abandoning their posts the penalty for desertion was death. The young soldier's mother heard what had happened and went to plead with Napoleon to spare the life of her son. Napoleon heard her plea but pointed out that because of the serious nature of the crime her son had committed he clearly did not deserve mercy.

"I know he doesn't deserve mercy," the mother answered. "It wouldn't be mercy if he *deserved* it."

That is the point about mercy: nobody deserves it. Everyone deserves true justice; mercy, on the other hand, is sheer gift. Mercy cancels out wrongs and transgressions – not because a sparkling defence has been found or excusing causes have been skillfully argued – but because that is the free response of the person who is grieved. Mercy does not suggest that the guilty are not guilty; it recognises the guilt but does not demand satisfaction for the wrong. In all this, mercy reflects the utter graciousness of the one who has been wronged.

Misery and mercy

In today's Gospel we have a magnificent story of the mercy of Jesus as he forgives the woman taken in adultery. It is interesting to note that the story is missing from the earliest manuscripts of John's Gospel. Some scholars argue that the delay in accepting the story as part of the Gospel reflects the difficulty many people had in the ease with which Jesus lets the woman off the hook, an easiness which was totally at odds with the strict penitential practices of the early Church. If this is true, it reflects an old problem many people had with Jesus and many people have with God: really believing in what Graham Greene has called "the awful strangeness of God's mercy." Does God forgive as easily as that?

In the Gospel story the woman is caught committing adultery. If it takes two to tango, it takes two to commit adultery, but the man seems to have had ready access to an emergency exit leaving the woman in the hands of the scribes and Pharisees. These men know the Law of Moses which stated: "If a man has intercourse with another's wife, both must die, adulterer and adulteress, and so Israel is rid of a plague." (Deut.22:22) The scribes and Pharisees are zealous about the execution of the Law which means the execution of the woman. They are in the moral majority for they clearly have the Law on their side. Thus armed they come to tackle Jesus on the issue.

Jesus' reaction to all the fuss is to start writing on the ground. But his questioners persist and Jesus responds not by taking issue with the law but by taking issue with the lawyers. When you remember the law but forget what the law is for, perhaps your memory is a little selective. Jesus seems to think that all victims can do with some form of allegiance and he refuses to join this moral majority. Jesus does not say the woman is innocent or argue that adultery should be taken off the books; but neither is he persuaded about the innocence of her accusers. He asks them to exercise their memories and check their own track-record on sin. If any are innocent, they can throw stones. And while they're all having a good think running their own home videos in their heads, Jesus goes back to his writing.

At least the woman's accusers are honest people for they readily recognise that they are not innocent accusers. So the procession of unemployed executioners is led away by the eldest – who is no doubt giving the example of necessity! Of course Jesus doesn't want them just to walk away but to exercise their forgiveness too. Jesus and the woman are left alone. As St Augustine described it poetically, "two are left: misery and mercy." And the woman hears good news from Jesus: "Neither do I condemn you. Go and sin no more."

Caught up in forgiveness

When we see that Gospel scene we can all imagine ourselves in the place of the woman caught in adultery, and probably have no trouble filling in the faces of our accusers who are ready to heave a stone or two in our direction. But that scenario is too easy. The challenge of the Gospel is not whether we can see ourselves as the woman who is caught in adultery, but see ourselves as *the man who is caught up in forgiveness.* Can we forgive as readily as Jesus forgives? Or do we dote on people's wrongdoing, reminding them of past failures, and lighting vigil lamps to their mistakes? Can we forgive and leave it?

We spend time wondering whether God can really forgive without hoarding the hurt. God's track-record on forgiveness is clear: he's had lots of practice and he's good at it. How about our track-record?

Grand Passion

Grand entrance

Jesus organises his own parade into the city that is destined to kill him. It seems puzzling – not only to go voluntarily to the place where your innocence will not protect you, but to enter the arena of your own execution in the midst of song and acclamation. Matthew tells us that all this commotion throws the city into turmoil as the people seek to discover: "Who is this?" The city people are told that this is the prophet Jesus of Nazareth, from up north in Galilee. The northerner has come to question the south; the countryman has come to take over the city; the prophet has come to confront established authority.

In spite of all the excitement, it is a serious business. The poet Clive Sanson tries to catch this as he imagines the owner of the donkey who yesterday saw Pilate come bouncing along the same road, armour shining, and half Rome trotting behind:

> Then today,
> Him and my little donkey! Ha – laugh? –
> I thought I'd kill myself when he first started.
> So did the rest of them. Gave him a cheer
> Like he was Caesar himself, only more hearty:
> Tore off some palm-twigs and followed shouting,
> Whacking the donkey's behind...Then suddenly
> We see his face.
> The smile had gone, and somehow the way he sat
> Was different – like he was much older – you know –
> Didn't want to laugh no more.

Grand passion

By the time the passion gets under way there is nothing to shout about. Processions that follow messiahs are triumphant affairs; processions that follow condemned criminals are timid by comparison, shabby affairs made up of those who have to be there and the curious who can never be mistaken for disciples. Matthew tells us that all Jesus' disciples deserted him: one betrayed him with a kiss; another denied him with curses. Confronted with fight or flight, their fear made the decision.

When the passion comes it brings with it a pressing question: can you still attach yourself to this man when all the authorities are ranged against him? Can you still believe in Jesus when you face the direction of Golgotha?

Jesus himself presses on to the end. When we speak of the passion of

Jesus we usually mean the suffering and death inflicted on him. But the passion is not just something that is done *to* Jesus by others, it is a power within Jesus, *his* passion, that enables him to face the violence and the pain. Jesus has a grand passion, one that consumes his whole person and drives him through this time of horror. He could have avoided coming south to Jerusalem; he could have compromised and settled for survival. But the passion that is in him is grander than his need for security and survival. He is a passionate man. His ardent love insists that he face the ultimate test of love. The cross.

Throughout his ministry Jesus has revealed the reaches of his own passion. His undying urge to do his Father's will. His preference for the poor and abandoned. His fury at a religious authority that only invents new burdens for people. His energetic love for those who are handicapped in life. His open disappointment with those who are economical with love and forgiveness. His way of having basketfuls and jars of plenty. His outlandish attachment to those who count themselves worthless. His loyalty to those who have deserted him. None of this emerges from a man who is timid and frugal in his ways; it reveals a man of grand passion.

In the end the cross comes as no surprise: it is the penalty for making a habit of such extravagant love.

The sign of the cross
The cross of Jesus stands at the centre of the Christian story as the sign of *the lengths love will go to* in its passion for others. If we ever wonder if we are really loved, we should look at the figure on the cross. It is difficult to maintain that we are unloved when we know that someone thought we were worth dying for. The cross is lifted up as a sign of our worth: somebody thought we were worth all that pain and suffering. And that somebody is Jesus, Son of God.

We remember the death of Jesus not as an arbitrary, heedless act of violence; rather, we honour his death as the supreme act of love. The love of one who "did not cling to his equality with God but emptied himself" to become as we all are; and as we are to show that, in spite of our sins and stupidities, God loves us. That is the heart of the passion story. All else is commentary.

The cross: did Jesus have to die?

The cross of Jesus

We gather to remember the passion of Jesus, to enter its mystery. We gather to hold holy the love that opposed violence and the love that endured violence, the love that made its way with a cross on its back. We gather to profess our gratitude for that love and to stand in solidarity with all those people whose courageous love makes them victims of violence.

The cross of Jesus has not been dismantled, the suffering he experienced has not ceased. The cross stands in the midst of life – not as ritual decoration, but as a reminder that this is the price the world exacts from those who confront its ways with the values of the Gospel.

Could Jesus have avoided the cross? Could he have made a detour around Calvary and continued on his way? Could he not have evaded assassination and settled for a quiet existence in his own region of Galilee? Did his forgiving love *require* the cross?

Jesus' commitment

It was not Jesus who looked for the cross; it was the world that looked to the cross as the way to eliminate him. The cross was not the idea of the Father; it was the final solution thought up by a world opposed to Jesus' way. God the Father is not a sadist who planned the destruction of his beloved Son; in letting go of his Son the Father had to be vulnerable to what would happen to his Son at the hands of others. All parents have to take that risk. God the Father, no less, did likewise.

Love does not demand the cross, but in the life of Jesus love ends up on the cross. *That is what actually happened.* That is what continues to happen to self-forgetful love. Love chooses not to avoid the suffering that emerges from its commitment. The avoidance of suffering is not love's governing passion. It cannot be.

Jesus could have avoided going to Jerusalem; he could have taken the advice of the disciples who warned him about the fate that would surely befall him there. But instead of avoiding Jerusalem, Jesus enters it publicly and loudly. He does not disguise himself and slip in through a quiet gate; he heads a parade.

He decides to confront the power that is set against him. And when he chooses to do that, like all people who confront oppression, *he makes suffering visible.* As Theodor Adorno noted:

> It is part of the mechanism of domination to forbid recognition of the suffering it produces.

Jesus brings suffering to the forefront. For Jesus to have avoided suffering, he would have had to avoid confrontation with the authorities. He would have had to suppress the real suffering of people and settle for the conspiracy of silence. That he refuses to do. His love makes itself vulnerable to suffering. He could only have removed himself from suffering by keeping himself untouched by other people's pain, by making himself invulnerable, by removing himself from human relationships.

But that was not why he had come. He had not come to be a mobile monument in stone; he was God's love in fragile human flesh and bone. He was God's passion, God's overwhelming love, God's risky adventure.

Remembering the passion

Today we recall the entry of Jesus into Jerusalem and we hear again the story of the passion. But why should we remember the passion of Jesus? Why keep alive the memory of such anguish and pain? Aren't we supposed to forget about past pain and hurts, and let them disappear if they can?

As Christians we are committed to be a people who remembers the passion of Jesus: "Whenever you do this, do it in memory of me." When a community chooses to remember suffering, their memory becomes a protest. Remembrance of pain demands a future that is more than a repetition of the past. That is why the memory of suffering is dangerous: in recalling the suffering of the victim there is a protest that this should not be repeated again. There should be no innocent victims.

That memory also serves to make us aware of the crosses that are in our midst. The memory of Jesus' passion educates us to pay attention to the suffering of others. The cross demands that attention should be paid. So today we pay attention to the suffering of Jesus and the suffering of all who are victims of hate and violence.

On parade

Engaging attention

They say that everyone loves a parade. We've probably all enjoyed watching some kind of parade make its way through the streets, celebrating a special occasion. When it comes to parades, nothing succeeds like excess: large floats, headline banners, loud music, dressed-up people and outlandish characters, all competing for our attention. The streets become the scene for a movable feast and with all the drama it becomes difficult for the passers-by to pass by a parade.

Of course, the whole point of a parade is to grab people's attention and hold it for as long as possible. The appeal is big and loud – making parades unknown for their subtlety. Often the parade is a demonstration to publicise people's concern. Sometimes, we watch unmoved; sometimes, we might be moved to join in. Parades and demonstration always try to *engage* the onlooker to be more than an onlooker and be moved to action. That is why parades are always public: they are always aimed beyond themselves.

But not everyone loves a parade. As Will Rogers proclaimed in 1924: "Parades should be classed as a Nuisance and participants should be subject to a term in prison. They stop more work, inconvenience more people, stop more traffic, cause more accidents, entail more expense, and commit and cause hundreds of misdemeanours." Parades make some people nervous, particularly those people in authority who might stand to lose if the parade is successful. And in today's Gospel we have a parade that makes some people very nervous.

Cheers and complaints

In today's liturgy we recall Jesus' parade and entrance into Jerusalem. In the Gospel Luke shows Jesus in control of events as he organises his own parade to the place where he has an appointment with death. Throughout his ministry Jesus had to face the prospect of Jerusalem which killed the prophets of old; now he has to face the reality as the city confronts him. But Jesus faces Jerusalem with style. So, it is on with the parade!

The disciples are told to go and fetch the required colt, and when they bring it back they cover its back with some of their clothes for a makeshift saddle. The fact that no one has ever sat on this colt shows how Jesus' presence is something completely new in history. As the procession moves off the people throw their cloaks on the ground – and early version of putting out the red carpet to welcome important people.

As the parade gets under way the disciples get into the spirit of things by praising God at the top of their voices for what he has accomplished in Jesus. The disciples organise an uproar of prayer, and a charismatic jamboree becomes an essential part of this parade. But not everyone loves a parade, and there are onlookers who remain unmoved by what is happening. The Pharisees suggest volume control, probably because this demonstration has messianic overtones. Is Jesus the liberator they've been waiting for?

Jesus does not think too much of the Pharisees' suggestion: he is in no mood for controlled enthusiasm. This is not the time for silence. The time for silence will come later. For the moment, the parade is on with all its loud rejoicing.

Another parade
The parade leads Jesus, as it leads us in today's liturgy, into the passion – the time of Jesus' ultimate trial and death. Jesus has a rough time ahead of him. The last supper when his disciples choose to have a seminar on which of them is the greatest. The talk about betrayal as if it is one man's problem. His chosen friends snoring through his loneliness and suffering. Being arrested by a friend's kiss. Being disowned three times by the one you've chosen to rely on most.

The time of being kicked around like a political football. Being flogged to placate a politician's conscience. Being handed over to a mob because of political cowardice. Making the way of the cross without the disciples. All the time being watched and stared at. Exercising a talent for forgiveness right up to the end. Taking a last breath when all your friends are at a safe distance. The last time for being. Death.

The parade which began outside Jerusalem leads to the cross as we hear in the reading of the passion. In the passion we will hear of another parade where the mood is different and the absences more noticeable.

Can we join the parade that Jesus began? We know where it is leading. Are we onlookers watching unmoved? Does it matter to us enough to join the parade? Today the Church asks us to be the parade, to proclaim that it *matters* what happens to him. We will not leave it to the stones to cry out. We demonstrate our love of Jesus; we demonstrate our care and our thanks that *we mattered so much to him that he faced Jerusalem*. So, we cancel the advice of the Pharisees and go public on our love of Jesus. So, let our parade begin!

At table

His table

It is near journey's end for Jesus. The hour has come and there is not much time left. The cross is still unoccupied but the public will not be deprived of their afternoon spectacle. Enemies have closed in and are just waiting to pounce. Pilate's wife is not the only one having bad dreams. Jesus' friends are getting scarcer by the hour, and he decides to have a last meal before the horror story begins. Before he is handed over to his enemies he gives himself away to his friends.

But when they all get together for the meal there is treachery in the room and it doesn't all belong to the company treasurer who will later prefer the company of the night. There is misunderstanding and confusion and hurt in the room: the apostles are unsure about what on God's earth is going on. A voice keeps telling them: "You do not understand what I am doing now. Later you will understand."

The scene in the upper room is not your usual friendly night out. There is something about the host which makes this meal different. After they have all finished eating the supper there is talk about the brokenness of the bread and the bloodiness of the wine. There is talk about a forthcoming death and the fact that there is a traitor in the room. At the table, there is a noticeable absence of the frivolity and easiness associated with friendly gatherings. Few people seem to know what is going on. Is this a celebration? If it is, why doesn't the host share a cup of good wine with his friends? Why instead does he wander off into the night to a garden to sip from a cup of grief – alone?

Did the final chapter of the story have to read like this? With a king who looked more like a clown; a prince of peace who looked more like the prince of fools; the lamb of God who would soon end like something strung up at the butcher's. Did Isaiah have to be right when he wrote: "There is no form of comeliness about him that we should desire him, and as one from whom men hide their faces we turn from him. A man of sorrows and acquainted with grief"? When he went to the garden why did his friends fall asleep? Why did they not stay awake to talk away the terrors of the night and help him through the coming nightmare? Why did his Father ask him to hold up the world when he could hardly hold up his head?

Jesus, the faithful one

In spite of all the rejection and disenchantment, the trial and the failure, Jesus made a mighty decision to stay faithful to his mission from his Father. He was not a theological robot programmed to act in a certain way; he had to decide himself whether to put himself on the line – literally – with his body and blood. Everything he ever did and said was brought to a head now: this was the hour. And Jesus said yes.

He got on his knees and demonstrated the parable of his kingdom: that in his upside-down world, the king was servant, and the one who ministered was master. And whatever was oppressive belonged to the creed of power not his gospel of love. And what he showed them on his knees, he continued to share with them at table. He gave them the most costly gift he could give: the gift of himself. It was at this moment that Jesus identified himself forever with bread and wine. He gave his followers more than food for thought; he gave them himself.

In spite of the hurt and the sorrow and the misunderstanding, Jesus accepted the fact that it was worthwhile to pay the price for who he was, and for what he stood. The price was himself, his own body and blood. That was the bill for the Last Supper, and Jesus picked it up.

The Last Supper was not a tragedy, but the resolution of tragedy. When Jesus approached the table he did not camouflage the difficulties of his own story: he included the tragedy and the comedy, the make-up of every story. Jesus gave us a powerful message that our befogged and befuddled humanity does not have to be denied to be accepted; rather, in its fragility it is uplifted and transformed by the love of the Lord.

Our table

Tonight we all bring our different stories here to the table of the Lord. And we know there will be times when we will be sore and hurt and wounded; when there will be no one to talk away the terrors of the night; when we will occupy the garden of grief alone. But Jesus has already travelled that route. He has shown us that it is worthwhile to pay the price for who we are and for what we stand; it is worthwhile to pick up our bill for having fellowship with him. And this night the Lord invites us again to copy what he has done for us. Wash the feet of each other. Give nourishment and hope to each other. Be bread for others; be life.

Let's do it.

THE SEASON OF EASTER

Protesting against death

Surprising death

Margaret is wondering whether to have an Easter holiday or not. Her boyfriend has just walked out of their relationship leaving her feeling rejected and abandoned. Perhaps a holiday will make all the difference. With no immediate family she doesn't have to plan herself around others. With a small income she knows she can afford it, if she is careful. A cautious jaunt, she thinks. But she's not sure. So she consults a friend who gives her the advice: "Enjoy yourself now while you can – you're going to be a long time dead."

Being a long time dead is what God protests against today. When we celebrate Easter as the most important feast of our faith we rejoice in a God who faces death frankly, and who outstares it with the power of his own love. Resurrection is God's protest against the finality of death; it is love outstaring violence; it is laughter in the tomb; it is the surprise of life overcoming the inevitability of death. Resurrection is God having the last laugh.

Today we exult in a God who refuses to leave the dead forever dead. Jesus did suffer a violent death; he was buried. But the Father has no intention of letting Jesus rest in peace! He gives death no permission to hold Jesus as the permanent victim of other people's violence. The resurrection is God's answer to those who think that prophets are expendable and that death will render them harmless. The Father's undying affection for Jesus sweeps death aside as he claims his beloved Son again. Nothing can come between them.

Resurrection in life

When we celebrate Easter we hold holy the memory of God's great act in raising Jesus from the dead. We believe that God's graciousness will be extended to ourselves and that our own death will not be the final word. Our faith educates our hope that we will participate in Jesus' resurrection on the last day. But a question raises itself: is our faith in the resurrection limited to remembering Jesus' resurrection and hoping for our own on the last day? What happens between times? What about today?

When we look at our world today we have to close our eyes and ears not to see and hear how suffering and violence continue to disfigure so many people. There are people here today who can feel their wounds. What does the resurrection of Jesus say to all this? Today. The challenge of Easter today is to understand the history of human suffering in the light of Jesus' resurrection. This means that we have to take God's part in *protesting against* the violence and the suffering that are accepted so readily *as inevitable*. As Christians we have to make our protest against death in the midst of life.

Death is not just a fate that we meet at the end of life. We see death all around us in the midst of life. This point was made movingly by the German theologian J. Moltmann in an Easter sermon when he said:

> Death is an evil power now, in life's very midst. It is the economic death of the person we allow to starve; the political death of the people who are oppressed; the social death of the handicapped; the noisy death that strikes through bombs and torture, and the soundless death of the apathetic soul.

Resurrection today

To accept this litany of death as inevitable is to empty the resurrection of its power for today. A resurrection faith faces the cross and protests against the finality of that violence. It educates us to see as God sees; to act as so many of God's chosen *do* act today when with enormous courage they refuse to genuflect to the powers of darkness that use suffering and death as their tools to keep power.

The resurrection of Jesus is a proclamation that this outcast from Galilee is the beloved of God who cannot be held in the keep of death *because someone else takes action.* Jesus did not raise himself; he was raised by God. The truth that God raised Jesus from the dead gives hope and help to all those who want that miracle repeated in the midst of life. They believe that God's work continues – not least because they believe Jesus' words: "I *am* the resurrection and the life." Today.

We can all catch something of the reality of the resurrection when we experience new life in the midst of hopelessness. We see it in hospital wards, when tired nurses hug people back from death. We see it in the men and women who risk their lives protesting against the mindless violence inflicted on their fellow human beings. We can see it in the beloved disciples who see in the dark what no one else sees. For all this we rejoice. It is Easter in our midst; it is the refusal to accept that anyone should be left for dead.

The cross: the Father's response

A mad rendezvous

When we face the death of someone we love we face an unspeakable loss. A future is mapped out for us where there will always be a large absence. Sometimes the finality of the loss is so great that there is a denial of death itself. People tell you how they "hear" the footsteps of their loved ones on the pathway, their key being turned in the lock. They "see" them on the street and follow them for a while, only to be confronted with the puzzled face of a stranger. Sometimes the denial takes the form of searching for the dead. Like Anne, the widow of the French actor Gerard Philipe, who went to the cemetery to look for her husband:

> I went to find you. A mad rendezvous...I remained outside reality, without being able to go in. The tomb was there, I could touch the earth that covered you and without being able to help it, I began to believe that you would come, a little late as usual; that soon I would feel you approach me.
>
> There was no point in telling myself that you were dead...You weren't coming, no you were waiting for me in the car. A mad hope, that I knew to be mad, and still it overtook me.
>
> "Yes, he's waiting in the car." And when I found it empty, I protected myself once more: "He's taking a walk on the hill." I went down to the house, talking to friends the while, looking for you on the road. Without believing in it, of course.

Expecting the dead to be dead

When Mary of Magdala goes to visit the tomb of Jesus she expects to make a rendezvous with death. It is very early on the first day of the week. It is still dark, but there is light enough to see that the stone has been moved from the entrance to the tomb. Mary's reaction is not immense relief that Jesus is not dead. She does not cheat herself with that mad groundless hope. The only conclusion she can come to is that some unknown people must have stolen the dead body of Jesus. Even in death Jesus is not allowed to rest in peace.

When Simon Peter and the Beloved Disciple hear Mary's story they run to the tomb. The account in John's Gospel is clearly written in favour of the Beloved Disciple. When Peter enters the tomb he sees the burial clothes; when the Beloved Disciple enters the tomb he sees and he believes. The disciple who was closest to Jesus in love is the one who is first to believe in him as the risen Lord. Perhaps the Beloved Disciple reckoned that if someone had stolen the body he would not have taken the trouble to strip the body first and then roll up the burial clothes. Or perhaps the evangelist John is simply telling us that beloved disciples are always the first to get to the heart of the matter. For the heart of the resurrection is the matter of love.

The resurrection: response of the Father

What we celebrate in the resurrection is God's liberating love for his beloved Son. Resurrection is the Father's response to the cross, his defiant answer to a world that hoped violence could keep Jesus in its hold. In raising Jesus from the dead God raised every value that Jesus stood for, every story that Jesus told, every preference that Jesus made, every purpose that Jesus followed. All this was given new life and new significance.

If death had spoken the final word about Jesus, it would only have been a matter of time before everything about Jesus would have been reduced to a curiosity, a forgettable footnote in the crowded history of lost causes. But God had the last word. As indeed he had the first.

The resurrection of Jesus was not a hysterical invention of people who refused to accept the death of their master. On the contrary, *resurrection is the original act of accepting Jesus' death.* The Father's act of raising Jesus from the dead is *the Father's way of accepting his Son's death.* Jesus is wakened to new life by the applause of his Father, by the sheer energy of his Father's love, by the loud shout of his Father's gratitude. The dead Jesus has no alternative but to rise to the occasion. The tomb can never be his permanent address.

The Good News is that the Father's affirmation is not confined to Jesus, it is extended to all who follow the way of the beloved Son. As Paul says in today's second reading: "When Christ is revealed – and he is your life – you too will be revealed in all your glory with him." In the meantime, however, we struggle to let some of that glory shine through our halting efforts to follow the Lord. We know the way of the cross leads to our own doorstep and that we are challenged to take it. It leads us to the Father's ultimate affirmation, to the God who will laugh us out of our tombs. Today let us bless the God who insists on having the last laugh!

Seeing in the dark: the beloved disciple

Out of darkness

The ancient story is told of a rabbi who gathered all his students together very early in the morning while it was still dark. He told them to pay attention because he had a very important question to ask them. The question was this: how could they tell when night had ended and the day was on its way back.

One student answered: "Could it be when you see an animal and can tell whether it is a sheep or a dog?"

"No," answered the rabbi.

Another student said: "Could it be when you look at a tree in the distance and can tell whether it is a fig tree or a peach tree?"

"No," answered the rabbi.

After a few more guesses the students demanded: "Well, then, what is it?"

"It is when you look on the face of any woman or man and see that she is your sister and he is your brother. Because if you cannot do this then no matter what time it is, it is still night."

For John, as we heard in his Gospel, the Easter story begins very early in the morning of the first day of the week when it is "still dark". But the Easter story has its finest expression in the new life in Christ, when, as John tells us,

> the night is over
> and the real light is already shining.
> Anyone who claims to be in the light
> but hates his brother
> is still in the dark. (1 John 2:8-9)

The Easter we celebrate is an invitation out of darkness into the light of the risen Christ. In that light we see him and recognise each other as brother and sister in the Lord. It is that light which enables us to tell that night has ended and day is on its way back. It is that light which summons us to leave loitering in the dark. From hanging around the graveyard it calls us to look for hope elsewhere. It suggests to us that we write other people's epitaphs too readily. When Jesus conquers death, nobody and nothing can be written off as a lost cause.

The love that sees in the dark

Easter began in the dark and began in the tomb. The story begins with someone whom many had written off as a lost cause: Mary Magdalene.

114

When she reaches the tomb she sees that the stone is rolled away, and she interprets this to mean that Jesus' body must have been stolen. She finds it easier to believe in the night-time antics of graverobbers than the night-time antics of a God who refuses to let death have the last word.

When Peter and the Beloved Disciple hear her story they immediately start running for the tomb, and we have a marvellous action picture of the Easter jog! The Beloved Disciple runs faster than Peter, reaches the tomb first, looks in to see the cloths lying on the ground, and then waits for Peter. Peter goes in and sees the cloths. The climax of the story is when the Beloved Disciple goes in and sees the same evidence: in contrast to Peter, he believes. He sees more than discarded cloths; he sees with the eyes of faith what this means. His is a love that sees through the dark.

One of the marks of John's Gospel is the special love between Jesus and one of the disciples. The Beloved Disciple is presented as the ideal follower of Jesus, the one who is closest to him at the Last Supper, and the one who stands at the foot of the cross when he dies. Now in running to the tomb on Easter morning, the urgency of his love gets him there first, and the sensitivity of his love makes him the first to believe. And later when Jesus stands unrecognised on the shore of Lake Tiberias, it is the Beloved Disciple who informs Peter: "It is the Lord". His is a love that gets him there first.

If Peter enjoys the "primacy of authority", the Beloved Disciple enjoys the "primacy of love". This takes nothing away from Peter: it just means that, in Paul's phrase, "if love can persuade" it can get you to the point quicker!

Seeing more

So we look to the quality of our own seeing and hope, so that when the time comes we too will have the love to enable us to see through the dark. In celebrating Easter we rejoice in the light that darkness cannot overpower; we celebrate that God raised Jesus from the dead and that he extends that homecoming to all of us; we bless God for the faith that challenges us always to see more in others because we love him.

In that Easter faith we can answer the question of the old rabbi. We can tell that the night is gone and the day is on its way back when we can look on the face of our brother and sister and see something extraordinary. We can catch a glimpse of the Messiah.

Not seeing, yet believing

Seeing Jesus
The first disciples of Jesus had the rare privilege of knowing him while he walked the roads of Palestine. They saw what he did; they heard what he said; they touched him and were touched by him. Travelling around with Jesus they saw him at work: preaching, healing, forgiving, challenging, praying, eating, moving on, struggling, suffering and dying. During the public ministry Jesus was gradually revealing himself through his verbs, through what he actually did. Sometimes we imagine that everything must have been clear to the disciples, but the Gospels tells us that many of Jesus' deeds and words puzzled and confused them. The *meaning* of much of what Jesus did and said was not available to the disciples at the time; they had to wait for something else.

During the public ministry the disciples could not *see for themselves* the whole truth about Jesus: they came to that truth only after the resurrection when they received from Jesus the Spirit of truth. As Jesus tells the disciples in John's Gospel: "The Holy Spirit, whom the Father will send in my name, will teach you everything and remind you of all I have said to you." (14:26) It is only when the disciples receive the Spirit of truth that they can fully answer the question, "Who do you say that I am?"

Not seeing, yet believing
When the disciples received the Spirit of truth, that new experience opened up the significance of their past with Jesus: they could now *remember with understanding* the mighty deeds and words of Jesus. They became the first witnesses who could testify from their experience to the truth about Jesus. As long as the early Christian community had the first followers of Jesus in their midst, the community's understanding of Jesus was rooted in those who knew him personally. But what happens when there are no more witnesses who knew Jesus at first-hand? Does the memory of Jesus fade away?

In Robert Browning's poem *A Death in the Desert* the last of the apostles, John, is dying. He looks over his life and wonders what will happen after the death of the last person to know Jesus personally. What will happen when

> there is left on earth
> No one alive who knew (consider this!)
> — Saw with his eyes and handled with his hands
> That which was from the first, the Word of Life.
> How will it be when none more saith "I saw"?

116

How can the Church speak about Jesus in a compelling way when no one can see him? This is precisely the problem that the evangelist John faces in today's Gospel. The apostle Thomas is absent when Jesus appears to the others, and he cannot believe that Jesus is risen because he cannot see him. This is a story for everyone who was not present with the disciples on Easter evening – and that obviously includes ourselves. Today's Gospel builds a bridge between those who saw Jesus and those who do not: "Happy are those who have not seen and yet believe." That is a blessing directed at us: we who believe in Jesus without seeing him.

Our own faith

We know from experience that it isn't easy to believe in someone we cannot see for ourselves. But we also know that many people who did see Jesus did not believe in him. Seeing does not necessarily lead to believing. The apostles have a unique place in the Church because they saw Jesus and believed in him, and they were commissioned to share their faith with others. Without the apostles' seeing and believing there would be no Christian faith. That is why, as we pray in the creed, one of the marks of the Church is that it is "apostolic".

We have no experience of the physical presence of Jesus, but our understanding of him is linked through time – through all the previous generations of Christians – back to the apostles themselves. It is a great chain of faith which is linked to the person of Jesus himself.

You may think that the chain gets weaker the more it is distanced from the time of Jesus, but the Spirit which Jesus gives is a *present reality* in the Church. The Spirit is the life of the Church, the power which keeps the memory of Jesus alive, and which enables each of us to have a living relationship with God.

So the sentiments expressed in the First Letter of Peter are addressed to us: "You did not see him, yet you loved him". The fact that we are gathered here today is a sign of our belief and a declaration of our love. Future generations depend on us to hand on what we have received so that they too can have life through the name of Jesus. If we all do that, there will never be an end to the story of Jesus.

Caring about faith

Believing and belonging

When we gather each week to celebrate the memory of Jesus, we help each other by our very presence at Mass. Turning up is an act of faith. Our faith gives us a sense of belonging to a large community: when we believe, we belong. We believe together. As Christians the principal object of our faith is Jesus the Lord, and though we are many in number we share our belief and trust in him. But the community of faith can never be a substitute for individual faith. As W.H. Auden remarked:

> The relation of faith between subject and object is unique in every case. Hundreds may believe, but each has to believe by himself.

Nobody can do our believing for us. Some people will believe in anything, because their belief costs them nothing. You can add random lists to their creeds and they will smile and nod agreement – not because they have faith, but because they have become accustomed to defending themselves against facing the complexity of the real. They don't travel on their belief; their commitment ends with their ready assent. This is not the innocence of simplicity; it is the disguise adopted by those who don't care *what* they believe in. As long as they're numbered among the believers they are content.

The discontented apostle

In today's Gospel the disciples are gathered in a locked room. The recent violence has made them security conscious. They have become runaways from a society they fear is hostile, so they lock themselves in what they hope is a safe house. God's grounded spies. For all their defensiveness, however, they cannot keep out the pressing love of the risen Jesus. He appears in their midst; his greeting is peace; their response is joy. For the evangelist John, Easter Sunday is Pentecost, and the gift of the Spirit is the breath of the risen Christ.

The disciples breathe in and the Spirit becomes part of them. But one of their number is missing – Thomas. When he arrives to hear the story, he refuses to believe what he hears.

Thomas is part of the apostolic group, but he is also a distinct independent self. He cannot be loyal to the group while being disloyal to his own inner self. That would render his loyalty worthless. For Thomas honesty is more important than loyalty. So he refused to become part of this company of believers, for it is not enough for him to shelter in a faith that he cannot credit for himself. He may want to believe, yearn to accept as true what the others say, but his wish cannot struggle into faith.

Doubt cannot be transformed into faith by willing it. After all, the other disciples only come to believe in the risen Jesus when they see him; it seems unreasonable therefore to criticise the absent Thomas for being afflicted with the same handicap. *The insistent honesty of Thomas is what makes him doubt.* For Thomas to say he believed would be play-acting and make-believe. It would be to make a religion out of role-playing, agreeing to act out a part that was expected of him but to which he could not bring his real self. For Thomas it is important *what* he is asked to believe in, more important than belonging to the company of believers.

Coming to belief

We learn from the Gospel that Thomas comes to believe in the risen Jesus in the same way as the other disciples – when he sees the Lord for himself. We can appreciate, however, that the character of Thomas is larger than the apostle Thomas: he stands for all those who have not seen the Lord but are asked to believe in him. The story of Thomas leads to the beatitude aimed at the generations of people who will not see the risen Lord: "Happy are those who have not seen and yet believe."

It is not that we are asked to do what the apostle Thomas could not do – believe in Jesus simply on the testimony of others. Thomas was not gifted by the Spirit, and no one can believe in Jesus without the Spirit of God. As we heard in today's reading from the first letter of John: *the principal witness to the risen Jesus is the Spirit* – "since the Spirit is truth." We can only pray "My Lord and my God" because we allow the Spirit of God to pray in us. In the grace of the Spirit we can proclaim Jesus our Lord.

If faith is one of the principal gifts of the Spirit, it is also a form of life that has to be nurtured, helped to grow, loved into maturity. It is not a precious stone that has to be locked in a vault – that kind of security consciousness is indistinguishable from death. Faith is a life, and like any life it can wither if forgotten or overlooked. Faith can die from a lifetime's neglect. We need to pray about our faith, think about our faith, live the life of our faith. Faith demands our active verbs. That does not mean that we will never have our doubts; but if like Thomas we care about what we believe in, that care in time will bring us into the presence of the living Lord.

119

Seeing and believing: Thomas

When a body dies

Christianity has its beginnings in the fact that some people met Jesus of Nazareth and were never the same because of their encounter with him. Something happened to them, and they didn't organise it. Because of him, they were changed; they saw themselves and their future differently. They claimed that their new identity and new direction in life was due to him. They said that without him they would have stayed the same. He was the sole reason for their new experience of life.

Think of the disciples. Before they met Jesus they all had their own jobs, their own identities, their own way of life. After they met Jesus all that changed. They didn't stop being themselves, but they saw themselves in a new way, and the direction of their lives was changed to following in his footsteps. They became known as *his* crowd!

But what happens to all that when Jesus dies? If your *identity* as a follower of Jesus depends on Jesus being around, what happens when there is no more Jesus? What happens to the *direction* of your life when Jesus is no longer there to lead you? What happens to your *enthusiasm* for the values of Jesus when Jesus is no longer around to clarify what they mean? Does life after Jesus mean life without Jesus? Does everything come to a dead stop?

From doubt to belief

Everything does come to a dead stop as today's Gospel tells us. After the death of Jesus the identity of the disciples and the direction of their lives changes dramatically. Now they are a group of men whose shared fear keeps the company together, and whose only direction in life is to lock themselves into their own no-go area. After the death of Jesus their lives are rooted in fear. They are deeply afraid they will have to face the same fate as their master.

It is into that desperation that the risen Christ comes. And he comes not to disown his disciples for abandoning him but to reclaim them with his peace. He shows himself to them. The resurrection doesn't make the marks of cruelty and suffering disappear: the risen Christ is *the wounded Christ.* He is Jesus who was crucified. The same. In his gift of peace the disciples experience great joy, and they are commissioned to share that joy when they release others from sin through the power of forgiveness. Again because of Christ, they have a new-found identity and a new direction to their lives. Now they have his Spirit.

But one of their number is missing. Being absent from the community means that Thomas missed meeting the Lord, and when he returns he cannot bring himself to believe in the disciples' story. His doubt is that of a man who is committed to the truth. Unlike Judas, he did not betray Jesus; unlike Peter, he did not deny him. There is a sparkling authenticity about Thomas: he refuses to say that he can understand or believe when he can manage neither understanding nor belief. Thomas is brave enough to have the conviction of his doubts, and rather than hoarding his doubts to himself he shares them with the community.

Later, the risen Christ appears again to his disciples and the purpose of the visit is clearly to pay attention to the doubt of Thomas – not to scorn it. Thomas is invited to inspect a wounded Jesus to discover the reality of the resurrection. But seeing Jesus is enough for Thomas, and he is the one who proclaims the basic Christian credo: "My Lord and my God." As Thomas is fearless in voicing his doubts, he is quick to proclaim his faith, and in John's Gospel it is he who makes the most important affirmation about who Jesus is – that he is Lord and God.

Teaching

In coming to believe in the risen Jesus the disciples experience a profound change: they become spirited followers of their Lord. They have seen the Lord, they have met him, they have eaten with him. They can testify to others from the authority of their own experience. As John says: "What we have seen and heard we are telling you so that you too may have fellowship with us as we have fellowship with the Father and with his Son, Jesus Christ." (1 Jn.1:3) The apostles have a unique place in the Church: they experienced Jesus at firsthand and were authorised to be his witnesses. And as we heard in the first reading they led many people to believe in the Lord through the power of their witness.

But what about all those people who never met Jesus or heard him or touched him? And we are numbered among them. Can we believe without seeing the Lord for ourselves? And *that* is why the story of Thomas is so important because it tells us that *it is possible to believe in Christ without having seen him.* "Blessed are those who have not seen and yet believe" is the teaching of the Gospel. The beatitude is for all of us who live in the absence of the physical Jesus but who believe in him as our Lord. And it is in the Lord that *we* have our identity as his followers and follow his direction in our lives. Like the apostles, because we believe in him, we know now *who* we are and *what* we must do.

Emmaus

Old experience, new meaning

Maude and Harry have been happily married for six years. It hasn't been bliss all the way, but they've become the best of friends in their struggle to live a genuine life together with their two children. One evening Harry is having a drink with an old friend, John, who was best man at his wedding. As they exchange notes on married life Harry tells John how he has loved Maude from the first moment he set eyes on her.

John contradicts him. He says: "Harry, old son, you've forgotten that I introduced you to Maude. Remember? You heard her talking at a party I was giving, and when you heard her rabbiting on you said that whoever married her would be marrying a mobile Oxford English dictionary!"

Which of them is right? John remembers the event as it was then. But Harry remembers it as something more – an event that led to where he is now. Because Harry is in love *now*, he takes that love back in time and invests the past with a new significance. His relationship with Maude *now* affects the way he remembers their beginnings: he gives their first meeting a significance it never had at the time because he reads it in the light of his present love. His love actually changes the past.

Because we change, we review our past differently. We keep re-interpreting the past in the light of what is going on now in our lives. What appeared to be a mountain at the time turns out to be a mole-hill; what appeared to be a chance encounter becomes the most important meeting of our lives. Often the *meaning* of an experience is unclear at the time of the experience. We have to wait for meaning. Only then can we understand.

Making sense of Jesus' death

In today's Gospel two disciples are struggling to make sense of a recent event: the death of Jesus. They leave Jerusalem over their shoulder as the place where their hopes met with final defeat. When a stranger joins them on the road, they tell the story of their disappointment. Jesus, the one they had hoped would set Israel free, is now dead. In their story it becomes clear that they cannot hold two things together: their hope in Jesus *and* his death. The death of Jesus cancels out their hope. They feel hopeless and helpless.

The two disciples cannot understand how the death of Jesus can be understood as anything more than a tragic end to a life of promise. Like most people they believe that if you haven't achieved what you set out to do *before* your death, you will never achieve it in death itself. When you are dead, it's too late for everything. Death is the end of the road of promise. So the disciples mourn not only the death of Jesus but the death of their relationship with him. Now they are ex-disciples of a dead prophet. With faces to match their story.

Only when they have finished their own story does the stranger begin his own. He invites them to look at the past again, this time in the light of scripture. He gives a wholly different interpretation of the same event as he sees the death of Christ as something which was essential for his glory. According to the stranger, the death of Jesus was the achievement of his mission – not the collapse of it.

As the stranger helps the two disciples to make sense of the past in a new light, they respond by inviting him to stay with them. When they go in to table they break bread together. The stranger gives himself away by giving himself away to them. He is the risen Jesus, and he leaves them with hearts that burn and with eyes that see. Not only does he help them to interpret the past in their new experience of him as Lord, he gives them a new future. They can now face Jerusalem even in the dark, and they return there to share their story with the others.

Bringing the past up to date
In their new experience of Jesus as Lord, the disciples' past is changed. They can now revisit the past with the new light and the new love that they have experienced. They take the light of Easter Sunday back into the darkness of Good Friday, and everything looks different now. Only the risen Jesus makes sense of everything that went before. In his word and in the breaking of the bread the past is brought up to date. The past is now interpreted in the light of the great truth that Jesus is risen and is Lord.

When we gather here each week to celebrate the eucharist we too listen to the word of God and break bread together. Jesus comes among us not as the stranger; rather, he comes to us in word and sacrament to give us new hope to face the future with faith in him. Our own stories may not sound very different from the two forlorn disciples on the road to Emmaus: we too may be covered in disappointment; we too may have a past that makes little sense to us. But we are invited to tell our stories to the Lord, to listen to him as he speaks his word, and to recognise him in the breaking of the bread. Only then can we look with understanding at the past, and with hope look to the future.

Understanding what is going on

Experience and meaning

A mother looks out of her kitchen window and sees her two sons fighting. It looks serious. When they see her hurry out of the house towards them, they disentangle themselves from each other's hold, hoping beyond hope that she will let the matter pass without comment. No such luck. She asks them: "What on God's earth is going on here?" She knows *what was happening* – they were fighting each other – but she is determined to find out *what is going on* between them. Only when she discovers that will she understand why they were fighting in the first place.

It is always frustrating to witness an event without knowing what it actually means. From our own experience we know the difference between having an experience and knowing what it means, between being part of an event and understanding its significance. Jesus himself made the distinction between those who "see and hear" and those who "perceive and understand". Being part of an event is no guarantee that we will understand it. As T.S. Eliot observed:

> We have had the experiences but missed the meaning.

Being opened to understand

In today's Gospel we see how the disciples cannot make sense of Jesus' recent death. Nor can they make sense of what is going on when Jesus appears to them. When Luke writes his Gospel he writes it to strengthen the belief that Jesus is the Christ, the Son of God. He has his own way of doing this, and when he comes to the story of the resurrection he chooses to emphasise how *only the risen Christ can make sense of the events of Good Friday and Easter Sunday.* By themselves the disciples cannot arrive at an understanding of what is going on; they need the risen Christ to uncover the meaning of all that is happening.

Luke demonstrates this dramatically in today's Gospel. The two disciples of Emmaus have returned to Jerusalem to be reunited with the assembly of Jesus' followers. Luke tells us that the two disciples "told their story of what had happened on the road and how they had recognised Jesus in the breaking of the bread." But the question remains: can the assembled disciples actually make sense of all that has happened?

This question is soon answered by Luke. While the disciples are still talking Jesus appears among them. Rather than rejoice in his presence, they are alarmed and frightened; rather than recognising Jesus, they think they are seeing a ghost. They are unable to make sense of what is happening in their midst, any more than they have been able to make sense of the recent events that have happened in Jerusalem. Luke serves notice that the appearance of the risen Lord is not by itself a compelling demonstration of his reality. *By itself* the appearance of Jesus does not open the disciples' eyes. It did not do that on the road to Emmaus and neither does it do it here.

Jesus appeals to the disciples' sense of touch, so that they see *who* it is they are touching. He appeals to their reason, "ghosts have no flesh". But it is only when he tells them what he meant when he was with them and opens their minds to understanding the scriptures that they come to believe in him. By interpreting what has happened the risen Christ draws the disciples out of their confusion. The disciples cannot do that for themselves; they cannot see for themselves; by themselves they cannot understand what is going on. Only the risen Christ can take the disciples from mystery into revelation, from confusion to understanding. That is his Easter gift.

Turning the experience into a message

In this new understanding the disciples become witnesses – not just eyewitnesses to what has happened, but witnesses to the meaning of all that has taken place. So when Luke tells of the preaching of the early Church in the Acts of the Apostles – like Peter's sermon we heard in the second reading – the evangelist shows how they disclose the meaning of the death and resurrection of Jesus. In all this Luke shows us how the understanding of the early Church is firmly based on the teaching of the risen Jesus. That is its unique authority.

The understanding of the Church today is based on the unique experience of the first disciples. We will always be indebted to them for their insight and courage. Happily, they did not keep their new experience to themselves, they did not hoard their new insight: both were shared with anyone who had ears to listen. The first disciples turned their new experience into a message of Good News for all people.

Every generation must make the message of Jesus its own and pass it on to others. It is a message enlivened by the witness of generations of Christians who have continued to have life in the name of Jesus. We keep the message alive only by giving it away. That way, the Gospel never dies.

Insisting on love: Peter

Looking for love

There is a marvellous *New Yorker* cartoon which depicts a moment of challenge in the life of one man. He is well on in middle years, his hair is in retreat, and thick rounded spectacles sit on his nose. Dressed in pyjamas and dressing-gown he stands inside his front door staring at something on the floor. The door is heavily reinforced with steel brackets and a variety of bolts and locks and chains. It is a picture of security gone mad. There is no letter-box to receive mail, but there is a peep-hole to see out. Clearly no one could penetrate this place without approval.

But something has got through this array of defences. A white envelope with a large red heart impressed on the back is lying on the floor. A valentine card has been slipped under the door. Our middle-aged hero stares in wonder. Is this a joke? Is it a flat letter-bomb? Should he claim it or push it back across the threshold? We'll never know!

Trying to get through to some people can call for impressive resources, not least patience and perseverance. It is particularly difficult with those people who live their lives in fear of *showing* their love. We get the impression that they could be accused of love only on highly circumstantial evidence. Sometimes we wonder why we bother when our tentative efforts are met with a look that could sink an aircraft carrier! But we keep trying in the hope that sheer effort will be rewarded. So we send out signals, hints, smiles, winks, sighs. One day when we are near exhaustion we might just ask the question: "Excuse me, but do you love me?"

Questions and affirmations

In polite society you are not supposed to go around asking people questions like "Who do you say I am?" or "Do you love me?" Perhaps because the answers might be deadening. Questions that go to the heart of the matter, particularly when the matter concerns what you really think of another person, are usually eased out of the conversation like slightly potty relatives are eased out of the room after they have misbehaved. In today's Gospel, however, Jesus is in good voice when he asks Peter three times if he really loves him.

Remember that before the crucifixion Peter had not exactly distinguished himself. Three times he denied being a disciple of Jesus and knowing anything about him. The man Jesus chooses to exercise primacy of authority is the one who is caught out by a servant girl as he lies insistently. He is the man who is arrested by a cock crowing in the dark.

As we hear from the epilogue of John's Gospel, after the crucifixion Peter and the disciples returned to their old trade of fishing. There is no suggestion that they believed themselves to have a mission to carry on after the death of Jesus. After Jesus had died their hopes went into the tomb and they returned to old, familiar ways. They try to cope with the loss of the one who had changed their lives.

After a long night's fishing the disciples come up with zero, and a distant figure on the shore tells them to try again. They pull in a marvellous haul. The Beloved Disciple identifies the figure as Jesus, and Peter in his excitement tries treading water to be with him. Peter has a wet breakfast with the Lord.

After the meal Jesus asks Peter three times about the reality of his love. Insisting on love is something of a mark with Jesus. Three times Peter affirms his love, as three times Jesus insists on it. And when Peter professes his love Jesus commissions him to care for his flock. Seeing the Lord is always a dismissal for ministry; loving the Lord is always a charge to care for others.

And that is what Peter does – as we heard from today's first reading. In his ministry of preaching and healing Peter gets through to many people, and the authorities become nervous at the ability of Peter and the apostles to work in the name of Jesus. In spite of the opposition Peter will continue insisting on his love for Jesus and this insistence will take him to martyrdom in Rome. In the end Jesus' question "Simon, do you love me?" becomes profoundly unnecessary. There is nothing circumstantial about Peter's love.

The question asked by love
So the question of Jesus is openly directed to each of us: "Do you love me?" But before Jesus puts the question to us he goes to enormous trouble to first assure us that he really loves us. He died making the point. When we're assured of that first love we might be less hesitant in declaring our own.

The question of Jesus stays with us hoping for an answer. The question comes from one who is more interested in our future prospects than our past failures. He doesn't pass the time in bitter recriminations. He's more interested in what can become of us. That kind of person is worth letting through our defences and locked doors. He's not a security risk. After all, his Valentine has already been slipped under the door.

"They never follow a stranger"

When a stranger comes

When the American film director John Ford was interviewed about his technique for making westerns, he stated that there was only one way to open a film to arouse people's interest. You must begin, he said, by having a stranger ride at full gallop into town. The peaceful life of the settlement is going to be disturbed by this stranger. The townspeople don't know who he is; they don't know where he's coming from; they have no idea why he is in such a hurry. And why *here?* For Ford, all these questions were provoked by a stranger whose arrival kicked up so much dust. The life of the settlement was then primed for conflict.

In the familiar life of the small town, strangers are often regarded with suspicion and resentment. Sometimes new arrivals have to wait years before they feel accepted as part of the community. Some always feel the outsider, no matter how long they stay and strive for approval. When it comes to voting for leaders in the community, people usually select those who know the community well, those who can be judged worthy of trust. They're not going to place their trust in someone they know nothing about.

In that sense people are like sheep. As Jesus says in today's Gospel: "They never follow a stranger but run away from him: they do not recognise the voice of strangers."

Authentic voice

One of the central beliefs of our faith is that Jesus was no stranger to our humanity. He was fully human. We believe that he was not an alien from outer space who arrived in our midst as a totally formed package of difference. As John announces in the prologue of his Gospel:

> He came to his own home,
> and his own people did not accept him. (1.11)

Born and brought up as a member of the chosen people, Jesus was to *become the stranger* because of the way he was aliened by his own people. Others, however, did accept him because for them he spoke with the voice of authenticity. They could see how he always paid attention to the real condition of the people he encountered.

There are some voices we recognise as real because we believe that the speaker is trying to face the complexity of life with honesty and courage. There are other speakers we suspect are just prattling on, tuned to making the right noises in an everlasting effort to be elected the official voice. In the end they just fleece people: they steal their hope to secure their own power. Today's Gospel gives us an image of Jesus as someone who hopes that people will come to recognise his voice as the one that does address who they are and where they are, one that leads them without disguise and without pretence. The first letter of Peter makes the same point when it speaks of Jesus: "He had not done anything wrong, and there had been no perjury in his mouth."

Clearly, many people do not want to hear the truth from Jesus; but if a price is demanded for ignoring his truth, Jesus does not exact it. "He was insulted and did not retaliate with insults; when he was tortured he made no threats but he put his trust in the righteous judge." Jesus places everything in the hands of his Father. In spite of the treatment he receives, he always refuses to give back as he has received. That doesn't make him into superman; it speaks to us of *his way of being human.*

To be a human being does not mean the same as being human. In virtue of our birth we are all human beings; but we have to learn what it means to be truly human in our world. Jesus teaches us that. He takes our inhumanity on his back and carries it to the cross. His way of the cross is his most authentic voice: it speaks of the shepherd willing to die for his sheep. He dies for what he believes in. He is his word.

Human like Jesus
As Christians we are all called to be fully human like Jesus. That is our vocation. We believe in the words of the Gospel that Jesus came so that we could "have life and have it to the full." To share in his way of being human. To speak our truth quietly and insistently, even when the opposition is ranged impressively against us. To have a way that meets people's meanness with the generosity of life in abundance. To have a heart that is capable of imaginative sympathy – of seeing the real muddle and conflict in people's lives. To have a mind that is not a computer record of past hurts, but is freed for other projects because it makes judgement the Father's business.

Jesus' way of being human keeps us all on our toes. Sometimes we do appreciate that his way is not strange to our condition; it is the human condition at its finest. Other times when we look at ourselves we feel helpless to move with that generosity of spirit. But the voice of Jesus forever calls us. It calls to a place deep within us, the place that recognises the voice of the one who loves us with an everlasting love. And when we hear that voice speak, we know it belongs to no stranger.

Shepherding

The shepherd

One of the most popular images of pastoral care is that of the shepherd who leads his large flock and protects them from harm. In the time of Jesus many herds consisted of thousands of sheep, their sheer number requiring highly skilled men to look after them and know how to cure their ailments. The flocks spent most of the year on the vast open uplands, from March to mid-November, and the winter was spent under cover. Hyenas, jackals and wolves roamed the hills, as well as robbers on two legs, and the shepherd was usually armed with a knife or a cudgel. The shepherd's care and courage were legendary. When the young David was anxious to convince King Saul that he was capable of fighting Goliath, he said:

> Your servant used to look after the sheep for his father and whenever a lion and a bear came out and took a sheep from the flock, I used to follow him up and strike him down and rescue it from his mouth; if he turned on me I seized him by the hair of the jaw and struck him down and killed him...God who has rescued me from the claws of lion and bear will rescue me from the power of this Philistine. (1 Samuel 17:34ff)

Shepherding was a hazardous occupation; outdoor living was rough. Sometimes the shepherds would build sheepfolds with dry-stone walls to make the watching and the counting easier; this also allowed them to spend more time in human company. During the long dry season, however, they had to move their flocks in search of new pastures and watering places, and because they trespassed so often on private land they were somewhat unpopular with landowners. In common with tax-collectors, they were forbidden to hold public office or give evidence in court.

Jesus the shepherd

The wandering figure of the good shepherd, anxiously tending his sheep to the point where he is willing to surrender his life for them, is the image Jesus uses about himself in today's Gospel. That mixture of tenderness and toughness, care and self-sacrifice, is one that summarizes his own practice of leadership. It is not a leadership of detachment and defensiveness; rather, it is a leadership of physical involvement and self-sacrificial love. In the good shepherd's foolish extravagant love, his own life matters less than that of his sheep.

The good shepherd is not an image of religious authority that is eternally pleased with its own importance, blind to the useless pain it causes in those it leads. The authority of the shepherd costs the shepherd, not the sheep. The image of the shepherd cannot be separated from how the shepherd actually cares for his own sheep. His concern is not untroubled, his courage is not bloodless, his love is not detached. When we see how Jesus *actually behaves* as a leader, we see his tenderness and courage.

> Jesus tackles his opponents, face to face.
> He confronts those who steal the dignity of the little ones.
> He names the wolves in sheep's clothing.
> He is willing to leave his enemies looking sheepish.
> He warns his followers about the rough terrain ahead.
> He goes there before them.
> He is defensive when people attack his own followers.
> He is realistic about people's wayward ways.
> He endures isolation and insult.
> He faces his own fear, but stays loyal.
> He risks being slaughtered himself.
> He does lay down his life for his sheep.

Pastoral care

In his life and in his death Jesus sought out the lost and the least and the last. When he wanted to speak of a tender God he told the people about a shepherd who, when he loses one of his sheep, leaves the other sheep and goes off in search of the lost one. The shepherd refuses to accept the loss of one sheep as "just one of those things". He searches for the lost sheep until he finds it, and then taking it on his shoulders he returns to share his joy with all his neighbours.

That is Jesus' image of pastoral care, a search that continues until a find can be made. We know, of course, that a search is not automatic after a loss. Many losses are not even registered. Where there is no love, there is no loss. Some people are regarded as "no great loss". Other people are encouraged to "get lost". But all of us hope that when we are lost someone, somewhere, will be looking for us. Like the good shepherd.

The good shepherd challenges our own way of leaving people for lost: "I have come to seek out and save the lost." Probably all of us know two or three people who have wandered away from the Church, who have lost their sense of belonging, who feel they have no community to belong to. How will they know they are welcome back if no one tells them? How will they be helped back if no one offers to make the journey with them?

Pioneers and settlers

Different types

If you have ever watched a Western you will have noticed that most characters in the film fit into two categories: the pioneers and the settlers. The pioneers are those who never like being tied down, who enjoy new faces and new frontiers, who are happy answering the call of the wide, open spaces. Their home is usually a covered wagon and they leave a litany of forwarding addresses in their trail. They always seem to be moving on, not least because sheriffs are usually nervous when they ride into town.

Then there's the settlers. They have stopped wandering and now have regular addresses. They've put down roots, built their homes, and surround themselves with familiar faces. They like the settled life and the security that goes with it. When they have to leave home they never stay away too long. They guard their homesteads with their lives from marauding wanderers. And usually all the authority figures – the mayor, the sheriff and the judge – are settlers.

You will remember that the first two brothers in the Bible, Cain and Abel, are a settler and a pioneer. Cain is the one who is settled, the farmer who tills the soil and waits on the produce from the land. Abel is the shepherd, the wandering figure who searches out new pastures for his flock. Although they are brothers, the shepherd and the farmer, the pioneer and the settler, they do not relate very well. Cain is jealous because the first-born lambs of the shepherd are accepted by God while his first-produce from the land is rejected. He takes Abel to the open country and murders him. The first killing fields. Doomed to be a fugitive Cain soon settles down again and he becomes the builder of the first city. The settler has landed again.

Jesus, the shepherd

Long before the chosen people settled as farmers, they had wandered from place to place living in tents and leading their animals from one pasture-land to another. At the time of Christ the shepherd was still an important worker, but he was not looked on with great confidence. The old rivalry between the nomads roaming with their flocks and the settled tillers of the soil was still alive. Shepherds were regarded as an unhappy mixture of gypsy and roaming thief, not least because their flocks sometimes ate their way through private property! Because of the roving nature of their job they could not honour the demands of the ceremonial law and so were regarded as religious outcasts; and because they were seen as untrustworthy, they were disqualified from appearing as legal witnesses.

The popular, romantic image of the shepherd that many of us have is a world away from the reality. It does not include living on the fringes of civilisation, the harshness and danger of the wilds, the smell of the unwashed, the large loneliness, and the sheer difference of a life which communed more with sheep than with people. The shepherd had a place in the folk-lore of the Israelite people but he had no place of importance in their society at the time of Jesus. Shepherds, donkey-drivers, and pedlars were all at the bottom of the social scale.

So when Jesus speaks of himself as the shepherd he is clearly allying himself with the vagabonds of society. Elsewhere he says: "Foxes have holes and the birds of the air have nests, but the Son of Man has nowhere to lay his head." He is the wandering prophet who has been rejected by his own settlement in Nazareth. He keeps moving, always having another address in mind, and he shakes a lot of dust from his feet. He never lingers on even when the people's hospitality is generous. He will not be tied down – except when he is taken to Calvary. He is a pioneer rather than a settler.

As the shepherd he is always going ahead of his flock seeking out new pastures. He takes on the risks and dangers of the calling, knowing that there will be a few wolves on the uplands with marvellous woollen outfits and make-up to outsmart anyone but a shepherd with an acute sense of smell – especially for the phony. The authority figures – all of whom are settlers – regard him with undisguised hatred. They will eventually ensure, just as at the beginning, that he is taken into the killing fields and murdered. They will tie him down at last. But he does not settle into death, and the tomb is a temporary stop. Clearly, you cannot keep a pioneer down!

A Church of pioneers and settlers
When you think about yourself, do you see yourself as a pioneer or a settler? Is the Church made up of both kinds of people? Like St Paul, who was a tent-maker and who was good at moving on, as we hear in today's reading, do we need more pioneers in the Church? Every community needs both kinds: people who call the community away from stagnation, and people who build up the community. Every person here has a vocation to do one or the other. Let us pray for each other's vocation.

The Way, the Truth and the Life

A sense of direction

Most of us manage through the day without being bothered by the question of life itself: what's the point of being here? It can take all our time and energy merely to cope with what the day brings, and we're happy to leave questions about the purpose of life to the armchair philosophers. However there are times when we are forced to pause because something happens that throws our routine into question. Like the sudden death of someone very close to us which leaves us in a large absence. Questions arise which are *our* questions. Things that we took for granted now look different from before; ventures we thought so important begin to look so insubstantial against the reality of loss.

We wonder where we are going, if anywhere. What direction do we take when our very sense of direction seems to have gone? We might feel that we're going round in circles but not really getting anywhere. Like the fish who were fooled by their owner when he pasted postcards onto the aquarium to give them the impression they were going somewhere.

An experience of profound loss always makes us question our own direction in life, and in today's Gospel John shows us that it is no different for the disciples. Jesus gives his final discourse before leaving his close followers for the last time. He counsels them not to be afraid, for he is going to prepare a place for them, and he will return to take them with him. And it is Thomas who voices their problem: what direction are they going to take in the absence of Jesus? What is to be their way when Jesus leaves them?

Jesus as the Way, the Truth and the Life

What Jesus does *not* do is give his disciples a theology handbook that will answer all their questions about God. Neither does he hand them a book detailing every law with an index classifying every sin. We might wish that he did, but clearly that was not his way. There are no maps into the future with specific routes clearly arrowed. Jesus simply points to himself: "I am the Way, the Truth and the Life." He alone is the gateway to God, the access to the Father.

Jesus is the Way by which we travel to the fulness of God. he does not say, "I have a way" but "I am the Way." This is not an easy saying. Only when we are united with him can we reach the Father, because he and the Father are one. We are not speaking about the unknown God of the Greeks or the invisible God of the Jews: we are speaking about the God who has made himself known in the person of Jesus of Nazareth. Jesus is the face of God, the heart of God, the word of God. God is *inseparable* from Jesus as the Father is inseparable from the Son. "No one can come to the Father except through me. If you know me, you know my Father too."

Jesus is the Truth. He not only speaks the truth, but the fulness of truth is found in him alone. This is the answer to Pilate's question, "What is the truth?" The truth is not some abstract system of thought but is embodied in the particular person of Jesus. The truth is not a theory, it is a person. Jesus is the truth about God as he is the truth about humanity. The one who walked the roads of Palestine and ate with sinners is God's gift of his true self to us.

As God looked to Jesus to reveal his true self, we look to Jesus to reveal God; He is the only true icon of God.

Jesus is the Life. As John announced at the beginning of his Gospel:

> Through him all things came to be,
> not one thing had its being but through him.
> All that came to be had life in him. (1:3-4)

We are because of Jesus. Our very life is his gift. This is why we regard life as sacred from its beginning to its end. We see it not as an accident of fate but as a unique example of God's gift. No one in this gathering is regarded as a mistake by the Gospel! Other people may see us as a large mistake, but the Gospel clothes us with a unique dignity. Jesus is the Life, and we all have our life in him.

The way ahead
But does all this help to give you direction, or do you remain as puzzled as the disciples? The disciples learn soon after Jesus leaves them that they don't have ready answers to everything. As we learn from the early divisions in the community, they all have to work together to find a way forward. There are many things Jesus did not tell them, and they have to try to face the future with honesty. Together.

Jesus *trusts* his followers down the ages to face the confusion and complexity of the world. That's why he doesn't leave answers to everything. There's still a lot of working out to be done. Looking to Jesus as the Way, the Truth and the Life, doesn't actually *solve* every question effortlessly. But Jesus knew that! Clearly he wants us to put our faith to work.

The apostle Paul

New beginning
In Syria there is a small village called Deraya which stands on the ancient road between Damascus and Jerusalem. Like thousands of other rural settlements, it looks remarkably unimpressive – as if history has kept its pledge to pay it no heed. Most of the Syrian inhabitants are not sure why their village is called Deraya, but Christians are. In Arabic the name Deraya means "the vision". Something that happened on the Jerusalem-Damascus road gave this village its name. For it was there, according to tradition, that the persecutor Saul encountered the Christ.

The small Catholic chapel in Deraya stands as a memorial to the most significant conversion in the early Church, when the man who went out of his way to hunt down Christians was confronted by the God who went out of his way to meet his persecutor. Saul believed that his vocation from God was the persecution of the Christian community. As he declared:

> I once thought it was my duty to use every means to oppose the name of Jesus the Nazarene. This I did in Jerusalem; I myself threw many of the saints into prison, acting on authority from the chief priests, and when they were sentenced to death I cast my vote against them...my fury against them was so extreme that I even pursued them into foreign cities. (Acts 26:9-11)

Whatever actually happened on the road to Damascus, Paul dates his new beginning from that experience. He never claimed that his change was just an afternoon episode: his conversion *began* on the Damascus road and continued throughout his life. For the first three years of his life Paul underwent a wilderness novitiate in the Arabian desert. After that he went to Damascus, where he managed to throw the Jewish colony into complete confusion. The new missionary escaped with his life when he was lowered from the city walls in a basket. That undignified exit was the first of many escapes.

Paul the apostle
Paul's story is picked up in today's first reading. He escapes to Jerusalem where he tries to join the disciples, but he is in for a rude awakening. The disciples are all afraid of Paul; they simply cannot believe that he has really changed. Given Paul's punishing track record, the disciples' suspicion seems all too reasonable. By his own admission, Paul had signed the death warrants of Jerusalem Christians; now he seems to expect ready admission into their inner circle. Barnabas, whose name means "son of

encouragement", takes charge of the new arrival. He introduces Paul to the apostles, telling them the story of his conversion and recent preaching.

We are not told if the apostles are impressed, only that Paul begins preaching in the city. He does the same favour for Jerusalem that he did for Damascus – he causes a riot and turns his hearers into willing assassins. Another deadly response, another security operation, another emergency exit. And when he is gone, Luke tells us, the churches in the region are now left in peace. With the dynamite shipped back north, the churches can breathe easily again.

But not for long. Paul refuses to go into hiding or retire from his new career; he cannot because he believes that he has been appointed by God to be an apostle and missionary. For all his belief in the divine authority of his appointment, however, the burden of his past never seems to leave him completely. Paul's apostleship is never effortless – he admits that he appears before people in fear and trembling. He is always anxious to prove that he is as good as the other apostles, that he preaches the same message, that he has been chosen by the same Christ, that he suffers more than they do for the sake of the Gospel.

The love of the apostle

That need to overcome any suspicions about his authenticity makes Paul an energetic preacher, a tireless traveller, a fierce debater. He is no "yes man" submitting to authority before he has thought through the propositions. He is a great example of authentic humanity: he is sensitive, impulsive, obstinate, moody, thoughtful, demanding, driven, caring. His idealism is tempered by his sense of realism, and his own struggle always serves to educate his spirituality.

Above everything Paul's great lesson to us is his abiding love. He was a man who longed for friendship and the affection of people. As he wrote in his second letter to the Corinthians: "I may have hurt you, but if so I have hurt the only people who could give me any pleasure...it was not to make you feel hurt but to let you know how much love I have for you." (2:2-3) It sounds like a lover's quarrel. The poet Robert Frost could have been speaking about Paul when he wrote:

> And were an epitaph to be my story
> I'd have a short one ready for my own
> I would have written of me on my stone
> I had a lover's quarrel with the world.

Encouraging others: Barnabas

A name that means something

In the fantastic world which Lewis Carroll describes in his book, *Through the Looking-Glass,* the young Alice meets a legion of very strange creatures. Among them is an old sheep who spends her time knitting while running a small shop which is packed with curious things. After peering around for some time Alice decides to buy an egg, and when she takes it with her it gets larger and larger and more human – complete with an enormous face. The large human-egg is called Humpty Dumpty, who finds it provoking to be called an egg. He asks Alice for her name.

"My *name* is Alice, but –"

"It's a stupid name enough!" Humpty Dumpty interrupted impatiently. "What does it mean?"

"*Must* a name mean something?" Alice asked doubtfully.

"Of course it must," Humpty Dumpty said with a short laugh: "*my* name means the shape I am – and a good handsome shape it is, too. With a name like yours, you might be any shape."

I suppose it has to be said that Humpty Dumpty has a point. Most of our names are not *descriptive* of who we are or what we're like: for the most part they are just convenient identity tags. Just from our name nobody could guess either the shape we are or the shape we're in! Sometimes we pick up nicknames which try to catch something of our peculiarity, although these are rarely flattering – least of all when they're accurate.

In the first years of the Church there was a young Jew from the island of Cyprus who became a missionary preacher. His name was Joseph but the apostles decided to give him another name. And the name they chose to give him describes accurately who he really was: they called him Barnabas, which means "son of encouragement".

Barnabas

The first Christian community shared everything in common, and the first thing we hear about Barnabas is that he sold his estate and laid the money at the apostles' feet. Luke describes him as a "good man, full of the Holy Spirit and of faith" whose encouragement resulted in many people persevering in their faith. And there was one man in particular who was helped by Barnabas: his name was Paul.

Remember that Paul had been the grand inquisitor and unrivalled as a persecutor of the Church. After his conversion Paul tells us that he spent three years in the Arabian desert in a long renewal course in the Spirit. When he emerged from the wilderness he went to Jerusalem to see Peter.

The apostles gave Paul a cool reception – no doubt because they found it difficult to believe that such an accomplished persecutor of their community now wanted to be numbered among them. With indecent haste the Church leaders ensured that Paul was soon back in Tarsus.

But one man encouraged Paul in his new life and decided to sponsor him. Barnabas had been appointed to superintend the Church in Antioch, the capital of Syria. He sought out Paul and invited him to come as his assistant, and for a full year they ministered there together. It was at Antioch that the followers of Christ were first known as "Christians". Clearly, Paul and Barnabas fulfilled the command of Jesus: "By this love you have for one another, everyone will know that you are my disciples."

Paul and Barnabas travelled widely together and, as we heard in the first reading, "they put fresh heart into the disciples encouraging them to persevere in the faith." Paul extended to others the encouragement he had received from Barnabas. For Barnabas saw something in Paul that no other apostle saw: he saw beyond the face of the persecutor into the heart of a man who was struggling to be an apostle. Barnabas called out the best in Paul. And he did that not from long distance but through staying with him for 1400 miles of travelling and preaching. That's a lot of sponsorship and a lot of encouragement!

The power of encouragement

Even the haughty Humpty Dumpty hopes that in the unlikely event of his ever falling that all the king's men will turn up to put him together again. He fondly hopes that someone will help him into the shape of his name. When Paul falls off his high horse it is Barnabas who turns up to help him into the shape of his new name. Barnabas lives up to his name, "son of encouragement," by helping Paul live up to his new name, apostle of Christ Jesus.

By his encouragement Barnabas actually gives shape to Paul's life. And he does that not with idle chatter or vague well-wishing but by staying with Paul. He promotes the best in Paul; he assists the possible; he invests his time and love and energy in the person Paul can become. That is encouragement.

We can all bless God for the people who invested in us, who encouraged us to be who we are. And we all need to pray that when the time comes we too can be a Barnabas.

Accounting for hope

The puzzle of hope

The scene is the courtyard of a prison. The time is dawn. A prisoner is led out to be shot: he is a priest who has been sentenced to death because he has opposed the Portuguese policy of slave-trade in the country's colony. He stands against an outer wall facing seven members of the firing-squad, all of them his own countrymen. Before the officer ties the blindfold he asks the prisoner for the traditional last request. The reply comes as a surprise: the man about to die wants to play his flute for the last time.

The firing-squad is stood at ease as they wait for the prisoner to play. When he does, the prison compound is filled with music that sounds all the more beautiful in this strange place. The officer is worried because the more the music plays, the more absurd his task appears to be. He orders the prisoner to stop playing, ties the blindfold, and gives his soldiers the command to fire. The priest dies instantly. But the music lingers on to puzzle his executioners: in the face of certain death, where does the music come from?

In today's second reading the early Christian community is told that their conduct should be such that their persecutors will be put to shame: "Always have your answer ready for people who ask you the reason for the hope that you all have. But give it with courtesy and respect and with a clear conscience, so that those who slander you when you are living a good life in Christ may be proved wrong in the accusations that they bring."

When people face persecution, hope is often the first casualty. That is why hope in the face of violent death is deeply puzzling to many people – particularly to those who aspire to kill not only the believers but what they believe in. What kind of hope is it that enables those who suffer to play music in the face of death? In the death of the martyr, the persecutor and the onlooker are always questioned by the hope that sees through death.

The help of hope

Hope is the virtue that enables us to look to the future with real confidence. It is not to be reduced to wishful thinking. We can all pass the time daydreaming, imagining a future that has nothing to do with reality. Wishful thinking has no bounds; it admits of no limitation; it is not criticised by what is actually possible. I can ask you to imagine a tartan elephant with six legs doing a highland fling. You can imagine that, but it would be foolish to hope that you will see it happen one day. Hope is grounded in life. As the Jewish writer Martin Buber observed: *"hope imagines the real."* That is the difference between hope and wishful thinking.

Hope is not limitless; it is limited by real possibility. Hope needs help if it is going to go beyond the expression of desire. If you hope for peace, for example, your hope needs all the help it can get if it is to be more than a cherished wish. Without help, hope remains an orphan – abandoned in the nursery of the mind.

Jesus has no intention of leaving his disciples behind him in a situation where they are left to hope without any help. Jesus promises his followers the Spirit, the Advocate, who will be with them forever. *The power of the Spirit is the help of Christian hope.* Without the Spirit, the followers of Jesus would be thrown back on their own resources, which are clearly inadequate when the going gets rough. The time of Jesus' passion proved that. With the help of the Spirit, however, the disciples can face the future with a power that is much larger than themselves. That power is the Spirit, the gift of God himself. The reality of the Spirit is the ground of their hope.

The unseen Spirit

Jesus warns the disciples that the world will not welcome the Spirit "since it neither sees nor knows him." Nevertheless the Spirit of God will be *in* the disciples, even though so many people cannot recognise its presence. The only way the persecutors and onlookers will catch something of the reality of the Spirit is when they see the courage and hope of the disciples in remaining steadfast in witness.

The hope of the disciples is something the world *can* see, but cannot account for. The disciples can account for their hope by pointing to the power of God's Spirit which funds them. They know that that power is not their own. Without that Spirit, there would be no music to puzzle the firing-squad.

Finally Jesus makes it clear that the Spirit he promises will be given not only to the present disciples but to all those who love him and keep his commandments. The Spirit which will sustain them through persecution and martyrdom is the same Spirit which is given to all who love Jesus. That promise is extended to each of us in our own struggle in faith. And that is why we are called on by the Church to pray again for a renewal in the Spirit at Pentecost. With that Spirit in us we can continue the ancient Christian practice of puzzling people with the hope that is in us.

Choosing to love

Being chosen

Before people go for a job interview they usually spruce themselves up, dust themselves down, then check with their family or friends if they look all right. Minor adjustments are made, assurances of "not to worry" are urged. On the way to the interview the hopefuls might even whisper a telegram to St Jude, traditional patron of hopeless cases. Résumés have already been sent on ahead, advance notice of past accomplishments that are supported by important signatories. The gaps have been covered as well as could be truthfully managed. All these reports now lie on the table in the interview room. Dry throats are watered, moist palms are rubbed, nervousness is covered with a ready smile. The interview begins. The agenda is themselves.

People go through all this anxiety and strain in the hope that they will be selected for the job. The prospect of failure and rejection is real, but the strenuous hope of being chosen gives them courage to face the probing questions. To be chosen is to be picked out, opted for, preferred, taken on. All this makes the risk of refusal worthwhile.

It is only when applicants are chosen for a job that they are free to take it or leave it. Before acceptance they are in no position to *choose* the job that is advertised. In applying they declare that they want the position; but wishes aren't choices. Only after acceptance have they the actual *power* to choose the job or not. That is why people forced by circumstances into a course of action always say, "But I had no choice in the matter." *Real choice presupposes the freedom and the power to commit oneself.*

Choosing

When John talks about the love of God in today's readings, he is clear what he means – "this is the love I mean: not our love for God, but God's love for us". The same message is underlined in the Gospel: "You did not choose me, no, I chose you". We don't have to turn up at an interview to discover if God will choose us or not: God has already made an everlasting decision to love us. God's love is not an issue, it is not a matter of speculation. It is there.

God's love is first, and it is only because of the primacy of God's love that we have the power and the freedom to choose God.

God has opted for us, he has declared his choice, he has taken us on. It is a decisive movement of love that began with the Father: "As the Father has loved me, so I love you. Remain in my love." The hope is expressed that we can come to appreciate God's choice of us. It is such good news that John is anxious to get the message through to us, simply and clearly. Can we remain in the love that chooses us?

God's love is based on choice: he loves because he chooses to love. The supreme example of that is in his Word, Jesus. If the supreme act of love is to lay down your life for the sake of others, Jesus shows that he could have no greater love. His love takes him to the cross, just as the Father's love raises him up. Jesus spends himself, he gives of himself until there is nothing left to give. He empties himself.

Choosing to give ourselves
In everything that he did Jesus kept on choosing to love. He did not choose *once* upon a time; he chose to love at all times. It drained him. That self-giving quality of divine love is one that can be seen in the lives of many people. One doctor saw it in a way that he can never forget. As a young medical student he watched an unusual operation in a London hospital:

> It was the first time that this particular brain operation had been carried out in this country. It was performed by one of our leading surgeons upon a young man of great promise for whom, after an accident, there seemed to be no other remedy. It was an operation of the greatest delicacy, in which a small error would have had fatal consequences. In the outcome the operation was a triumph: but it involved seven hours of intense and uninterrupted concentration on the part of the surgeon. When it was over, a nurse had to take him by the hand, and lead him from the operating theatre like a blind man or a little child.

That kind of self-giving and concentration on the needs of another reflect something of the quality of God's love in Jesus. Jesus hopes that we will choose to keep on giving ourselves in love, even when the giving hurts, even when we feel we have nothing left but our exhausted presence. But it's that *kind* of love that mirrors God's kind of love. As Jesus said himself, the love that costs nothing can be managed by anyone, for everything is on credit. The bill for authentic love is the giving of the self, the communication of the self, the handing over of the self.

We have to admit that few of us have the freedom or the power to accomplish this. We can only choose to try, confident that our struggle is backed by God's energetic love. Somewhere in the struggle we can hear the voice of God cheering us on.

143

Arguing for Christ: Paul

Absence and loss

The prospect of saying farewell to some people can become the only pleasure of a long, boring evening. Saying farewell to those we love, on the other hand, is often postponed for as long as possible. It's a fact of life that in the presence of some people our whole life is enhanced, while in the presence of others we pray for wings! When the time comes to let go of those we love we always find it difficult. That is all the more true when someone we love is dying. We mourn for the dying and we wonder how we will cope in a future without them. We hope they will stay on because we are afraid that our world will collapse around us. Like Dylan Thomas pleading with his father,

> And you, my father, there on the sad height,
> Curse, bless, me now with your fierce tears I pray.
> Do not go gentle into that good night.
> Rage, rage against the dying of the light.

In today's Gospel Jesus is aware of the deep anxiety of his own disciples as they face the reality of his final departure. They are who they are because of him. Without him who will they be? Jesus prepares them for the day of his going, as the liturgy prepares us for the feast of the Ascension which we celebrate on Thursday. Before he returns to his Father Jesus counsels his disciples not to be afraid. Go he must. But in his last will and testament he leaves them more than his absence: he leaves them his word and his peace and the promise of the Advocate, the Holy Spirit, who will help them in the future to be his apostles.

Arguing for Christ: Paul

In his last will Jesus did not leave his followers answers to every question in life. He knew that they would have to endure many struggles, that they would have to face ambiguity and confusion, difference and disagreement. They would not see eye to eye on everything; they would have different memories of Jesus; they would emphasise different things. In the conflicts that would arise they would have *to put their faith to work.* That is why they would need the Advocate, the big lawyer! We only need a lawyer when there's trouble, and it wasn't long before the Advocate was needed to settle conflict in the early church.

During their year's mission in Antioch Barnabas and Paul had great success receiving many Gentiles into the Christian faith. However their success gave rise to conflict in the community when members of the

Jerusalem community argued that all converts first had to be circumcised and obey the detailed Law of Moses. Paul vigorously opposed this group, arguing that obedience to the Law does not bring anyone salvation: that is achieved through faith in Jesus Christ. However, those who argued that all Gentiles must obey the Law had an influential lobby, and Paul tells us in his letter to the Galatians that they even influenced Peter:

> When Peter came to Antioch I opposed him to his face since he was manifestly in the wrong...When I saw they were not respecting the true meaning of the Good News, I said to Peter in front of everyone, 'In spite of being a Jew, you live like the pagans...so you have no right to make the pagans copy Jewish ways!' (Gal 2:11ff)

You can hear the conflict in Paul's account of what happened. When Luke tells the story of the Council of Jerusalem which was called to settle the question, he tidies up the conflict and all we get is the resolution! Paul, on the other hand, is clearly not embarrassed by having to argue his case openly and oppose very powerful and respected members of the Church. Paul puts his faith to work and argues for Christ, and it is largely through the Spirit working in him that the Church spread so rapidly among the Gentiles. Paul took Christ from within the precincts of the Jewish faith and introduced him to the pagan world.

Facing real confusion
We should take heart from the conflict of the early church because we know from experience that there will always be some confusion and disagreement in our complex community. Not everything is heavenly clear, and that is because we are here on earth! And that is why we need the Spirit. In the lives of all of us we have to work through confusion and aim for peace. The Church we belong to continues to grow and has to face new questions honestly in the light of the Spirit.

We are neither alone nor helpless. We have the word of God and the presence of the Spirit to help us do what the Church must always do: face the real confusion and aim for peace. It will not be until the heavenly Jerusalem that we will know total peace. Meanwhile we face the real world with confidence because we have great gifts in our community: the word of God, the presence of the Spirit, and leaders who still argue for the freedom of the Gospel.

Heart problems

Where is the light?
So, Jesus has gone back home. His work is done and he has left us, although not abandoned us. He has left us to work at our Christianity, to work out the consequences of our faith, to take on the terrible freedom of forming our own lives and being responsible for them. We have put out the light of the paschal candle; but we can extinguish the light there in the belief that that light burns somewhere else – that we have caught the light ourselves, and that it burns in our own hearts.

You may have heard the ancient tale of God's original problem: where to conceal his most precious possession, his own image. He called three wise counsellors, to listen to their suggestions. The first advised God to put his image on the top of the highest mountain on earth, where it would be safe forever; God, however, declined the suggestion. The second wise man proposed that God should put his image in the depths of the deepest sea; but God saw submarines in his mind's eye and said no. The third suggested that God hide his image on the far side of the moon; but God smiled to himself and said that even there man could reach it. Then God had his original idea: "I know where to conceal my image," he said. "I will put it in a place where people will never think of looking; I will put it into their hearts. There, it will never be discovered." And the three wise men nodded in agreement; they knew that God was indeed right.

The image of God, the light of God, is in the place where we rarely look: in our heart. We believe God's presence is within us – not as a hiding-place, but that we might discover him at close quarters. When St Augustine discussed the ascension in the fourth chapter of his *Confessions* he made the same point: "He withdrew from our eyes that we might return to our own heart to find him." When the light goes out on the paschal candle, do we find that light nearer home, in our own heart?

The home of God
In today's Gospel the disciples are invited to take to heart the great vision of a discipleship of all nations, and to let that vision shape their mission. With the departure of Jesus, they are invited to take a lot of people to heart. We know from experience that it is not enough to take Christ to heart. When Christ comes to dwell in our heart, he never comes alone. He arrives complete with entourage and baggage: he brings his loves and his values and his hopes; he brings his dreams and expectations. He also brings disciples and strange friends and hangers-on; he brings the poor and the

---

blind and the crippled; he brings the outcast and the stranger and the legion of the overlooked.

Christ never comes alone. And when he comes we realise that the visiting team may look more like a circus parade than a divine procession. Like the innkeepers of the world, we might be tempted to put up a "no vacancy" sign, to tell Jesus that we have no room in our heart for his busload of supporters and for his theological baggage. But one thing is certain: we cannot take him in and leave the rest outside.

Long before his ascension, Jesus took a lot of people to heart. He suffered because of his passionate love for others. He paid a price for taking so many people to heart. But he treasured them, in all their pettiness and lopsided resolve, with all their thin aspirations and crazy ambitions, with all their private preoccupations and hidden fears. With all of this, his heart began to look more like an emergency-ward than a treasure room.

The challenge

The challenge of Jesus is to open our hearts to his kind of people. When we let them in, he slips in among them. Who will take to heart the poor and the elderly, the sick and the Scrooges of this world? Who will risk making the fragile people the adornments of the treasure rooms of their hearts?

We know many people do this. The quiet people who nurse and wash and dress the decay of old age, those who do the daily rounds in mental clinics and hospitals, those who choose to work in slums and ghettos. Their large heartedness makes the rest of us humble, and our own troubles and preoccupations seem so paltry compared with the huge demands they face with commitment and humour.

We can only try to make more room in our heart for Jesus' people, and we can do that in the Gospel truth that he will be at the heart of that enterprise. For the rest, we can only pray the unofficial prayer of the ascension:

> You chose us, Lord, you must recall;
> We never claimed to know it all.
> So long, Jesus,
> Here come the amateurs.

147

B The Ascension

Endings and beginnings

Endings

Some people like stories to reflect their orderly view of the world: with a beginning, a middle and an end, having a pattern and purpose that can be seen and understood; having a conclusion that ties up all the loose ends, leaving people with a sense of completion and satisfaction. When the book is closed there are no more questions to be asked. It is finished.

Other people prefer their stories open-ended, because they believe that life is like that: with a variety of loose connections and accidental happenings; having a development that can never be fully grasped; not having a tidy ending, because tidiness can never contain either the muddle or the mystery of things. When the book is closed the questions do not cease.

Depending on your own point of view and preference, you can read the story of Jesus' ascension as a story that completes everything or as a story that leaves everything open-ended. Of course the ascension does complete the mission of Jesus: it is the last act of the cycle of Jesus' life, death and resurrection, celebrating the return of Jesus to the Father. The ascension is also open-ended, for it marks the beginning of a new time when the apostles have to live in the absence of the Jesus they knew. They have to come to terms with the fact that Jesus will never again walk with them on the roads of Palestine, healing the sick and the wounded, preaching about the kingdom of God. That time is over. He is gone.

"Why are you men of Galilee standing here looking in the sky?" The show isn't over, the curtain hasn't fallen, the action isn't completed. The ending of the Gospel of Mark emphasises this: "Go out to the whole world; proclaim the Good News to all creation." That process is open-ended. It is still going on.

Part of us and beyond us

Not only is the process still continuing, but we don't really know if we are at the beginning of the Christian movement, in the middle of it, or near the end of it. It could all end tomorrow in a nuclear mushroom. It could continue for thousands of years. We don't know. All we know is that we are somewhere between the beginning and the end and that we are addressed by the same challenge to keep the story of Jesus alive.

We are in-between people, we find ourselves in the middle of a complex variety of stories which compete for our attention. None of us can begin at the beginning of those stories, because we are middle people. None of us started from zero: we were all born into a world that was already in motion; we found ourselves in the midst of a history we did not

148

originate; we were ushered into a family and a tradition we did not form. We inherited the times we live in. We could make a start for ourselves only because we were given a start by others. Before we owned anything we owed everything.

The story of Jesus was a power that was given to us, a gift of life to help us shape the world. The story does not simply reflect how things are, but calls us beyond ourselves to a kingdom that is larger than the boundaries of geography and nationality and culture. It is like the story of the people who spoke to the man with the blue guitar:

> They said "You have a blue guitar,
> You do not play things as they are."
> The man replied "Things as they are
> Are changed upon the blue guitar."
> And they said then "But play you must
> A tune beyond us, yet ourselves,
> A tune upon the blue guitar
> Of things exactly as they are."

Following the tune

The story of Jesus is always played upon the blue guitar, for the story is "a tune beyond us, yet ourselves". The story of Jesus' ascension reminds us that Jesus is beyond us – sitting at the right hand of God. But the same story also reminds us that the Lord was working with the apostles by confirming their word by the signs that accompanied it. Beyond us, yet ourselves.

The Gospel beckons us, calls us on, challenges us to move beyond the boundaries that are set by our own fear and weakness and sinfulness. That won't take us into the clouds, but it will provoke people to stare in wonderment at us for moving on. Our stories are not finished, the last word has not been written, the final scenes are still open-ended. Where the future is a mystery there is still hope; it is only when the future looks like an endless repetition of the past that there is a feeling of hopelessness. That is not Gospel, for it is not the tune that is beyond us, yet ourselves.

Departure

Goings and comings

Life is busy with entrances and exits. People come and people go; people arrive and people depart; people are born and people die. Most societies usually mark the time of birth and death with rites and ceremonies. Births and deaths are registered because they are of public importance. They affect other people. New arrivals are greeted and cooed over; new departures are prayed for and mourned. The only thing we know from witnessing death is the parting. As the poet Emily Dickinson wrote:

> Parting is all we know of heaven
> And all we need of hell.

The last we know of people in life is their death. This is what the apostles believed when Jesus died and why they felt so shattered and forsaken. His death was hell for them because it meant a future without hope. In their experience of him as risen Lord, however, their faith was renewed and their hope was reborn. But they still had to face the fact that he would walk among them no longer, for he had to return to the Father. It is to mark that time of Jesus' return that we celebrate the ascension.

In today's readings we have two stories of Jesus' final departure. Both stories are written by St Luke. Luke brings his Gospel to a close with the story of Jesus' ascension. He also opens his second book, the Acts of the Apostles, with the story of Jesus' ascension. In doing that Luke tells us that Jesus' return to his Father is the completion of his mission, while at the same time it marks the beginning of a new age. The ascension is an ending and a beginning.

The ending

Death was not the final departure of Jesus. Our faith proclaims that God raised him from the dead and that he let himself be known to his chosen followers so that they could experience new life in him. That new experience will become the ground of their preaching to others. As Peter says in his first sermon: "God raised this man Jesus to life, and all of us are witnesses to that." (Acts 2:32)

In Luke's Gospel when Jesus appears to his disciples he does not breathe the Holy Spirit on them and commission them to go out and preach to all nations. Rather, Jesus tells the disciples to stay in the city of Jerusalem. They are to go nowhere preaching in his name because they are not yet *empowered* to do so. For Luke Jesus has to go before the Holy Spirit comes. His going means the coming of the Spirit.

The disciples are not yet ready. They cannot witness to Jesus because they cannot fall back on their own resources to minister to other people. Their own resources are not enough for ministry. First they must have a new wardrobe, a new outfit! They must be "clothed with the power from on high." Before that can happen Jesus must go. So, he takes them to Bethany, blesses them, and his ascension marks the time of the end of his appearances. It also celebrates the completion of his life's mission. It is over. Now is the time of the Spirit.

The beginning
You remember when Jesus began his public ministry how he was first invested with the power of the Holy Spirit. In his baptism Jesus received power and authority from the Father through the experience of the Spirit. It was in that power, "Filled with the Holy Spirit" (4:1), that he began his public ministry. The Spirit marked the time of Jesus' new beginning, his time of ministry, his time for reaching out to others and ministering to them with power.

That same process of investiture is repeated for the followers of Jesus. The only difference is that now *Jesus* sends the Spirit from on high. When the disciples receive that Spirit, like Jesus they will be empowered to minister to others and exercise a new authority. This is the beginning of the Church, a beginning which is made possible only in the Spirit of God.

And we believe that as the Spirit made the beginning of the Church, the same Spirit empowers the community of believers today. The Spirit makes a new beginning for us. That is why the approaching feast of Pentecost is so important: it is not only a memory of the beginning of the Church but a celebration of the Spirit at the heart of the Church today. Without the Spirit, we are thrown back on our resources. Clearly our own resources are not enough. We can minister to people in Jesus' name only in the Spirit.

Each of us here is a part of the Church; each of us has a different role to play in the power of the same Spirit. That is why Paul prays for the Christian community at Ephesus that they may be blessed with the Spirit of God. Without it, the community dies. With it, we have life and power. As the feast of Pentecost approaches we pray for a new outfit: that we too will be clothed with the power from on high. Without that outfit we can go nowhere – like the apostles before Pentecost we have to stay put because we have no resources for ministry. With that outfit, we can go anywhere in the power of the Spirit.

Waiting together for the Spirit

Waiting

Standing in the rain waiting for a bus to arrive is no one's idea of a pleasant way to pass the time. Waiting for an important letter to arrive, for exam results, for people to turn up, are all activities that few of us actually enjoy. There are times in the lives of all of us when there is nothing to do but wait. But spending our time waiting is often regarded as a waste of time: we'd rather be doing anything than just waiting around. Sometimes we feel guilty when someone says to us: "Don't just sit there, *do* something!" But sometimes the only thing to do is to wait.

One of the reasons we feel frustrated is because we have no control over what happens. We feel passive and powerless. But there are times when waiting can be a positive experience. When parents wait for the birth of their child their waiting is full of hope, because what they are waiting for has already begun to take place in the womb. What they are waiting for is quietly taking shape in a tiny bundle of life. So too in the history of God's people: the community wait for the fulfilment of a promise that God will come.

> My soul is waiting for the Lord,
> I count on his word.
> My soul is longing for the Lord
> more than watchman for daybreak.
> Let the watchman count on daybreak
> and Israel on the Lord. (Ps. 129:5-7)

Waiting together

In today's reading from the beginning of the Acts of the Apostles Luke shows us three groups of people that wait together for the coming of the Spirit. The three groups are the eleven apostles, the women from Galilee, and Mary with the brothers of Jesus. The gathering of these three groups into *one* community that waits in the upper room is very important for Luke: from the very beginning this community serves to demonstrate the unbroken continuity between the life of Jesus and the life of the Church. Together they will constitute the basic community of the Church.

The Eleven enjoy a unique importance because they were chosen by Jesus and were with him "Right from the time when John was baptising until the day when he was taken up from us" (Acts 1:22). But the apostles' experience does not cover the whole of the Gospel – which is why the other two groups are so important. The women from Galilee were the first to hear the message of the resurrection in the empty tomb – something not witnessed by the apostles. Mary was the first in the Gospel to hear God's message about Jesus and, together with Joseph, was responsible for the formation of Jesus' early life. Neither the apostles nor the women from Galilee cover this time of the Gospel. But *together* they all do.

The apostles *and* the women *and* Mary bring the Gospel in its entirety into the beginning of the Church. One of the brothers of Jesus, James, will play a very important part in the early Church as head of the church in Jerusalem. Now all these figures are united in prayer as they wait for the coming of the Spirit.

Together around the word
They all come together because of the word of God in Jesus. Waiting on the Spirit is not their own idea; rather they wait on the basis of the promise of Jesus. They are a community gathered around that promise, and their presence affirms the hope of each person there. They are not just passing the time. They are expectant that something new will happen in them, and they are attentive to the present moment through prayer.

At the beginning of the Gospel Luke showed us that Mary's response to the word of God was to let it happen. Let it be. Let it become. Let it take shape in her. Now Luke shows us at the beginning of the Church how the whole community responds to the word like Mary first did: they wait attentively to let the word of God happen in their lives. They have a conviction that the word will happen where they are, not somewhere else. And they wait together because together is the place where the Spirit comes.

And that is what we are invited to do as we approach the feast of the Spirit in Pentecost. We are challenged to *wait together around the promise of Jesus;* to share the conviction of the first community that the Spirit of God will happen here, where we are. The promise of Jesus which gathered the first community is the same promise which gathers us together. We have all come here to pray as a community for the blessing of the Spirit. And like the first community, we have the word of God at the centre of our assembly. So we wait. We wait in the knowledge that someone wants to reach us, someone wants to visit us with power.

Our prayer is to let it be. Let it happen. Let what God has said be done in us. Only in that way is the work of God accomplished in the world of today and tomorrow.

A dicey business

Past and present

Rachel is a German Jewess who lives in New York City. Her friends know her as an intelligent vivacious woman, funny and warm and always welcoming. Most people who know her envy what they see as her charmed life: with a family who clearly loves her, with emotional and financial security, she appears to have nothing to fear. What nobody knows is that each morning of her life Rachel faces a crushing torment. When her sons leave for school and her husband leaves for work, she becomes deeply depressed. She says: "I feel lonely, abandoned, petrified. I need hours to compose myself. All my emotions are engaged around the absence of my family. I keep asking myself: what if they don't come back and I am left alone?"

Rachel could not understand her fear. She sought help. After many weeks of journeying into her past she uncovered an old fear. In the late 1930's, when she was six months old, her mother was struggling to keep the two of them alive. Each day her mother had to leave home and join the endless queues for food, and face the German bureaucracy that was making it increasingly difficult for Jews to survive. While her mother was absent each morning, Rachel was left alone at home. Penned in by the crib, the only thing she could do was wait for her mother's return.

One day her deepest fear was realised: her mother did not return. Rachel never discovered what happened. She was taken by relatives to New York where she was brought up by her mother's younger sister. Rachel discovered what she was facing in her adult life was the pain of that original loss. The re-opening of the wound was painful, but in the pain there was insight. As she says now: "I have to grow to forgive the past. If I can't do that, I'll never be able to live freely in the present. I've shared my fear with the family, and they are enormously supportive."

Uses of the past

Rachel had to journey into the past to make sense of the pain of the present. The insight didn't abolish the pain, but at least the source of the pain was located and identified. And that is one of the uses of the past – to draw aside the veil that covers the present tense.

One of the ways we try to make sense of the present is by consulting the past. When we try to figure out why things have turned out the way they have, we often search the past for an explanation. So, ancient voices are listened to with a new attentiveness, old texts are consulted with a new eye, past events are scrutinised anew. That human effort of making sense of the present by rereading the past is one that was used widely in the early

Church – thus things are seen to happen "so that the scriptures might be fulfilled."

So, in today's first reading we hear Peter saying: "Brothers, the passage of scripture had to be fulfilled in which the Holy Spirit, speaking through David, foretells the fate of Judas, who offered himself as a guide to the men who arrested Jesus...In the Book of Psalms it says: 'Let someone else take his office.'"

Peter is claiming the past as a reinforcement of the present. A past, once skimmed over, now becomes part of the Church's sequence of references; what was said before becomes personal territory. The past takes on a new significance *because of what is happening now.* As the past throws light on the present, so the present captures the full meaning of the past. In that sense we can see how the past is not dead: it just bides its time until the full truth can be discovered.

Bringing the past up to date

The activity of bringing the past up to date is one that we all engage in from time to time. We review the past in the light of a new experience, and in the process we begin to see a shape to our story. Certain people and dates become more important, an encounter once regarded as forgettable is seen to be directly related to what is happening now. We begin to see how our previous history contains pointers to our present situation, how everything is connected. A pattern slowly emerges. Things begin to make sense.

In today's first reading you can see the attempts of the early Church to make sense of all the recent happenings. They scour the past for signs, indications, clues. But when they come to look to the future of the Church and choose a successor to Judas, their faith takes a riskier turn. They nominate candidates, pray together, and then draw lots. As one commentator put it: "a little prayer, and then roll the dice!"

Their faith is an enterprise which needs the support of the past but also the willingness to take risks in the present. For all its worth, the past cannot provide solutions to all their needs. The time comes when the disciples must go through the door into the dark, without being sure if the future will confirm their choice to be the right one. Our venture in faith, like theirs, needs the support of the past and the readiness to roll the dice. We have to take the risk. By definition, the future is a dicey subject.

155

Dying for Christ: Stephen

Appointment with hate

When he was still a young boy, the Jewish writer Elie Wiesel was deported with his family to Auschwitz and then to Buchenwald where his parents and little sister died. In his first book, *Night,* he gives a memoir of these experiences:

> Never shall I forget that night, the first night in camp, which has turned my life into one long night, seven times cursed and seven times sealed. Never shall I forget that smoke. Never shall I forget the little faces of the children, whose bodies I saw turned into wreaths of smoke beneath a silent blue sky. Never shall I forget those flames which consumed my Faith forever. Never shall I forget that nocturnal silence which deprived me, for all eternity, of the desire to live. Never shall I forget those moments which murdered my God and my soul and turned my dreams to dust. Never shall I forget these things even if I am condemned to live as long as God himself. Never.

Seventeen years after he left the concentration camp Wiesel returned to Germany to make a kind of pilgrimage to the source of his pain. That journey of return may puzzle many people but, as he observed himself, the criminal is not alone when he returns to the scene of the crime: he is joined by his victim and they are driven by the same curiosity – to relive the moment in time that stamped their past and future lives.

After all those years Wiesel was certain that he would find his hate intact. He had avoided all contact with Germans and he was now returning to their country to keep an appointment with hate. When he landed on enemy territory he walked the streets staring into people's faces trying to perceive the invisible: trying to guess what they had done during the war and whether their paths had crossed in the concentration camps.

When he taped a programme for radio he was surprised when he listened to it later. There was no hatred or bitterness in his voice, just a concealed anger. When he met different groups of people he was puzzled by his attitude. He had come to Germany to keep an appointment with hate but it had failed to turn up. He was left confused and hurt and worried that he was no longer capable of hating. Perhaps that is for the reason he writes: "In our heart of hearts we hate only what resembles us. The first murder was a fratricide."

Stephen, the first martyr

In today's first reading we hear how Stephen did not survive his captors but was stoned to death and became the first Christian martyr. We first learn about Stephen when we hear about the conflict in the Jerusalem Church between the Hellenists and the Hebrews. The Hellenists were Greek-speaking Jews who came from communities settled outside Palestine and who went to their own synagogues in Jerusalem where the scripture was read in Greek. The Hebrews were the Palestinian Jews and in their synagogue the scripture was read in Hebrew. The Hellenists complained that their widows were being overlooked when it came to welfare support, whereas the widows of the Palestinian Jews were looked after well. To answer the problem the apostles called a full meeting of the disciples to elect seven men of good reputation who would care for the needy while the apostles concentrated on preaching. The men elected were the first deacons whose ministry was to assist the apostles by serving at table where gifts for the needy were distributed. And the first worthy to be chosen was Stephen.

Stephen is described as a man full of faith who preaches in the name of Jesus and works wonders among the people. However it is not long before he comes into serious conflict with his fellow Greek-speaking Jews. Stephen is brought before the council where he is charged with claiming that Jesus will destroy the Temple and change the Law. In his own defence he makes a long speech accusing his accusers of resisting the Holy Spirit; finally, he tells them his vision of Jesus standing at the right hand of God. When they hear this the council go into uproar, rush Stephen out of the city and stone him. The final scene is witnessed by Saul: Stephen forgives his executioners before he is killed.

Like Jesus his master, Stephen's final act is not a scream of hate but a word of forgiveness. His last act is a refusal to mirror the hatred he sees in his executioners. His martyrdom is not an appointment with hate but with forgiveness. And forgiveness turns up to keep the appointment – dead on time.

There is no doubt that the way of Stephen's dying prepared for the conversion of Saul, because the voice of the forgiving Christ echoes in the voice of the dying disciple. But perhaps there is more. We do not know if a shadow came over Saul when he witnessed the killing of Stephen. We do know that he could not deny being closely linked to this anguish. Did Stephen's violent death *say* anything to the silent watcher? Every killing of another human being is an accusation: in the death of Stephen, was Saul accused of persecuting Christ? In the death of the first martyr, was there the birth of the last apostle?

The Spirit of all sorts

Locked doors

The French writer Jean-Paul Sartre wanted to explore the agony of many human beings who feel trapped in the midst of life. He wrote a play about hell, and gave it a suitable title: *No Exit.* Three people arrive in hell, which consists of a large sitting-room with mirrors around the walls. There is no exit in the room, and no intermission in the action. The three characters are on stage all the time since they are condemned to spend eternity together without leaving the room.

They pass the time reflecting on what has happened in the past, but they cannot use that to change their lives now. As they remain locked within the room, the final line is, "Let's go." But they can go nowhere. For them hell is being tied to a past and a present that cannot be changed. They have no prospect of a future that is different from the present time. All they have is mirrors. And that is hell.

It is one thing to be locked in a room with no exit. It is another thing *to lock yourself* in a room because you believe that the world beyond the door is hostile, and that if you leave the room you will meet with certain death. The world may not get into your room, but neither can you get out. In today's Gospel this is the scene John writes to depict the condition of the disciples following the death of Jesus. Since the crucifixion they have been bunched together behind locked doors. They have locked themselves in: this is an assembly that fear has gathered together. They are in a room that just mirrors their fears and provides no exit for them. For them, it must have been hell.

Enter the Spirit

However, the evangelist John shows us that there *is* an exit from this paralysing fear through the peace that Jesus brings. Into this room of trapped people Jesus comes with peace. He breathes the Holy Spirit on his disheartened followers. As the risen Jesus breathes on them, the disciples breathe in the Spirit. The Holy Spirit is the breath they take on Easter Sunday evening, the breath that gives them all new heart.

Only in the gift of the Spirit is fear changed into freedom. Only in the Spirit are the disciples empowered to understand the past anew and see the future with hope. The Holy Spirit *is* the exit from the hopelessness of being locked into a cruel and fearful past. The Spirit is the exit that leads into the streets and the market-places where legions of people may seem to walk freely, but where so many feel trapped in their own lives. Through the disciples of Jesus the Holy Spirit will reach these people. For the disciples are commissioned to breathe out as they have breathed in: to share this new Spirit with the multitude of peoples whose lives are hell without it.

It is Luke who demonstrates the effects of the Spirit in the ministry of the apostles. As we heard from the first reading, Luke reserves the story of the Spirit to the feast of Pentecost, the fiftieth day after Easter. At that time Pentecost was a Jewish feast which celebrated the ancient covenant which God gave to his chosen people through Moses. There was a tradition that the covenant was given to the people on the fiftieth day after the exodus – that was why it was called *pentekoste,* from the Greek word for fiftieth. *What Luke does is to make Pentecost into a Christian feast,* when God renews his covenant with his people through the power of the Spirit. In that power the apostles speak a new word to all those people from unpronounceable places. All the places mark out the reaches of the Roman empire; all the people are Jews who come to celebrate the important feast. For Luke it is the feast of the Holy Spirit, when all these people are offered a new opportunity to renew their relationship with God. It is a time for new beginning, a time of new creation. Through the Spirit a whole new life is possible.

The Spirit of variety
The same Spirit of God is in our midst here. As St Paul says, it is the same Spirit "working in all sorts of ways in different people". The Spirit is not shy of difference, but is free to deal with people as individuals: there is a variety of gifts. That great variety emerges from the one Spirit in which we were all baptised. It's not that our differences are smothered by the Spirit; rather our differences are funded by the Spirit who works not to standardise everyone to factory proportions, but to make variety his mark. He is the Spirit of all sorts.

Part of our own task is to discover how the Spirit has gifted us in individual ways, and to appreciate the Spirit's different gifts in other people. In the Spirit difference has a future. Hell is where everyone is the same because nobody has a future different from the present. There is no variety of gifts in hell. If hell locks everyone into the same room with no exit, the Spirit of God is the power that frankly opposes that condition of hopelessness. Today we are all gathered in the one room. Here. There is an exit. Before we say "Let's go" we invoke the Spirit to awaken us to the gifts he has graced us with, and we thank him for their variety. When we do that we can all go in peace.

Witnesses for the defence

Truth and wisdom

Frederick Edwin Smith, 1st Earl of Birkenhead, was a famous British lawyer and politician. He was regarded by many as a man who was too clever for comfort. As Margot Asquith said of him: "Very clever, but his brains go to his head." Smith was conducting a lengthy and complicated case before a judge whom he regarded as slow and rather dim. As the case drew to its close, the judge let it be known that some of the issues involved were no longer clear to him. Smith gave the judge a short and clear account of all the issues and their implications. As Smith sat down, the judge thanked him courteously, but added: "I'm sorry, Mr Smith, but I regret that I am none the wiser." Smith rose wearily to his feet again. "Possibly, my lord," he said "but you are better informed."

Information doesn't add up to wisdom; knowledge doesn't necessarily lead to good judgement. Like the judge in the story, we can possess all the information available but still be no wiser about what it actually means.

In today's Gospel we hear Jesus give his final address to his disciples. He promises to send them a good lawyer! Lawyers are needed only when there's trouble, and there is plenty of that knocking at the door. Soon there will be arrests, charges, court scenes, trials, accusations, sentences. Jesus promises his disciples that the lawyer he will send will lead them out of confusion and bewilderment into the complete truth. This lawyer is no human advocate; he is the Spirit of truth who comes from the Father. Jesus consoles his followers with the promise:

> I still have many things to say to you
> but they would be too much for you now.
> But when the Spirit of truth comes
> he will lead you to the complete truth.

No human advocate

One of the fascinating characteristics of John's Gospel is how he presents the story of Jesus as a lawsuit between God and the unbelieving world. Witnesses are ranged on either side to argue the case. And the case at issue is: is Jesus the Messiah and the Son of God? God's witnesses are his Word in Jesus, the great prophet John the Baptist, the signs and mighty works of Jesus, and finally the Holy Spirit and the apostles. That is the group of witnesses who support the claim that Jesus really is the Son of God. The opposition is represented by the unbelieving Jews, who bring their own testimony against the claim.

When Jesus' trial gets under way, the accusers are invited to bear witness regarding the evil that Jesus is alleged to have committed. Jesus boldly challenges the officer in court: "If I have spoken wrongly, bear witness to the wrong; but if I have spoken rightly, why do you strike me?" No one takes up the challenge. According to John's account Jesus wins the most important lawsuit in history. And because Pilate declares Jesus innocent three times, the judge is convicted of perverting justice when he hands Jesus over to be crucified. The trial of Jesus is seen as a masquerade; the innocent one is handed over to be executed.

When Jesus dies, however, the lawsuit is not finished. His claim to be the Messiah and the Son of God is confirmed in his resurrection, when the Father raises the innocent one to glory. But there are still many who do not accept the evidence. The principal advocate for Jesus' claim is now the Holy Spirit. He is the big lawyer who advances the claims of Jesus before the court of the unbelieving world. And the Advocate's principal witnesses are the apostles – those who have been with Jesus right from the beginning of the ministry.

The lawsuit continues
What we celebrate at Pentecost is the coming of the Advocate, the one who enables the apostles to be witnesses to Jesus' claims in the world. Before the coming of the Spirit, the apostles were incapable of acting as witnesses; they were frightened men who were too confused and hurt to act as effective witnesses on behalf of Jesus. With the help of the Spirit they are graced with a new courage. Their courtroom is the market-place of the world, and they are willing to testify to the truth of Jesus' claims to anyone who has ears.

As we know from experience the lawsuit still continues, the case is not closed. There will always be opposition to face, there will always be a jury to persuade. The Spirit continues to be the Advocate, calling on generations of Christians to come forward as witnesses in the case.

We are the witnesses. To us it is given to continue the case on behalf of Jesus. The disbelieving world still looks to Jesus' witnesses to make their case – not so much by the quality of our information, but by the quality and courage of our lives.

The world is not dying from lack of information. It might be dying from not having life in Jesus' name. The evangelist John finishes his case on behalf of Jesus when he tells his readers that he has advanced his cause "so that you may believe that Jesus is the Christ, the Son of God, and that believing this you may have life in his name." So the case continues.

The language of the Spirit

Spirit and energy

Archbishop Anthony Bloom recalls the time when he was discussing Christianity with a learned Japanese writer. The writer told Bloom: "I think I understand about the Father and the Son, but I can never understand the significance of the honourable bird." Many people might sympathise with the Japanese writer, for the Holy Spirit has traditionally eluded the attention of scholars and preachers like a bird in flight resists capture. We cannot capture the Spirit or cage it, allowing it to limp out only on special occasions like baptism and confirmation. The honourable bird is still in flight. Like the wind you hear the sound of it, but you do not know whence it comes or whither it goes. But you do know when it's been around.

Our own language tells us that it's difficult to contain or even describe spirit, but usually spirit-talk suggests life and movement and energy. We rarely hear people talk about a high-spirited turtle or an inspired tortoise. A high-spirited horse, yes, which is rearing to go. We talk of the creative energy in inspiration, an energy which has the power to break through barriers, break records, go beyond the expected and the mediocre, break through the locked doors of convention and not be bound by restrictions. However, very little of that language describes what was going on behind locked doors somewhere in Jerusalem two thousand years ago.

Outdoors in the Spirit

A group of dispirited followers of Jesus had gathered and locked themselves in an upper room, probably the same room where the last supper was held. There was more perspiration than inspiration in the room. There was fear and suspicion. The room was occupied by a group of followers who were afraid that they would suffer the same fate as their master. So they listened to every step on the stair; they waited for the knock of the executioner; they prayed that no one would discover their hiding-place and that the world would leave them safe in their sacred enclosure.

In contrast there is the powerful image of the Holy Spirit as one who is not shy of the boundaries and the barriers that people erect. He is not halted by locked doors or locked hearts; he doesn't exclude himself from the restrictive areas people settle in. When the Spirit comes, it is not like a spring breeze that whispers unnoticed through a room; it is more like a hurricane that lays flat all the precious protections against its force. And the Spirit takes this group of dispirited followers and fires them with a new energy and a new enthusiasm and a new authority.

The presence of the Spirit makes the disciples open their lives to others:

they don't just decorate their sacred enclosure, they leave it and pass over into the lives of other people with the gifts of Gospel and peace and forgiveness.

The disciples go outdoors. They go to the market-place where people gather and there they proclaim to all how they have been changed by the power of the Spirit. They tell a *Magnificat* and proclaim how God has worked wonders in them. At first the crowds think that the apostles are drunk – no doubt because they're sure it takes some kind of spirit to transform these men. Whatever it is, everyone acknowledges that something happened to dramatically change the outlook and behaviour of the followers of Jesus. The name of that experience is Spirit.

The crowd's second reaction is a joyous one when they realise that the apostles are speaking their language. Perhaps we've all heard people say to us in a mixture of relief and enthusiasm: "Now you're speaking my language!" When that happens there is communion, where before there had only been misunderstanding and division. The apostles got through to people, they spoke the deep language that is in all of us and which rarely gets spoken. It is the language in search of understanding; it is music in search of a melody. St Paul spoke of it as inarticulate groaning, the cry of the spirit within us. The apostles reach people in this profound language. It is the language of the Spirit.

Spirit language
After Pentecost the Church struggles to live the language of the Spirit. In today's second reading we hear Paul reminding the divided community at Corinth that their diverse gifts are for the good of the community. It is the one dynamic Spirit which is the source of the community's gifts.

And the Spirit which fired the apostles and which enthused Paul is the same Spirit which fires and enthuses us. The Spirit does that in our own mundane attempts to work at forgiveness and love and understanding. That is the language of the Spirit. Forgiveness, love and understanding form a language which everyone understands and needs to hear. That is the language we are invited to speak and the promise is that when we speak it people will recognise it as their own language. They can truly say that we are speaking their language because it is the language which has no boundaries, and no special dictionaries are needed to understand it. It is the language of the Spirit. It is the call of the honourable bird.

So much love

God so loved the world

In the dark of night a cautious diplomat from Jerusalem meets an outspoken prophet from Galilee. Nicodemus is genuinely impressed by the reports he has heard about Jesus, but as a member of the Great Council he is unwilling to risk open support. He has his future career to think about: so it is that darkness is his cover and secrecy his insurance. But Jesus' response to this caution on tiptoe is not more caution: he makes a clear declaration about God's attitude to the world: "God loved the world so much that he gave his only Son...For God sent his Son into the world not to condemn the world, but so that through him the world might be saved." And that includes Nicodemus.

Jesus meets the personal caution of Nicodemus with the affirmation of God's universal love. At the heart of the Gospel we hear that God's relationship with the world is rooted in love. It is not rooted in suspicion or condemnation as rumour has led so many to believe. It is God's radical love which gives our world its importance; it is that same love which gives all of us our essential dignity. God's love is all the more significant because it is fully aware of the sin and the brokenness and the stupidity that are part of our lives. It is not a love that protects itself from facing the negative side of life; it is a love that faces the complexity of the real.

That same truth is underlined in today's first reading when we hear God and Moses in conversation. Moses admits to the truth that the people are headstrong with a litany of sins and faults to their names. But this does not alter God's nature of being "a God of tenderness and compassion, slow to anger, rich in kindness and faithfulness." Whatever happens, God's love is never at issue.

A love that abides

At the centre of the mystery of God is his everlasting love and fidelity. Given the shabby response of the world, the constancy of God's love is very difficult to grasp: a love that continues to be faithful even when it sees continued infidelity in those it loves. God's ceaseless love of the world is so great that he sent his beloved Son among us. The Son's faithful love is so great that he faced the ultimate infidelity – being put to death by those he loved. But God's love survives the death of Jesus: God raised his Son and sent his Spirit so that we could share the very life of the love of God. God is love. In honouring the Trinity today *we celebrate the awesome stubbornness of God's extravagant love for our world.*

It is of the nature of God that his love abides forever. And if there is one thing we all ache to experience in our lives, it is the love we can depend on, the love that is not withdrawn when misfortune comes, the love that sees beyond our frailty and faults because it sets no limit to forgiveness. None of us has experienced the fullness of this authentic love, yet it is to that love that our whole being aspires. We can catch glimpses of it when we look at our own experience of love in the community. As St Paul says in today's reading: "Live in peace, and the God of love and peace will be with you."

Love and importance

The Father, Son and Holy Spirit, all three persons reveal the fullness of the unity of God's love. We experience something of that love when it is communicated in simple ways through the people of grace we meet in our lives. Most of us have experienced it first in the generosity of our parents' love, one that is so important in the growth of every child of God. The Irish writer Clare Boylan reflected in a radio interview on the lasting power of her parents' love:

> My parents did two things for me: they gave me a sense of my own importance and they let me know that I was loved. I think that a lot of parents don't want to give children a sense of their own importance in case it becomes over-inflated; but we were always told that we were absolutely marvellous and that if anyone said otherwise they were wrong. That gives you tremendous confidence – and it lasts. If your parents have given you these two things – a sense of self and the love – you have them all your life. If not, you're forever looking for them...I don't think anything else matters.

Love is the essential atmosphere for every child to grow in, and when that love is sure any hardship can be faced. We are all children of the one God, and love is the essential atmosphere for our continued growth. But we are all responsible for playing our own part: none of us can retire from the task of helping to make our family and community a place where God's love gives shape to what happens. That is why Paul encourages the divided church in Corinth: "Be united; live in peace, and the God of love and peace will be with you."

None of the Trinity retires from the task of loving the world. God's love is sure and everlasting. As children of the one God we never grow out of the need of his love. Neither do we outgrow the responsibility to share it with others.

Growing into mystery

Understanding each other

John and Josephine have just celebrated their fortieth wedding anniversary. Since their four children have left home and married, they have spent seventeen years on their own, a time they describe as "a new growing towards each other." When they were asked why they still enjoyed each other's company, Josephine replied: "We've always had a healthy respect for each other's differences. And we're still growing to know each other better. I just wish that we could have communicated with each other years ago the way we do now. But perhaps our easiness with each other now could only come about because of all the struggles we went through."

The longer we are acquainted with people, the more we grow to realise how little we know them. Family and friends continue to surprise us, reminding us that they are always more than our understanding of them. We can all give instant impressions of people after knowing them only for a week, but if we're honest with ourselves we have to admit that our clarity is born of ignorance. We can have epic conversations about a new acquaintance, but the lengthy talk is mostly guesswork, makeshift images built from a few clues.

Unless we settle for stereotypes, understanding other people is a lifetime's task. It is hardly surprising, therefore, that when it comes to understanding God we can become paralysed by the sheer magnitude of the mystery.

The mystery of God

The more we discover about God, the greater becomes the mystery of his presence and love. The considerable knowledge of the Church can never dispel the mystery of ages. Mystery means that we can never say the final word about God; there is always more to discover, there is always more to share, there is always more to experience. In that sense the mystery of God invites us never to abandon the endless task of growing to understand the power behind the world we live in. And each year, Trinity Sunday calls us to reflect on the life of God.

As Christians our principal entrance into the mystery of God is the person of Jesus. He is the Way, the Truth and the Life. He is the image of the invisible God, the firstborn of all creation, the Word made flesh among us. As Jesus said to the apostle Philip: "He who has seen me has seen the Father." Jesus is God's adventure among us. To make our journey to God we begin with him. And the Good News we heard today tells us that Jesus has promised to accompany us until the journey to God is completed: "Know that I am with you always, to the end of time."

In the person of Jesus the mystery of God has a face, a voice, a language, a love, a life. In the pages of the Gospel we meet Jesus' friends and enemies, his enthusiasms and dislikes; we are caught up in his struggle for what is right; we are challenged to keep alive the values he cherished. In the three years of his public ministry the light from light shone among us. In Jesus we are still able to taste and see the goodness of God. God's particulars are revealed in him. "He who has seen me has seen the Father." To look on the Son of God is to begin to understand the mystery of God.

The feast of Pentecost that we celebrated last week reminded us that we cannot begin to understand the truth of God unless we are gifted with the power of the Spirit. Even the apostles could not recognise the full truth about the Jesus they knew and loved without the gift of the Spirit. The same is true for us: to understand Jesus we need the Spirit. To reach the Father we need to go via the Son. So it is the mystery of the Trinity that is at the heart of the Christian life of faith. Which is why we begin and end everything in the name of the Father, and of the Son, and of the Holy Spirit.

The mystery of ourselves
Today's second reading reminds us that we are not God's slaves living in fear: we are children of God, heirs as well. We have been granted the privilege of inheriting the glory of God, we have been given the right to belong. So, we can move around with the easiness of sons and daughters who have to share in our Father's inheritance. And if God is a mystery, it is hardly surprising that his children are of similar strain.

If we are all made in the image and likeness of God, it should come as no shock to realise that it takes a lifetime to work out and understand each other. We know that we learn best about people when we really *want* to know them for ourselves, refusing to be satisfied with second-hand accounts. Our love for people prompts us to know them better; our love for God urges us to deepen our understanding of him.

Loving is the highest form of understanding. Our journey towards God and towards each other is made along the same road. And when we journey that road in love and respect, the way we travel assures us of our destination. That is the Gospel.

Living in approachable light

No easy answers

In 1947 a young German writer died in a Swiss sanatorium. His name was Wolfgang Borchert. During the war he had become sickened of the excesses of the Nazis and he became consumed by illness contracted at the front and in Nazi prisons. Before he died he wrote feverishly and among his writings is an address to God:

> "Ho, you are old, God, you're old-fashioned, you can't cope with the long lists of our dead and our agonies. We no longer really know you, you're a fairytale God. Today we need a new one, one for our misery and fear. Oh, we've searched for you, God, in every ruin, in every shellhole, in every night. We've called for you God, we've roared for you, wept for you, cursed for you. Where were you then, dear God? Where are you tonight?
>
> "The theologians have let you grow old. Your trousers are patched, your soles are worn out, and your voice has grown too soft – too soft for the thunder of our times. Live with us, at night, when it's cold and lonely, and the stomach hungers in the silence – live with us then, God. Have you completely walled yourself up in your fine churches? Can't you hear our cries through the shattered windows, God? Where are you?"

You might find those sentiments blasphemous, but the cry of the German soldier is not too different from the cries of the psalmist who screamed on his bed of pain for God and heard only the echo of his scream come back from the darkness. When we are confronted with the stark reality of other people's pain and their longing for God's comforting presence we are reduced to silence. There are no easy answers.

The Trinity

The Trinity might seem a world away from the trenches of human suffering and yet if it is to mean anything the two must be connected. Usually the subject of the Trinity is guaranteed to excite nothing more than a shrug or a weary smile. As working examples, the triangle is tired and the shamrock is long wilted: besides, both treat the Trinity as a problem to be reckoned with rather than a mystery to be entered into. However, when it comes to talking about the Trinity we must face what Thomas Aquinas called "the misery of language". The appeal of silence becomes attractive, but it is the silence of God which is the problem for so many.

All religions recognise that God is beyond every name, that he is the Absolute One who lives in unapproachable light, who is beyond all reach and all description. In the Christian tradition the Absolute One is called the Father of our Lord Jesus Christ. We believe that the Absolute One has chosen to reveal himself in his Son.

Everything the Father is he gives the Son. Everything the Son receives he gives to the Father in return. This gift between the Father and the Son is called the Spirit of God. The Father does not keep anything from the Son; the Son does not withhold anything from the Father. This bond of unity between them, the vibrancy of this love, this is called the Spirit of God.

The Son is the Word of the silent God, he is the visibility of the invisible God. The Son is the Father made visible. "He who has seen me has seen the Father." Whoever sees Jesus sees the Father because *the Son is everything there is to see about the Father.* Jesus is the one who lived in approachable light, he is the one whose name we can get right. He is the one who calls us friends.

In the life, passion and death of Jesus we have the icon of the Absolute God, we have the image of the invisible One. Jesus is the one who walked among us, who was truly human, who suffered the loss of his own friends and who suffered the absence of God. The cry "My God, my God, why have you deserted me?" echoes loudly in the silence of the Gospels. It is the same cry as the German soldier; it comes from the same place within which longs for the comfort of God's presence in the midst of horror and desolation.

It is the scream of God. And in his scream we can hear our own. It is "deep calling on deep". Jesus is the cry of God to us and our cry to the Absolute One. In him God and humanity meet. Through him we can approach God and call him our Father. Through Jesus we can touch God; we can look on the face of God and live.

God living with us

At some time in our lives we can all make the prayer of the German soldier who pleads with God: "Live with us, at night, when it's cold and lonely, and the stomach hungers in the silence – live with us then, God." What we hunger for is not a new argument about the Trinity but the experience of a God who loves us. And the promise of Jesus in today's Gospel is that he will share the love between himself and the Father with all his followers. That God will live with us in the power of the Spirit.

We believe that the Spirit of God is alive in us. The Spirit of God lives in us and experiences our hunger and loneliness and helps us voice our prayers. We can rejoice that God still chooses to dwell with us and groans within us as we struggle towards the peace of his kingdom.

Remembering to eat

Remembering God

Many of the prayers made by the people of the Old Testament are centred on reminding God, in case his divine memory is slipping, of the promises he made to save them. When the chosen people face new trials, their insurance against disaster is the promise of God to see them through their time of pain. They hold fast to that word of promise. Every new experience of want or suffering serves to keep alive the memory of God's promises. Thus their prayers of intercession are made to jolt God's memory, to play back his promise, to hold him to his word.

But what happens when the people come into plenty? Do they remain faithful to *their promises* to God in the midst of prosperity? In today's first reading Moses reminds his own people of the need to remember God: he notices that as the people get richer, their memories get poorer. In the midst of comfort God appears as unnecessary as a fire-brigade at a picnic.

If the people do not want God to forget them in their affliction, God does not want the people to forget him in their affluence. So, he reminds the people that when they are safely installed in their new homes with security devices to keep out the uninvited, with their two-car garage, excellent salary, fringe benefits, and enlightened retirement plan, they should still remember who it was who hauled them through the wilderness when they had no baggage but the memory of slavery, and nowhere to go but away from Egypt. If that memory is not kept alive, then it will be as if God no longer existed because people are not disposed to remember how he adopted them and cared for them in their need. Prosperity has made them a thankless people.

Remembering to eat

In the desert the people learned that they could not continue their journey without being sustained by the word of God. This experience was to teach them that they could not live on bread alone: when the bread ran out and the water dried up, their very survival depended on the word of God making new life possible for them. It was the creative word of God which brought them the manna – their daily bread – referred to as "the grain of heaven" and "the bread of the mighty" (Ps.78:24f). The people collected as much as they needed for the day; they were forbidden to hoard any of it. The next day the arrival of the bread was seen as a new sign of God's continuing favour.

In today's Gospel John picks up the theme of the manna and contrasts the bread the Jewish ancestors ate in the desert with the new bread of life given by Jesus. In the person of Jesus there is a new word of God and a new bread from heaven. Now the Word of God has become flesh, and the bread of heaven is the very life of Jesus himself. To eat this bread is to have a share in the life of God himself; it is to participate in eternal life.

It is at the Last Supper that Jesus gives himself away as food and drink to his followers: "This is my body which will be given up for you. This is my blood which will be shed for you. Do this in memory of me." During the last meal of his earthly life Jesus charges his disciples to keep his memory alive by gathering together to break bread. Whatever else they do, *his followers must remember to eat in his name.*

Remembering Jesus

Most of us don't have to remember to eat: our stomach has its own way of telling us when it's time. But we do have to remember to eat in the name of Jesus – which is why the Church asks us to gather in community each week to keep the memory of Jesus alive. Our eucharist is a celebration of thanksgiving for what Jesus has done. Lest we forget what he has done, we assemble to hold that memory sacred. That is why after the consecration we pray in the eucharistic prayers:

> Father, we celebrate the *memory* of Christ, your Son. (I)
> In *memory* of his death and resurrection...(II)
> Father, *calling to mind* the death your Son endured...(III)
> Father, we now celebrate this *memorial*...(IV)

Each of the eucharistic prayers expresses the purpose of our gathering: the refusal to forget what Jesus has done in his body. We keep the memory fresh; we celebrate it anew; and in celebrating we receive new life for our own journey in faith. Whether we live in the midst of affliction or affluence, we come together as a community to profess that what Jesus did for us has a continuing importance. Today. Our celebration of the eucharist keeps us from being a thankless people.

In celebrating the eucharist we celebrate a *dangerous memory:* the memory of suffering, passion and death. We recall Jesus' radical values that put him in opposition to so many of his own people: his talk about God and the kingdom; his insistence on forgiveness; his opposition to religious sham; his commitment to peace; his willingness to die to overcome sin. In receiving the body and blood of Christ we become his body in our world. As St Paul says: "Though there are many of us, we form a single body because we share in this one loaf." In communion we share with Christ and with one another; we become one with his memory. That way, his memory never dies.

A sign that is enough for us

"Until the day I drink a new wine"

For all of us there comes a last time for doing the litany of familiar things that we do always. There is the last time we see our family and friends; the last time we write a letter, hear a name spoken, share a family meal. Perhaps it is a mercy that most of us don't know when the last time arrives, that we are never sure when our goodbyes have the accent of finality. Even the dying can still hope that they will feel again the comfort of human touch, will hear the blinds being drawn, will smell the promise of breakfast. There is always a crazy hope that there will be another time.

In today's Gospel Jesus prepares for the last time with his friends: he knows that the final moments are upon him. This is to be the last opportunity for him to share with his followers. Preparations are carefully made; the last meal must be celebrated in peace, to savour the gift that will be offered. The gift is a surprise. Jesus gives himself. Literally. "Take it, this is my body ... This is my blood ... I shall not drink any more wine until the day I drink the new wine in the kingdom of God."

The close association that Jesus has had with his followers is about to come to an end. That fellowship will be renewed in full only in the kingdom of God, when they will all drink a new wine together. In the meantime, the followers of Jesus must gather to share a simple memorial meal. Until the fulness of the kingdom the sharing of that meal must satisfy their hunger for God, their longing for the presence of Jesus. The meal of fellowship has to be enough for them. As it has to be enough for us.

The action of the Mass

Jesus faced the darkness of his last time by gathering his friends and sharing with them the gift of himself. After the resurrection they would gather to keep his memory alive, to hear again the stories that love remembered, to break the bread of life that would nourish them in their journey to the kingdom. Down the ages the Christian community has shared that memory as life. That is what we do today

The Eucharist is not something we come to watch; rather, it is something we come to do. We gather as a consecrated people to do something together. In the action of the Mass we hold holy the memory of Jesus, we share the bread that is broken, we accept the cup that is held out to us. Week by week throughout the year we strengthen each other by our sharing and our faith, so that all our time is consecrated to the Lord. Until the fulness of the kingdom, when we hope to see the Lord face to face, this simple meal has to be enough for us.

"This will be enough for me"

We are all seeking God. We all need the witness of each other's love and faith at this simple meal. In Ingmar Bergman's classic film, *The Seventh Seal*, the quest for God is set against a medieval world threatened by plague. After fighting in the crusades, a knight makes the return journey to his native land. He survives a shipwreck, but Death lets him know that he is doomed to die within a certain time. The knight wins a little more time at a game of chess, but he is sick of heart: he wants to believe in God, yet he cannot manage by himself to reach faith. He seeks for signs of God's presence, but there is none he can see. It is the time of the Black Death; God seems to be absent from the troubled streets of every town and village.

On his journey the knight meets a peasant couple and their child, and shares a simple meal with them. The only food they can manage to gather is wild strawberries – this they share, together with fresh milk.

The love in the young couple's welcome and regard, the fruit of their love in the sleeping child, Mikael, all this is greater than the food and drink that is shared. In the simple actions of sharing the meal the knight sees the presence of a love that has eluded him. The husband picks up his lyre and plays music that mocks the plague that surrounds all of them.

In that meeting place the darkness begins to lift from the knight. He has been gifted with more than food; he has been graced with more than fellowship. He prays his thanks when he says:

> I shall remember this moment. The silence, the twilight, the bowls of strawberries, the milk, your face in the evening light. Mikael sleeping, Jof with his lyre ... I'll carry this memory between my hands as carefully as if it were a bowl filled to the brim with fresh milk ...And it will be an adequate sign. It will be enough for me.

"Give them something to eat yourselves"

Reflection

The Brothers Grimm tell the story of a man who had three sons, the youngest of whom was called Simpleton, and who was despised and mocked by everyone. The father wanted wood for the fire and he asked his eldest son, who was the brightest of the three sons. Before he went his mother gave him a sweet cake and a bottle of wine. When he entered the forest he met a little grey-haired old man who greeted him and asked him for something to eat. The eldest son said: "If I give you my food and drink I'll have little for myself. Go away!" He left the little man standing and went on his way. But when he started to knock down a tree he cut himself and had to return home and have his arm bound up.

After this the second son went into the forest, with the cake and the bottle of wine his mother had given him. The little old man asked him for a piece of cake and a drink of wine but the second son said: "What I give you will be taken from myself. Away you go!" He left the little man standing there. But when he started to hew down a tree he struck himself in the leg and he had to be carried home.

Then Simpleton asked if he could go for the wood. His father reminded him bluntly that he couldn't do anything right because as the youngest son he was as thick as a tree! But Simpleton insisted and his mother gave him a cake made of cinders and a bottle of sour beer. When he came to the forest, the little old man told him of his hunger and thirst. Simpleton answered: "I have only a cinder cake and sour beer; if that pleases you, we will sit down and eat." So they sat down and ate and drank together. Afterwards the little man said: "Since you have a good heart and are willing to divide what you have, I will bring you good fortune."

Needless to say Simpleton eventually inherits a kingdom because once upon a time he shared his food and drink with a little grey man who was hungry.

Today's scripture

In today's second reading we are in the real world of Corinth in southern Greece in the year 57 A.D. Of course there were no churches then and the only place where the Christian community could meet was in a large room of someone's house. The only people with large rooms were the rich. The eucharist was celebrated after the common meal, but the problem was that while the rich were eating and drinking well, the poor were overlooked and left hungry. Rather than bringing people together the eucharist underlined the divisions already in the community. So Paul wrote to them:

"when you hold these meetings, it is not the Lord's Supper that you are eating, since when the time comes to eat, everyone is in such a hurry to start his own supper that one person goes hungry while another is getting drunk. Surely you have enough respect for the community not to embarrass poor people?" (1 Cor 11:20f)

By contrast, in today's Gospel the poor and the hungry are neither overlooked nor embarrassed. At first, however, they are almost dismissed by the apostles. When they are confronted with such a large number in such a lonely place the apostles' reaction is to send the whole crowd away to look for food and shelter elsewhere. How can they answer the vast hunger of so many people? How can they minister to the needs of so many with so little themselves? And yet that is precisely what Jesus challenges them to do: *"Give them something to eat yourselves."* The apostles remind Jesus of the poverty of their resources: they have five loaves and two fish. That is all.

Jesus takes the little they have and shows how the little they have is more than enough to answer the hunger of the crowd. In telling the story Luke uses the language associated with the eucharist as he speaks of Jesus saying the blessing...breaking...and handing to his disciples. Luke does not say that Jesus multiplies the loaves and fish. The miracle is that when the apostles share the little they have in the name of Jesus they discover that the crowd is satisfied. There is no need to send anyone away. In fact there is enough left over to feed another crowd!

Teaching
Sometimes when we are faced with people's needs and look at our own resources we can sit down in a state of depression, believing that we have nothing to give. The hunger of people is so vast and our abilities are so small: what can we do? But all care and all ministry is a sharing from poverty. None of us has all the answers; none of us is millionaires in mercy and compassion. Like the youngest son Simpleton in the fairy tale we might have only a cinder cake and a sour beer; but the good news is that that is enough for the hunger of the old man. It is also enough to inherit a kingdom.

We are challenged to be the body of Christ. Jesus shared himself; he gave himself away; he became bread for all who hunger and thirst for the presence of God. And the promise of the Gospel is that if we share our poverty then we too will inherit a kingdom prepared for us from the beginning of the world.

THE
SEASON OF
ORDINARY
TIME

The witness of John

The Baptist sect

One of the curious facts of modern life is the growing number of cults and sects which compete for our attention alongside the major religions. Perhaps that is not so curious when we appreciate the genuine longing of many people for something to believe in that is greater than the wage packet. When people speak of cults, they usually refer to unorthodox religion or to the excessive admiration of an individual person. Most cults are movements which have broken away from mainstream religion; they often arise from the supposed failure of those religions to address the personal needs of their followers. Because of this, cults usually stand as a critical challenge to institutional religion.

It is worth noting that when the Christian movement began, it was regarded in most places as an eccentric cult focusing on Jesus of Nazareth. One of the problems the early Church had to face was another cult, the Baptist sect, who believed that John the Baptist, not Jesus, was the Messiah. The Baptist sect argued that their master was superior to Jesus for two main reasons: firstly, John the Baptist was prior to Jesus and that priority gave him superiority; secondly, Jesus submitted to John's baptism of repentance making him inferior to John. Faced with these arguments, the early Church had to respond and clarify its own position in regard to John the Baptist.

John, a witness for the light

In today's Gospel we see how the evangelist John faces these charges. John takes the point that priority does indeed mean superiority, and shows that Jesus is superior to the Baptist because he pre-existed him! So, John the Baptist declares: "A man is coming after me who ranks before me *because he existed before me.*" Jesus is the Word who existed from the beginning; *all* that came to be had life in him. As for Jesus submitting to the baptism of John, the fourth Gospel drops the account of Jesus' baptism; instead, John the Baptist is seen to interpret the meaning of the baptism by affirming that the Spirit of God rests on Jesus.

In John's Gospel the Baptist is treated in a different fashion from the other Gospels. There is no mention of his austere dress and diet; he does not confront the religious leaders with his fiery criticism; he does not send his disciples to ask Jesus *if* he is the Messiah. In John's Gospel the Baptist speaks only about Jesus and reveals to others the mystery of his person: "I am the witness that he is the Chosen One of God." John is a man sent by God. He says of Jesus: "I did not know him myself". No one can know

Jesus by himself. The Baptist knows him because the truth about Jesus has been revealed to him.

When the religious leaders send messengers to John to find out who he really is, he protests that he is not the Christ, not Elijah, and not the Prophet. John keeps declaring *who he is not* in order to say *who Jesus is.* All that he is not, Jesus is. The Baptist is wholly subordinate to Jesus, a truth that is declared in the prologue to the Gospel: "He was not the light, only a witness to speak for the light." (1:8)

If the Baptist appears to speak negatively about himself it is for the purpose of directing attention to Jesus. He is not the centre of his ministry: when Jesus comes, the Baptist points his own disciples in the direction of Jesus, releasing them from their attachment to him. In the Gospel of John, the Baptist plays a unique role: he is the first Christian witness, the first person who leads others to Jesus whom he identifies as the Messiah. The relationship between the Baptist and Jesus in John's Gospel is summarised poetically by St Augustine:

I listen; he is the one who speaks.
I am enlightened; he is the light.
I am the ear; he is the Word.

Being a witness

We can see how the evangelist John defends the truth of the Christian faith against the Baptist sect, those who believe that the Baptist was the Messiah. John the Baptist is a witness to the light; he is not the light. He is the first of many witnesses to Jesus – a host of people who give testimony to the truth about Jesus. Later in the Gospel Jesus tells his own disciples that when they receive the Spirit of truth, "you too will be my witnesses" (15:27).

And that charge is given to each of us. We have all been baptised in the Spirit; we have all been called to witness to Jesus. We are asked to point away from ourselves to Jesus; we are challenged to lead others to the person of Jesus. The best way to do that is through our own genuine attachment to the Lord. Many people need help to come to Jesus. None of us comes to him alone. If only we had the courage to speak about Jesus to each other. Most people are moved when others share with them what *really matters* in their lives. Perhaps we have lost the courage to say any more what matters to us; perhaps we doubt if anyone will care.

We should take courage to share what we believe. With Cardinal Newman, we know that we believe because we love. In the power of that love, let us share our belief with each other.

Discipleship: the introducers

Eli and Samuel

The time is the 11th century B.C. The place is the shrine in the small town of Shiloh, where the ark of God is kept. One day Eli, the high priest, is sitting by the doorpost of the shrine when he notices a woman praying. She is praying out of the bitterness of her soul, weeping. The high priest watches her lips move, but hears not a word. He thinks the woman is drunk and promptly tells her to leave the wine alone. But the dazed-looking woman is not drunk and explains her story that she is barren. Her husband's other wife has provided a healthy brood of children. The old priest listens as the woman tells her story of grief and resentment; she tells too of her promise to God that if she bears a male child she will give him back to serve God all his life.

Eli is moved by her sad tale, and he introduces her to her new future as a mother. He will pray too, and God will surely answer their prayers.

Their prayers are answered. The woman, who had waited so long, prayed so hard, hoped so strenuously, does become a mother. She calls him Samuel, because God has heard her. After she weans Samuel she keeps her promise and brings him to the shrine, leaving him to be reared by the priests. The child helps with the religious services and also looks after Eli, who is now very old. He can no longer see, but the lamp of God has not yet gone out. When Samuel hears a voice in the night he assumes the old priest is calling him. Samuel has no knowledge of the word of God, but the old priest has grown to recognise its strangeness and its power. As he introduced Samuel's mother to the promise of God, he introduces the young boy to the word of the Lord. So Samuel learns to respond: "Speak, Lord, your servant is listening."

The introducers

Eli's place in the scheme of sacred events is to introduce others to the Lord and to their new vocations. Samuel grows up to be the last of the great judges and the first of the king-makers. If Samuel has books named after him, Eli is remembered and honoured as the one who was there when new beginnings took place. And ten centuries later, the same is true of two other men: John the Baptist and Andrew.

In today's Gospel we see John the Baptist introducing two of his own disciples to Jesus; in doing this he introduces them to their new future. The disciples follow Jesus and stay with him. John points away from himself to the Christ. That is his role. In the fourth Gospel this man sent by God runs the first introduction agency for those on the lookout for the messiah.

Andrew is one of the two disciples. He leaves his master, John, to follow in the footsteps of his new master, Jesus. He needs John the Baptist to point him in the right direction, to make a new start. And what John the Baptist did for Andrew, Andrew does for his brother, Simon. He shares his experience with Simon, tells him that he has met the Christ, and introduces him to Jesus.

In the other three Gospels Andrew is known simply as "the brother of Peter". But in the fourth Gospel Andrew has the special function of introducing people to Jesus. Before the feeding of the five thousand, Andrew discovers a small boy who has five loaves and two fish; the disciple introduces the boy to Jesus, who takes the little food, blesses it, and offers it for distribution. The last appearance of Andrew is just before the Passover festivities in Jerusalem. Some Greeks speak to the apostle Philip and express their desire to meet Jesus. Philip tells Andrew, and together they introduce the delegation to Jesus. Like Eli the high priest and John the Baptist, Andrew's role is to bring others into the presence of the Lord.

The introduced

When we reflect on the beginnings of our own Christian faith, we recall the people who introduced us to Jesus. Most of us can think of a particular person who enabled us to begin our journey in faith, as we can think of others who introduced us anew to Jesus. None of us goes alone to Jesus: access to Jesus is always mediated through people. Before we meet Jesus, first we meet a litany of other people. We all come to Jesus by way of generations of Christians who shared their experience of Jesus, people who were themselves introduced to Jesus by others. Thus the story of Christianity is a story of a great chain of witnesses linked through the apostles to Jesus himself.

Of course we have to play our own part in introducing others to Jesus. We don't have to be great missionaries to do this; if we believe that Jesus is worth knowing, we will bring others into his loving presence by our quiet witness. In that way the Christian faith grows, and there will never be an end to it. Because somewhere, someone like the apostle Andrew will be bringing another person to meet Jesus of Nazareth.

"You will be called by a new name"

What's in a name

The woman is at a wedding reception looking her best. She had spent the morning stationed in front of the mirror, persuading wrinkles to disappear, making hiding-places for grey hairs, and highlighting her best features. The mirror agreed that the end result was a credit, and our friend went off to the wedding wondering how the other women would fare in the looking-glass war.

Now she is greeting relatives and friends at the reception. She is delighted when her niece says to her: "Oh Aunt Penelope, you look a real picture!" And then she hears another voice from behind her: "Hey, you in the red hat! Move out of the way so we can get a picture of the couple!"

Aunt Penelope loses some of her stature, as we all might. None of us likes being addressed as "Hey, you" and identified by something we're wearing. We like people to get our name right, and we get touchy when they spell it wrongly. There's a lot in a name. As T.S. Eliot believed, it is important even for cats:

> When you notice a cat in profound meditation,
>   The reason, I tell you, is always the same.
> His mind is engaged in a rapt contemplation
>   Of the thought, of the thought, of the thought of his name:
>   His ineffable effable,
>   Effanineffable,
> Deep and inscrutable singular Name.

Jesus, the real bridegroom

The prophet Isaiah knows very well how important names are to people – which is why he tries to cheer up the despondent Israelites by telling them: "you will be called by a new name...no longer are you to be named 'Forsaken', nor your land 'Abandoned', but you shall be called 'My Delight' and your land 'The Wedded'." The good news is that the Israelites are not going to be stuck with their old name "forsaken" – for there is going to be a wedding. And just as the bride changes her name in the wedding, so the Israelites are going to get a brand new name.

Isaiah promises that the time *will* come when God will take his people to himself like a bridegroom takes his new bride, and there will be great rejoicing in this new relationship. So it is that Israel waits for the day and the hour when this great event will take place. They wait for the big wedding.

182

In today's Gospel we hear from John that the wedding is on. At the festival of a Jewish wedding in Cana Jesus reveals his glory through his first great sign. It's an unusual wedding – for there are two bridegrooms! There is the bridegroom just married, and there is Jesus who is the *real* bridegroom. He is an invited guest at the wedding, but Jesus is the long-awaited bridegroom of Israel. Jesus will transform this private Jewish wedding into a great sign to show that the time has come when God will take his people to himself in a new way. Jesus has come as the bridegroom to claim his bride, Israel.

During the wedding feast the wine runs out and Mary expects Jesus to do something about it. Jesus' negative answer to Mary underlines the point that he cannot be bound by family relationships, but only by his Father's will. Mary's final words, "Do whatever he tells you," recognises the supreme authority of Jesus and what he must do himself.

There are six, large stone jars used to provide water for the Jewish ritual of cleansing. Jesus tells the servants to fill these to the brim, and after they do this they discover that the water has been changed into wine. All 120 gallons of it! When the steward tastes it he compliments the bridegroom for keeping the best wine until last – but he is complimenting the wrong bridegroom! Again the wrong name. Jesus is the one who has supplied choice wine in abundance, and in doing so has revealed his glory. When the disciples see what has happened they believe in Jesus.

Out of his fulness

The story gives us a marvellous image of the loving relationship we have with God through Jesus. Jesus has come to claim us as God's own, and he is generous in the gifts he brings. There is nothing mean about Jesus in the story: not a thimbleful of plonk, but gallons of the choice stuff! Luke has the same point in his Gospel: "Can the wedding guests fast while the bridegroom is still with them?" (5:34). It is not the time of fast, but the time of feast. And the feast is generous: "out of his *fullness* have we all received" (Jn.1:16).

Of course the ultimate generosity of Jesus is shown when he dies for the love he has – when the bridegroom lays down his life for his bride. Jesus gives his whole self in love. He gives us his body and blood in this Eucharist – so that we can be united with him and with our Father. So, let us rejoice today that we know the name of the bridegroom and that he knows our name in love.

Discipleship: united under Christ

Called

A full-page advertisement appears in the Sunday papers. It is headed by pictures of a doctor, a lawyer, a musician and an army officer. Underneath is written in bold: *"A vocation. What if you don't have one?"* The text continues: "It was the first time I felt envious about anything," a young man told us recently. "I looked around the dining hall and realised with some pain that there were two sorts of people here: those who had vocations, and the rest of us who did not. The first group knew exactly where they wanted to go and how to get there. Their lives, I naively imagined, would be unswerving and purposeful, rich with certainty and fulfilment.

"By contrast I felt muddled and irresolute. I found myself mentally trying on different jobs but, like secondhand clothes, none seemed to fit."

Only in the next sentence do we find out what the advert is for: "What, you may well ask, was this young man doing at the Army Officer Selection Board?"

The advertisement tries to kill the idea that a young man who is uncertain has no place in the army. Uncertainty, it argues, is not feeble mindedness. After all, how can you commit yourself to something you know nothing about? The army, so the argument goes, will give this unsure young man time to make up his mind about the future. He will have time to discover if he really has what the recruiting officer calls "a vocation for the Army."

The first disciples

When Matthew writes of the call of the first disciples, there is no suggestion of any hesitation on the part of the four fishermen. Matthew does not tell us why they follow Jesus. His story is simple: Jesus calls them and they follow him. There is no hint about where they are going; there is no detailing of what discipleship will involve. Nothing is promised; nothing is signed. Matthew is clearly not interested in these questions; he is more concerned to show that the disciples are called by Jesus and how their discipleship requires the leaving of everything that occupied them until that moment.

Obviously things did not happen as abruptly as that. The disciples did not leave the security of their homes and jobs on the spur of the moment to follow a stranger they had never seen before. In their accounts Luke and John allow time for the disciples to find out about Jesus before they are called. The absence of any of this detail in Matthew points to the fact that he wants to focus on something more important: the beginning of Jesus' public ministry. With John the Baptist now in prison, the great voice of the wilderness is silenced. It is time for Jesus to begin. Matthew shows that Jesus is the fulfilment of the prophecy of Isaiah. Jesus is the great light that has dawned; he is the one who begins his mission in Galilee of the Gentiles, a mission to all peoples.

Matthew keeps the focus on Jesus and shows the authority of his word and the power of his healing. Discipleship is centred on Jesus. Because of *who* he is, others will change. Jesus alone is the source of discipleship. Without the person of Jesus, discipleship is meaningless.

Who are you for?

Like Matthew, Paul is insistent in today's reading on Jesus as the focus of Christian discipleship. Jesus is the great light, and no one, however exalted, can take his place. Paul confronts the dissension in the Christian community at Corinth because they are making lesser lights into the great light. The church is divided into factions – not over doctrinal differences but over personalities. Some are following Apollos, an eloquent and enthusiastic teacher who attracts the well educated to Christianity. Some, mainly Jewish Christians, rally to the name of Peter. Some stay loyal to the memory of Paul, preferring his passion and bluntness.

This division of the church is destructive and Paul argues for unity under Christ. Christianity is Christ. It was Christ who died for the sins of others and all Christians are baptised in his name. Paul wants the community at Corinth to be a *Christian* community, not a collection of factions and not slaves to personality cults. No leader, however important, can attach disciples to himself. As Paul says later, there is only one foundation of the Christian community: "For the foundation, nobody can lay any other than the one which has already been laid, that is Jesus Christ." (3:11)

Paul resists any attempt to make Christian discipleship a matter of following this or that Christian leader. For Paul, only one person gets the incense and that person is Jesus himself. Religious leadership is about leading others to Christ: it cannot be reduced to smiles and styles. Religious authority does not lead others to itself but to the Lord. It does not exult in itself or point to itself. It points to Christ. For Paul and Matthew there is only one answer to the question "Who are you for?" The Christian must answer, "I am for Christ".

The story of Jonah

The fugitive prophet

One of the most intriguing stories in the pages of the Bible is the tale of Jonah, the runaway prophet. Jonah is commanded by God to go to the great city of Nineveh and tell the people that God is going to destroy them in forty days. Jonah believes that because God is merciful, the city will not be destroyed – hence he will look a buffoon after his all-to-be-wiped-out speeches. If this is Jonah's first mission, it is also his first refusal: instead of going to Nineveh, he decides to go to Spain on a runaway package holiday. At least in Spain no one will laugh at him for being a failure.

Jonah makes the mistake of thinking he can travel out of God's reach, but he is in for a wet surprise. He buys his ticket, boards the ship, and settles down to sleep for the voyage. There is a great storm and the ship threatens to break up. While all the sailors are busy praying and throwing cargo overboard, Jonah is fast asleep. The captain orders him to get up and pray, and when Jonah sees how close disaster is for everyone, he admits that he is the cause and tells the sailors to throw him overboard. Since tossing passengers overboard is not a permissible pastime for sailors, they are reluctant to oblige; but when the seas grow rougher, they change their mind. With Jonah overboard, there is calm again.

And then Jonah, who is not famous for keeping his mouth shut, meets a whale, not famous for keeping its jaws shut. The image is clear: Jonah is taken into the depths to be born again. If the hero is to pass onwards he must first pass inwards. Something in Jonah has to give, something in Jonah has to die. Illumination will come only after the experience of annihilation. So God sends Jonah on a renewal course for three days.

Another chance

Jonah has the opportunity to repent. He is out of his element, he is in the depths, he must face himself and what is asked of him. He prays, he reflects, he remembers; and then he promises to fulfil the word of God. When that happens, he is delivered out of the depths and the blubber-bus deposits him on land. When Jonah is back in his element, the Word of God is addressed to him a second time: "Up! Go to Nineveh, the great city, and preach to them as I told you to."

Jonah obeys. He goes into the city and tells the people that all of them will be destroyed in forty days. There is no ambiguity about his message; it is proclaimed as certain. Everyone pays attention. The king and his ministers command the people to renounce their evil behaviour: "Who knows, God may yet repent and turn from his furious anger?" (RSV) They hope that if they repent, so too will God.

God repents when the people repent. Everyone is overjoyed. All except one. While the people rejoice, Jonah leaves the city. To sulk. As he suspected from the beginning, God has a controlling habit of forgiveness. He argues again with God: "That was why I fled...I knew that you were a God of tenderness and compassion, slow to anger, rich in graciousness and mercy, relenting from evil." He asks God to take his life. He has been put to shame. The prophet has been proved a failure.

Jonah decides to sit in the hot sun until he dies. But God causes a tree to grow, to shade his prophet. Jonah feels better. But God causes the tree to die, and then Jonah feels sorry for the tree. God has the last word: he asks Jonah why he is sorry for the tree. Should God not feel sorry for Nineveh, where many thousands of people live?

Repentance

With that question from God, the story of Jonah comes to an end. Jonah is obsessed with being right and he is willing to see all the people perish to be proved right. But the prophet has to learn that *the point of prophecy is not accuracy but repentance.* True, Jonah has been made to look foolish; but his foolishness is much less important than people's repentance. He has to learn that it is never too late to repent, and that it is always good when the give-them-hell prophet is proved wrong.

The story of Jonah holds out hope for all of us. In the story everyone repents: Jonah himself, the people of Nineveh, even God. The good news is that no one is tied to a planned fate, no one is doomed to embrace disaster. By choosing to repent we can change our lives. Repentance is good news because it means that nothing is settled, nothing is sealed. Punishment that has been planned can always be cancelled. Things *can* change. If God can begin again, so we can begin again and again and again.

That is Gospel. That is good news. And repentance need not be a crusty, grouchy affair. As Jonah experienced himself, you can still have a whale of a time!

187

A sense of belonging

Homeland

Edgar Reitz, the German film director, tells the story of how he went home with a friend to visit his mother and while they were there his mother told a story he had never heard before. The story was of a man from their town who had left his house one day saying he was going up the road to the local inn for a drink. But he never returned home, and no one ever heard of him again.

Reitz was intrigued by the story because he was interested in what would make someone leave home without telling anyone, and what would keep him from ever coming back. He was interested in what makes people leave the place they belong to, and what makes some of them come back. Why do some people leave home never to return? What draws some people back – if only to rediscover why they left?

Reitz decided to make a film on the theme. He has called it *Heimat,* which means "homeland", and it lasts for 15 hours and 36 minutes! The film is a chronicle of one family and one small village in Germany from 1919 until 1982. One of its many appeals is how it depicts the great sense of belonging the people have in the small village of Schabbach when they are born into a place their family have lived for generations. They are born into a particular memory that associates them with people and places and little stories. They are able to call on all this, which gives them a sense of belonging, and a hold over their identity. The film shows how in the passage of time that sense of belonging slowly disappears.

But no matter how far people travel from home perhaps there is always some hope that they can go back. As the poet Robert Frost wrote:

> Home is the place where, when you have to go there,
> They have to take you in.

No local prophets

In today's Gospel Jesus returns to Nazareth where he has been brought up, the place which gives him the identity of Jesus of Nazareth. We know that Jesus left home to go and see John the Baptist, and we know that his whole life-style changed after his time with John. Jesus didn't stay in the wilderness to live a hermit's life with John: he received a prophetic anointing in his baptism to announce the new age of the kingdom of God. So he became a travelling preacher.

By the time Jesus returns to his home town his reputation has arrived before him: when he goes into the synagogue on the sabbath as he usually did, this time he is invited to preach. He chooses a passage from Isaiah which gives a beautiful summary of the programme of his new mission: to announce good news to the poor, proclaim liberty to captives and new sight to the blind; to free the oppressed and to proclaim a year of favour – which was a time when all debts were cancelled and all property returned to the rightful owners (cf. Lev.25:8-55).

Jesus points to himself as the fulfilment of ancient prophecy: today the text becomes true in the hearing of his own townspeople. At first their reaction is approval of his words, but then they remind themselves of his identity and say "this is Joseph's son, surely." The neighbours don't allow Jesus' wisdom to interfere with their memories of him. When he presents himself to them for the first time as the prophetic preacher, they remind themselves of his address and pedigree. They won't allow Jesus to grow up so they lock him into the past and into a former identity.

Perhaps the neighbours have a vested interest in focusing on who Jesus was to them, rather than who he is now. It's much easier having a carpenter around the house than a prophet; it is much easier talking about broken chairs than broken lives. The neighbours want to keep Jesus at the level they can handle him at; they want to keep him reasonably harmless. After all, he's only a carpenter!

Jesus reminds them that no prophet is accepted in his own homeland, and as if to prove him right the local crowd become so enraged they try to throw him off a cliff. But Jesus escapes, and it is no surprise that he never returns home again.

New home
We all need a place to belong to and people we can call our own. Usually we call that "home" where you are accepted in love for who you are, but also encouraged to *become* the person you could be. Perhaps the last people to accept our changes are those who live with us: they're so used to the old ways they can't believe in real change.

Jesus had to leave home to become the person his Father wanted him to be. He couldn't rely on his own folks to foster his new life and new mission. So, he established a community, a body of people, who would recognise as St Paul says their need of each other. That's us. We're home for each other, pledged to support the growing life of the Spirit in each of us. In this gathering here everyone should feel welcome, and everyone should have the freedom to grow. Welcome home.

Sermon on the Mount: the beatitudes

The heart of a nobody

Before he discovered his vocation as a painter, the Dutch artist Vincent van Gogh studied for the priesthood. He longed to dedicate himself to helping other people, and after a short spell in England as a lay preacher and teacher he studied theology and then took up training as an evangelist in Brussels. He failed to be recommended and left to do missionary work among a poor mining population – an experience which gave him what he called "a free course at the university of despair."

He gave away the few possessions he had to share the life of the poor and was dismissed for taking the Gospel too literally. Only when he became penniless and experienced rejection did he discover his true calling as a painter. He decided that his mission would be to bring consolation to people through his art. As he wrote to his younger brother, Theo:

> What I want to aim at is this. I want to do drawings which touch people. I want to progress so far that people will say of my work: he feels deeply, he feels tenderly. What am I in most people's eyes? A nonentity, somebody who has no position in society and never will have. Very well then, I should want my work to show what is in the heart of such a nobody. This is my ambition which, in spite of everything is founded less on anger than on love.

Van Gogh produced over 700 drawings and 800 oils, only one of which was sold during his lifetime. His incapacity to overcome his loneliness led him to suicide, and only after his death was his work appreciated. In his paintings, even the dirtiest corner of life has a ray of light. He succeeded in his ambition to show the world what was in the heart of such a nobody. Through his art he has ministered to untold numbers of people throughout the world.

Blessed are the little

In today's three readings we hear of God's preference for the nobodies of this world. The prophet Zephaniah speaks of the humble and the lowly, those who find refuge and shelter in the Lord. Paul warns the Christians at Corinth not to become puffed up with their own wisdom because God has a habit of choosing what is weak and foolish by human standards: he uses "those who are nothing at all to show up those who are everything." And Matthew gives us the great jewel of his Gospel – the beatitudes, which celebrate the little people whose lives illumine the truth of the Gospel.

Those who are called "blessed" or "happy" in these beatitudes can hardly be described as fortunate or lucky people in the eyes of the world: the lowly, the mourners, those deprived of justice, those who are persecuted and abused. In structuring the beatitudes in the way he does, Matthew is not offering an unusual programme to happiness; rather, he is describing what happens to Christian discipleship when the kingdom breaks in this broken world. The beatitudes speak of a variety of experiences that disciples undergo as a result of their involvement in living the Gospel. The result of this involvement might appear to the world as senseless suffering, but Jesus says that it is good. He heaps blessings on those who struggle to love the truth of the Gospel.

Jesus, a life of beatitudes
The best commentary on the beatitudes is Jesus' own life. To be authentic to his own calling, Jesus gives up power and prestige to follow the way of powerlessness. He is gentle with the kind of people that others write off as hopeless cases. He mourns when he sees how so many choose to be blind when God visits them. He experiences hunger – not just the hunger that is satisfied by bread but the hunger that can be satisfied only by doing what is right.

Jesus has a habit of scandalising the religious authorities with the readiness of his mercy and forgiveness. His single-mindedness in pursuing his mission sees him through times of hurt and terror. He is driven to make peace between God and humanity. In the end he is abused and persecuted in the cause of right and handed over to death. He ends up on another mount dying for what he believed in. *But in all this Jesus is blessed:* God raises him on the third day.

Jesus experiences all this as an *outcome* of a life lived in the love and enthusiasm of God. All this happened to Jesus because he was personally gripped by the reality of the kingdom. If his disciples, to whom the beatitudes are addressed, are gripped by the same reality then they too will have to face similar experiences. And Jesus says that they will be blessed because they will experience the fullness of the kingdom of heaven.

Everyone here has some experience of the cost of discipleship. Some will know what it is like to be accounted as a nobody because of their fidelity to Jesus. But as Paul tells us, Christ is our wisdom and freedom. As Christians we are pledged to share the wisdom of one who was counted a nobody himself. In doing that we will continue "to shame the wise" by declaring the foolishness of God. We will continue to show the world what is in the heart of such a nobody.

Power and authority

Power and authority

The imposing figure of G.K. Chesterton, English writer and wit, was often seen squeezed behind a table in London restaurants. Chesterton always joked about his large bulk, saying that it gave him the consolation of offering his seat in the train to three ladies. During one of his literary lunches Chesterton was expounding on the relationship between power and authority. He described the difference: "If a rhinoceros were to enter this restaurant now, there is no denying he would have great power here. But I should be the first to rise and assure him that he had no authority whatever."

Power without authority always looks dangerous; authority without power always looks comical. If power is the ability to cause or prevent change, to influence people and events, it is important that those who exercise it also enjoy the authority that justifies them in what they do. For many people, particularly those who have suffered under military regimes, power is associated with force and compulsion and violence. The power that identifies itself only with force makes victims of all its subjects. That is the power of Chesterton's rhinoceros.

People rightly oppose the power that exploits, manipulates, bullies into conformity. But power need not be destructive. We remember how Gandhi and Martin Luther King and Archbishop Romero used the power of nonviolence to oppose powerful systems. The fact that all three were assassinated did not belittle their power: their moral authority, exercised on behalf of a suffering people, made them forces for good. So too with the power that parents can exercise over their children. This is power allied to love, a force that is exerted on behalf of others.

The power and authority of Jesus

When the evangelist Mark begins telling his story of the ministry of Jesus, he shows us how Jesus is invested with the power of the Spirit at his baptism and thus acts with authority. The power that moves Jesus has its source in God; the authority that Jesus displays, both in his actions and words, is the authority of God himself. When Jesus begins teaching, the people are deeply impressed; they can see for themselves the difference between how Jesus teaches and how other religious leaders teach. When Jesus teaches, something actually happens! It is not a matter of words decorating the air. Jesus' teaching creates an impression because people can see the change for good it effects in the broken and the crippled and the dispossessed.

In today's Gospel Jesus' teaching is seen in action. In the first public work of the ministry there is a confrontation between two super powers: the power of God and the power of darkness. While Jesus is teaching in the synagogue, he is interrupted by the shouts of a man possessed, a man who has no authority over his body or spirit. He is possessed; he is not in charge of his own life. When Jesus speaks, he commands the power that dominates this man's life to leave him alone. At Jesus' command, the man is freed. The people are astonished and marvel at Jesus' *teaching:* "Here is a teaching that is new and with authority behind it."

When Jesus teaches, he shares not only his wisdom but his power. Jesus' actions are his principal teachings. That is his unique authority. He uses his power to liberate people from the evil forces that dominate their lives. And when others see what he is *doing* with his teaching, they begin to wonder who this Jesus really is.

The authority that liberates

At the beginning of his ministry Jesus seems to meet with unmixed approval and success. You can hear the applause. But later, as we know, things will change and the applause will die down. When people want to shelter from his teaching and ignore his worth, they will distract themselves by focusing on his background, his address, his family, his supporters. His listeners will haul in the usual array of defence mechanisms to protect themselves from his insight. They will begin to question his authority, criticise his values, denounce his preferences. Jesus, however, seems to be aware that the road from approval to violence is a short one, and that he is not excused from facing the rejection that all the prophets before him had to face. All that goes with the territory.

The important point is that Jesus stays committed to using his power for good. He continues to exercise his authority to liberate those who are bound up and to confront those who lay burdens on the weak. Applause or no applause. No matter what the opinion polls say, Jesus struggles on. If he receives his authority from elsewhere, he looks elsewhere for his approval and support. Ultimately he is responsible to the Father, from whom all power and authority come. In the meantime Jesus can only hope, like all religious authority hopes, that the Father will not be alone in the business of approval.

Rejection and love

Facing rejection

The Greek philosopher Diogenes was regarded by many who knew him as a somewhat eccentric teacher, not least for his belief that virtue consisted in the avoidance of all physical pleasures, that pain and inconvenience were conducive to goodness. When Alexander the Great visited Diogenes in Corinth, the philosopher was living in a large earthenware tub in one of the city suburbs. Few people could accept either his teaching or his way of life. Diogenes was once noticed begging from a statue. When someone asked him the reason for this pointless conduct, he replied: "I am exercising the art of being rejected."

Diogenes experienced plentiful rejection in his time; whether he ever became accustomed to being rebuffed remains an open question. In today's Gospel we see how Jesus, after preaching in the synagogue in Nazareth, is rejected by his own townspeople. Some of them are awed by his gracious words, while others are more concerned about his pedigree and address. The neighbours of Jesus are no different from any neighbours. Jesus, for all his mission to mankind, still has to face local suspicion, gossip, behind-the-curtain omniscience, experts in character demolition, locals who believe that nothing special can emerge from the neighbourhood without their spotting it first. Prophets are accepted provided that they came from backwoods somewhere else; there is nothing so unpromising as the local backwoods.

Jesus' response

Jesus accepts from experience that a prophet is not accepted in his own country. He is not free from local prejudice, he is not above the normal, haphazard way that people look at other people and events. People get tangled in his roots; they cannot see the tree for the roots. They complain that Jesus performs no local wonders while at the same time letting him know that they disbelieve in him anyway. When Jesus tells his own people that his mission is addressed to all people, they become angry.

Jesus refuses to share their small-mindedness, their meanness of vision. He will be no part of their pettiness. In responding to his neighbours, Jesus makes it clear that he is not going to live down to their expectations

Like many groups, the neighbours want Jesus to be different in the same way that they are different. They expect Jesus to share the same exclusive outlook as themselves – as R.D. Laing observed, "Sanity is a matter of having the same diseases as everyone else." Jesus is different: he does not share their clannish idea of salvation, their mean image of God, their suspicious view of each other. God is always more than people's expectations. Jesus may share their nervousness about local boys making good, but he has good reason to be nervous about the cost of making good in such an environment of threat.

When your local audience suddenly becomes a mob, you have reason to be nervous. Jesus' audience is at such a loss for words that they do what many mobs did before them, they try the final solution of beating your opponent to death. But Jesus makes himself scarce, learning, so early in his public ministry, the art of knowing when to run. He is not looking for an executioner; he is shy of threatening mobs intent on his death. So he escapes to live and preach another day. And in Luke's Gospel, Jesus, not surprisingly, does not return home again.

Rejection and love
The harsh reality of the Nazareth experience seems a world away from Paul's description of love in today's second reading: "Love is always patient and kind: it is never jealous; love is never boastful or conceited; it is never rude or selfish; it does not take offence, and is not resentful. Love takes no pleasure in other people's sins but delights in the truth; it is always ready to excuse, to trust, to hope, and to endure whatever comes."

The quality of love "to endure whatever comes" can be seen in Jesus' whole ministry. If love is always patient and kind, it has to face impatience and unkindness. If love is always ready to excuse, it has to face those who are prompt to condemn. If love takes no pleasure in other people's sins, then it has to face those who delight in the weaknesses of others.

Love has a tough programme. We know this from experience. But what else can meet rejection with such endurance and greatness?

Sermon on the mount: sharing the light

The last Christian

The novelist Graham Greene tells a story, a fantasy which takes place in the distant future when the whole world is governed by a single party. The opening scene is a sordid little hotel in New York. It is late at night. An old man, tired, down-hearted, wearing a shabby raincoat and carrying a battered suitcase comes to the reception and asks for a room. He signs the register and disappears up the stairs. The house detective looks at the register and says to the clerk:

"Did you see who that was?"

"No."

"It's the Pope."

"The Pope? Who's that?"

Catholicism has been successfully stamped out. Only the Pope survives; he is doomed to rule over a Church that doesn't exist. All the cardinals, bishops and priests have met their fate at the firing squad. But the Pope has been authorised to live because he is useful in demonstrating how dead the Church is, and because there is always the possibility that some survivor will betray himself by getting in touch with him. But there are no more survivors.

In the end the world Dictator gets tired of the game and he wants to put an end to it in his own lifetime. He wants to go down in history as the man who, with his own finger on the trigger of the revolver, puts an end to Christianity. The Dictator tells him that he is going to die – the last Christian who still believes. The Dictator takes a revolver out of the desk drawer and, while the Pope is praying, shoots him.

But something happens. In the second between the pressure on the trigger and the Pope dying, a thought crosses the Dictator's mind: "Is it just possible that what this man believed in was true?" In that question another Christian is born.

The light of the world

The story illustrates a truth: that Christianity cannot die. Even if the world succumbed to a regime of atheism, there would still be pockets of belief. There would still be spies of God who would keep their faith intact and pass it onto others, even though they risked their lives in the process. There would always be people who would share their light: that instinct has been the driving force of Christianity.

In today's first reading the importance of sharing the light is stressed. The background to the reading is important: the exiles have returned but they have a complaint against God: "Why have we fasted if you did not see, why mortify ourselves if you never notice?" (Is.58:3) The prophet tells them that genuine fasting is related not only to God but to their neighbour. Their fasting should include sharing their food with the hungry, sheltering the homeless, and clothing the naked. When they do these things *"Then* your light will shine like the dawn and your wound will be quickly healed over." The practice of their religion must include God *and* their neighbour.

The theme of sharing the light is repeated in the Gospel as Jesus continues to instruct his disciples. Discipleship is not only about a right relationship with God but also about a right relationship with other people. Discipleship is not a personal privilege; it is for the benefit of others and the glory of the Father. If the disciples stop witnessing then they become like flat salt that is wholly useless.

Jesus compliments his followers by calling them the light of the world. He is confident that his disciples have something which is worth showing and sharing. Light is not a private energy; it is not for hiding or hoarding. What's the point of lighting a lamp in a house without windows and putting the light under a tub? When people are shuffling around in the dark it is little consolation for them to know that the inside of the tub is well lit! The light should be put "where it shines for everyone in the house." And the purpose of all this sharing is not to light up the disciple but to lead others to praise God.

Puzzling people with the light

When we as Christian disciples share our light in the witness of our lives, that witness can puzzle people into wonder. In Graham Greene's story the quiet witness of the last Pope puzzles the Dictator into wonder. That is the beginning of faith. A real Pope, Paul VI, made the point eloquently in his exhortation, *Evangelization in the Modern World:* "Through this wordless witness these Christians can stir up irresistible questions in the hearts of those who see how they live. Why are they like this? Why do they live in this way? What or who is it that inspires them? Why are they in our midst? Such a witness is already the silent proclamation of the Good News and a very powerful and effective one. Here we have the initial act of evangelization." (21)

As disciples of Christ, our witness should lead others to wonder. As Paul VI observed, that is the first act of spreading the Gospel to others. If we hide our light we puzzle no one. When we share it with others, another Christian is born.

Job, Jesus, and suffering

The afflicted man

Once upon a time, in a faraway land, there lived an upright and blameless man called Job. He had a loving wife, seven sons and three daughters, and the largest estate in the kingdom. He never abused the power and privilege he enjoyed: he used his wealth for hospitality and his influence for helping the needy. No one who went to Job's house for help left disappointed. But Job's piety and sanity are put to the test. In a series of disasters he loses his family, his friends, his fortune, his possessions. Messengers keep coming to him to tell him tales of horror, of loss, of tragedy. Job rents his robe, shaves his head, and falls to the ground, praying: "The Lord gave and the Lord has taken away; blessed be the name of the Lord." The only thing Job does not lose is his faith in God.

Job is then afflicted with sores, from the soles of his feet to the crown of his head. His wife tells him to curse God and die, but Job keeps faith in God. The man who was described as the greatest figure in all the east is now afflicted with disaster and sickness. What has Job done to deserve such a terrible fate? Why is he chosen to be God's victim?

Why does Job have to suffer? Why should an innocent man face such a fate? In Old Testament times it was thought that suffering was directly connected with people's conduct, and that anyone who suffered had sinned. This view is represented by Job's friends who come to console him. They argue that Job must have sinned; he should admit his guilt before God. Job protests: he has not sinned, he has always loved God and his neighbour, honouring them both. He even challenges God to have the matter cleared up in a court of law.

Why suffering?

Although Job refuses to believe that his suffering is a consequence of sin, he has no answer to satisfy himself. He shares the eternal question of the persecuted: "Why me?" As he shares the absence of an answer. He holds fast to his faith in God but loses all his reasons for hoping that things will ever change. He settles for despair and, as we heard in today's first reading, turns to a weary philosophy:

> Months of delusion I have assigned to me,
> nothing for my own but nights of grief.
> Lying in bed I wonder, "When will it be day?"
> Risen I think, "How slowly evening comes!"

Job is never graced with an answer to the question of suffering, although his fortunes do change for the better. This man, who interrogated God and suffered a sorrow he did not deserve, is a symbol of all the innocents in history who wonder at their pain. As Jacques Maritain observed: "It is a lucky man who knows why he suffers." Job is familiar to all of us; if few of us share his innocence, all of us share his hurt and anguish and bewilderment. We have all lived through some of his questions and some of his despair. And we still wonder: why suffering?

The witness of Jesus

When Jesus is confronted with concrete human suffering, he does not stay with the question "Why suffering?" but moves to heal the afflicted. In today's Gospel people are crowding around the door bringing with them the legion of the inform and the broken. No doubt each of them has questions about the why of suffering, but all of them share the same hope that Jesus will care for them. Their hope is not misplaced; Jesus attends to their plight and heals them. Early next morning he seeks out a lonely place and prays there, but the apostolic search-party finds him to tell him that everyone is looking for him. Once the word is out about Jesus, every anxious Job in town emerges with his hurt showing. Jesus has an emergency ward on his hands. And he knows that it will be no different in the next town. So he faces the sick with the love of God. That is why he has come.

The questions of the suffering Job are not answered in the Gospel. Jesus may have his own questions about the endless suffering that surrounds him, as he will have his own questions when his own suffering becomes passion. But whatever his questions are, Jesus stays committed to caring for the sick. That is his witness. And that must be the enduring witness of his followers.

Through the witness of Jesus we hold fast to the truth that God loves us in our weakness and fragility, in our sickness and suffering. We can see a reflection of God's care in the commitment of doctors, nurses, healers, hospital chaplains, and all the people who tend to the suffering of others. They are God's compassion in flesh, God's care in motion. No doubt all of them have reason to wonder, to protest, to be angry when they see the innocent suffer. But they carry on. That is their enduring witness. Like Jesus, they know that the schedule of care must be kept.

Working hard; catching nothing

Mobile ruins

There are times in the lives of all of us when we come face to face with the stark reality of our own shortcomings and failure. We see our sins writ large, and we know that we can't fall back on our own resources to put things right. We feel disabled in a very real way, and the prospect of change is more than a dream away. Our energies are crippled and our hope is in the emergency-ward. There doesn't seem to be any way forward. We might wonder if anyone has noticed the cause of our depression.

Emily Dickinson put it well when she wrote:

> A great hope fell.
> You heard the noise?
> The ruin was within.

When we carry our ruins within us we have no reason to go sightseeing for the architectural ones. We can just journey within and the sight is enough to keep us busy. We can all pass the time inspecting the details of our own ruins, and prospecting for a few new ones! And it's a short trip from there to wondering whether God could possibly have time for the likes of us. Why should God be *bothered* with accomplished sinners like us?

Unworthiness and forgiveness

Similar thoughts appear in our readings today. Isaiah has a vision in the temple in Jerusalem and becomes acutely aware of the holiness of God. When his attention turns to himself, however, it's not much of a vision: he says, "What a wretched state I am in. I am lost." Isaiah sees the holiness of God as a beautiful reality that highlights his own sin and leads him to depression. However Isaiah doesn't stay around the temple nurturing his depression; he accepts the forgiveness of God when it is offered. His *conviction* of the reality of God's forgiveness frees him to respond to God's challenge. He is no longer preoccupied with his own unworthiness; God's forgiveness has released him for mission so that he can offer himself: "Here I am, send me."

The same story is told in the Gospel. Peter and his companions are professional fishermen and do their work at night when the fish come to the surface. They have worked hard at the right time but have caught nothing. Now the expert fishermen are being told by a carpenter to put out during the day! Peter obeys the word of Jesus, and the word of Jesus comes home to him when they do indeed catch a giant shoal of fish. Peter recognises the hand of God in what has happened and at the same time realises his own sinfulness. And his pastoral advice to Jesus is to go away and not be bothered with the likes of him.

Happily, Jesus does not take Peter's advice to put distance between himself and sinners. Jesus has not come to be a hermit with an unreachable address in the desert; rather, his whole mission moves in the opposite direction, for he has come "to seek out and save the lost." (Lk.19:10) So, Jesus travels *into* people's lives, not away from them. He entertains sinners, he enters their homes, meets their families, eats at their table, listens to their stories, and calls them to a new way of life. Throughout his life Jesus is never far from sinners. And on the cross he will die between two of them.

And Jesus wants Peter to share that mission with him, so he calls Peter away from fixation with his own sinfulness and preoccupation with himself. Peter has acknowledged his own unworthiness. That is enough. Jesus moves the conversation on and invites Peter to see himself as a leader who will bring people close to God. Jesus draws out the worth in Peter and challenges him to do the same by becoming a fisher of men. Can Peter draw out the best in people? And if it doesn't make any sense for a fisherman to be far from fish, it won't make any sense for Peter to be far from people. So, Peter follows Jesus.

Forgetting the past
There is a marvellous teaching here for all of us. Jesus doesn't write us off because we are sinners; he is broadminded when it comes to working with people because he doesn't believe that people should be summarised by their sin. Jesus has other plans because he believes that sinners have a future, not just a past. He can see beyond the sin to the worth of the sinner. As St Paul proclaims: "Christ died for our sins". Christ thought we were worth enough to die for.

Even though Paul admits his own destructive past in persecuting the Church, he is *convinced* that the love of Christ has overcome that. So he writes to the Philippians: "I believe nothing can happen that will outweigh the advantage of knowing Christ Jesus ... All I can say is that I forget the past and strain ahead for what is to come."

As we too will stop doting on our past sinfulness only when we are *convinced* of the central Gospel message: Christ died for our sins.

Sermon on the Mount: the new vision

Matthew the scribe

Any new movement or community which emerges from an older tradition has to face the problems of its own identity and direction. How different is it from the old community? How similar? One of the problems which the early Church had to face was its relationship with Judaism. Jesus was a Jew and his early followers were all Jews: they upheld the Law of Moses and they honoured the traditions of their own people. But there is also discontinuity with that tradition when it comes to healing on the sabbath, attitudes to Samaritans, and fasting.

Matthew himself is a Jewish convert living in Syria and writing his Gospel in the 80's for a mixed community of Jewish and Gentile converts. He has to hold both these groups together in the community – both the convert Jews who respect the tradition of the Law of Moses, and the convert Gentiles who have their own traditions.

Matthew was probably a scribe himself – a man of learning whose study was the written and oral law. He clearly respects the Law and he also respects the authority of the scribes and the Pharisees (23:2), but he is openly hostile to those scribes and Pharisees who oppose Jesus (23:15ff). Matthew is probably referring to himself when he writes in his Gospel: "every scribe who becomes a disciple of the kingdom of heaven is like a householder who brings out from his storeroom things both new and old." (13:52) Matthew is a scribe who became a disciple: he shows us his respect for the old Law *and* his enthusiasm for the new vision of Jesus.

Continuity and discontinuity

Matthew is writing in the 80's when the Christian community is facing heavy criticism from the official Jewish leadership: they claim that the teaching of Jesus is destructive of all that is cherished in Judaism. Around the year 85 one of the prayers read in the synagogues is a formal curse on everyone, especially Jewish Christians, who believe that Jesus is the Messiah. Jewish Christians are now expelled from the synagogues, and this expulsion, instigated by the Pharisees, increases the hostility of Christians towards them.

So when Matthew writes his Gospel he is anxious to show that Jesus does not come to abolish the Law and the Prophets; rather he is their completion. Matthew shows the continuity with the ancient tradition. But he also shows the discontinuity when Jesus says: "You have heard how it was said...but I say this to you..." Jesus completes the Law but he also goes beyond it. Because Jesus is who he is, he has the authority to put before people a new vision.

Jesus confirms the old Law in its condemnation of killing, but he goes much further in condemning the motivation that often leads to killing: anger. He asks his disciples to take responsibility for the charges made against them. If their brother has something against them, they should leave their gift at the altar and attend to that complaint first. Reconciliation is more important than sacrifice; the duty to make peace is more urgent than the duty to offer worship to God. If people are not reconciled then no amount of liturgy is going to disguise that brokenness.

Jesus confirms the old Law that adultery is wrong, but he goes much further in saying that a man who looks lustfully at a woman has already sinned. Women can be violated by men's attitudes, not just by physical acts. Women are cheapened when they are treated simply as sex objects, and Jesus asks his disciples to forego that kind of violence.

Jesus' respect for women is also evident in his teaching on divorce. The Law of Moses allowed for divorce, but it wasn't possible for a wife to divorce her husband. The legal debate was over what reasons the *husband* could use to gain a divorce. According to the strict school of thought, divorce was possible only if a wife was unfaithful to her husband; according to the lax school, a husband could divorce his wife "even if she burnt his food in cooking it." (*Mishnah*, 'Gittin', ix.10) Jesus' prohibition on divorce puts the husband and wife on equal footing: *both* are equally obliged to make the marriage work.

A radical vision

In all this Matthew asserts that Jesus' authority is greater than the authority of Moses. Jesus' demands are more radical; his vision sharper; his expectations are greater. Moses made concessions because of the hardness of people's hearts; Jesus has hope that people's heart condition has improved since then.

When we see our own record of doing good against the demands of Jesus in the Gospel, we can all come away feeling helpless. Our own efforts look so shabby against the clear unambiguous demands of the larger vision. But Matthew is not writing his Gospel to grind his readers into the dirt or make them feel helpless. He is calling the community of believers to face the vision of Jesus with a willing heart and a ready spirit. None of us can do this alone. That is why we are here, gathered in community, to pray that God will fund our efforts to bring that vision down to earth.

Questioned by a leper

Questioning the healer

Sometimes we communicate what we mean not so much by what we say as by how we say it. We've all had the experience of someone saying good morning to us in a tone calculated to wither a cactus. When the leper in today's Gospel says to Jesus "If you want to you can cure me", what is the tone of his question? Is he saying: "Go ahead, you can do it. All you have to do is marshal your resources. Don't worry, you can cure me."

Or is the leper taunting Jesus: *"If* you want to, you can cure me." The if is in front of the want, not the cure. The leper does not doubt Jesus' power to cure, he doubts his good will. He questions whether Jesus *wants* to cure him. Has the leper been a religious and social outcast for so long that he doubts whether anyone has the will to bother with him?

When people question our good intentions we tend to get flustered. How does Jesus react to the leper? The translation we read says that Jesus feels sorry for him, but many of the early Greek manuscripts say that Jesus fumed! The New English Bible tries to compromise and says that Jesus reacted with "warm indignation". Jesus protests when he says "Of course I want to! Be cured!" Then he sternly orders the man to say nothing to anyone. Jesus tells this man to keep his mouth shut, but he broadcasts the story. And while the cured man now moves around freely, Jesus hides in places where nobody lives. Somehow, they seem to have changed places.

What kind of Jesus?

This brief encounter between Jesus and the leper, with its strained exchanges and emotions, gives us a fascinating insight into the ministry of Jesus. It gives us the opportunity to ask ourselves: what kind of Jesus emerges from Mark's portrait? Mark, the author of the first Gospel, is well known for presenting a very human Jesus. In his Gospel Jesus demonstrates human feelings and strong emotions; he is critical, angry, impatient, fearful. This portrait prompts questions about our own understanding of Jesus.

a) Do you think of Jesus as a person who never gets ruffled?

b) Is he the kind of person who never sweats over anything?

c) Does Jesus have his *own* reactions to people and events?

d) Does he ever blow up?

e) Does his anger show when the people he tries to help question his good intentions?

f) Does he ever become tired when people treat him like a magic wonder-worker, a mobile relic, without accepting his teaching that no amount of healing is going to exempt people from suffering and brokenness?

g) Is he ever afraid of people's limitless expectations?

h) Does he get annoyed when people misrepresent him, so that he tells them to stay quiet? Better say nothing than run around giving false impressions.

i) Is he ever surprised at the trust people put in him?

j) Does he get nervous when people begin to use him for their own peculiar causes?

k) Does he bless God when someone gets his name right?

l) Does the pressure ever become so intense that he makes for somewhere that has no addresses, because no one lives there?

m) Do professional healers need time off?

n) Does Jesus ever get tired of living in an emergency ward where people come to bleed him? So much that he goes to a lonely place where nobody can bleed him.

The human Jesus

These are a few of the questions that are raised by Mark in his Gospel. They have a timeless quality about them, for they address our own understanding of Jesus. Mark's portrait of Jesus is often blunt and shocking, which is why Mark's Gospel was appointed to be read so rarely in the liturgies of the Church. The work of Mark has waited a long time before being accepted fully into the *celebration* of the Church's life; but its insight into the humanity of Jesus is one that touches many people more than the high theology of John or the brilliant teachings of Matthew.

Mark believes that Jesus is the Son of God, but he also portrays him in such a human light that everyone can identify with him. Immersed in the strengths and limitations of humanity, the Jesus we meet in Mark's Gospel is alive, real, always struggling to be authentic. For many Christians, it is Mark who gives the most moving account of the Lord's commitment to a broken and fragile humanity. In previous centuries Mark has been ignored; but now the Church is rediscovering his work, like a lost treasure.

And the good news is that when we rediscover the Gospel of Mark, we rediscover the person of Jesus.

Beatitude and warning

Sermon on the level

In today's Gospel we see how Jesus, after choosing his apostles on the mountain, comes down with them and stands on a level place. Like Moses, who descended the mountain to deliver God's word to his people, Jesus descends the mountain to announce his word. In the presence of the crowds, he addresses his disciples. He speaks the four beatitudes and the four woes. Each beatitudes is balanced with a warning:

> **Blessed are you**
> who are poor
> who are hungry
> who weep
> who are hated
>
> **Woe to you**
> who are rich
> who are full
> who laugh
> who are honoured

In the sermon Jesus tells the poor and the hungry, the mournful and the reviled, that the kingdom of God is for them. They have the first invitations to enter the kingdom; they are God's preferred people. Jesus later speaks of the kingdom in terms of a magnificent banquet where the guest list is composed of a human panorama of rejects. The banquet in the kingdom is for the forgotten people, the ones most precious in the eyes of God.

The Gospel and the fairy tale

In the upside-down kingdom of Jesus, which has more affinity with the world of the fairy tale than the world of conventional wisdom, it is the eldest son, the one who has everything going for him, the one who inherits the earth's bounty, who is rich and highly regarded, who ends up with empty hands. It is the youngest son, the one who is the summary of weakness, the one with the least going for him, who is forced to rely on any help that comes his way, who eventually inherits the kingdom.

In the Gospel and the fairy tale, it is the reject, the forgotten one, the despised one, who eventually finds rest – like poor Lazarus who, after a lifetime of being ignored, ends up in the bosom of Abraham to live happily ever after.

In his sermon Jesus does not give a blanket support to poverty, weeping, hunger and hurt: these are not desirable states to be sought after, and only a masochist would argue otherwise. As Archbishop Helder Camera commented: "Saints may be found in slums, but we cannot retain slums in order to make them the breeding ground of saints." Destitute poverty is not a condition to be sought after, it is a condition to be avoided; it deprives human beings of their basic dignity. That said, it still remains true that Jesus' preference for the poor has a social basis.

Jesus' own life

The best commentary on Jesus' sermon is Jesus' own life. Jesus did not live his life *as if* he was blessed by God; he lived out his life in the constant awareness that God did indeed bless him. In the course of that life he experienced poverty, not only the poverty of deprivation, but the poverty of standing alone against the crowds, the poverty of total reliance on his Father. He experienced hunger, not just the hunger that can be answered by bread, but the hunger that can only be satisfied by doing what is right. He had reason to weep and mourn not only at the loss of a dear friend but at the lost opportunities of his own people. He was no stranger to being held up as a clown for the amusement of all; he knew the experience of rejection, betrayal, and abandonment.

All this was experienced by Jesus in the course of his mission; it wasn't adopted as some precious theological posture. It was the *outcome* of a life dedicated to God.

The beatitudes are not prescriptions for becoming poor or hungry or mournful or afflicted. They are addressed to those who are already involved in committing themselves to the kingdom, and they give instances of what happens when the kingdom arrives in this broken world. They speak of a variety of experiences that people go through as a *result* of getting involved in God's way of doing things. So, there is the promise that God can handle the poverty, the hunger, the tears, the rejection.

The promise is that God handles all these things, lifting his people *out of them*. That is the Good News. God is not committed to keeping his people at the level of being hurt and wounded – if that were true the beatitude would read, "Blessed are you who weep, for you shall weep even more." The vision of the God of the beatitudes is the vision of a generous God, one who reverses the tragedy. "Blessed are you who weep" is the tragedy; "for you shall laugh" is the comedy. And it is the comedy, not the tragedy, which is the promise.

Sermon on the Mount: love of enemies

Getting stung

The story is told of a holy old man who used to meditate every morning under a large tree on the banks of the river Ganges in northern India. The place he chose was near a site of pilgrimage where Hindus came to wash in the sacred river and cleanse themselves from sin. One morning, after he had finished his meditation, the old man noticed a large scorpion floating helplessly on the strong current of the river. The scorpion became caught in the tree's long roots that extended into the river bed. The more it struggled to free itself, the more entangled it became in the twining roots. The old man reached out to free the captive animal and, as soon as he touched it, the scorpion lifted its tail and stung him wildly. But the old man reached out again to free it.

A young man was passing and saw what was happening. He shouted out: "Old man, what's wrong with you? You must be mad! Why bother risking your life to save such an ugly useless creature?"

The old man turned to the onlooker, and in his pain there was a question: "Friend," he said, "because it is the nature of the scorpion to sting, why should I give up my own nature to save?"

The story of the old man and the scorpion raises a problem that we all face: do we take our cue for action from the treatment we receive from others, or do we continue in the way of graciousness even when we get stung ourselves?

The way of the disciple

In today's Gospel we hear Jesus address himself to the question of how his disciples should conduct themselves when they are faced with hurt and hatred. Jesus again develops the Law that he has received: "You have learnt how it was said ... but I say to you ..." Jesus quotes the ancient law of retaliation, the *lex talionis,* which fixed the boundaries of vengeance. The Law stated: "Anyone who injures a neighbour shall receive the same in return, broken limb for broken limb, eye for eye, tooth for tooth. As the injury inflicted, so will be the injury suffered." (Lev.24:19f)

This might sound a savage law but it was introduced as a legal practice to limit blood feuds between communities. In traditional tribal life if a man of one tribe injured a man of another tribe there could be outright war in which *all* the members of both tribes were involved. There were no limitations on the revenge the offended tribe would take against the family and tribe of the offender. The law of "an eye for an eye" *limited* the retaliation to the penalty of the same injury. In its time, therefore, the law was merciful because it stopped whole families being wiped out.

Jesus, however, revokes this law saying that his disciples must not be provoked into taking retaliation for the wrongs done against them. The disciples must not allow another person's hostility to be their cue for action. Their cue for response is taken from the nature of their discipleship, not from the wrong they have experienced.

Jesus confirms the ancient Law that you should love your neighbour, but rejects any interpretation of the Law that permits people to hate their enemy. This is a long way from the biblical advice on capturing the enemy's town: "Yahweh your God having handed it over to you, you will put the whole male population to the sword. But the women, children, livestock and whatever the town contains by way of spoil, you may take for yourselves as booty." (Dt.20:13f) That policy of extermination shows how radical Jesus has departed from his own tradition.

The Law enjoined the Israelite to love his neighbour, but a neighbour was understood as a fellow Israelite. Jesus rejects this limitation of love: in asking his disciples to love their enemies he is lifting *all* limitations to love. No one is excluded from Christian love – not even the one who persecutes the disciple.

A disciple's love

Jesus argues that the love his disciples give people is not related to the love they receive from others: it is not a social contract or a fair bargain. The disciple loves because that is what the nature of discipleship involves. A disciple is the son of the Father – and look at the Father's graciousness. He does not withhold the sun and the rain from those who oppose him; likewise, the disciple must not withhold his love from those who oppose him.

The love is offered not because Jesus thinks that it will *change* the enemy into something else: certainly, love might confuse him! Love is offered because that is what a disciple of the kingdom should do. His script proceeds from who *he* is, not from what he receives from others.

Jesus does not believe that love transforms enemies into instant friends. Love didn't solve all Jesus' problems with his enemies. In the end he was the one who reached out to free others and was stung in the process. He was stung to death. But he stayed with his supreme value because that emerged from who he was as the Son of the Father. Love is his way and it stays his way no matter what appears on the agenda. Even the scorpions.

Who can forgive sins?

Four persistent men

In today's Gospel Mark continues his story of Jesus' early ministry in the region of Galilee. After his tour of the synagogues, Jesus returns to Capernaum – probably to Peter's house, which serves as his base of operations. His return is eagerly awaited, for the house is soon overflowing with people who have come to listen to the word.

Four men arrive on the scene, carrying their paralytic friend; but the crowd is in no mood to budge or give way. The new arrivals, however, are men of resource who are not going to be diverted from their task: if they cannot get in the door, they can always get in through the roof. They carry their charge up the external stairway of the house, make a hole through the layer of beams, brushwood and earth, and then lower him to the feet of Jesus.

It must have been a bit of a surprise to Jesus – being showered with parts of the roof and having his teaching interrupted by such a dramatic entrance from on high! But then Jesus is the kind of teacher who has the art of *making what is happening the subject of his teaching*. The paralytic is not an unfortunate diversion from the word of God; rather, his presence becomes the opportunity for a new word. Jesus is frankly delighted at the persistent faith of the four friends. Because of their faith, their bold and insistent belief that Jesus can help their paralysed friend, Jesus forgives the paralytic his sins.

Who can forgive sins?

Now the real trouble starts. The scribes, who are always numbered among the traditional enemies of Jesus, have enjoyed a front seat in all the drama. They question what Jesus has done: "How can this man talk like that? He is blaspheming. Who can forgive sins but God?" They are spokesmen for the traditional Jewish belief that only God is capable of forgiving sins. Jesus moves in to question their attitude – not because he is the Son of God, which he is, but because he believes that the scribes are wrong both about God and about the nature of forgiveness.

Many people agree with the scribes in limiting the forgiveness of sins to God. God does forgive sins, but is he the only one to do that? Do we believe in a God who wants to hoard the practice of forgiveness to himself? If we believe that the forgiveness of sins is God's exclusive right, it lets us off the hook about bothering to forgive those who have sinned against us. For Jesus, forgiveness is not the exclusive right of God, it is the shared duty of all who would follow him. Jesus wants everyone to *imitate* God's practice of forgiving sins, not sit back and leave the business of forgiving to God alone.

When Jesus teaches his disciples to pray to the Father, he makes an essential part of that prayer the commitment to forgive: "Forgive us our trespasses as we forgive those who trespass against us." So too he will instruct his disciples, "Whose sins you shall forgive, they are forgiven." Jesus is committed to extend the practice of forgiving sins. That is why he vigorously opposes the scribes who would limit forgiveness to God. The scribes are wrong; Jesus is their corrective in what he does.

Forgiveness

For Jesus, forgiveness is the most profound healing a person can experience, yet is easier to effect than the healing of the body. We know from experience how people can remain disfigured and paralysed in spirit when they live without forgiveness. We know how our unwillingness to forgive others can keep them imprisoned and chained. Jesus opposes that with all his might. God's forgiveness is not an issue: God forgives. As we heard in the first reading:

> No need to recall the past
> no need to think about what has been done before.
> See, I am doing a new deed,
> even now it comes to light; can you not see it?

There is little point in questioning God's generosity in the matter of forgiveness, wondering whether he hides from sinners. The problem is not with God's forgiveness but with our own. The theological question is not whether God forgives, but whether we do. God's track record on forgiveness is impeccable; he is an accomplished forgiver who has been practising the art since the beginning of time. Jesus' concern is to involve us in the same work, in the same commitment to forgive those who sin against us. This is one of the new deeds that God is doing in the person and ministry of Jesus. The scribes didn't see this new deed coming to light. Hopefully, we do.

Measure for measure

Saul and David

The principal characters in today's first reading, Saul and David, are the leading figures in a heartbreaking story: a story of friendship, betrayal and misfortune; a story of ambition, power and madness. Saul is the first king of Israel. Before being marked as God's anointed, Saul cared for his father's animals; he was a shepherd, a simple countryman, who never aspired to rule over anyone. One day the prophet Samuel tells him that he is marked by destiny to become king; but from the first day of his kingship Saul seems afflicted by war and internal division. He becomes melancholy, isolated, withdrawn; he has no inherited experience to rely on, no trained mentor to teach him what to do.

As Saul's power gradually declines, so his melancholia increases. The one thing that calms him is the music of his new page, a shepherd boy called David. But if David disarms the king's sadness, his many abilities and bravery on the field of battle provoke jealousy in Saul. David appears to steal the show; he is praised by the people at the expense of the king. Saul loves him, but he also hates this new talent who is now married to his youngest daughter. Worse still, David has been secretly anointed as king by the same prophet who anointed Saul. To be free of David, Saul decides to eliminate him, but members of the king's own family warn David to make himself scarce.

In spite of being exiled and hunted everywhere, David still loves Saul and never seeks to harm him: all he wants to do is to sing the king out of his depression. Three times David has the opportunity to kill his father-in-law. In today's first reading David steals into Saul's tent and finds him asleep, his spear stuck in the ground beside his head. David's companion offers to kill Saul with his own spear, but David commands him to leave the Lord's anointed in peace. David takes the spear and the pitcher of water from beside Saul's head. Their absence, he hopes, will speak its own message.

Measure for measure

Saul is puzzled by David's loyalty and attachment, by his refusal to treat his father-in-law as an enemy. David believes that, even though Saul was put in his power, he has no right to raise his hand against the Lord's anointed. Not only that, but since David himself is the Lord's anointed and will occupy the throne of Israel, he is unwilling to justify assassination as a form of diplomacy. That could grow into a national habit, and David wants to die in his bed of old age! The future king has an eye to his own survival; thus he treats the demented Saul in the way that he hopes his future subjects will treat him. A case of measure for measure.

In the Gospel Jesus enjoins his own disciples to follow the basic imperative of loving generously: "Love your enemies, do good to those who hate you, bless those who curse you, pray for those who treat you badly ... Give and there will be gifts for you ... because the amount you measure out is the amount you will be given back."

The measure of love

Jesus does not ask his disciples to fall in love with their enemies – that would be wholly unrealistic. The followers of Jesus are challenged to be determined about their enemy's welfare, to be stubbornly gracious, and to refuse to pay back violence with violence. Hatred can be defeated only by love; injury can be healed only by forgiveness; evil can be controlled only by goodness. That may not reflect conventional wisdom, but it is Jesus' wisdom in action. It was also David's response to King Saul's aggression.

In his own life Jesus had to work hard at honouring his own ethic. That process was not a painless or bloodless affair: it cost Jesus everything. He offered love first, even though he knew that the return would never measure up to what was offered; he never bargained love for love; he never became involved in stock-taking returns. Above all, he made a habit of confusing his enemies with love.

Jesus expects us, his followers, to share the gifts we have received. Love is offered because someone somewhere is shuffling through a loveless life. Mercy is given because someone somewhere is cloistered in his wrongdoing. These are gifts which create worth in another person; they build temples in wasteland; they introduce people to the forgotten geography of paradise; they stop the contagion of meanness.

Love creates its own reality, its own force for goodness. It enables us, time after time, to refuse the offer of putting a spear through the heart of our sleeping victims.

Sermon on the Mount: "Do not be anxious"

The age of anxiety

Sometimes we wonder what it would have been like to live in another age. We imagine a simpler time when life was uncomplicated, when the major issues were the weather and the crops, and bewilderment was confined to the identity of the stranger just arrived in the village. Whether life was ever that simple is doubtful. But we know for sure that today we live in a complex world and that the more complicated the world becomes the more insecure we feel about the future. We are shocked when we discover that the systems we create to support us prove too fragile to bear the weight of our hopes. We awake to the knowledge that the future can no longer be taken for granted. That is why those who document our time call it an age of anxiety, one that is marked by disquiet and misgiving.

We are all aware of the *social anxiety* about whether we can control the nuclear force we have created, about the security of jobs, about terrorism and violence, about standards of service and justice in the community. There is *religious anxiety* about change in the Church, about the endless suffering in a world created by God, about the future of belief itself. There is *personal anxiety* that we feel from time to time about how our lives are going, about our families and our health, about separation and loneliness, and about a host of other things.

There are many people who lead lives of quiet anxiety and who never say what haunts them or troubles them. W.H.Auden tried to capture this affliction in his poem *The Age of Anxiety* where he wrote about

> ...this stupid world where
> Gadgets are gods, and we go on talking,
> Many about much, but remain alone,
> Alive but alone, belonging – where? –
> Unattached as tumbleweed.

"Do not be anxious"

In today's first reading we hear how the people of Israel believed they were alive but alone, belonging to no one. Unattached. While they were in exile in Babylon they were deeply anxious and afraid believing that God had abandoned them and forgotten them. But the prophet addresses their anxiety assuring them that even if a mother forgot her baby at the breast, God would not forget his own. This is one of the rare female images of God in the Bible: the tender, caring mother whose love keeps memory alive, who could never abandon her children to live in the anxiety of separation.

And today this song of consolation, this word of the Lord, is addressed to us: "I will never forget you."

In today's Gospel we hear the voice of Jesus speak similar words of comfort: Do not be anxious. "I am telling you not to worry about your life and what you are to eat, nor about your body and how you are to clothe it. Surely life means more than food, and the body more than clothing." But we hear another voice say to us: That's all very well. But when a mother doesn't have food or clothes for her children she cannot leave them hungry and naked while she meditates on the birds of the air and the flowers in the field. When children are not fed, they die of hunger; when they are not clothed, they die of exposure. If you are poor and hungry you are always anxious, because you are never certain about your daily bread. Poverty and anxiety go hand in hand.

Anxiety and trust

Jesus is not suggesting that being his disciple means that we will have a care-free life without a worry in the world. That would be wholly unrealistic. Jesus himself will be anxious and afraid when his passion gets under way and he has to look death in the face. What Jesus argues against is an anxiety that consumes us, that steals all our energy and leaves us feeling abandoned by God. When Jesus faces the cross he must trust in a God beyond the cross; he does not ignore his own fear but puts it in the framework of his belief in God. His fear is not the *ultimate* reality. God is.

As his disciples Jesus asks us to see beyond our real fears to a God who knows us and values us. That is not easy. When we are anxious it is difficult to pay attention to anything other than our anxiety. Many people are exhausted simply from coping with what life brings them; they feel they have no heart left for God because they have nothing left to give. Jesus asks us to place our anxiety in the larger perspective of the kingdom and put it in God's care. If our heart is set *first* on the kingdom then everything that happens is seen in the light of the heart's priority. Nothing can alter God's love for us. Nothing. And that is why we pray in each eucharist: "protect us from all anxiety as we wait in joyful hope for the coming of our saviour, Jesus Christ."

Letters from Christ

Subscribing oneself

Lord Erskine, British politician and lawyer who became lord chancellor in 1806, was noted for the brevity of his letters. He had a standard practice for dealing with letters asking him to subscribe to various causes. "Sir, I feel honoured by your application to me, and I beg to subscribe" – here the reader had to turn over the notepaper – "myself your very obedient servant." Whether anyone took up Lord Erskine's ample subscription remains a mystery.

Subscribing oneself is what Paul recommends to the Christian community in Corinth. An important and wealthy city, Corinth was the capital of the Roman province of Achaia, the southern part of Greece. Because of its position on the great trade route between Rome and the East, it was a city of great commerce and wealth; and like many great cities Corinth was renowned for its culture and notorious for its immorality. Its cosmopolitan community and its strategic position made it an important place in the spread of Christianity.

In the winter of 49 A.D. Paul arrived in Corinth after his unsuccessful visit to Athens. He remained in the city for eighteen months, working as a tent-maker and living with a Jewish couple who had been expelled from Rome. As a result of Paul's preaching a large Church was formed at Corinth, mostly from the poor and the slaves. After leaving the city, Paul seems to have received little but bad news about what was happening among the Christian community in the province.

Paul's apology

The early Corinthian Church was divided by factions, it had little sense of sin or of the need of salvation. A second visit by Paul failed to achieve any reform, and, after he had been publicly insulted, he sailed back to Ephesus. Paul wrote at least four letters addressing the problems of the Corinthian Church; only two of these letters survive. In the section we hear today Paul faces the charges levelled against him by false apostles: that he is no true apostle, having brought no letters of recommendation with him from the other churches. In defence of his apostleship Paul writes his moving apology, arguing that the true proof of his apostleship is the converts produced by his preaching:

> You are yourselves our letter, written in our hearts, that anyone can see and read, and it is plain that you are a letter from Christ, drawn up by us, and written not with ink but with the Spirit of the living God, not on stone tables but on the tablets of your living hearts.

Good News to the world

Paul calls out the best in his converts, affirming them in their new identity as letters of Christ to the world. They are not only the messengers of Christ but the message of Christ. For Paul, the message of Christ is inseparable from the person of the Christian. How can the world hear the message of Christ if the Christian is silent? Every Christian is a message that should be seen and read by everyone. Paul values the importance of each individual Christian, and he hopes that all Christians will subscribe *themselves* to the spread of the Good News.

In that sense every Christian is a missionary – one sent to others. We are all letters of Christ addressed to the people we meet. Some of us may be difficult to make out, a puzzle of scribble to those we meet; some of us may communicate little of the joy of the Gospel; some of us may never get round to delivering the message that Christ has written in our hearts.

When we look at Paul we see how Paul's own energetic life for Christ was the best proof of what he wrote. The truth of his writing shone through his troubled and spirited life story. And his hope for every Christian community is as valid today as it was in the middle of the first century. We should take courage from God's choice of us; we should not be timid about the message we have received; we should share the Good News that is part of our very being. All of us have benefited from the witness of other Christians who have been letters to us. It would be a pity if our generation had a postal strike.

The language of the heart

Hypocrisy

The scene was market day in the city of Athens. Everyone was busy trying to find that elusive commodity called a bargain, and they were not averse to using their tongues and elbows to aid them in the task. In one corner of the market, however, there was a strange quiet: someone whom most people admired and respected walked among the crowd. He was a famous man, who had condescended to patronise the market place. People moved aside to let him have his walkabout. He wasn't a film or television star – the time was still B.C. Neither was he a member of the royal household. He was an orator renowned for his eloquence and patronage of lost causes.

There was something very odd about his appearance. In spite of being a rich man, he wore tattered clothes; he dressed in rags with the diligence and care other people dress in formal clothes. He was clearly pleased at the theatrical impression he was making on the onlookers, until a voice in the crowd hailed him: "Antisthenes, Antisthenes, I can see your pride through the hole in your cloak." For once, the great orator had nothing to say.

If hypocrisy tries to make a profession out of deceit, humility is a matter of honouring the truth about ourselves and other people. Humility is a candid acceptance of reality, an unfussy recognition of what is true. In today's Gospel Jesus names as hypocrites those who notice faults in others but who are blind to their own shortcomings, thereby passing themselves off as something they are clearly not. In his teaching Jesus touches on an important subject in all personal relationships: how self-criticism is an essential part of genuine relations with other people.

Self-criticism

To be critical of others, while at the same time lacking any sense of self-criticism ourselves, is a profitless pastime. To exact high standards from others, while readily finding excuses for our own lack-lustre performance, can only be a fruitless exercise. Apart from anything else, it makes us appear little more than insufferable. Our criticism of others may be true, but the accused may regard us as having no more self-awareness than could be stuffed into a thimble. Telling the truth about others is rarely sufficient recommendation in itself – the process may be nothing more than scapegoating. And at the end of that process we usually end up with a victim, not a convert.

This does not mean, however, that we are condemned to silence, rendered incapable of making our reservations felt about people and issues. Other people will pay more attention to what we have to say when they detect that we are aware of our own shortcomings and that our criticism does not emerge from self-righteousness.

When our own scars of conscience glow in the dark, others will be more inclined to heed our words.

The language of the heart

We know from experience that people can greet criticism with reactions that vary from eyebrow raising to nuclear war. How do you tell the truth to people without stealing their dignity or leaving them in the casualty department? The Gospel says: "A man's words flow out of what fills his heart." Which leads to the question, what fills our hearts? What kind of heart is behind the way we criticise others?

The way we offer criticism depends on our heart condition. William Penn, the great Quaker and champion of religious tolerance, made the observation: "They have a right to censure that have a heart to help." That insight makes good commentary on the Gospel. When people know that our heart is behind our censure, that what we say comes from a genuine attempt to help them, they might take heed. But if they doubt that, they appeal to us: "Oh, have a heart!"

In the language of the Gospel, criticism must come from the store of goodness in our heart. If that goodness is absent, we would be better keeping silent. Sharing a bad heart converts no one. Sharing the goodness in our heart, however, is no guarantee that others will greet our criticism with applause. But then Jesus was rarely applauded when he exercised his critical mind. Like him, we have to soldier on – even when the ratings go down. After all, as the Gospel also says: "the fully trained disciple will always be like his teacher."

219

Sermon on the Mount: acting on the Word

House on rock

The story is told of an American naval officer who longed for the day when he could command his own ship. The day came when his hope was realised: a great destroyer was commissioned and he was named its captain. Everyone who knew him appreciated how much this meant to him and they celebrated the occasion with great rejoicing.

On the maiden voyage everything was going like a dream until the third night brought a fierce storm. The great destroyer was lashed by huge waves and buffeted by gale-force winds, but the captain was able to maintain his course. What came to disturb him was not the weather but a light that seemed to be converging on the bow of his destroyer. He ordered the signalman: "Send out a signal and have that ship alter its course twenty degrees to the south."

The signalman sent the message; in return a message came back, "You alter your course twenty degrees to the north." The captain, a little disturbed by this message, told the signalman: "Send the message, 'This is Captain Cunningham and I order you to alter your course twenty degrees to south.'" The message sent, a reply came back: "This is Third-Class Seaman Jones, you alter your course twenty degrees to north."

The captain was infuriated by this impertinence and sent another signal: "You had better alter your course. I am a destroyer." The message came back: "You had better alter your course. I am a lighthouse."

A name is not enough

In today's Gospel Matthew concludes the sermon on the mount with the image of a sensible man who built his house on rock and a foolish man who built his house on sand. Like the lighthousekeeper and the captain, there is little doubt about which party is more vulnerable to the elements – no matter what his title or rank. Jesus warns those who hear "these words of mine" and fail to act on them that they are fooling themselves and will surely incur destruction. "These words of mine" refer to the teaching of the sermon on the mount, which constitutes the law of the kingdom of heaven. This is the Law of Moses reinterpreted by Jesus. For Matthew, Jesus is the new Moses, whose authority as lawgiver is supreme. Anyone who follows this law, who not only listens to his words but obeys them, will build his life on a secure foundation.

That foundation consists of obedience to the word of God spoken through Jesus. Matthew, writing for his own church, directs an attack against certain Christian charismatics who think that addressing Jesus as

"Lord, Lord" is sufficient for the kingdom of heaven. Even though they have gifts of prophecy, exorcise demons and work miracles, all this will not guarantee them admission to the kingdom. For all their presumed familiarity with the risen Jesus and exercising authority in his name, they are not known by the real Jesus: "I have never known you; away from me, you evil men."

Real foundation

Matthew warns his community that they might be fooling themselves when it comes to religious matters. By extension, the warning is addressed to us. None of us wants to build what we believe to be a sure religious structure only to discover that we have built a house of cardboard, which comes tumbling down because it lacks a real foundation. The prospect of getting it all wrong is frightening. The prospect of all our religious activity leading to Jesus' personal disapproval makes us nervous and worried.

But perhaps that nervousness and uneasiness will serve us well. It can send us back to the drawing-boad, to review the groundwork of our Christian life. We can all suffer from the illusion that the particular religious practices we follow serve to secure our place in the kingdom. We can say: "But I do the novenas to St Jude, Our Lady of Perpetual Succour, and St Joseph. I do the nine Fridays, the five Tuesdays and the six Saturdays. I've joined the charismatic movement and I'm involved in shared prayer, dialogue homilies, sunset meditations and sunrise exercises. I even diet for God during Lent. It must all add up to something."

The Gospel tells us that it does, if it is based on the sure foundation of the word of God. Just as a destroyer cannot command a lighthouse to move twenty degrees to the south, we cannot command the word of God to move out of our way. It is the word that shows us the way. Without it, we are all sunk.

Sabbath conflict

The importance of the sabbath

In Judaism the sabbath became a weekly observance to mark the close of the seven day week, a day when all Jews would abstain from any kind of work. It was a humanitarian custom, one which guaranteed slaves a rest from their labours; it was a religious festival, a hallowed time, since by abstaining from work, people imitated the sacred rest of God on the seventh day. Observance of the sabbath was a practice that distinguished Jews from foreigners; it became an important part of Jewish national identity. Thus they made the day holy by gathering in holy assembly in the Temple or the synagogue, to offer sacrifice or interpret the Holy Scripture.

The keeping of the sabbath was a sensitive issue in Jewish tradition, not least because it was the most distinctive of Jewish customs. It was one which, like Catholics going to Mass on Sunday, was known by people who knew nothing else about the religion. How important it was can be measured by the fact that two hundred years before Jesus Jewish fugitives in the first great national revolt had allowed themselves to be massacred rather than bear arms on the sabbath.

The sabbath marked the separateness of the chosen people, and to attack that sacred tradition was to attack the national image of the people. And to do that with any people is to court disaster.

Jesus and the sabbath

The purpose of the sabbath observance was positive: it was a release to benefit the people, not a device to trap them if they made the wrong move. The danger was that the purpose of the sabbath was lost under the weight of rigid prohibitions which the interpreters put on it. Among the thirty-nine types of prohibited work were reaping, threshing and preparing food – all of which we see the disciples transgressing in today's Gospel. Visiting the sick, clapping of hands, healing unless it was to save life were also included in the list of prohibitions.

The Pharisees appear on the scene to object to what the disciples are doing, and Jesus takes up the cause of his followers. He quotes the incident where David and his followers ate bread which was reserved for the priests; when David's human need was in conflict with the letter of the Law, the need was upheld (1 Sam 21:1ff). And there is a greater than David here. Jesus focuses the attention on genuine human need rather than observance of the interpretation of the Law. When people remember the Law, but forget what the Law is for, then they abuse the whole purpose of the Law, which is for the good of the people. No human regulation should override the fundamental purpose of the Law; and when the Law becomes a master to be served slavishly rather than a servant to be employed wisely, then it negates itself. It becomes a god which demands sacrifice, and the sacrifice is usually human.

Jesus further clarifies his position when he takes the initiative and heals the man with the withered hand on the sabbath. Again the Law is subservient to the pressing need of the individual. Jesus puts the case clearly when he asks whether the sabbath, which honours the work of God, is a day for saving life or destroying it. And the implication is that to refuse to save life is to destroy it. The argument is that when confronted with pain and loss, we cannot take refuge in the thicket of the Law to support our innocence. If we do, it will be our so-called innocence which will constitute the crime.

Law and responsibility

Jesus' argument makes pastoral sense: the Law can never liberate anyone from the responsibility of human concern – not even for a day. Jesus does not wait to heal the man on the morrow; he gives the man rest from his suffering on the day of rest. Where helping is concerned, there is no forbidden time. The only time for helping is now: tomorrow is always unnecessarily late. And if the Law justifies the wait, then the Law itself is in need of healing.

Jesus knew well that the Law can be used as a weapon as well as a shield, and when used as a weapon it is nearly always the poor and the broken who are the casualties. And Jesus knew that the Pharisees were using the Law as a weapon against him. While Jesus was healing the sick man, the Pharisees were plotting against Jesus. It is a strange Law which outlaws healing but permits plotting someone's death –strange work indeed for the sabbath. It is Jesus, not the Law, who heals the man. The case against Jesus is dismissed, but the case against the Law continues to be heard.

"For you and for all"

God and the Gentiles

Throughout this year the Gospel readings for Sunday are taken mainly from Luke's account. Unlike the other evangelists, Luke was not a Jew: he was a second-generation Christian who associated with those who had first hand knowledge of the original Good News. From his two-volume work, the Gospel and the Acts of the Apostles, Luke's character emerges as a highly sympathetic and sensitive person of wide interests. Both his books are dedicated to Theophilus, whose title ("your excellency") indicates that he held high office in the Roman government. Luke's purpose in writing was to supply Theophilus, and other Gentiles like him, with the truth about Jesus and the Christian movement.

Luke's interest in God's abiding concern for all the people, not least the Jews themselves, is evident throughout his writing. From the very beginning of his Gospel, Luke shows how the angels (2.14) and the old prophet Simeon (2:32) witness to the good news that God's salvation is for *all the people*. When John the Baptist begins to preach he quotes the prophet Isaiah, who longed for the day when "All flesh shall see the salvation of God." And when Luke gives Jesus' genealogy he traces the lineage not just to Abraham but back to Adam. Jesus is not only the fulfilment of Israel's destiny but the destiny of all peoples.

In today's first reading we have the earliest expression of God's salvation coming to the Gentiles. Solomon, who had built the Temple, entreats the God of Israel to listen to "foreigners". He makes the appeal that salvation will come to all Gentiles who will believe in the one true God.

The Roman centurion

In the Gospel it is a foreigner, a Roman centurion, who entreats Jesus' help, and he does this through a Jewish delegation. He is an officer in the army of Herod Antipas. Like a number of Gentiles, the centurion is attracted to Judaism – perhaps because of its worship of one God and its high moral standards. Not only is the centurion sympathetic towards the Jews, he is the one who built their synagogue. Now he seeks the help of the Jewish elders by sending them to plead with Jesus to heal his dying servant.

Jesus goes with the Jewish elders, but before he reaches the house he meets another delegation from the centurion – this time composed of his friends. They express the courtesy and faith of the centurion by telling Jesus that he has no need to enter a Gentile house; all he has to do is to speak his word and the dying servant will be cured.

It is fascinating to note that in Matthew's account of this story and in

John's the centurion/royal official goes to Jesus personally to seek his help. In Luke's account the centurion and Jesus never meet. Luke heightens the drama: the centurion stays at home and sends his word of pleading through others. *In Luke's story two words meet:* the expectant word of the Gentile and the powerful word of Jesus. Both words are effective. Jesus is astonished at the centurion's words: "I tell you, not even in Israel have I found faith like this." And the centurion's faith in Jesus is shown to be well placed: when the messengers return they find the servant in perfect health.

"For you and for all"
You can see how this story serves Luke's purpose in presenting Jesus, the Son of God, as the saviour of all peoples. Jesus is sent not only to the Jewish race but to the human race. He is the light to enlighten Israel and all peoples. The faith of the Gentile centurion proves to be a model for everyone in the kingdom. And it is not surprising that when Luke writes the Acts of the Apostles, the first Gentile convert to the Christian faith turns out to be a Roman centurion.

At each eucharist, before we receive the body of Christ, we pray like the centurion in today's Gospel: "Lord, I am not worthy to receive you, but only say the word and I shall be healed." We use the language of his expectant faith to express our own. The body of Christ, which is given "for you and for all", is offered as a source of new life.

As the centurion shared his faith, so we are challenged to share ours. Like him, we are asked to risk our faith in public. We remember with thanksgiving how others have shared their faith with us. Like the centurion's servant, who knows how each of us is helped by the faith of those who love us?

Mercy, not sacrifice

The mercy of God

All the writings of the Bible are consistent in celebrating the great truth of the mercy of God. When we speak about mercy, we usually mean clemency or forgiveness; the ancient biblical understanding of mercy, however, was much richer. Mercy conveyed both compassion and fidelity. Compassion was understood as tenderness in action, like the instinctive attachment of a mother for her child. Mercy was also signified as a relationship between two beings, one which implied fidelity. The mercy of God meant the loving kindness of God for his people, one which held him faithful to his covenant.

In today's first reading the prophet Hosea criticises the people whose loyalty to God's covenant has no substance. They take part in a ceremony renewing the covenant and are convinced that the Lord will come automatically, like the spring rains watering the earth. Hosea proclaims God's anger at this mechanical liturgy, which is unrelated to what happens outside the sanctuary. Hosea lists their wrongdoing:

> There is no fidelity, no tenderness,
> no knowledge of God in the country,
> only perjury and lies, slaughter, theft,
> adultery and violence, murder after murder. (4:2)

The prophet rejects the divide that exists between liturgy and life. Worship of God is intimately connected with how people behave outside the liturgical precinct. Because people's behaviour is opposed to God's covenant, their liturgy becomes unacceptable to him. What God wants is mercy, not sacrifice; true obedience, not incense. Sublime liturgy is no substitute for loving kindness.

The complaint of the Pharisees

If ancient Israel was too confident in the sufficiency of the sacrificial system, the Pharisees are too confident in the sufficiency of observance of the laws of purity. The Pharisees, the separated ones, prided themselves in keeping distance from sinners and avoiding table fellowship with such types. In today's Gospel they complain to Jesus' disciples about their master's habit of eating with tax collectors and sinners. Matthew the tax collector has just responded to Jesus' invitation to follow him by providing a banquet to mark the occasion. The new disciple's associates, described as tax collectors and sinners, eat with Jesus and his disciples. For the Pharisees, this is an occasion of ritual uncleanness.

The reproach of the Pharisees is met by Jesus' affirmation about his own prophetic mission: "I did not come to call the virtuous, but sinners." Jesus is free to call whom he pleases from those who know their need of him. As a tax collector Matthew was in the service of his country's conquerors and would have been despised as a traitor. He and his associates were classed with robbers and murderers, were forbidden to act as a witness in any case, and were debarred from the synagogue. These are Jesus' table companions; it is from this group that he calls Matthew. And Matthew becomes not only a follower of Jesus but a symbol of hope for all sinners who can have a new future with Jesus.

The requirement of mercy
Jesus shares nothing of the Pharisees' disgust of sinners. The Pharisees' obsessive concern for their own spiritual health has disabled them: they have no reach in them for those who need help and healing. Their orthodox piety, like the liturgy of ancient Israel, is unrelated to the needs of their neighbours. Jesus quotes Hosea when he says, "Go and learn the meaning of the words: 'What I want is mercy, not sacrifice'." The faithful love that God shows his people is to be reflected in the mercy that his people show their neighbour in need.

Jesus does not reject liturgy or orthodoxy but their dissociation from daily life. If liturgy and orthodoxy exclude God's people then they exclude God; both have to be open to Jesus' world of concerns. When we gather in community to celebrate Jesus as Lord, we also gather to acknowledge each other as brothers and sisters of the same Lord. When we celebrate God's loving kindness to us, we also pledge to give others reason to celebrate our loving kindness to them.

When that happens, mercy enlivens the heart of our liturgy and the heart of our life.

227

Family troubles

In the beginning, exile

All ancient religions and cultures have stories which portray the beginning of the world. The story of Genesis invites us to imagine a garden where there was complete harmony between man and woman, between human beings and God, between the human world and the world of animals and nature. In this garden peace presides over everything. But there is a veto on eating from the tree which yields knowledge of all things, including death. The woman is tempted by the serpent to eat the forbidden fruit; the promise is made that "your eyes will be opened and you will be like gods, knowing good and evil."

The offer made, the woman makes her decision: she takes the fruit, eats it, and gives some to her husband who does the same. Their eyes are indeed opened, but to no obvious advantage; rather than becoming divine they experience a rude awakening in beholding each other's nakedness. Their eyes testify to their knew knowledge and lost innocence: ashamed of themselves and afraid of God, they hide parts of themselves from each other and then hide themselves from God. Cover-up becomes the new governing rubric in relationships.

Genesis teaches us a profound truth about sin: when we sin we cannot face each other openly. Neither can we face God. In the story of Genesis God has to seek out the first human beings. So the question of a questing God: "Where are you?" When the man and woman finally emerge from their hiding-place they are banished from the garden into the chaos that exists outside its gates. The first human beings are the first refugees; they are banished from their home, condemned to make do in a world that is no longer under their authority. In the beginning there was the exile.

Jesus the refugee

That experience of distance from God dominates much of the prayer of the people of Israel. In the fulness of time, however, God sent his Son. But, as we learn from the Gospels, Jesus was not accepted by his own people. He was an exile in his own homeland, a refugee forced to flee from his own town. In today's Gospel, Mark tells us that Jesus' own relatives think that he is demented. No doubt they cannot understand why Jesus does the things he does, why he associated himself with so many undesirables. Jesus brings home the kind of people that any normal parents might regard with undisguised horror. The relatives make their disapproval known; they want to take charge of him. They do not yet understand that Jesus has his charge from someone else. His Father.

A second group arrives, lawyers from Jerusalem who oppose Jesus by claiming that he is possessed, that his miracles are performed through the power of the prince of devils. Jesus, in turn, registers his own complaint against his accusers: in ignoring the obvious good that he does, in twisting the truth to fit their own destructive prejudice they sin against the Holy Spirit. The scribes deliberately call good evil and evil good. That is sinning against the Holy Spirit because it is knowingly rejecting the light.

Finally, Jesus' mother and brothers arrive. They stand "outside". Jesus is surrounded by a group listening to his teaching. The family send in a message to Jesus; they do not join the circle of those listening to Jesus. When Jesus receives the message he asks: "Who are my mother and brothers?" He looks around at those sitting in the circle around him and says: "Here are my mother and brothers." Jesus makes it clear that his real family is determined not by blood relationships but by fidelity to the will of God.

Jesus' new family
Jesus is not disowning his family; he is acknowledging a relationship that is higher than the physical bond. He establishes a new family of relations, no doubt hoping that his own relatives, like everyone else, will come to accept him for who he is. Clearly his relatives have trouble accepting the change that Jesus has undergone – from becoming a village carpenter to a mighty prophet. As John says in his Gospel: "Even his brothers did not believe in him." (7:5) Jesus has to face that misunderstanding and rejection. It is part of the cross he has to bear.

Things change for the better after Jesus' death and resurrection. When Luke tells of the birth of the Church in the Acts of the Apostles, he shows Jesus' disciples praying "together with several women, including Mary the mother of Jesus, and with his brothers." (1:14) Jesus' blood relatives are shown to have joined forces with his new family of faith. They are no longer "outside" the circle; they are united with the followers of Jesus who have come to recognise him as their Lord. That recognition made in faith is central to the life of the Church.

The Good News is that we are part of Jesus' new family. We are his mother and brothers and sisters – if we do the will of God. Doing the will of God may alienate us from our family and relatives, but the witness of Jesus always points us towards a more important relationship. That is why we gather each week as a family of faith: to bless our Father and gain strength from our brothers and sisters.

Otherwise Engaged

Serenity or emptiness

It is a Saturday afternoon in a quiet square in London. A quiet man named Simon is alone in his living-room and is carefully unwrapping a new set of opera records. He handles them with the care of a man who is clearly longing to listen to them. He walks over to the very expensive hi-fi set which dominates the room and puts the first record on, listens, and adjusts the level. He then settles himself on a large sofa. The sound of Wagner fills the room.

Then there is a knock on the door. The knock is the first of many, and a whole series of people keep knocking in the form of an upstairs lodger, a worried brother, a troubled friend, a sad old school mate, and finally Simon's wife. They all try to engage Simon in the cares of their world. He is polite and listens to them all; but he can hardly contain his indifference about what is going on around him. He simply wants to listen to Wagner. Eventually his wife becomes furious at his indifference and quotes her new friend's diagnosis of Simon:

> He says you're one of those men who only give permission to little bits of life to get through to you. He says that while we may envy you your serenity, we should be revolted by the rot from which it stems. Your sanity is of the kind that causes people to go quietly mad around you.

The story of intrusions and accusations make up the play, *Otherwise Engaged,* by Simon Gray. The questions it raises are all too real: is it good or bad to be like the character Simon and protect yourself from being drawn into the confusing and untidy world of other people? When people come to you, of course you are never rude: you conceal your dismay behind courtesy and wait quietly for an ending. At the end of the play when Simon does sit down to listen to his new recording of Wagner you wonder a question: is the music of Wagner all he needs for a serene life or all he has left of an empty one? Why should we be bothered? Why not be otherwise engaged?

Paying attention

In today's first reading we meet Elijah, the great Hebrew prophet. He was trying to escape from a terrible famine and drought when he met a widow at the city gate of Sidon. She was preparing the last meal for herself and her son before they resigned themselves to death. She had enough to bother about without worrying about Elijah's hunger, but he told her not to be afraid, for her flour and oil would not be spent until the drought ended.

From then on Elijah lodged in the upstairs room as a favoured guest. But when the widow's son died the distraught woman blamed Elijah. He did not run and leave her in her misery; instead he stretched himself over her son and prayed that God would restore the dead child to life. The child revived and the relieved mother declared that Elijah truly was a man of God.

That story is the background for Luke as he tells us how Jesus raised the widow's son to life. Jesus is approaching the town when he sees a funeral procession coming out of the town gate. The dead man is the only son of a widow. She is supported in her plight by a large group of her neighbours. Nobody asks Jesus to do anything. Jesus could just watch the procession heading for the grave without getting involved in other people's tragedy. No one screams at him to do something. He is not expected to be drawn into the widow's experience of loss. He has his own schedule to keep.

But Luke tells us that Jesus is moved at the sight of the widow. Jesus moves first because he is first moved. He tells her not to cry and then gives her a reason not to cry. As his hand touches the stretcher carrying the dead body, the funeral procession comes to a stop. At his word of command, the dead man sits up and begins to talk. Jesus gives him to his mother. The people respond to this by praising God and recognising how God has visited his people in the person of Jesus. Truly Jesus is the prophet of God.

The moved mover

In both these stories from scripture there are people who bother about other people. There are people who do not distance themselves from other people who are in pain. The poor widow shares the little she has with a hungry prophet; he in his turn shares the touch of life with her dead son. In the Gospel the neighbours of the widow of Nain declare their sympathy for a woman who is now very alone in life. At the heart of it all there is the figure of Jesus who does not let loss and grief pass him by. He is not the unmoved mover. He is reached by the pain of other people. He is not otherwise engaged. By the power of his word there is new life and new hope.

What do we do when we are confronted by the concrete suffering of other people? How do we react when the music we are listening to is interrupted by an anxious visitor? What happens when we seem to be overwhelmed by people eager to share their confusion? Do we put on a louder record? Are we otherwise engaged? In the end we must allow the Gospel to question us.

The Twelve

Family history

The head of a prominent family in Boston was retiring after a long and distinguished career in publishing, and his family wondered what to give him as a gift to mark the occasion. After much discussion they agreed to present him with a history of the family, that being one of his lifetime interests. The family employed a well known biographer to do the research and write the story. The book was to be printed at a private press.

The biographer interviewed members of the family, consulted old records and letters, and started to shape all the information into a readable story. The daughter of the family, whose idea the whole venture was, shared a worry with the biographer: "It's my great-uncle George," she said. "He was the black sheep of the family and no one ever speaks about him. He died in the electric chair after he had been found guilty of murder. If you're going to write an accurate history, you can't miss him out. Maybe you could minimise the embarrassment."

The biographer assured his worried client that he would take care of great-uncle George and still write an accurate history of the family. When the book was finally printed, she was relieved to read: "Uncle George occupied a chair of applied electronics at a famous government institution. He was attached to his position by the strongest of ties, and his death came as a real shock."

The Twelve

Writing up family history could present problems for all of us; creative writing might appear an appealing option when we come to certain names. When Matthew writes his Gospel he displays no interest in the biographical details of the apostles. The same is true of the other evangelists. The twelve apostles, the first members of the Christian family, appear in the Gospels as little more than a list of names. Apart from Judas, the only four who stand out among the Twelve are the two sets of brothers, Peter and Andrew, James and John.

In the New Testament story of the early Church Andrew disappears from the scene; James is martyred in the early 40s; John is identified as the beloved disciple in the Fourth Gospel. Peter is the only member of the Twelve about whom we have any significant knowledge.

Although each Gospel states that Jesus chose twelve apostles from among the larger group of disciples, we know little about them as individuals. There is even some variation in the four lists of their names. Perhaps the evangelists were deliberately avoiding what we would call "personality cults". The apostles were chosen by Jesus to be his accredited witnesses. Their experience of Jesus who walked the roads of Palestine was unique in the history of the Church; but they were important *as apostles* in the measure that they pointed others to the person of Jesus. This might explain why, although they were revered in the early Church, there was no organised nostalgia about their time.

The Church moves on in the life of faith; each community of believers must give birth to its own apostles. The apostles of every age must be as self-effacing as the apostles of the first age: they must point others to the living Lord.

The call to everyone

We are all called to holiness, we are all called to follow Jesus, we are all called to make Jesus known to all peoples. Like the chosen people of Israel we are counted a kingdom of priests, a consecrated nation. We cannot spend our time in nostalgia, looking back to the days when Jesus walked the roads of Palestine with the Twelve. We must minister to our own time, take responsibility for our own mission. This is a matter for all of us. As Cardinal Newman wrote:

> He called us first in baptism; but afterwards also; whether we obey his voice or not, he graciously calls us still...Abraham was called from his home, Peter from his nets, Matthew from his office, Elisha from his farm, Nathaneal from his retreat; we are all in course of calling, on and on, from one thing to another.

The call takes us on and on, not back and back. It is a call to future. This doesn't mean that we cannot look back at our own Christian family history, in the course of which we will bump into a legion of great-uncle Georges; rather, it means that we refuse to be fixated by what has been. Our responsibility is today and tomorrow.

The growth of the kingdom

The limits of language

Sometimes when we try to find words to express something important to us – like how we felt when we fell in love – we soon bump into the limits of language. We try to express ourselves as clearly as possible, all the time aware that our words seem to diminish the truth we are struggling to make known. We falter, we stammer, we keep on trying. We say: "If only I had the right words ... What I'm trying to say is ... Well, it's something like ... Sort of ..." As T.S.Eliot observed:

> It's strange that words are so inadequate.
> Yet, like the asthmatic struggling for breath,
> So the lover must struggle for words.

When we want to explain anything, we have to say how it is *like* something else. All good teaching opens up the unknown by starting with what is known, because to speak about what is strange we have to begin with what is familiar. When Jesus speaks about the kingdom of God he never says what it actually is, he speaks about what it is like. Words cannot capture the mystery of the kingdom, but they can paint a picture of what the kingdom is like.

So it is that Jesus uses parables when he teaches the crowds. In today's Gospel Mark tells us: "He would not speak to them except in parables, but he explained everything to his disciples when they were alone." This doesn't mean that Jesus gives one message to the crowds and another to his disciples. By definition parables are never enough; there is always more to say because the subject can never be exhausted. Besides, the followers of Jesus have a bigger investment in getting his teaching right. Their shared commitment involves living out their understanding of what Jesus teaches.

The like of the kingdom

In the first parable of today's Gospel Jesus compares the kingdom of God to what happens when seed is sown by a farmer. Once the seed is sown, the farmer waits for harvest time. The cycle of growth follows its own secret rhythm; how it all happens the farmer does not know. Even though nothing much seems to be happening, the miracle of growth is taking place. The farmer cannot improve the crop by staying awake at night and worrying; the seed is nurtured in its own silence. The harvest will not be rushed; neither will the kingdom of God be advanced by those restless for instant results. Just as the harvest comes in its own time, so the kingdom will reach its completion in God's appointed time. It is God's kingdom, not ours.

In the second parable Jesus compares the kingdom to a mustard seed that grows into the largest shrub so that the birds of the air can shelter in its shade. In the ancient world the size of the mustard seed was a byword for the smallest and most insignificant thing anyone could imagine. According to the Koran: "God will bring good and evil to light, even if they are no bigger than a mustard seed." In Jesus' parable the contrast is made between the smallness of the seed and the exuberance of its growth. Unremarkable beginnings can make for mighty achievements. Littleness is no index of importance. The small mustard seed grows to become a shelter for all the birds of the air.

It is worth noting that the phrase "birds of the air" was a traditional Jewish expression for the Gentiles, all the non-Jews. In today's first reading, for example, the prophet Ezekiel speaks of the universal openness of God's welcome in the image of the tree where all birds can find a resting place.

> Every kind of bird will live beneath it,
> every winged creature rest in the shade of its branches.

Similarly in Jesus' teaching: the kingdom of God is open to all peoples. The greatness of the kingdom, which grows from such a small beginning, is for the benefit of all peoples; *it is not the exclusive domain of any one flock.*

Rejoicing in God's work

When we think of the small beginnings of Jesus' ministry in Galilee to the spread of his message throughout the world, we can appreciate the vast growth that has taken place in history. The seed which Jesus planted has indeed grown: who could have guessed in Galilee in 27AD what would emerge from Jesus' ministry? From small beginnings – Jesus' preaching, his attention to the afflicted, his quiet transformations, his unusual company of followers – there did indeed arise the greatness of the kingdom of God.

God's work still continues, not only in the Christian churches but in people and places unknown and unrecognised by us. At the heart of the familiar God works in so many ways. His kingdom grows of its own accord; how, we do not know. This doesn't mean that we can be complacent, but it does save us from cynicism and despair. We have reason to rejoice in God's work, that his kingdom still attracts and welcomes so many different people. We are part of that kingdom.

And we shouldn't be surprised if we seem to be sharing the shade with some really strange birds.

Showing love

Hospitality

In the Gospel of Luke you will notice that Jesus is never far from a dinner table. This is not because Jesus is always hunting for food but because he is always hungry for fellowship. Throughout his ministry Jesus uses the social occasion of a meal as a graced opportunity to challenge some people with his teaching and to comfort others with his healing. Jesus always shares more than food with his table companions; he shares himself. And in sharing himself he is the source of conflict for some and good news for others.

Jesus is severely criticised for making a habit out of eating with sinners. His chief critics are the Pharisees, whose name means "the separated ones". The Pharisees are frankly appalled that Jesus openly associates with sinners; they are careful to segregate themselves from sinners lest they become unclean. When it comes to a choice of dinner partners Jesus is highly indiscriminate: he'll eat with anyone! He doesn't demand that people first mend their ways before they eat with him; rather, Jesus uses the meal as a *way of coming to fellowship with him.* In the context of the meal Jesus brings sinners to a true understanding of their worth before God and offers them peace through the forgiveness of their sins. In that sense a meal with Jesus is always an opportunity for change and renewal.

As a guest at a public dinner Jesus would expect to receive three customary marks of hospitality. There was the kiss of greeting which was the normal courtesy between a host and guest. This was a sign of welcome and mutual acceptance. The guests would then have their heads anointed with oil. Originally this anointing was reserved for kings to mark them as sacred – as we heard in the first reading when King David was anointed. However, this practice later became a way of marking guests as sacred while under the protection of their hosts. Finally, when guests entered a house they would leave their sandals at the door, and their feet would be washed as an act of service. Thus welcomed, the guests would then take their places at table.

Jesus in the house of Simon

In today's Gospel Jesus is a guest in the house of Simon the Pharisee. The first thing Jesus does is take his place at table: the three marks of hospitality are missing. These are supplied by an uninvited guest, a woman whose reputation is well known – she is probably a prostitute. She comes prepared to minister hospitality to Jesus and she lavishes on him the fulness of her care. Her tears wash his feet which she dries with her hair;

she covers his feet with kisses; she anoints them with the ointment. In all this she does not say a single word. Her language is in her body as she demonstrates her love for Jesus.

The host looks at this extravaganza and is shocked. Remember that Simon is a Pharisee, "a separated one": for him contact with sinners means uncleanness. And here is this lady of the night slobbering over Jesus. But Simon is cautious: he talks to himself about it. He wonders if Jesus really is a prophet if he can let this woman with a bad name *touch* him. That is Simon's complaint. It is very difficult to kiss people or anoint them or wash them without touching them! Simon has avoided all three and, therefore, has not touched Jesus.

So Jesus confronts Simon with the real question: *"Simon, do you see this woman?"* That is the problem. Simon does not see a woman: he sees a bad name; he sees a whore. True, the woman does have a bad name. But is that all she is? Because something is true it does not mean that it is the whole truth. We can use the truth about people to ridicule them and destroy them. When we use a truth about people to make them seem cheap we hide a larger truth that makes them worthy. There are ways of using the truth to destroy the truth. And there is a massive difference between telling the truth and telling the truth with love. Simon sees a destructive truth and fastens onto it.

Showing love

So Jesus tells Simon that he prefers the extravagant love of a streetwalker to his untouchable welcome. From Simon there was no kiss, no anointing, no washing. Nothing. He has no reach in him. In contrast the woman is free to show love because she has experienced the forgiveness of Jesus. "The man who is forgiven little shows little love." Simon is not free to *show love* either to Jesus or the woman. And when the story ends the conflict is not resolved between Simon and Jesus. The woman goes in peace. She is the kind of woman who makes up Jesus' support group as he continues his wandering mission.

In dining at Simon's house Jesus has confronted his host with the question of how he sees other people. That question is addressed to us also. Do we see other people in such a way that encloses them in their wrongdoing? Like James Joyce who accused some of his friends in Dublin: "You hold my follies hostage." Or do we see others like Jesus does – in such a way that allows them a future? Forgiveness promotes change in people; it funds them for a new future. Let our sharing around the Lord's table help us to do that.

Intimidation and worth

Facing intimidation

No individual, no group, no nation likes being pushed around. We all like to arrive at our decisions without being intimidated by a stronger party into submissive agreement. Even if our decision turns out to be a blunder, we tend to prefer the freedom to make our own mistakes over being forced to do what others judge to be right. When someone stands at your door and makes you an offer, while his armoured tanks take up position at your gateway to concentrate your attention, that is usually understood as an offer you can't refuse. But some people do refuse. And depending on your point of view, they are madcaps or martyrs.

The point is illustrated well in a story about Philip 11, who was king of Macedon around the middle of the fourth century B.C. Philip was the kind of leader who always managed to claim by conquest what he failed to win by diplomacy. He had subdued all the major Greek city states, all of them except one. Sparta had remained stubbornly independent and Philip decided to make them an offer they couldn't refuse. This was his message: "You must submit without further delay. If I bring my army into your land, I will destroy your farms, I will slay your people, and I will raze your city." The Spartans' reply was one word, taken from Philip's threat: *"If"*. They had no intention of being intimidated by Philip, and he decided to leave them alone.

The disciple's response

When push comes to shove, people react differently. In today's first reading Jeremiah refuses to be intimidated by terror from every side. That doesn't mean that the terror doesn't get to him – he is a prophet, not a robot; it means that he has no intention of allowing the terror to write his script and dictate who he is. Jeremiah has been abandoned by all his friends who now try to discredit him. He is thrown into prison for his preaching, and the army council threatens him with death if he doesn't change his tune. But Jeremiah refuses to be bullied into agreement because he believes that "the Lord is at my side, a mighty hero". What keeps Jeremiah sane amidst all this persecution is the profound belief that God cares for him. And, less spiritually, the frank hope that God will clobber all his enemies in good time!

In today's Gospel Jesus appears in strong voice against intimidation. He does not disguise the truth that his disciples will be confronted by those who threaten, bully, and intimidate others into submissive agreement. Jesus' advice is clear: not only does he want his disciples to refuse to submit to the merchants of death, he tells them not to be afraid of them: "Do not be afraid of those who kill the body but cannot kill the soul".

The followers of Jesus are going to come face to face with terrorism, with the kind of violent intimidation that gives them an offer they can't refuse. Jesus tells them to refuse it. They have a real choice: disown Jesus and love, or profess him and face certain death. That is a fearful prospect. Yet Jesus says: "Do not be afraid." How can the disciple *not* be afraid? What power is available to the disciple to overcome that fear?

Fear versus worth

Jesus argues that the Father cares deeply for the true disciple. He takes the example of a sparrow, which was regarded as almost worthless. Sparrows were sold in the market-place as food for the poor – two for a penny, and five for two pennies. The fifth was thrown in for nothing. "Yet," Jesus says, "*not one* falls to the ground without your Father knowing. So there is no need to be afraid; you are worth more than hundreds of sparrows." Jesus' point is very important: do not be afraid; *you are worth*. According to Jesus your own sense of worth is strong enough to overcome your sense of fear.

If you believe deep down that you are worthless, there is no point in defending anything. Anyone can intimidate a sparrow; anyone can intimidate those who regard themselves as worthless. But if you believe that *who you are* and *what you stand for* add up to some worth, then you will be willing to take on those who would rubbish you and your values. That is Jesus' point. Your real worth before God is a more powerful force than your real fear of your persecutors. That sense of worth can outdistance the hate of all your oppressors. That is why Jeremiah and Jesus and all the Christian martyrs can face their persecutors with awesome courage: they all know that their true worth can never be killed. God's everlasting love is the only real offer they can't refuse.

The challenge to confess the name of Jesus is one that is issued to every generation and every Christian. The intimidation we experience may not be one of terror and persecution, but it can still be felt when we come face to face with those who resent the Gospel. When it comes to Christian values, the raised eyebrow and the scornful silence can be ways of trying to brow-beat the believer. Eyebrow-raising and crucifixion are different only in the degree to which they display disapproval.

We can face that kind of intimidation only when we believe in our worth before God. Our real sense of worth can overcome our real fear. The Father offers us his everlasting love. When we keep that offer in mind, all the other offers begin to look very tacky indeed.

Storm in Galilee

Galilee

Most people who visit the Holy Land on pilgrimage are struck by the beauty and simplicity of Galilee, the region where Christianity was born. For many pilgrims, the most memorable time of their visit is a quiet walk on the shores of the Sea of Galilee or a journey by boat between the lakeside towns. In the stillness you can hear the echo of so many of Jesus' words which were spoken around the shores of the lake. The surrounding countryside gives you a sense of place for many of the familiar stories about Jesus, and your faith and imagination can fill in the deserted places with people who still long to see Jesus. In a curious way, even though Galilee is a foreign place to visitors, Christians are struck by a sense of belonging to this place. Visiting Galilee is like going home and discovering it for the first time.

After he left his home in Nazareth, Jesus settled in the town of Capernaum on the west shore of the Sea of Galilee. Unlike Nazareth, which was isolated from the main roads, Jesus' new home was on the main route from Damascus to Egypt and would have served as a good base for his ministry. Capernaum was a customs post: merchants and traders would have stopped there, no doubt exchanging goods and stories. For the locals, the warm climate and the fertile soil made for plentiful crops, including figs and grapes and olives. In addition to all the fruit-growing and farming, the lake industries included trading, tanning, fishing and boat-building.

Most of Jesus' ministry in Galilee was around the shores of the lake. He spoke of the sea, the land around it, the people who lived in the region. He used Peter's boat as his pulpit when the crowds became too large, and he crossed the lake many times – no doubt with Peter as his captain.

Fear in a storm

In today's Gospel Jesus suggests to his disciples that they cross the lake to the other side. The sun has set; soon it will be nightfall. The pressing crowds are left behind, but what lies ahead is no picnic. The lake is normally calm, but because of its position – about seven hundred feet below sea level – it is subject to sudden windstorms which sweep down from the surrounding hills, rush through the narrow gorges that break upon the lake, and whip up the saucer-like sea. This is what happens in today's Gospel: the rapid change of weather causes the waves to break into the boat so that it starts to fill.

In the midst of this chaos Jesus is fast asleep on the small bench at the back of the boat, his head on a cushion. The disciples have no intention of letting Jesus doze through a disaster; the boat is sinking and, perhaps like most fishermen, the disciples cannot swim to save their lives. They wake Jesus with an accusation: "Master, do you not care? We are going down!" Jesus wakes up, rebukes the wind and commands the sea to be quiet. After rebuking the tempest Jesus rebukes his disciples for their large fear and little faith. In the midst of the calm there arises the central question about Jesus: "Who then is this?"

The question about Jesus' *identity* arises from seeing what Jesus actually *does*. People begin to wonder about *who* Jesus is when they witness *what* he does. If everyone had been washed overboard, for example, the question would not have arisen. The question is posed; the answer, however, will be understood only after the resurrection.

Lord of chaos

We believe with St Mark that the answer to the question "Who is this man?" is that he is the Son of God. That proclamation of the identity of Jesus is at the heart of our Christian creed. But the question remains whether our faith in Jesus will stay with us even during threat and danger and storm. The experience of the disciples on the Sea of Galilee is a graphic one: they feel all at sea, they feel up to their neck in difficulty, they feel powerless to withstand the environment of threat. For sure, their experience is not alien to us.

We believe that Jesus accompanies us on our journey to God, that he is "on board" with us. Sometimes, when we see such disorder and chaos around our world, we might wonder if Jesus has chosen to sleep through disaster – even though we know that his presence is no insurance against our own fear and anxiety. To journey with Jesus is to journey through storms, not around them. The peace of our Galilees will be disturbed. But we know that the disciples of Jesus went on to face shipwreck and hardship and rejection. Ultimately, many of them came face to face with a violent death and martyrdom. What kept them going is what keeps us going: a strenuous belief that Jesus is Lord of all chaos, a stubborn faith which tells us that there is no storm that will not be stilled at last by the peace of his presence.

In the meantime, we struggle on and hold on to our hats!

Discipleship: the identity of the master

Associating with failure

The scene is a desolate street in London. It is a wet, murky night and the rain is bouncing off the street. A few lights glimmer from some shabby houses nearby as a man walks down the street with his coat collar high around his neck. He shivers with the cold and pulls his wet coat around his body. He comes to a stop under a lamppost. Somewhere a dog whines in the background and a door bangs shut. Our hero takes a packet of cigarettes from his pocket, and as he lights one he exhales a long self-comforting whiff of smoke. He smiles to himself, slowly gathers himself together and makes his way through the deserted streets. And a voice says from the screen: "You are never alone with a Strand cigarette."

When that advertisement first appeared on television in the early sixties many people thought that it was the opening of an Alfred Hitchcock thriller – an unidentified man slouches down a street and pauses to light a cigarette. It worked as an interesting advertisement for a new cigarette. Everyone who saw the advert remembered it, but very few people bought the cigarette. It was an early case of "nice video, shame about the song". Strand cigarettes were taken off the market in a matter of weeks because they were associated with a lonely man, a deserted street, a dismal night, and a run-down area. Who wants to associate themselves with that package of neglect? Nobody. People didn't buy the cigarette because they didn't want to buy into the shabby world associated with it.

Suffering for identity

Nobody wants to follow in the footsteps of someone who is heading nowhere. Few people are willing to risk following a person who looks as if he is shaped for failure; few people want to join a movement that looks primed for collapse. We know from experience that in the presence of some people our life is fuller and richer when we're with them. They make an impact on us and we enjoy being in their company. So when a small group of men left the security of their familiar ways to follow Jesus, their new direction indicates the impact Jesus must have made on them. If Jesus made no impact on them they would have no reason to follow him.

We tend not to seek out those people who, as one observer put it, "when they enter a room it's like someone just left." When Jesus entered a room something happened. He generated something in people. He gave them hope. He gave them new life.

When people make an impact on us we become interested in who they are and we want to know more about them. Because of the impact Jesus made on people, many became interested in discovering who Jesus really was. *Because of the impact of his presence, people became interested in the question of his identity.* It is a measure of the effect Jesus had on people that they were concerned to get his name right. (That is why when people can't remember our names we begin to wonder what impact we had on them!)

In today's Gospel we see Jesus actually promoting the question about his own identity. He risks asking his disciples who people really think he is. Asking that question is always dangerous because the answers you are likely to hear will rarely match the answers you hope to hear. People think that Jesus is John the Baptist, or Elijah, or one of the ancient prophets come back to life. The crowds seem to think that Jesus is really someone else – an old prophet having another go! Clearly the replies are not encouraging.

After getting horrendous replies to his first question Jesus moves on to ask his own disciples: "Who do you say I am?" The question we tend to ask, "Who do you think you are?", doesn't put the questioner at risk. Jesus, however, risks his question. Peter answers that he believes Jesus to be the Christ. But, given the popular overtones of this title within a tradition which spoke of triumph rather than suffering, Jesus insists that he has to suffer for his identity. Because he is who he is, he cannot avoid suffering. It's not that Jesus plans it; rather, he knows that suffering is inevitable if he is to face the future honestly. And he states further that those who become his followers will have to suffer for their identity like their master.

Willingness to suffer
Most people like to keep the subject of suffering outside normal conversation. Jesus brings it to the centre – no doubt because the question is central for himself. He refuses to cover up the truth; he will not cheat his followers with a banal optimism that refuses to face the real. He does not seduce his disciples with empty promises but opens them to the question of their own willingness to pay the price for who they are as his followers.

The disciples still follow Jesus. It is a measure of his continuing impact that they stay with them. The disciples are not following someone who is programmed for failure: they are not idiots. They follow someone they sense is not kidding them; someone who faces the real with enormous courage and commitment. Every commitment to love means a willingness to suffer for a while. And it's that kind of commitment that Jesus still expects of all who follow him.

Hospitality and its reward

The tradition of hospitality

The modern traveller has become accustomed to the easy availability of roadside cafes, motorway services, motels, country inns, city hotels. In the days of Elisha the prophet there were no guest-houses or fast-food stops. Those who travelled beyond the territory of their own family or tribe had to depend on the hospitality of strangers to survive. As we see from today's first reading Elisha is lucky in his travels: he meets a woman of means who invites him to break his journey and eat at her house. The hospitality must have been good because Elisha makes a habit of stopping there on his travels.

The woman sees that Elisha is a holy man, and she asks her husband's permission to build an attic on to their house so that the prophet can have his own room when he stays with them. The husband must have agreed because the next we hear about Elisha is that he is resting in the upper room. The prophet wants to repay the hospitality of his hostess and he asks his servant for some ideas. His servant tells him: "Well, she has no son, and her husband is old." The servant is astute: he knows that the woman is entertaining this holy man because she hopes that she will receive the special blessing of a child. Her hope is fulfilled. The new guest will be her child. And soon the attic of the prophet will become the nursery of the newborn.

The woman receives her reward. In the words of Jesus in today's Gospel: "Anyone who welcomes a prophet because he is a prophet will have a prophet's reward; and anyone who welcomes a holy man because he is a holy man will have a holy man's reward." The woman's reward for welcoming a holy man is the best she can have: a family.

Jesus and hospitality

In the tradition of tribes who move from place to place to find new grazing lands for their cattle, hospitality becomes a matter of life and death. Their modern equivalent might be the migrant workers who leave home to find jobs in different areas and countries. All these people depend on welcome if they are to thrive. In the sacred tradition of Israel hospitality was regarded as one of the chief responsibilities of a caring people. The stranger, the outsider, the wayfarer, anyone outside his home territory – all were regarded as people who needed special care. The reason for this was enshrined in the Law: "If a stranger lives with you in your land, do not molest him. You must count him as one of your own countrymen and love him as yourself – for you were once strangers yourselves in the land of Egypt. I am Yahweh your God." (Lev. 19:33-34)

One of the important values of the tribe is the fact that its social security is the tribe itself: everyone can look to the tribe for help. But when the tribe becomes *settled,* people's security moves away from the tribe to their own work and their own land. They can no longer look to the tribe because everyone is looking after his own property! By the time Jesus is born, the people of Israel have long settled into the land of Palestine. They are no longer nomadic; they are landed. And their values have changed.

As soon as Jesus is born Matthew portrays him in the Gospel as the one who is born into a place where he is not accepted: he has no security, and must be taken to Egypt for safety and shelter. At the beginning of his life Jesus is marked as the one who must depend on the hospitality of others. As an adult Jesus learns that he cannot depend on the acceptance of his own family when he begins his ministry as a prophet. He takes to the road with his own band of itinerant supporters. As they leave their own region of Galilee behind them, they become a travelling people who have to depend on others' hospitality to receive them and welcome their message.

Hospitality's reward

When Jesus is welcomed into towns and villages by people who see him as a holy messenger from God, the people receive a holy man's reward: the poor hear Good News, the sick are healed, sinners come to know the forgiveness of God. The people receive their own reward for *the hospitality of a faith that welcomes Jesus.* Their hospitality is not a matter of bed and breakfast and goodbye; it is the act of opening their heart to the visit of God who comes in the person of Jesus. Jesus' presence rubs off on them; they catch something of his goodness and values; they are changed because of his visit.

When Jesus and his disciples faced closed doors and closed hearts in other towns, all that the people receive is a cloud of dust.

The ultimate support that Jesus looks for is our openness to the Gospel. His promise stands good for all who listen to his word today. Jesus doesn't want us to give an offering to his messengers in the hope that they will go away and leave us in peace. Supporting your local prophets means first listening to what they say. But it also means taking practical responsibility for supporting them in their ministry. One of the characteristics of the Church is the generosity of the people towards their ministers and so many pastoral projects. Jesus says that responding to all this has its own reward. People won't lose by their generosity to the cause of the Gospel. As Jesus tells his messengers: "Anyone who welcomes you welcomes me; and those who welcome me welcome the one who sent me." In the end, it is God who is our guest.

Desperation and faith

The quality of desperation

In today's Gospel Jesus returns to the west shore of the Sea of Galilee, a journey from Gentile to Jewish territory. He is on home ground again. On his return a large crowd gathers round him, and out of the press of people one person comes forward, a Jewish official. Jairus has an important position in the local community, supervising services in the synagogue; but he hasn't come to Jesus to talk about the process of ritual. In spite of his religious status, Jairus falls at the feet of Jesus and begs him to save the life of his twelve-year old daughter, who is seriously ill.

Jairus is a desperate father: his love for his daughter makes him a beggar, craving the help of the one person who can restore her to full health. His dignity is cast aside; his longing is expressed in his whole body fallen at the feet of Jesus. Such is the quality of his desperation. Jesus says nothing, he promises nothing. His action speaks for itself – he goes with Jairus. And the crowd press forward into the new drama.

The walk to Jairus' house is interrupted by a secret sufferer. Out of the press of people a woman comes up behind Jesus. She suffers from an incurable haemorrhage, an affliction that makes her, and anyone she touches, ritually unclean. She has already exhausted all attempts at a natural cure, and the long and painful treatments have exhausted her savings. She is all spent. All she has left in life is a saving dream that Jesus can cure her. She jostles her way through the crowd that is heading somewhere else, hoping that if she can touch Jesus' clothes, that contact will be enough. Such is the quality of her desperation. Such is the quality of her faith in the power of Jesus.

The quality of Jesus' healing

When the woman touches Jesus' clothes, she senses that she is cured of her complaint; but she is not allowed to disappear back into the crowd. Jesus insists on asking who touched his clothes. Clearly Jesus doesn't want to be treated like a mobile relic, a magical touchstone that requires no relationship. He continues to look around the crowd. His question and his look bring the woman forward. She is frightened, falls at the feet of Jesus and tells him the whole truth. It is only when she meets the person of Jesus that her action is approved and her cure confirmed. The purpose of the personal meeting is not to humiliate the woman but to commend her for her faith and let her go her way in peace.

The bleeding of twelve long years has now stopped, but that good news is interrupted by messengers from Jairus' house with the news that the life of twelve short years has come to an end. The beloved daughter of Jairus is dead. This time, Jesus does speak to Jairus: "Do not be afraid; only have faith." Taking with him only his inner circle of disciples, Jesus goes to the house and is greeted by the wails of the mourners. When he expresses his belief that the girl is not dead but asleep, the mourning becomes mockery. The scoffers are thrown out; only the girl's parents and the three disciples accompany Jesus into the girl's room. This small community of faith assembles to face the large loss. At the command of Jesus the girl rises from the bed of death, and Jesus tells the astonished witnesses that a snack for the girl would not go amiss. For Jairus, after all, there was no need to be afraid.

The quality of our faith
It is worth dwelling on the detail of the stories because they give us an insight into the mystery of Jesus. They tell us about a man who has a fierce kinship with those who suffer, who does not disappoint those who look to him for help. Like Jairus, there are many people who suffer on behalf of their loved ones and who feel powerless when they are confronted by the pain of those they love. Unlike Jairus, there are many parents who have attended the funeral of their young children

There are mothers and fathers who continue to grieve secretly, turning to their memory of loss long after everyone else has forgotten the source of their pain. Their children are no less precious to Jesus than the daughter of Jairus. To Jesus, these children are asleep in death. As the risen Lord he will come to awaken them. That is our faith. That is why the words addressed to Jairus are addressed to all of us: "Do not be afraid; only have faith."

The Gospel story of Jairus' daughter is given to all of us as Good News. It is offered to us *today* to nourish our faith in Jesus, to enliven our hope in his power over death itself. We know there are those who mock that belief, professional mourners who believe that death must have the last word in every human story. There is no place for that attitude in the community that gathers in the Lord's name. In this eucharist we support each other in our shared faith, we confront real loss with Jesus at our side. And when the loss is deeply felt, we too need to hear the words of Jesus: "Do not be afraid; only have faith."

Discipleship: leaving home

Called away

Some people don't like travelling too far from home. At home they feel secure in familiar surroundings where they can relax in the easy comfort of what they know. Home is where they are walled, roofed, lit, warmed, loved, fed, located and identified. They are happy where they are and the prospect of leaving all this – to seek food, shelter, welcome and companionship from strangers – is one which holds no appeal. Why bother taking to the road where "home comforts" will be few?

On the other hand, some people regard home as a wall-papered trap. There are those who believe that it's more difficult to break out of some houses than break into them! They feel tied down, constrained. Their longing is for leaving. They tolerate the present as a necessary evil. The world beyond the front door has an appeal that makes home seem dull and boring. They are happiest when they're on the road, with home over their shoulder.

Perhaps most of us are somewhere between these two groups: we enjoy both the security of home and the adventure of travelling. So when things go wrong while we're travelling we can console ourselves by remembering our home base, and when we're feeling confined at home we can look to the leaving. But what happens when we feel *called to* something that *calls us away from* the world of the familiar? What happens when we are invited to make a choice that means leaving those we love? These questions bring us to the heart of today's Gospel.

Competing loyalties

Jesus himself has answered a call that has taken him away from his own family and home in Nazareth. From the moment Jesus begins his public ministry his family fades into the background. His mission projects him onto the world scene and he finds that those who are really related to him are those who hear the word of God and keep it. His new family is connected directly to his mission. At the beginning of today's Gospel we see Jesus putting his own region of Galilee behind him as he resolutely begins the journey to Jerusalem. The beginning of that journey is the turning-point in Luke's Gospel: Jesus has started down a road that will lead to the ultimate challenge of his mission: the cross. If Jesus is to be faithful to his mission, he cannot turn back.

It is in the context of the journey to Jerusalem that Luke shows how Jesus faces a number of questions. The first thing Jesus meets on the road is the inhospitality of the Samaritans who regard Jerusalem as the wrong address to be heading for. Why should they be gracious to a group of Jews who are travelling to a theological mistake? Two of Jesus' disciples think that the way to respond to religious difference is to incinerate your opponents. Jesus doesn't think much of a pastoral strategy that cannot be distinguished from a holocaust. His answer is to keep moving and not be distracted from his ultimate goal. Jerusalem.

As they journey on, Jesus is questioned by three prospective disciples. Jesus warns the first that to follow him means following an itinerant who has nowhere to lay his head – a clear warning that inhospitality is going to be a regular problem. The second and third questioners want to follow Jesus but have prior claims: one has to bury his father while the other has to say goodbye to his parents. In Judaism family loyalty is a matter of religious duty. But Jesus is seen to say "no" to these previous attachments which call people back to the home they have left. There is a dramatic urgency in Jesus' challenge: the disciple has to decide which has priority, loyalty to family or loyalty to mission. To be freed for his mission the disciple must be freed from past ties. For the sake of the kingdom he must be prepared to sacrifice security, duty, and affection.

Resolving to continue

At first, Jesus' response seems very harsh but we must appreciate that Luke is presenting the radical requirements of following Jesus as Jesus begins his own journey to Jerusalem. And Luke does that in a way which highlights the conflict both master and disciple face. The commitment of the disciple must be single-minded because *all disciples must face their road to Jerusalem.* And the probability is that they will have more to deal with on their journey than the inhospitality of some villagers!

Through Luke's Gospel Jesus is seen to warn all disciples that it will take enormous courage and resolve to keep travelling along a road that leads to hardship and trial. He hopes his followers will have the resolve to keep going.

When Jesus arrives at journey's end and the cross looms large we see that he prays for the resolve to continue. He too is tempted to give up and return to the quiet security of Galilee. But he literally hangs in there. The journey to Jerusalem which he begins in today's Gospel is seen as a route which all his followers have to take. No matter where we live. It is not a journey that is plotted through a map; it is an inward journey that is plotted through our experience. For each of us it is our journey to God in the footsteps of Christ.

"My yoke is easy"

Failure

In his campaign for the presidency of the United States, the socialist reformer Norman Thomas had many distinguished supporters, but he lacked the popular backing essential for his election to office. Looking back at his record of failure, he commented: "While I'd rather be right than president, at any time I'm ready to be both." But he never was. Like many people, he failed to achieve his goal; but, unlike many people, he refused to allow his personal failure to destroy his sense of purpose.

Although Jesus never ran for office or sought to join any religious or political party, he had to face rejection and failure. From the Gospel we learn that Jesus' ministry in his own province of Galilee has been largely unsuccessful; but this is something he comes to accept as the will of the Father. Jesus is able to face the failure of his work because his inner purpose is to do his Father's will. He has something to fall back on. To face failure with no inner resources is to face an empty self. But Jesus sees in his failure a particular wisdom: that his Father is making a positive choice to reveal his truth to the little ones, while hiding it from the legion of the self-important.

Perhaps Jesus thought that the rabbis, who referred to themselves as "the disciples of the wise", would be quick to see in his teaching the wisdom of God. Perhaps he expected that those who had been educated in the word of God would be first to recognise that word when it bumped into them. But Jesus is frankly disappointed. There is, however, a teaching in his disappointment; he learns that his Father overlooks the learned and the clever to settle his favour on the simple, on those who have received no formal training in the Law. When it comes to revealing who he is, the Father looks to those who exercise no power and enjoy no prestige in the community. He looks to people like the disciples.

"My yoke is easy"

Those who are regarded as experts in the word of God, the scribes and the Pharisees, often criticise Jesus and his disciples for openly flouting the Law. Jesus heals on the sabbath and he refuses to check his disciples when they do what is considered work on the sabbath. He knows that there are many people who regard the 613 commandments of the Law an insufferable burden to bear, and who are treated as religious outcasts because they are unable to bear the full yoke imposed by the lawyers.

Remember that in Jesus' time there are whole groups of people who are dismissed as sinners because they follow what are regarded as dishonourable callings – people who lead life-styles that do not permit them to observe the small print of the Law. Among these groups are shepherds, donkey-drivers, pedlars, tanners, and tax-collectors. All these people are deprived of civil rights, forbidden to act as a witness in court, and refused entry into the synagogue. They are at the bottom of the social heap. Ignored. But Jesus has a word for them and for all those who are bowed down by an interpretation of the Law that leaves them mugged into senselessness:

> Come to me, all you who labour and are overburdened, and I will give you rest. Shoulder my yoke and learn from me, for I am gentle and humble in heart, and you will find rest for your souls. Yes, my yoke is easy and my burden light.

Jesus has no intention of doing away with the Law; but he refuses to support the lawyers who spend their time manufacturing new burdens for broken people. Jesus offers all these people an invitation: "Come to *me*...learn from *me*...and you will find rest for your souls." Jesus makes *himself* the centre of his own teaching. He is the Wisdom of God, and personal fidelity to him will be the mark of the true disciple. God has chosen him to be the one who enshrines the fullness of revelation and who embodies the new Law of God.

Only Jesus

It is interesting how this problem appears again in the early Church when the first council is called in Jerusalem to decide if new converts have to obey the Law of Moses. It is Peter who settles the matter by arguing *against* those who insist that Gentile converts must fully obey the Law: "It would only provoke God's anger by putting a yoke on the neck of the Gentiles which neither our fathers nor we have been able to bear." (Acts 15:10) Peter admits honestly that the disciples of Jesus could not bear the yoke of the Law: *why should they demand of others what they have never managed to do themselves?* Peter concludes by focusing on the person of Jesus: "Remember we believe that we are saved in the same way as they are: through the grace of the Lord Jesus."

Peter's argument "silences the entire assembly." That is the effect of his honesty on all present. Peter keeps the memory of Jesus at the centre of his argument: like Jesus, he utterly refuses to be a party to imposing laws without taking into account people's capacity to keep them. Peter keeps the memory green of the disciples' own inability to live that Law. Now they have a new Law that is found in the person of Jesus himself. That is why all of Peter's preaching directs his hearers to the person of Jesus. Jesus did not say: "Come to the Law, and you will find rest for your souls." He said" "Come to me...learn from me...and you will find rest." And that is what we do in this eucharist.

Content with weakness

Facing the locals

When people from obscure backgrounds suddenly emerge as important public figures, journalists and television crews often seek out the family and neighbours of the new star to discover what they think of the local hero. Mixed impressions are usually given: delight is shown, congratulations are forthcoming, surprise is admitted, polite disbelief is registered, resentment is uncovered. Some neighbours, afraid of admitting their surprise, will declare confidently that they saw it all coming: if they didn't spot it first, it isn't worth knowing. Others are reluctant to acknowledge local greatness; they urge caution and hint that nothing much will come of all the hoo-ha.

In today's Gospel Jesus returns to his home place of Nazareth. This is not a social visit: like other towns in Galilee, Nazareth has to hear the Good News of the kingdom. When Jesus teaches in the local synagogue, many of the townspeople are astonished at the performance. They wonder at the origin of Jesus' teaching and the nature of his wisdom, as well as the miracles that are done through him. From the unanswered questions about Jesus' wisdom, the neighbours move to more familiar territory and focus on what they do know about Jesus. Whatever their wonder, they are not going to allow Jesus' wisdom to interfere with their memories of him.

So, the neighbours support each other in a chorus of distractions. Irrelevant issues are solemnly brought to the centre of attention: the job Jesus worked at, his mother, the presence of his sisters. Of course, the neighbours have a vested interest in focusing on who Jesus was rather than the Jesus that confronts them now: it's easier having a carpenter around the shop than a prophet loose in the town. So, once a carpenter, always a carpenter. Memory proves to be a useful fiction: it keeps Jesus at the level where they can handle him safely.

Mark summarises the reaction of the Nazareth community to their fellow citizen: "And they would not accept him." For them, the sheer ordinariness of Jesus cancels out his new wisdom and works. Nothing kills like frozen familiarity.

The reaction of Jesus

How does Jesus react to the locals? He says to them:

> A prophet is only despised in his own country
> among his own relations
> and in his own house.

This is a hard saying. The other evangelists soften it saying, "No prophet is accepted in his own country." In Mark's version Jesus is rejected by his own relations and by those in his own house. Mark has already told us that Jesus' relatives believe him to be out of his mind (3:21): now the rejection seems to be complete.

Jesus' experience of rejection in Nazareth renders him powerless to do any miracle among his own people. This is an extraordinary statement about the human Jesus: people's lack of trust limits his ministry. Jesus is profoundly affected by the way people react to him. He is not a robot, programmed for flawless performance, indifferent to all responses. Distrust disables him. So he moves elsewhere, refusing to be enslaved by his failure to reach his own people. And he never returns to Nazareth again.

Content with weakness

By coping with discouragement and failure, Jesus points beyond himself to the power of the Father. The cross of Jesus becomes the most striking symbol of weakness pointing beyond itself, beyond the brokenness of Jesus to the glory of the resurrection. New life emerges out of dereliction. This theme, so constant in the writing of Paul, is applied by the apostle to his own life.

Paul shares a very personal experience. He has come to learn that his own weaknesses are not a problem for God, as if God has no truck with poor achievers. Paul's human limitations, which refuse to go away, not only force him to be more realistic about himself, *they also force him to change his image of God.* Paul discovers through his own handicap that God's grace does work through human frailty: "So I shall be very happy to make my weaknesses my special boast so that the power of Christ may stay over me, and that is why I am content with my weaknesses...For it is when I am weak that I am strong."

Being content with our weaknesses is not an attitude that comes easy to most of us, educated to be content with nothing less than perfection. We might still suspect that God disassociates himself from those who are beaten down by their own limitations; but, like Paul, we have to learn that God isn't like that. Failure and human weakness give God immense scope to act out his own purposes.

Nazareth was the beginning of a new road for Jesus. Paul's thorn in the flesh was the occasion for a whole new way of looking at God and at himself. And we know from experience that when we admit our failures and limitations, that exercise in honesty can mark the beginning of a new understanding. If God can take failure in his stride, we might even end up boasting about God's fantastic style!

Discipleship: going forth

Constructive dissatisfaction

Many stories of adventure begin because someone is dissatisfied with life. Whatever the hero is looking for, he knows that it is not where he is. Here is not enough. That puts where he lives under question. If someone tells you to *seek* for justice, the presumption is that justice is not *here* now. The seeker has to make a choice: does he stay where he is and learn to live with his dissatisfaction, or does he leave home and search for what he hopes to find? If he stays he will be incomplete, but if he goes he risks losing everything he has. That conflict is important because without it many people would never start off! Being dissatisfied can be a very constructive experience: it can move people to seek for what is best.

Often when our hero leaves home he is poorly prepared for his journey. The temptation is to take everything he can carry – including a parachute, just in case he has a spectacular fall! But if he takes everything he has, he will discover only what he has already known. Dorothee Soelle puts it well when she writes:

> He who takes the most with him and leaves little behind, and therefore remains much the same as he was before, has less chance of finding what he seeks...He who does not give up anything cannot find anything...To find what is sought requires the complete renunciation of this world; compromise brings destruction.

That radical challenge to leave behind the guarantee of shelter and support and set off without provisions is one which rings out in today's Gospel. And Jesus believes that his disciples can take that risk for the sake of the kingdom of God.

Setting out and coming back

When Jesus sends out the seventy-two you might wonder how ready they are for the demanding task ahead of them. There is a picture of Jesus who must trust his followers if his outreach is going to be extended. He has to organise a movement because he doesn't have all the time in the world. Jesus must depend on the various talents of his followers; he must depend on their understanding and their resolve to get it right. Perhaps if we were in charge of that first outing the seventy-two would still be waiting to graduate! There is a clear urgency about the task: Jesus says, "Start off now".

As he gives his missionary instruction Jesus seems under no illusion about the territory: compared to the wolves roaming around, his own crowd are like lambs. He charges them to lead the radical lifestyle of the wandering preacher who must face homelessness and renunciation of family and property. They are not to be encumbered by extras nor be delayed by roadside chats. When they enter a house they should bless it with peace, and if they are welcomed they should not try to adjust the menu or fix better accommodation: all that takes time!

To tell a group of Jews travelling in foreign territory that "you must eat and drink what is set before you" is a radical demand indeed. In all this Jesus tells his disciples that they must depend on the *shalom* they bring, the peace of the kingdom. If they have no money they cannot stay at the local inn when people reject them; they must travel on until they are made welcome. They depend on the *shalom* they bring, and they depend on the hospitality of the strangers who receive them. They have something to offer the people in their teaching and healing; in return for that *work* the people have something to offer the disciples in welcoming them. Hospitality, therefore, is not just a social virtue; it is a response to the word of God which seeks to enter. So inhospitality to the disciples is a rejection of the word of God.

On their return the disciples are delighted that their mission has actually worked! Their joy demonstrates that people do welcome the word of God and *that the word of God is their real resource for mission.* Jesus counsels them to rejoice not because their mission has worked but because their names are written in heaven. If they rejoice only when their mission has worked, what happens to their joy when their mission fails? Jesus faces that question fully when he says at the Last Supper:

> 'When I sent you out without purse of haversack or sandals, were you short of anything?' They said 'No'. He said to them, 'But now if you have a purse, take it; if you have a haversack, do the same; if you have no sword, sell your cloak and buy one.'

There will be a time of crisis when the disciples can no longer depend on the hospitality of those who yearn for peace. In that time the disciples will have to hold fast to words of God like those we heard in the first reading: "Like a son comforted by his mother will I comfort you." There will be times as we know when the scorpions will bite us, and when the wolves will have their day. That is when we need to believe what Jesus tells us: that our names are written in heaven. There, nobody can wipe them out.

The seed that struggles to grow

The creative word of God

From time to time we all bump into the truth about ourselves that there is gap between what we say and what we do, between what we profess to be and how we actually behave. Often we notice this inconsistency more easily in others. One of life's disappointments is to discover people who will promise you anything without holding themselves accountable for what they say. Their word is worthless. But sometimes our own words are no bargains either: we lie, we draw back, we decorate the truth with so many disguises that it becomes unrecognisable.

In sharp contrast to the fragility of the human word, the word of God is seen to be always effective because of who God is:

> God is no man that he should lie,
> no son of Adam to draw back.
> Is it his way to say and not to do,
> To speak and not to fulfil? (Numbers 23:19)

For God, to speak is the same thing as to do, to promise is the same thing as to fulfil. God's word creates what it says; he speaks the world into existence; when he says "Let there be...", there is. From today's first reading we hear about the great power of God's word. As the rain waters the earth and makes all things grow, so the word of God accomplishes what it is sent to do. It is not an empty word; it is a powerful word which brings about the purposes of God. As God's word made the first beginning, so it also makes new beginnings.

The word of Jesus

One of the ways the evangelists show that Jesus speaks the word of God is by showing us how Jesus speaks with authority, unlike other religious leaders. So we see Jesus in the Gospels speaking a word that is seen to be effective. In his healing ministry he *speaks* people better – so much so that the centurion can send him a message: "Say but the word and my servant will be healed." Jesus commands; he rebukes; he orders. When he speaks, something happens. People who are open to his creative word are seen to leave his presence changed: something happens to them. In that change they see themselves differently, they see Jesus in a new light, they can face the future with new hope.

But there is another word that Jesus speaks, a word that is *offered* to others and depends on their response if it is to be truly effective. This word is like a seed that is sown by Jesus, a seed that depends on the condition of the ground if it is to grow and bear fruit. This we hear in the parable of the sower.

In the interpretation a variety of responses to the word of God is explored through four types of hearers. Firstly, there are those who hear the word without understanding it, and the word is easily taken from them by those who oppose its power. Secondly, there are those whose first enthusiasm for the word cannot withstand trial because the word has never taken root in them. Thirdly, there are those who hear the word but are overcome by a litany of distractions and lose it. Finally, there are those who hear the word and understand it, who take it to heart and make it their own, and yield a harvest through their persistence.

The last group of hearers are the model for true Christian discipleship: in giving the word of God a secure place in their heart, in making efforts to understand it, their co-operation ensures that this word becomes an event in the Christian life. Discipleship enables the preached word to become a fruitful *thing,* not just a word.

Underlying the parable there is a telling confidence: in spite of all the obstacles present in the various types of soil, the good news is that the seed does succeed in growing and producing a rich harvest. The word of God preached by Jesus, despite apparent failure and repeated opposition, will indeed enjoy great fruitfulness – symbolised by the hundredfold of the harvest's yield. The message of Jesus will be heard and enacted; the word of God risked in so many unlikely places will not be an empty word but will bear fruit.

Our own response

Today the word of God is still scattered generously, with throw-away style. God still risks his word, hoping that people will take to it, welcome it, and make it their own. How would we describe our own responses to the word? Does it take root in us? Do we make serious efforts to understand it and know what it's asking of us? Do we welcome it with great show and then go our own sweet way anyway? Do we hear it and then smother it with our own concerns? Only we can answer the questions when we allow the parable to question us. And no one can do that for us.

But we should be patient with ourselves. Like all seeds, the word of God takes time to grow. The sower knows that he has to wait for the weather, the secret workings of the soil, the slow thrust of life, before he can see the crops emerge. The sower cannot deny the time the whole process takes. God who sows the seed knows what it means to plant his word in different people in different situations. It all takes time. But if we take the time to nourish the word, God will wait on the gradual process. It might take us a lifetime. But if we allow the seed to struggle to grow in us, we will grow too. Eventually the word of God and our own word might become one. And that would be a harvest indeed.

"Go, prophesy to my people"

Confronting division

In today's first reading we are introduced to one of the great characters of the Old Testament, a layman called Amos, farmer turned prophet. Amos came from a small village in the hill country of Judah, about five miles southeast of Bethlehem. He experienced a call from God – what form that took we do not know. All we know is that the experience wrenched him away from his work on the land, impelling him to work as a prophet in another country. Amos was a simple man, but he was no simpleton with straw coming out of his ears. He was a critical observer of the social and religious scene, the first prophet to commit his work to writing, a telling communicator who knew how to proclaim his message with biting clarity.

The time was around the middle of the eighth century B.C. Amos was sent to the Northern Kingdom, Israel, which had reached the summit of its material power and prosperity. The land was full of plenty, the cities were elegantly built, the palaces were strongly defended and the rich had their summer and winter villas adorned in costly ivory. At the same time there was widespread corruption and immorality. The poor were afflicted, exploited, even sold into slavery. There was an absence of justice and pity in the land: the judges were corrupt, the innocents were betrayed.

In the midst of all this luxury and misery, religion flourished. People thronged to the shrines at festival time to practice elaborate ritual. Amos regarded the religious services as a counterfeit enterprise abhorrent to God. So he spoke the word of God:

I hate and despise your feasts,
I take no pleasure in your solemn festivals.
I reject your oblations,
and refuse to look at your sacrifices of fattened cattle.
Let me have no more of the din of your chanting...
But let justice flow like water,
and integrity like an unfailing stream. (5:21-24)

Staying loyal

So it was that the outsider Amos used his talent for disturbing the peace. He went to the shrine of Bethel, which was the sanctuary of the king, a chapel royal. There he came face to face with Amaziah, the priest of Bethel. He was exasperated by the preaching of Amos and accused him of being disloyal – an old trick to discredit the prophet who opposes the status quo. The royal functionary telegrammed the king: "Amos is plotting against you...The land is unable to endure all his words."

In today's reading the priest tells the prophet to go home and leave the royal sanctuary in peace. Amos replies with the story of his own experience. He has never belonged to the official guild of prophets. He was a shepherd; now he is God's spokesman. The single cause of this radical change was a compelling event: "The Lord took me." To Amaziah's command: "Go home", Amos rejoins with God's command: "Go, prophesy to my people Israel."

Amos states simply that he did not become a prophet by self-appointment or by royal appointment; he was conscripted by God for the declared purpose of announcing his message. Therefore, he is not torn between two competing loyalties: his loyalty to the word of God has clear priority over any other loyalty in his life.

The authority of the Gospel

In today's Gospel Jesus summons the twelve apostles and sends them out on a missionary tour. Like the prophet Amos, the chosen followers of Jesus have to carry the word of God as a challenge to others. In that mission the apostles have the authority and the power of Jesus. They have to travel on that.

So, they are not to rely on their own resources but on the authority that has been given to them and the hospitality that will be offered them. With no bread and no money, they have to depend on the kindness of others: *that vulnerability makes their message their real resource.* If they have bread to eat, it means that people are not only hospitable to them but to the word they preach. If they are not accepted, they have no option but to move on. And when a town rejects their message, the apostles are to shake the dust from their feet – a symbolic act performed by strict Jews returning to Palestine after journeying abroad.

Both the prophets and the apostles have to rely on the authority and the power given to them. In taking to the road, they will test their message on foreign soil; they will see if their conviction can pass beyond the boundaries of national difference and personal indifference; they will discover if their vocation can survive the official stamp of disapproval. For it is not only the message that is being tested, it is the messenger.

This process continues every day in the life of the Church and the world – every time a preacher braces himself to declare the word of God, every time a Christian goes public on the values of the Gospel, every time any man or woman takes a stand against injustice.

Discipleship: the virtue of disloyalty

Difference

It's more than likely that we've all had someone say to us: "Yes, but you must realise that we have our own way of doing things here." One of the principal ways any group maintains its identity is by asserting its difference from other people. That pride in difference shows itself in badges and flags, attitudes and beliefs, collected stories and traditions. Whatever the nature of the group – a tribe, a trade union, a political party, a religion, a race – loyalties within the group can foster the growth of its members. But intense loyalty can also promote hostility towards outsiders.

The real danger comes when members of one group believe that *their difference gives them the right to lord it over other people.* That usually spells violence. In Shakespeare's *The Merchant of Venice,* the old Jew, Shylock, asks the question why a Christian can mock him and scorn his nation:

> And what's his reason? I am a Jew. Hath not a Jew eyes? Hath not a Jew hands, organs, dimensions, senses, affections, passions, fed with the same food, hurt with the same weapons, subject to the same diseases, healed by the same means, warmed and cooled by the same winter and summer as a Christian is?

Old Shylock protests that Christians aren't *that* different from Jews. There is no difference between people – of race, of colour, of creed – that gives any group the right to rubbish other people. But can you maintain the identity of your group while still respecting the dignity of outsiders? If you need help from those outside your group, does that say something about your group's claim to self-sufficiency? These questions make for today's Gospel.

Extending the boundaries of compassion

In the parable of the Good Samaritan Jesus faces the old antagonism between his own people and the Samaritans. As John says in his Gospel: "Jews have no dealings with Samaritans." The Samaritans were despised as the half-caste descendants of northern Jews who had intermarried with foreign settlers. That racial difference made for religious difference, and when the southern Jews returned from exile in 520 B.C. they refused to allow the Samaritans to help them rebuild the temple. In response the Samaritans established their rival priesthood and temple. The breach was soon complete. Each group's loyalty to its own tradition served to nourish its hostility towards the other group.

The Jewish lawyer's question, "Who is my neighbour?" gives Jesus the opportunity to confront this old hostility. For the traditional Jew, to love one's neighbour was understood as loving someone who belonged to the Jewish community. A neighbour was someone within the boundaries of your own racial and religious circle. To love outsiders while rejecting their beliefs was totally alien to their tradition.

Jesus' story tells of three travellers on the same road who see the same naked and wounded man by the roadside. The question is: how are they going to react to what they see? Will their seeing oblige them to act? Two Jewish officials, a priest and a Levite, continue their journey as if the purpose of living is to hurry on. At this point in the story, the hearers who thought of their community as priests, Levites, and Israelites – like many Christians think of the Church in terms of bishops, priests, and lay people –were probably expecting the hero to be an Israelite. But the shock to the system is that the hero is a despised Samaritan, the one who is publicly cursed in synagogues. The one whose evidence is not acceptable in a court of law. He is the one Jesus holds up as the neighbour in the kingdom of God. He is the one who went beyond the limits of religion to extend the boundary of compassion.

Love as disloyalty

In the parable Jesus questions his own people's attitude to the Samaritans. When someone says to him, "Yes, but we have our own way of doing things here" Jesus' response is to question that way. In the parable he is questioning an attitude that has been taken for granted for hundreds of years, one which is enshrined in tradition and law. And Jesus is challenging the lawyer *to be disloyal to that tradition.* If your religious tradition invites you to despise other people then you must be disloyal to your tradition. If loving your neighbour means being disloyal to your tradition then disloyalty itself becomes a virtue. The ultimate loyalty is love.

We know from experience the weight of inherited hostility. We know that to help some people is not only an act of love but an act of defiance against the bigotry that passes for religion. Jesus tells us that as his disciples we must be disloyal to those who would educate our hate. If religion needs hate to nurture it, who needs that kind of religion? The Gospel comes to challenge our hate and to promote our love. And that challenge is always to extend the boundaries of our love to include our traditional enemies. If the Gospel does not liberate, then Christ died in vain. He died so that *everyone* could have life in his name.

Leaving the final judgement to God

Instant judgement

Ibn Saud, the first king of Saudi Arabia, was faced with a problem of judgement. A woman came to him demanding the death sentence for a man who had killed her husband. The man had been in a palm tree gathering dates when he had slipped and fallen, killing the woman's husband beneath. Ibn Saud inquired: was the fall intentional? Had the two men been enemies? The widow knew neither the man nor why he had fallen, but, in accordance with the law, she demanded the blood price due to her. "In what form will you have the compensation?" Ibn Saud asked her. The widow demanded the head of the guilty party. The king tried to dissuade her, pointing out that she needed the money and that the execution of this man would benefit neither her nor her children. But the woman was insistent, arguing that it was not right that the man who had killed her husband should be allowed to live in the community of good people. He should be rooted out instantly.

Ibn Saud said: "It is your right in law to demand compensation, and it is also your right in law to ask for this man's life. But it is my right in law to decree how he shall die. You shall take this man with you and he shall be tied to the foot of a palm tree; then you yourself shall climb to the top of the tree and cast yourself down from that height. In that way you shall take his life as he took your husband's." The king paused for a moment. "Or perhaps, he added, "you would prefer to take the blood money?" The widow took the money.

The good hope

That demand for instant judgement, for rooting out those who have done harm in the community, for bringing the last judgement into the present tense, is something that is seriously challenged in today's scripture. The author of Wisdom tries to answer the pressing question: why does God allow the bad to flourish? Why is God so patient and moderate with Israel's enemies? He argues that God's moderation is not a result of weakness: his justice, after all, has its source in strength. But how does God actually use this sovereign strength? The answer is that he *disposes of it* in favour of governing with "great lenience". So God's mercy is heaped on everyone in sight, even on traditional enemies. And in this there is a purpose:

> By acting thus you have taught a lesson to your people
> how virtuous man must be kindly to his fellow men,
> and you have given your sons the good hope
> that after sin you will grant repentance.

The people are asked to share in the same spirit of God and act with kindness to their fellow human beings. The argument is that God's leniency will give the people of Israel the good hope that when they wrong God, they too will surely benefit from his forgiveness. This same hope is enshrined in the Our Father: "Forgive us our trespasses as we forgive those who trespass against us."

The scandal of God's patience and forbearance with wrong-doers appears again in the Gospel. The kingdom of heaven is compared to a farmer who is confronted with a serious problem: his field is alive with wheat and a poisonous weed, darnel, which can only be distinguished from the wheat when the growth is advanced. The farmer's servants want to weed out the darnel, but the farmer tells them to leave it alone; he is worried that uprooting the weeds will endanger the wheat. He orders that no premature attempt be made to separate them. Thus both the wheat and the darnel are allowed to grow, and only at the final harvest are they separated.

A mixed community

The message of the parable is something that Jesus lived throughout his ministry. He reached out to all sorts of people, mixing with whores, priests, crooks, scribes, politicians, children, tax-collectors. Religious separatism was something Jesus refused to advocate, making it his business to seek out and save the lost. The Pharisees, those whose very name means "the separated ones", criticised him for associating with the wrong crowd. But Jesus knew that all communities are a mixture of the good and bad, the crooked and the cracked. And further that it isn't always easy to tell which is which. In the end Jesus is the one weeded out by the authorities and thrown on to the killing fields.

The message of the parable still challenges the Church today. It is not the place of the Church to set up inquisitions, support witch hunts, organise purges to free the field for its own approved supporters. The Church is not God. *As Christians we have no authority to pronounce the final judgement on anyone.* The last word cannot be said about anyone until death, and then it is God's part, not ours, to say it. Paul underlines the same point when he tells the church in Corinth: "There must be no passing of premature judgement. Leave that until the Lord comes". (1 Cor.4:5)

Paul, like Jesus, was aware that we can get it terribly wrong about people. There might be another story, another perspective, another time. After all Paul got it terribly wrong about Jesus when he went around weeding out his followers. Paul himself changed from being a real weed to a real apostle, even though some people thought that the last word had been said about him. But if the final judgement is precisely that – *final* – the good hope is that there will be some changes before then. And that hope should never be denied anyone, least of all by the followers of Jesus.

Service and solitude

Aiming for rest

In the year 1799 Napoleon Bonaparte returned to Paris after an unsuccessful campaign in Egypt. To compensate for loss abroad, he overthrew the executive power at home and was appointed First Consul. In his new capacity, Napoleon often worked a sixteen hour day, and he expected that the Council of State would have the stamina and the zeal to match his own. One night when the councillors began to doze off, he reprimanded them: "Let's keep awake, citizens. It's only two o'clock. We must earn our salaries."

These superhuman efforts were much applauded by Napoleon's supporters and admirers, but not by the royalists. One admirer, singing the First Consul's praises, remarked: "God made Bonaparte and then rested." An old count commented: "God should have rested a little earlier."

If God has his time for rest and relaxation, his Son seems to have more difficulty managing the same in today's Gospel. The apostles have returned from their missionary campaign; there are no casualties. After Jesus hears their report of what they have done and taught, he says to them: "You must come away to some lonely place all by yourselves and rest for a while." This is to escape the traffic of people coming and going, which is so constant that the apostles can't find time to eat. So, Jesus and the apostolic party climb into a boat and aim themselves for peace in some lonely place.

The schedule of care

Lonely places are hard to come by when people are intent on keeping you company. Jesus and the apostles become fugitives, but their escape into privacy doesn't come off. If enjoying privacy depends on the ability to control the amount of access people have to you, Jesus is not very able in that direction. But he is up against impressive opposition. The people can easily see where the boat is heading and their energetic need gets them there first.

Jesus doesn't have the heart to play hide-and-seek with the crowds. The apostolic party disembarks. They give themselves up. The game is over.

So much for their attempt at a package holiday. But by not turning the boat around, by not sending away the besieging crowds, Jesus gives his apostles a profound teaching on the tenderness of God for his people. He demonstrates the truth of his own teaching, "Ask, and you will receive. Seek, and you will find." The crowds have asked and they do receive; they have sought him out and they do find him. When the crowds seek Jesus at a time when Jesus is seeking privacy, there is no question which need has priority. The schedule of the crowd becomes more important to Jesus than his own.

That's the kind of person Jesus is; that's the kind of God Jesus reveals; that's the kind of pity Jesus hopes his own apostles will show in their time.

Rest and recovery

Of course, this Gospel passage is not an argument against apostolic havens or holidays; rather, it does serve to highlight the urgent love of Jesus for people in need. Jesus' original plan for the apostles underlines the importance of spending time apart and the value of rest and recovery. The apostles are not automatons; they have to rest sometime. If no rest is ever taken, if no time is ever reserved for recovery and renewal, the apostle will simply end up a burnt-out case with nothing to offer but his guilty exhaustion. And that offer is no good to any crowd.

We all need to get away, to be by ourselves, to have our time of quiet. We can easily accept the impulse to go off by one's self, so long as it is expressed by writers and artists and others. For many of us, however, solitude is commonly seen as a state of pain. It is something to run from as we hunt down companionship and things to do. Let one half of a married couple retire to another room, shut the door and gaze fixedly at a far wall, and the other half is likely to pursue with the anxious question, "Are you sick?" or "Why are you mad at me?"

Sometimes when we find ourselves alone we don't know how to cope. Like the New York journalist who discovered how little prepared he was to cope with solitude when he was left rattling around his apartment for a weekend while his wife and children were away on a trip. "It wasn't so much a question of liking or not liking it," he recalled, "but simply feeling incompetent at it."

Solitude can make us uncomfortable; resting can make us feel guilty, especially if we have been brought up to honour a work ethic that equates idleness with laziness. Stillness is something we have to learn in time. For God speaks to us not only in the urgent cries of other people but also in the "still, small voice." And to hear that voice, we have to be at one with the stillness.

Discipleship: welcoming the Lord

Gods as guests

In Greek mythology the story is told how the father of all gods, Jupiter, once visited the earth with his son Mercury. They disguised themselves as weary travellers and knocked on many doors in their search for shelter. Time after time they were ignored and left in the street. Eventually they came to a small cottage which was the home of an old couple Philemon and Baucis. When the two travellers knocked on the door, it was soon opened and they were welcomed inside. The old man filled a bowl with hot water so that his guests could wash; the old woman put on her apron and started to prepare a meal.

While all this was happening the conversation flowed easily but no identities were revealed. When all was ready, the hot stew was placed on the table, with a pitcher of wine. But as the wine was drunk it renewed itself in the pitcher, and the old couple were struck with terror when they realised they were entertaining gods. They implored forgiveness for their poor hospitality but the gods invited them to make a wish. After they discussed it between them the old couple expressed their shared prayer: "Since we have passed our life together in love and concord we wish to die at the same time so that neither of us has to live in grief." Their prayer was answered, and when they grew very old they both died in peace.

Welcoming the Lord

The story of a god who comes among his people and is disguised as a traveller is one which appears in many religious traditions. In today's first reading we hear how Abraham does more than entertain three strangers; in welcoming them he is really welcoming the Lord. Abraham displays the warmth of Bedouin hospitality as he rushes to meet the travellers, bows profoundly, washes their feet, invites them to rest while he attends to the menu, and then waits on them at table. As a Bedouin wife Sarah prepares the meal and then waits inside the tent while the others eat outdoors. In her culture men and women do not eat together. But from where she is she hears the good news that God will visit her again next year and she will have a child. So the hospitality of the old couple is rewarded as God answers their deepest desire.

In the imagery of Genesis the Lord God walks and talks and eats with his chosen ones. By depicting God in human form the writer shows us in a simple way a truth about almighty God – how he is involved in the life and struggle of his people. But when we move to the Gospel and see Jesus visiting people and talking with them, we see that this is not imagery but the literal truth. Jesus is not disguised as a human being; he is a human being. As St Paul says in today's second reading: the mystery of God, which was kept secret for endless ages, is now revealed in Christ. In the person of Jesus, the Lord really does walk among his people. In Jesus we can see the face of the living God.

In telling the story of Jesus' visit to his women friends, Luke underlines the importance of the guest: Martha addresses Jesus as *Lord* while Mary sits at the *Lord's* feet. This is not a casual visit. In response to Jesus' presence, Martha becomes fully engaged in preparing a meal while Mary becomes fully engaged in listening to the Lord. The scene of Mary sitting with her guest is a world away from Sarah being locked away from her guests! It is also a world away from the religious practice of the day: women were not instructed in the Law by the rabbis because they could be neither a teacher nor a disciple. But the word of Jesus is for men and women: so Mary adopts the disciple's posture.

Martha, however, thinks that her sister should be doing something more important than listening to Jesus and she asks him to tell Mary to help with all the serving. In which case Jesus can sit alone and talk to himself! But Jesus is not allowing Martha to write his script, for he regards Martha as a woman who bustles her way into distraction. She is anxious about so many things that she cannot focus on the real priority of the moment. In all her fret and fuss Martha is missing the one thing that is needed now: to welcome the Lord by listening to the word that he speaks.

Welcoming the word
It is Mary who exemplifies the true disciple who greets the Lord with hospitality. Remember when Jesus talked about the word of God as a seed, he described the good soil as those who "hearing the word, hold it fast in an honest and good heart, and bring forth fruit with patience." That is Mary. Martha exemplifies another response to the word, those who are "choked by worries" so much that the word cannot bear fruit.

We are all invited to welcome the word of God and give it our full attention. The way we continue having God as our guest is when we welcome his word and attend to it. When we do that it means we can act on it ourselves. And, as we do here in this Eucharist, we can then sit at the Lord's table and be the guest at his banquet. In that way, we are the Lord's host and his guest.

Finding the genuine article

Stumbling on treasure

In the spring of 1947 a Bedouin shepherd called Muhammed the Wolf was shepherding his goats on the western shore of the Dead Sea. One of the boy's goats had strayed, and to follow it he had to climb a steep cliff. Passing a cave in the rock face, he threw a stone inside; and when he heard the sound of breakage he became frightened and ran back to get his friend. Together they returned and entered the cave. Inside the cave they found several large clay jars; inside the jars, wrapped in a length of linen, was one of the greatest of modern archaeological discoveries: the Dead Sea scrolls.

The two young shepherds had stumbled on a marvellous treasure, but they did not realise it. They tried to sell the scrolls in Bethlehem to a merchant, but he refused to give them the twenty pounds they were asking for. It wasn't until four scrolls came into the hands of the Syrian patriarch in Jerusalem and three scrolls were smuggled out of the country to the United States that the treasure trove came to light. Among the ancient manuscripts was the rule of the Qumran community and fragments of scripture. A Carbon 14 test on the linen wrappings of the scrolls gave them the median date of 33 A.D.

At around the same date, some miles north of Qumran, Jesus of Nazareth told a story about a farm-worker who stumbles on a great treasure which has been hidden in a field. This man appreciates the value of his find – probably a jar full of money and valuables. He is an astute character: the first thing he does is to bury the treasure again, then he sells everything he owns to buy the field. He experiences the great *joy* of discovery; he knows the *value* of his find; he is prepared to pay the *cost* for possessing it.

Searching for treasure

Jesus told another parable about a man who discovers a great treasure. Unlike the farm-worker, this man does not stumble on his find but discovers it after a long search. He is a wealthy merchant who has devoted his life to hunting for treasure in the shape of fine pearls. It is worth noting that in Palestine pearls were a byword for what was supremely valuable. Elsewhere in Matthew's Gospel Jesus says: "Do not give dogs what is holy; do not throw your pearls before swine". (7:6) Pearls were the ultimate valuables.

The merchant in the story has no intention of decorating the pigsty with pearls; he is collecting the finest he can lay his hands on. He is an expert; he knows precisely what he is looking for. When he comes across the finest pearl he has ever set eyes on, he is in no doubt what to do: immediately he sells everything he owns, so that he can possess the pearl that is without peer. The cost has been everything, but when he owns that pearl his search has ended.

268

The authentic article

In both parables both men appreciate the true value of what they have discovered and are willing to pay the cost of everything they have for the new treasure. To outsiders looking at them, the two men might appear totally unhinged in risking *everything* on this one venture. But both are certain about the wisdom of what they must do; for them, the folly would be in passing over the main chance. In the parables Jesus is asking the crowds if they perceive the kingdom of God in the same way: do they really see it as a treasure that is worth more than everything they now value in life? If the kingdom of God is not perceived as the authentic article, people will not bother renouncing anything to attain it.

Jesus' own perception of life differed sharply from so many people's. He was constantly challenging people to see and see again in order to understand anew. To that purpose his stories turned much of popular wisdom on its head, and this was done in the hope that his listeners might catch something of another way of living in God's world. In effect Jesus had what Solomon prayed for – a heart to discern the ways of the people and the ways of God. But more than this, Jesus had the determination to close the gap between the two ways.

We know that Jesus had to give up everything he valued – his family, his home, his security – to do his Father's will and preach the kingdom of God. For Jesus there was no treasure greater than his Father's will: when he uncovered what it was, he renounced everything to make it his own. His own family and neighbours thought his ways either puzzling or foolish; and when he gave up his own life, even his disciples could not understand this ultimate folly. But there was a purpose in it: even in death Jesus kept hold of his treasure.

None of us can gain anything of value without renouncing something. Perhaps what we have to renounce first is our perception of what real treasure in this life really is. Few of us will chance on the crock of gold at the end of the rainbow, or win a lottery, or stumble on an oil-field in the backyard. But we have all stumbled on treasure. Like the two Bedouin shepherd boys, we may have problems appreciating our find wrapped in the ordinary stuff of life. The real treasure of life is under our noses – in the people we share life with, in the opportunities we face every day to exercise the values of Jesus. None of this might appear a glittering prize, but it is in the heart of the ordinary that we discover the presence of Jesus. He is the authentic article. He is hidden in the common-place, hoping that we'll stumble on that truth before long.

The bread of life: hunger and power

Bread

There is much in ordinary life that we take for granted, much that we appreciate only when there is a shortage. Then everyone scrambles for the remaining resources. As a Palestinian Jew, Jesus was brought up in a religion which hallowed everyday things, such as bread and wine, because they were appreciated as gifts from God himself. Food was a holy thing, and the Law required people to say a prayer of thanks every time they had eaten. The rabbis taught that a meal without a prayer was a meal that was accursed. Bread was the essential, basic food: "to eat bread" in Hebrew meant "to have a meal". The poor ate barley bread, the rich ate the bread of wheat. Whether of barley or wheat, bread was to be treated with respect: if crumbs were "as large as an olive", it was forbidden to throw them away.

An unknown author has a simple poem in praise of bread, an appreciation of this food of life:

> Be gentle
> > When you touch bread.
> Let it not lie
> > Uncared for – unwanted.
> So often bread
> > Is taken for granted.
> There is much beauty
> > In bread –
> Beauty of sun and soil,
> > Beauty of patient toil.
> Winds and rain have caressed it,
> > Christ often blessed it.
> Be gentle
> > When you touch bread.

Jesus feeds the crowd

In today's Gospel we see Christ blessing bread. A large crowd of Galileans, impressed by the wonders of Jesus' healing, has followed him into the hills on the far side of the lake. At the sight of the droves of people, Jesus turns to Philip, who is from the locality, to ask where food can be bought. Philip does some quick arithmetic and calculates that six month's wages wouldn't even make a dent in the food bill. Andrew has spotted a small boy who has five barley loaves and two fish, but this poor man's lunch doesn't appear to the disciple to be much of a resource. What the disciples have to learn is that Jesus is not only resourceful, he himself is the resource.

The disciples tell the people to sit down. Jesus takes the food the boy is willing to share; he gives thanks to God for it; he then gives the food to the waiting people. When everyone is satisfied, nothing is lost: the scraps are collected "from the meal of five barley loaves." At the end of the story the emphasis is on *the bread*. With Jesus as the resource, the bread of the poor is seen to be enough to satisfy the hunger of so many people. In the hands of Jesus, shortage becomes abundance, deficiency becomes plenty, nothing is lost of what has been given to him.

After the crowds take the food, they want to take Jesus by force and make him king. Their action is the kind of suspect gratitude that Dr Johnson described as " a lively sense of favours still to come." But Jesus is not going to be tempted to exercise that kind of fragile power and authority. In the Gospels of Luke and Matthew Jesus fights this temptation in the wilderness; here in John's Gospel, the temptation comes not from the devil but from a crowd of Galileans. But Jesus knows when to run. He does, into the hills.

Hunger and power

Jesus is happy to satisfy the hunger of the crowd by offering them the bread of the poor; he is not happy to satisfy their hunger for power by agreeing to become their king. There are some hungers Jesus refuses to satisfy: the hunger for domination is one of them. He is bread that is offered, a lordship of care that is a sign of God's ultimate reign when all will be fed. He rejects the lordship of domination, the destructive power of which he sees all around him.

Perhaps Jesus believes that the power which lords it over other people is one that keeps bread from the hungry, a power that steals the community's resources to secure its own superiority. This is something we are beginning to appreciate ourselves – especially with our massive defence spending. And that spending is related to other issues, not least the hunger of many people. As President Eisenhower observed: "Every gun that is made, every warship launched, every rocket fired signifies, in the final sense, a theft from those who hunger and are not fed, from those who are cold and are not clothed."

The power that dominates with force steals from the hungry multitudes. In saying no to the Galileans who would make him king, Jesus gives us the model of Christian leadership – one that must forever escape from being made in the image of secular power, because it must be free to offer itself to *all* the multitude. That is Jesus' challenge to us all. Only when we share the little we appear to have, will we discover how much we have left over. That truth can only be discovered by doing it.

Discipleship: praying persistently

Arguing with God

The Jewish tale is told of a man who argued with God. It happened one day in the synagogue when Ben Ezra was pouring out his prayer so vigorously that the rabbi grew worried and said to him: "You are a headstrong man, Ben Ezra. Perhaps you argue instead of pray."

Ben Ezra replied: "Listen, rabbi, and I will tell you what I have been saying. To the master of the universe I say this:

> These are my sins and I confess them. I argued with my wife, but you know my wife! I lost patience with my children, but what parent doesn't? I cheated a little in the shop, but just a little. How small my sins are, Master of the universe, but they are mine and I confess them. And now, consider your sins. Sometimes you dry up the skies and our crops wither in the fields. Other times they burn up because you send too much sun. You let the rains come before a poor man has his roof repaired. You do not stop war and the young men die. The marriage bed is empty, and there is no child in the womb. You take away the light from the eyes of a child and he is blind. You take away our loved ones and we are left alone until we too must die. These are your sins, Master of the universe, and they are great. But I will make you a proposal. You forgive me my little sins and I will forgive you your great ones.

"That was my proposal, rabbi, and I ask you what was wrong?"

The rabbi did not answer for a long time. And then he looked at Ben Ezra and said, "No, it was not wrong. But why, oh why, Ben Ezra, did you drive so small a bargain? For sins like these you could have asked him to send the messiah. You could have asked him to redeem the world!"

Praying persistently

In today's first reading it is Abraham, not Ben Ezra, who is busily bargaining with God over the number of just people needed to save two cities from destruction. There is a comical picture of Abraham as a shrewd and persistent bargain-hunter at a Dutch auction – where the price decreases – fifty, forty-five, thirty, twenty, ten. Sold to the canny patriarch! Abraham is the street-wise character who presses God for the best deal possible. God is portrayed as a patient dealer, who is not as testy and difficult to deal with as people might imagine. As Abraham wonders whether God will get angry at his final markdown of the original price, God agrees not to destroy the cities for the sake of ten good people.

An equally generous picture of God emerges from Paul's letter that we heard: "God has forgiven us all our sins and cancelled every record of debt we had to pay." Paul argues that God has done that in a very dramatic way: he has nailed all our debts to the cross of Jesus. *How can God hold onto our record of debts when he sees Jesus' record of love?* In the Jewish story of bargaining with God, the rabbi told Ben Ezra he should have upped the stakes by asking God to send the messiah. As Christians that is precisely what we believe God did. In the cross of Christ, all our sins, small and great, are forgiven.

However, that image of a generous and forgiving God is not one that people readily believe in. That is why, when Jesus teaches his disciples to pray, he insists that they relate to God as Father, *Abba,* and approach him in the confidence of children who know they are loved. To press home his point Jesus uses another character who is bold in the pursuit of what he wants. This one is up and about in the middle of the night hunting for a bread delivery, and he argues his case through the letter-box until the sleepy owner of the house eventually gives in to be rid of the midnight racket! That is Jesus' model of the smart disciple: the one who doesn't know when to quit. True disciples are very hard to get rid of!

Praying according to belief

Jesus believes that persistence in prayer is worthwhile precisely because the God we believe in is not some sultry, withdrawn figure who is unmoved by what he hears. Behind Jesus' advice on prayer is his image of a God who really does want to help and to save. *Because* Jesus believes in God as a loving Father he believes we should relate to him and talk to him as a loving Father.

But people say: "Yes, but I've done the nine Fridays, the five Tuesdays, and the three Saturdays. Also the novena to St Jude. I've joined the charismatic movement; I'm involved in shared prayer, dialogue homilies, and sunset meditations. And still I come up with zero!" Jesus' answer is that it is still worthwhile to keep on asking, to keep on seeking, to keep on knocking, because God is more than silence: he is also Word, and he will reply.

In the end Jesus will stake his own life on that belief. His passion and death are the most powerful appeal to his Father for the sake of all of us. In the end Ben Ezra received his answer from God. For God did send the messiah in Jesus, and he did hear the cry of the messiah's appeal to forgive us all our sins. And that is our most precious bargain.

When a little is enough

Getting away from it all

Once upon a time, in 1337 to be exact, there lived a famous Italian scholar and poet who, though he enjoyed life in the big city, found that all the stresses of urban life were turning his brains to mush. Petrarch had taken minor orders and was living in Avignon, at that time the seat of the papacy. He had made a name for himself at court, but one day he packed everything and took off for a quiet retreat in the country, there to find some peace and nurse his troubled spirit. He had time to enjoy solitude, even time to write about its attraction:

> Not to be crowded, pushed, put upon, trod on;
> not to be dragged to banquets when you aren't hungry;
> not to be forced to talk when you'd rather say nothing;
> not to be greeted at awkward moments;
> not to be clutched and held at street corners;
> not to spend the day, according to fashion's foolish decree, gazing at passing crowds.
> Think what it means not to grow old amid such boredom...

Petrarch's getaway shocked his friends and admirers in Avignon, who thought him quite mad to bury his talents in the wilderness. His escape to the wilds of Vaucluse, twenty miles away from civilisation, caused a sensation; even some bishops tried to persuade him to leave the solitary life to the monks and return to court. But Petrarch was insistent: what he was looking for could only be found in solitude, he said. And what he was looking for was himself.

Solitude and a large crowd

In today's Gospel we hear how Jesus tries to make his getaway to a secure hiding-place. John the Baptist has just been executed at Herod's Court, and when Jesus hears the news about the cruel death of this great spiritual leader, he withdraws to a lonely place: literally "to the wilderness". He tries to escape to the one place that is uninhabited by people, the same kind of place where John the Baptist himself lived. But as the crowds sought out John the Baptist in the wilderness, so the crowds now seek out Jesus. They seem to have a nose for hide-outs. And when Jesus sees them, he has no spirit to play hide-and-seek. He knows why they are looking for him. They have come with their family and friends who are afflicted and troubled; they have come with their hope that he will do something. Jesus takes pity on them and heals their sick.

Jesus' desire for solitude has been overtaken by his compassion for the many people who look to him for help, and he is still ministering to the sick when evening comes. Meanwhile the disciples see a problem with having such a large number of people on their hands and they give Jesus the benefit of their pastoral advice: "Send the people away and they can buy food in the villages." And when all the people go away, Jesus can be left in peace.

There is no suggestion in the Gospel that the crowds are actually looking to Jesus to supply them with food; but Jesus sees no problem anyway. He challenges his disciples: "Give them something to eat yourselves." They point to the little they have, but Jesus takes the little they have, raises his eyes to heaven, blesses it, and gives it to the disciples to give to the crowd. Matthew does not say that the crowd or the disciples are "astonished" or "amazed" – usual reactions in a miracle story. Matthew is telling us something else: the real miracle is that the little food Jesus and the disciples have is sufficient for everyone there. Indeed, they have more than enough. Although Jesus and the disciples are tired and have been deprived of their peace and only have enough food for themselves, still – with the blessing of God – they have sufficient resources to match the needs of the people.

Giving what we can

Jesus and the disciples give the crowd all they can: that is Jesus' lesson in pastoral practice. When Jesus faces the concrete needs of an expectant people, he does not see the need to send anyone away; but when he sees the brutalising power of Herod at work, he feels the need to go away himself. We do not know how the death of John the Baptist affected Jesus, but we do know that John played a unique role in the formation of Jesus' life. His violent death must have saddened Jesus and, by necessity, left him wondering about his own future. From the Gospel we learn that the news of John's death makes Jesus want to withdraw.

This is an important insight about Jesus. He needs a time of peace and quiet, to gain strength from his Father to face the forces that will oppose him to death. He is not a robot. He feels the need to withdraw, to gather his thoughts, to marshal his resources, to pray. Yet his need for peace is not overriding; it is superseded by the needs of others.

We can all readily sympathise with Jesus' need to get away. Like the poet Petrarch, we all experience the longing "not to be crowded, pushed, put upon, trod on." We need our time of quiet, our getaways, our holidays. If we don't answer that need, we can all become burned out or burned up. And God has no need of us as burnt-offerings. Like that we are no good to anyone. We can only give what we can, and the great teaching of today's Gospel is that even the little we give can be more than enough. To say more might be criminal. And that is the kind of plenty that no one needs.

The bread of life: food that endures

Longing for food

The film producer Alfred Hitchcock is well known for the tense atmosphere he was able to produce in his many thrillers. Among his friends Hitchcock was well known for the tense atmosphere he created when he waited for his dinner. One evening he was very disappointed when he saw the very small portions that were being served at a private dinner he attended. After dinner the host said to him, "I do hope you will dine with us again soon." Hitchcock replied, "By all means. Let's start now."

Some time later Hitchcock watched with fascination as his wife prepared a cheese soufflé. After she had put the dish into the oven, his eyes remained glued to the oven door. "What is going on behind that door?" he asked every few minutes, lowering his voice to a whisper in case a sudden noise should prevent the soufflé from rising. By the time the dish was ready, and Mrs Hitchcock opened the oven door to reveal a perfect soufflé, Hitchcock was in a state of nervous exhaustion. "No more soufflés until we have an oven with a glass door," he said. "I can't stand the suspense."

Longing for food is more than a popular human pastime. In today's first reading the whole community of Israel complain to Moses and express their longing for good food. They have their new freedom, but the menu that goes with it offers very small portions. The slavery of Egypt is behind them, but they now remember the country of bondage as the place where "we were able to sit down to pans of meat and could eat to our heart's desire." And they express their complaint to Moses, "As it is, you have brought us to this wilderness to starve this whole company to death!"

The bread of God

The Israelites are tempted to make a U-turn to Egypt, to follow the compass of their stomachs rather than focus on the way to freedom through wilderness. Slavery with good food looks more attractive to them than freedom on a starvation diet. God hears the complaints of Israel and promises that they shall eat meat and have bread to their heart's content. In the morning there is "a thing delicate, powdery" on the surface of the desert. When the people ask Moses what it is, he tells them it is "the bread the Lord gives you to eat."

In today's Gospel reading another crowd follow the instructions of their stomach and express their longing for food. This time it is the crowd of Galileans who, on the previous day, ate to their heart's content when Jesus offered them a meal of barley loaves. Now they follow Jesus to Capernaum, his base on the shores of the Sea of Galilee. The crowd is hungry again.

Jesus tells his hungry pursuers that they are only following him because they have enjoyed the food that physically satisfies them; they should work, he says, for the food that endures to eternal life. The one work which earns this food is believing in the one God has sent. The Galileans promptly ask Jesus for a sign to aid their belief in him – a sign like the manna their fathers ate in the desert. When Jesus points out that it was God, not Moses, who supplied the manna, he compares himself to the God who now gives bread from heaven. Jesus declares that he himself is the bread of life, the bread came down from heaven. Whoever believes in him will never be hungry.

The table of the Lord

The promise that Jesus held out to the Galileans is one that is held out to us today. It is a promise fulfilled in the eucharist that we now celebrate. If there is one thing we all share in this assembly, it is the same hunger. We hunger for a love that does not disappoint; we hunger for a word that does not fade away; we hunger for bread that does not fail to satisfy. In this Eucharist the love of a tender God is offered to us in word and sacrament.

The Vatican Council emphasised this great truth when it declared that the Church "never ceases to partake of the bread of life and to offer it to the faithful from the one table of the Word of God and the Body of Christ" *(Constitution on Divine Revelation, 21)*.

In this gathering, this local Church, we are nourished by God's word and the bread of life. The word spoken is opened up to us, the bread offered is broken for us to share.

This is not something we come to look at, like a still-life painting in an art gallery; rather it is something we come here to do. The Eucharist is a word that flows into deed; it is an *action*. It is the act of sharing in the bread of life, participating in the life of Jesus himself.

We continue to return here because we are hungry for God, because the food that physically satisfies is not enough for us. There will be times when we will wish we were elsewhere, times when what happens here will leave us untouched, times when we will be distracted by a litany of worries that refuse to go away. No matter. Sometimes we have to be content with the act of faith that brings us here, a public admission of our need for God and the people of God. In coming here we declare that we cannot fall back on our own resources: we need Jesus, the bread of life, to sustain us. Staying hungry for his bread means that we do indeed long for the food that endures to eternal life. That is what Jesus asks.

Discipleship: learning not to be dead

The living dead

In Samuel Beckett's play *Happy Days* there are only two characters, a middle-aged couple called Winnie and Willie. Willie is out of sight most of the time; he has very little to say for himself. In the first act we see Winnie buried up to her waist in sand, but in spite of her condition she chatters on and on. She still has the use of her arms and she rummages through a big black bag which holds her possessions, everything from a toothbrush to a revolver. She believes in the importance of things: "Ah yes, things have their life, that is what I always say, *things* have a life."

In the second act Winnie is buried up to her neck, but despite that she rabbits on unstoppably exclaiming: "Oh, this is a happy day!" She cannot reach out to anyone; neither can she be reached by anyone. She has no relationship with anyone as she is caught up in a world all of her own. Nothing gets near her; nothing that happens means anything to her. Winnie is alive, but she is dead.

The scriptures speak of a death which happens to people who are still alive. It is a creeping death which comes on those whose lives are empty of any human relationship. Being dead is something that people can learn to live with. The living dead is not a "video nasty" but a biblical portrait of those who have become accustomed to caring for no one. It is the portrait of the prodigal son who took his share of the inheritance to live with money but without relationship. So when he came home his father said: "This my son was dead and is alive again." In biblical terms, not to care is to be dead already. It is to be buried alive like Winnie and the prodigal son.

The rich man who died twice

Like the prodigal son, the young man in today's Gospel wants the inheritance divided between himself and his brother. He brings his request to Jesus since rabbis were expected to give judgement on the whole range of the law which included civil, criminal and religious questions. But Jesus refuses the role of the judge: instead, he communicates as the storyteller, inviting the young man to take his wisdom from the story rather than his rights from the law. Instead of dividing the inheritance between the two brothers, Jesus focuses on why the *inheritance* has divided the two brothers.

Where Jesus is, a story is sure to follow. A rich farmer is blessed with an abundance of crops. His reaction is not to rejoice with others but to talk to himself until he has worked out a way to store all this abundance and keep it secure. In chattering away, like the character Winnie, his talk is directed to himself and his touch is limited to what he owns. He rummages in his big black bag of possessions: *his* crops, *his* barns, *his* grain, *his* goods. He thinks that he owns his soul and his own future. His world is seen in terms of what he owns.

The rich man is dead already. He is buried up to his neck in his own grain. His world is unrelated to the fortune or fate of any other human being. He decorates his grave with his own possessions which give him a loveless advantage: he thinks that they will insure his future when in fact they will go to anyone but him. When the announcement of his death is made, people can ask the question that was asked of someone else: "Dead? But, how can they tell?" The rich man dies twice: he dies in life and he dies leaving it. His funeral only confirms what has happened a long time ago.

God very rarely appears in parables, but he appears in this one and he calls the rich man a fool. The rich man is a real *idiot,* a word which comes from the Greek, *idiotes,* meaning "the one who is alone". Although he is made in the image of his creator, he does not live as the creator does who gives himself away. As Paul says in today's reading, our new self must be renewed in the image of its creator. God's creativity moves out to others; he shares his richness with others. In the end, God gives *himself* away.

And that is why the rich man is an idiot, the one who is alone: he does not share any of his goods with others or any part of himself with others. Not even his conversation.

Living creatively

In contrast to the rich fool, Jesus spends himself. He spends his whole life sharing his talent for forgiveness, his insight, his love, his pathos, his energy, his imagination, his prayer, his stories. The list is endless. All these qualities create new life for others. Jesus keeps nothing to himself because he regards nothing as *his:* he says that everything he is and has comes from the Father. What Jesus owns, he owes.

That way of living creatively is something Jesus hopes for in his own disciples. He doesn't want his followers buried up to their necks chattering away mindlessly while the real world goes by. As his disciples, the inheritance that Jesus has given us is not to divide brother from brother: that would make us rich fools. The inheritance that we have received is one that we are pledged to give away. In Gospel terms, that makes us rich and smart!

Faith and fear

After the storm, the whisper

The year is around 860 B.C. The place is the northern kingdom of Israel. The Kingdom is ruled by King Ahab, and Ahab is ruled by his wife and queen, Jezebel. Under her influence Ahab has built pagan temples and opened his palaces to the hundreds of false prophets and cronies Jezebel has employed as part of her travelling circus. A strange man of unknown age appears on the scene. He wears a garment of haircloth and a leather loin-cloth. His hair is so long it serves as his cloak. He is unemployed, homeless, and a bachelor. He is Elijah the Tishbite, citizen of Gilead. We don't know how, but Elijah becomes fully employed as the prophet of the God of Israel and is chosen to confront the infidelity of the monarchy. When Jezebel is off on one of her trips, Elijah challenges her prophets to a public contest on the top of Mount Carmel.

The king and the assembly of people watch the trial of strength between Elijah and all the queen's men. No voice heeds the prayers of the false prophets; but when Elijah speaks, a fire appears and burns up his offering. The crowd shouts: "The Lord, he is God; the Lord, he is God." Meanwhile, Elijah exploits his win and has all the false prophets dragged into the valley, where they are put to death. When Jezebel returns from her shopping trip to learn that her cronies have been wiped out, she sends Elijah a telegram to say that he will join them by the following day. Elijah takes to his heels and flees into the wilderness.

The prophet makes a forty-day trek across desert terrain until he reaches Mount Sinai, where Moses had first received the Law from God. Elijah wants to die; he is deeply depressed, alone, hunted, hiding in a cave, clinging to his faith in God. Then he has an extraordinary encounter with God – as we heard in the first reading. When Moses came to this place, the fire and the earthquake indicated the presence of God. Now there is a great storm involving wind and earthquake and fire. But God is not in any of these elements. The storm quietens, and there is only the sound of a gentle breeze. God comes to Elijah in a "still small voice". (RSV) From now on God will not communicate through spectacular events of nature but through the word given to his chosen ones.

The one who has come

The wonders Elijah worked, and the extraordinary manner of his ascension to heaven, have given him a unique place in Jewish sacred tradition, which states that he will reappear to announce the arrival of the Messiah. At the circumcision of a Jewish child it is the custom to place a chair for Elijah in the belief that he will safeguard the child. At the Passover meal, an extra cup of wine is poured for Elijah and an empty chair is reserved for him at table. During the meal the door is flung open to let him in. And one of the songs that is sung expresses the hope:

> Elijah the Prophet
> Elijah the Tishbite
> May he come quickly to us
> With the Messiah.

The belief that Elijah's coming would herald the presence of the Messiah was a belief held by all Jews at the time of Jesus. Some wondered if John the Baptist might be Elijah; some wondered if Jesus might be. When Matthew is writing his Gospel, some fifty-five years after the completion of Jesus' mission, he expresses the Christian belief that Jesus is the Messiah and the Son of God. Matthew is facing a real problem: many of his Jewish converts feel estranged from their former partners in the faith, some of them are wavering, some renounce their faith when they are excluded from the synagogue. Matthew writes his Gospel to support them in their new faith in Jesus.

The doubts that Matthew's church is experiencing are expressed movingly in today's Gospel. Jesus is praying to his Father. His followers are separated from him. It is night. They are in a boat which is battling against a heavy sea and strong winds. All seems lost. The boat clearly represents the church, while the night storm represents the opposition the church is facing. Jesus calls to them and tells them not to be afraid, and then he comes to them over the water. When Peter tries to do the same as Jesus, *even he* is seen to begin to doubt Jesus' power and to panic. But Jesus supports him, then asks him, "Man of little faith, why did you doubt?" The storm ceases. Now all the disciples can acknowledge that Jesus is the Son of God.

When Peter "felt the force of the wind, he took fright and began to sink". Matthew tells his struggling community that even if their faith falters and they panic when they look at the surrounding danger, Jesus – even though he is with the Father – will come and save them. This is Gospel. This is good news indeed.

Neither Elijah nor Peter had the faith to match their zeal, but God supported both of them in their dangerous tasks. That promise is extended to all who put their faith in God and in his Son, Jesus Christ. Often when we feel that we are battling against the odds, we wonder why Jesus always seems to be off somewhere else. And even though we know that we won't be asked to walk on water, we get that sinking feeling all the same. In that plight we are not thrown back on our resources. In this community gathered in faith, we have the word of God and the bread of life and the support of each other. That has to be enough to keep us afloat.

Forgiveness at the ready

Delayed forgiveness

Frederick William I, King of Prussia, ruled severely as monarch from 1713 until 1740. He created a powerfully centralised government, in every department of which he scrutinised operations and exercised the final power of decision. He became deeply disappointed in his son, the future Frederick the Great, who was more interested in culture and music than military superiority. The father's disaffection turned to hatred, and his treatment became so harsh that the young prince decided to run away. But he and his accomplice were caught and faced a court-martial. The prince was sentenced to solitary confinement; his accomplice to life imprisonment. King Frederick decided that the sentence of life-imprisonment was too lenient; he had the accomplice beheaded in the presence of his son. This drastic measure had the desired effect: the prince asked the king's pardon and applied himself to military studies.

When the king was on his deathbed, the attending priest warned him that if he wished to go to heaven he would have to forgive all his enemies. The king's thoughts turned to his favourite enemy, George II of England. "In that case," he told his wife reluctantly "write to your brother and tell him that I forgive him. But be sure not to do it until I am well dead."

Being well dead is a little late for forgiveness. A message of forgiveness telegrammed from the cemetery is a classic case of too little too late. But the image does summarise what we find ourselves doing too often: hoarding hurt, watching over our aging grudges as if they were valuable antiques. So it is that forgiveness gets delayed. Sometimes we delay so long that we are left standing at a graveside quietly whispering forgiveness to a lowered coffin, wishing we had found enough courage to speak our peace long before the ritual farewell.

Forgiving readily

We rarely think of a God who gets depressed at our hardened attitudes, a God whose good mood changes to sadness when he sees how mean we are with the forgiveness he offers so generously. In today's second reading Paul tells us how not to grieve the Holy Spirit of God:

> Never have grudges against others, or lose your temper, or raise your voice to anyone, or call each other names, or allow any sort of spitefulness. Be friends with one another, and kind, forgiving each other as readily as God forgave you in Christ.

Paul was the one who had grieved the Holy Spirit. He was the man who persecuted Christ by hunting down the disciples with military precision and determination, chasing them into foreign cities, arranging their trials and attending their executions. Paul was committed to the violent oppression of the infant Christian community until he was confronted with a large paradox – the forgiveness of the one he was persecuting. The persecuted Christ forgave him readily. That experience overwhelmed Paul; it turned his life around; it gave him a sense of his own worth stronger than the sense of his own sin; it committed him to sharing the forgiveness he had received from Christ.

Paul hoped that other Christians could come to the same truth that he had experienced. The hurt God who forgave Paul did not delight in Paul's wrongdoing nor fasten onto his wrongdoing. Like the Father in the parable of the prodigal son, God's forgiveness does not reduce the wrongdoer to a servant but reaffirms his worth as a son. This is appreciative grace. Paul saw how Christ moved beyond his sins and called him to new possibilities. That delighted Paul. He appreciated it so much that he started doing the same himself. He hoped that forgiveness would catch on.

Becoming good at forgiveness
We know from our experience that there is a kind of forgiveness which is used as a putdown to humiliate others, which exploits people's shame, which dotes on their past wrongs. This kind of forgiveness is a new sin. The forgiveness Paul writes about is a reflection of God's forgiveness: it is readily given, it is not begrudged, it is offered freely.

Paul has a deeply held belief that if we keep God's forgiveness in Christ before us, that saving image will always help to shape our forgiveness. If the forgiving Christ stands before us, it becomes more difficult to refuse forgiveness to those who have hurt us.

Our faith tells us that God has made an eternal habit of forgiveness; he is a professional forgiver, not least because he has so much practice. The only way we can become accomplished forgivers is to forgive readily. Practice makes perfect. When we forgive readily, we don't hoard hurt and grudges, we don't assemble a junk-room of spitefulness. Not only does that keep our lives uncluttered, it is also a sure way of cheering up the Holy Spirit of God.

Discipleship: faith enough to dare

Trusting against the odds

When Alexander the Great came to the throne at the age of twenty he was a worried man. Alexander's sister had just been married, and his father was murdered at the wedding reception by one of his own nobleman. The young king was surrounded by enemies; his first task was to put down the rebellion in his own kingdom of Macedon and then quieten the opposition by proving his ability as a soldier and leader. He did that with unusual speed.

While he was leading his army of 40,000 men through Asia Minor, Alexander became dangerously ill. His physicians were scared to treat him because if they didn't succeed the army would suspect them of malpractice and make them shorter by a head! Only one man, Philip, was willing to take the risk; he had confidence in both the king's friendship and his own medicine.

While the medicine was being prepared, Alexander received a letter from an enemy of Philip, accusing the physician of taking a bribe from the Persian king to poison his master. Alexander read the letter and slipped it under his pillow without showing it to anyone. When Philip entered the tent with the medicine, Alexander took the cup from him, at the same time handing Philip the letter. While the physician was reading it, Alexander drank the contents of the cup. When Philip saw the charge in the letter he threw himself down at the king's bedside, but Alexander assured him that he had complete confidence in his integrity. After three days Alexander was well enough to appear again before his army.

Given what happened to his father, Alexander was trusting against the odds. But his decision to take the medicine wasn't a decision in the dark: although he couldn't see what would happen, he believed in what he *could* see – Philip's loyalty – and acted on that belief. Alexander was sure that Philip was hoping for the same thing as himself: his own recovery. As the letter to the Hebrews puts it: "To have faith is to be sure of the things we hope for, to be certain of the things we cannot see."

The faith to dare

In today's reading we heard Abraham described as a man "who was already as good as dead". He is an old man and his wife has passed child-bearing years a long time ago. For these two nomadic pensioners, the prospect of having their own children and their own land seems highly unlikely. But their faith in God enables them to believe in what they cannot see, to build up a vision of what the future will be like. They act on that vision of faith and they are rewarded with a son. They set out for their promised land "without knowing where they are going". Their map is their faith in God.

When Abraham and Sarah reach their promised land, they live there as strangers, not with the rights of citizens who belong there. They believe that their descendants will enjoy being citizens of the land. But Abraham looks even beyond that as he looks out of his tent: he looks to another city where the founder and the architect and the builder will be God. Abraham's faith enables him to see these things not as part of his experience now, but "in the far distance". As Tennessee Williams noted: "Time is the longest distance between two places." Abraham looks to another time and to a place in which he can settle as a true homeland. In that homeland, he will share the address of God.

Abraham's deep faith in God enabled him to dare. Wherever he went he took his treasure with him; his treasure was part of him; he could not be separated from it even in time of trial. Abraham's real treasure was his faith in God, and his heart was in the same place as his treasure. That is something which Jesus hopes will be true of his own disciples. Jesus says that "where your treasure is, there will your heart be also." But the question that asks to be answered is: *What is our real treasure?*

Treasure that will not fail

So, what is in our treasure boxes? What do we value most in our lives? If we were all to list honestly what we *really* value then we would be giving ourselves away. Jesus does not say "Where your heart is, there will be your treasure also." He makes a much more practical suggestion: he knows that if you want to know what is in people's heart you *first* find out what is in their treasure boxes! See what people put their trust in and then you know the condition of their heart!

The Gospel asks us: is our treasure the treasure that will not fail us? The kind of treasure Jesus talks about is the kind that cannot be stolen or destroyed. If we were all being burgled at the moment, would we still have our treasure?

Abraham risked everything, but his risk was funded from his treasure – his faith in God. Alexander the Great risked his life taking the medicine from Philip, but his risk was funded from his treasure – his belief in his physician's integrity. Jesus risked everything, but his risk was funded from his treasure – his great love of the Father. Is our treasure rich enough to fund the risks the Gospel asks us to take?

Going to the dogs

Making your presence felt

In 1919 the people of Plymouth voted in their new member of parliament. The new M.P. was born in the United States, but this was not the reason why the majority of the British parliament was antagonistic towards its new member. The new M.P. was a woman, Nancy Astor, the first woman to gain a seat in the House of Commons. Since Lady Astor believed in making her presence felt in the House of Commons, she regularly interrupted other speakers – particularly on the rights of women. When rebuked for her constant interventions, she protested that she had been listening for hours before interrupting. A colleague whispered to her: "Yes, Nancy, we've all *heard* you listening."

In today's Gospel we heard a pagan woman listening to Jesus and we saw how she made her presence felt. She comes across as one of the most attractive characters in the pages of the Gospel: a mother who is tormented by the torment of her daughter, a woman who takes to the streets to make her plea to Jesus, who refuses to take his silence for the last word, who organises a one-woman protest in the path of these runaway men. She is the only person in the Gospels who has the wit to outwit Jesus. And in the end, she gets what she wants.

To heal or not to heal

Jesus withdraws from Jewish territory and crosses into the region of Tyre and Sidon, present-day southern Lebanon. He is escaping from his opponents who are exasperated at the way he allows his disciples to break with the tradition of the Jewish elders, ignoring the laws about clean and unclean. If Jesus is trying to escape from this problem, he is heading for a large disappointment: he comes face to face with the same question in larger form. A pagan woman comes to him, hoping that he will have mercy on her and heal her daughter. Matthew calls her a Canaanite – the name given to the older inhabitants of Israel who were dispossessed by the Hebrews. This woman symbolises all those who are regarded as unclean by Jesus' own people. Will Jesus fraternise with her or not?

The silence of Jesus suggests a refusal to minister to this woman's needs. This is how the disciples interpret it, and they plead with Jesus to do *them* a favour by getting rid of this mobile nuisance who is screaming after them. Jesus explains his exclusive mission: he is sent only to the lost sheep of the House of Israel. This woman, therefore, is not his problem. She is outside the territory of his pastoral concern.

The woman, however, has no intention of bowing to these theological niceties which leave her out in the cold and abandon her daughter to a life of torment. She stops Jesus in his tracks by kneeling at his feet. "Lord," she says, "help me." Jesus responds by telling a harsh parable, one which voices his own people's traditional attitude to the likes of this woman: "It is not right to take the children's food and throw it to the dogs." Only Jews have a right to be treated as "children" of God; the Gentiles, like this woman, are "dogs".

The woman is not diverted by this offensive rebuff; rather than getting into a scrap about Jewish-pagan relations, she hangs on to the reason why she is there. She tells Jesus that even the dogs can eat the scraps that fall from the master's table. The scraps from the table become dog food. And this woman kneeling at the feet of Jesus lets it be known that she will be satisfied with dog food. In her response she has outwitted Jesus in a way that none of his learned opponents ever managed, and he has the grace to give in. The woman gets what she came for; her daughter is healed.

Going to the dogs

Only twice in the Gospels does Jesus leave Jewish territory. Although his attitude to the Gentile woman seems out of keeping with the way he normally relates in the Gospel stories, it probably does reflect strict Jewish-Christian thinking in the early Church. All the first Christians were Jews, many of whom still regarded Gentiles as unclean. In the Acts of the Apostles we learn that even Peter had to be converted to a new attitude. As he admits to his first Gentile converts:

> You know it is forbidden for Jews to mix with people of another race and to visit them, but God has made it clear to me that I must not call anyone profane or unclean. (10:28)

At first, the Christian community at Jerusalem had no mission to the Gentiles. Nobody went to the "dogs", as they were called. But Paul comes on the scene as the apostle who rejoices in the fact that his vocation is to go to the dogs. He himself was a strict Pharisee, and he too has had to be converted from his attitude to non-Jews. He leads by his example when he spearheads the early Church's mission to the Gentiles. Paul sets the example for the whole Christian Church. If we believe that Christ died for everyone, then no one is a dog. No one should be excluded from the all-embracing reach of God's love.

And that is why the Canaanite woman in the Gospel is so important for all of us. She is the teacher of the servants of God. Through her demand for attention and dignity, the voice of God questions us all.

The bread of life: wisdom and folly

Two hostesses

The soldier and writer Thomas Edward Lawrence, better known as Lawrence of Arabia, is remembered for his exploits while leading the Arab revolt against the Turks in the First World War. He led raids on the Damascus-Medina railway, captured various key posts, and in 1917-18 fought his way through Palestine to Damascus. After the war he returned to Oxford to write an account of his experiences. The title of his book, *Seven Pillars of Wisdom,* comes from today's first reading, taken from the Book of Proverbs.

The reading imagines Wisdom as a woman who has built herself a house and erected seven pillars. She is a generous hostess, laying a plentiful table of meat and wine, despatching her maidservants to proclaim her invitation from the city heights. All who lack wisdom are invited to leave their folly behind them and head for the banquet where a different menu awaits them:

> Come and eat my bread,
> drink the wine I have prepared!
> Leave your folly and you will live,
> walk in the ways of perception.

As opposed to Lady Wisdom, there is another hostess called Dame Folly. She is childish and knows nothing. She sits at the door of her house, on a throne, inviting passers-by to her banquet. But when the guests enter the house of Dame Folly, they are unknowingly heading for the valley of darkness. There is only one course on her menu: death. Eating at the table of Lady Wisdom brings life and new perception; eating at the table of Dame Folly brings only death.

Jesus, the host of God

In the second reading the Christians at Ephesus are encouraged to leave foolish ways behind them and live in the ways of wisdom. Instead of drugging themselves with drink, they should be filled with the Holy Spirit. Whether together or alone, they should be a people whose heart always sings praise and thanks to the Father. To live like this is to love the new life of wisdom in the Spirit.

When it comes to the Gospel of John, Jesus is the Wisdom of God in the flesh. He embodies it in his person. Jesus is the Way who, like Lady Wisdom, invites people to come and eat the bread that nourishes them for life. Jesus' dream is not only to invite people to the banquet of life but to *be* the banquet of life. Himself. His dream is to give his flesh for the life of the world. Not surprisingly, when he shares this dream with his listeners, they cannot understand how it can be.

How can Jesus' dream be reality? How can he give his flesh as real food and his blood as real drink? Is this just an empty dream? Lawrence of Arabia wrote in *Seven Pillars of Wisdom:*

> All men dream: but not equally. Those who dream by night in the dusty recesses of their minds wake in the day to find that it was vanity: but the dreamers of the day are dangerous men, for they may act their dream with open eyes, to make it possible.

Jesus' dream to share himself as food for others is no vanity of the night: he acts his dream with open eyes; he makes it possible on the cross in the total giving of self. It's helpful to remember that for Jesus, the word "body" meant more than it means to us – it meant the entire person. Also, in Jesus' day, blood was regarded as the principle of life – when a person lay wounded and bleeding, the loss of blood meant the person often died. When Jesus says, "This is my body, my blood, given for you", what he is saying is, "This is the totality of my being, all that I am, all that I hope to be." This is a great summary of Jesus' message: a self-giving love that is offered without holding anything back. This is offered as the food of life.

"Do this in memory of me"
In the sacrament of the Eucharist we draw life from the body and blood of Jesus. "Do this in memory of me." The act that we do in this assembly is the deed of memory: we not only recall Jesus, we consume his memory as the food of life. We are nourished by real food and real drink: in eating and drinking we have new life in him. We eat the Wisdom of God; it becomes part of our very being; it becomes our resource for leaving folly and living a life of wisdom.

"Do this in memory of me." These words summarise what is expected of us. It has been pointed out that the words of consecration make excellent marriage vows. When husbands and wives struggle to enflesh the words, "My body, given for you", when they struggle to reach out to each other in gentleness, in trust, in love, they are realising in a special way, "Do this in memory of me." When we try to leave folly and break out of our selfishness, when we try to be bread broken for others, we realise the words, "Do this in memory of me." When that is done, the Wisdom of God takes flesh again.

Discipleship: the prophet's conflict

Jeremiah, the prophet

The place is the city of Jerusalem. The year is 588 B.C. The city is surrounded by Babylonian soldiers who are feared as "the foe from the north". All the outlying defence posts of the city have already fallen and the survivors have been thrown into exile. From the walls of Jerusalem the people can see the Babylonians – their weapons, their uniforms, their faces, their intent. The people under siege hope that God will intervene and save them from the coming catastrophe.

Inside the walls of Jerusalem there is a prophet called Jeremiah. Years before he had predicted the catastrophe: he had sounded the alarm but everyone had ignored him. He even walked the streets of Jerusalem with a wooden yoke around his neck to warn people that they would soon be under the yoke of the enemy. And when false prophets chased him and broke the wooden yoke, Jeremiah put on a new one made of iron. He uses pantomime to get across his point; he screams, he prays, he shouts, he warns, he weeps. Jeremiah complains that all the reaction he gets is stone-walling: "They have made their faces harder than rock." (5:3)

Wherever he goes, Jeremiah is always fighting the establishment: the king, the princes, the army, the politicians, the hired prophets. He shatters their fragile serenity; he increases their collective anxiety. They try to discredit him, they call him a madman; they throw him into prison in the guards' courtyard.

But even there Jeremiah is busy! Instead of wailing at the walls he tells the soldiers that they are wasting their time practising their swordplay and spear-throwing. They might as well play darts for all the good it will do. And as we heard in the first reading, the king's war cabinet complains: "he is unquestionably disheartening the remaining soldiers in the city, and all the people too, by talking like this." Jeremiah is clearly no good as a military chaplain so he is thrown into a well of mud. Only when a black slave from Ethiopia pleads with the king does Jeremiah get hauled out of solitary confinement and thrown back into prison. Where he continues where he left off!

Prophetic conflict

Jeremiah is a pacifist. He tells the people not to fight but to surrender. He has a religious reason for doing this: he believes the people are defenceless because God has withdrawn his protection. He believes the people are responsible for what is happening because they have forgotten their promises to God. To forget their promises is to bury their identity as the people of God; to forget is to deny the past and the present its meaning.

He rails against the false prophets who give easy answers to difficult questions, who appeal to popular taste at its lowest, who cheat people with their cheap optimism. Jeremiah warns the people: "They speak of peace when there is no peace." But the people do not listen to him and Jeremiah is hurt and angry. He is angry at God for making him the prosecutor of his own people. As a witness of God he becomes the victim of the people. Jeremiah is everyone's favourite victim. Even God's. As he complains in prayer:

> You have overpowered me; you were the stronger. I am a laughing-stock all day long, they all make fun of me...Why ever did I come out of the womb to see toil and sorrow and end my days in shame?

Jeremiah is the supreme example of the prophet who is isolated because of his fidelity to the word of God. He is in conflict with his own people, with himself, even with God. It's all very well to say what you mean, *but if what you mean is not what is wanted, what happens to you?* What happens when the word that you speak and the values that you cherish cause division even within your own family? And Jesus warns in today's Gospel that even families will be divided among themselves because of him.

The death of the prophet

The opposition that Jeremiah brought proceeded from his fidelity to his mission. The fire that Jesus brought proceeded from his fidelity to his mission. Neither of them introduced conflict as a way of passing the time. They both paid the price with their own lives. Jesus warns that his own disciples must face the real conflict that the Gospel will surely bring. Standing for something inevitably means standing against a lot of other things. And as Jesus suggests when the lines are drawn up there can be a lot of familiar faces on the opposite side.

Every community needs its prophets. The prophets today don't get treated any better than in the past. They rarely appear as popular figures because their popularity ratings are rarely high. They are not appointed by the community, so the community cannot sack them when they don't like what they hear. Often they end up like Archbishop Romero – slaughtered by the power that fears them. In the end the death of the prophet is his last accusation and challenge. We must pick up where he left off.

Peter, the rock

Simon Peter's authority in the earliest tradition

It is unusual to think of the first Bishop of Rome as someone called Simon Johnson, who came to be called Rocky by his friends. Simon was a Galilean fisherman from the small village of Capernaum on the shores of the lake. He was the first person Jesus called to follow him. The apostle's full name was Simon Bar-Jonah, which means Simon Son of John. Johnson. Just as the two brothers James and John were given the nickname "sons of thunder" because of their thundering temper, Simon is given a new name which reveals something of who he has become. The new name is Cephas in Aramaic, or Petros in Greek, taken from the root word for "rock". Matthew shows us in today's Gospel that Simon's new name is given to him by Jesus; he also tells us that the Church is founded on the inspired confession of Simon, who henceforth will be known as Cephas.

All four Gospels were written after Peter's lifetime; all of Paul's letters, however, were written *before Peter died,* so they give us the earliest testimony we have about Peter. When Paul writes to the Galatians about his conversion he tells them how he first "went up to Jerusalem to visit *Cephas* and stayed with him for fifteen days". (1:18) By the time Paul has been converted, the name Cephas has replaced the first apostle's proper name. Cephas is seen as the acknowledged leader – that is why Paul goes to see him first. Paul sees himself as having been appointed by God to be the apostle to the Gentiles, and he is openly disappointed when he discovers that Cephas has stopped eating with the Gentiles because of pressure from others in Jerusalem. Paul tells us how he takes a stand against Peter: "When Cephas came to Antioch, I opposed him to his face, since he was manifestly in the wrong." (2:11)

Although Paul opposes Cephas, it is important for him to get Cephas on his side. Both Paul's group *and* the Jerusalem group try to win Peter's support. *Peter is clearly, then, the major figure whose support matters most in times of controversy.* He stands as the figure of authority who has the power to bring both groups together and so avoid a division in the early Church.

Simon Peter's authority in the Gospels

In the Gospels Peter is first in all the lists of the apostles. Not only is he the first to be called, but Jesus's mission in Galilee has its base in Peter's house in Capernaum – where Jesus cured Peter's mother-in-law. He is seen as the spokesman for the apostolic group, their acknowledged leader. In the story of Jesus there is no other figure that is mentioned as frequently as Peter. And the Gospels are realistic in their memory of him: he is not only the one who confesses who Jesus is, he is also the one who denies Jesus; he is not only the one who expresses faith in Jesus, he is also the one who falters in that faith. He has to be helped by Jesus in all that he does, but the Gospels indicate that he is Jesus' choice to lead the community in the future. He is the one who will return and strengthen the brethren.

Matthew shows us that Peter is chosen by God to receive enlightenment about Jesus – not flesh and blood, but the Father in heaven is the source of revelation. In response to God's choice of Peter, Jesus elects to build the Church on this rock. Like Eliakim in the first reading who is given the keys which open and close access to the king, Peter is given the keys of the kingdom of heaven. He is given authority "to bind" and "to loose", terms which mean to forbid and to permit. This makes Peter the ruler of the Church, the one whose decisions in faith will be confirmed by God. As God makes Peter his choice, so Christ is seen to make Peter's decisions at one with God's. Matthew later extends this authority to the whole body of disciples when Jesus says to them all: "I tell you solemnly, whatever you bind on earth shall be considered bound in heaven; whatever you loose on earth shall be considered loosed in heaven." (18:18)

The Petrine figure in the Church

Given the division in the Church today, the universal community of Christians clearly needs the Petrine figure, who will summarise in himself the unity of the whole Church. That is why the role of the papacy is at the centre of discussion between Roman Catholics and other Christians. We believe that being in communion with the Pope, the Petrine figure, is as important today as it was in the early Church. Too often, however, we tend to see the figure of the Pope as the one who uses his keys, the symbol of his authority, to keep people out. But keys open doors as well as close them, they give access as well as prevent it. And many non-Catholics are hoping that the Petrine figure can still become the great symbol of unity in the Church by using his authority in the service of unity.

This work of unity is something that can be seen practically at work in the second Letter of Peter. In spite of the real differences between Peter and Paul, Peter speaks movingly about "our brother Paul, who is so dear to us" (3:15), and goes on to defend Paul against those who distort his words. Peter functions as the great unifier, the one who holds the different factions together, the one who is the first in the defence of those who have received a mission from God to spread the Gospel. He lives up to his new name; he really is a rock.

Take your choice: Joshua and Jesus

Joshua, our contemporary

The outstanding figures of Israel's early history, Abraham and Moses, belong to a time when the people were desert nomads, living with their flocks on the steppe country and moving on when they needed new pastures. It was a dramatic change to their way of life when they became settlers on the land. They gave up their tents and built houses; their security, which previously had been centred on belonging to a travelling community, came to be centred more on the land. They became property owners. At the turning-point of this history there stands the towering figure of Joshua, the man who succeeded Moses as leader of the people of Israel.

Moses had led the children of Israel out of bondage in Egypt, led them for forty years in their desert wanderings, and moulded them into an organised community based on the Law. But Moses was not permitted to enter the Promised Land; that role was reserved for his disciple and chief-of-staff, Joshua. It was he who commanded the invasion and conquest of Canaan after leading the people across the river Jordan. After the invasion, he partitioned the land and allotted defined districts to each of the Israelite tribes.

Joshua is celebrated as the bravest field commander in Jewish history. At the North American military academy of West Point, Joshua's name appears in the Hall of Fame. His story is one long military adventure or one long tale of violence – depending on your point of view. And his story is unfinished. As the Jewish writer Eli Wiesel has observed:

"Joshua's concerns remain ours, his anguish is our anguish. May one go too far to assure one's survival? His name evokes Shiloah, Hebron, Jericho – and so many other biblical names that have re-entered international diplomacy. Joshua must have spent sleepless nights over the West Bank. His present is our past, and also our present."

A choosing people

When Joshua is an old man, and the country is resting from war, he calls all the tribes of Israel to the ancient sanctuary at Shechem. The story is told in today's first reading. All the elders, leaders, judges and scribes are called to listen to the last farewell of their distinguished leader. He does not recall his military victories, nor does he ask the people to cherish what he has done for them. Instead, he asks them to choose whom they wish to serve: the God of their ancestors or the false gods of the land they now inhabit.

It's as if Joshua wants to be remembered not as the great military commander who brought his people to the Promised Land but as the prophet who brought his people to choose God again. This inner battle of faith seems to preoccupy him more than his military campaigns ever did. He gives the people the opportunity to close the book on the past or recommit themselves to the God of Israel.

Joshua is tired; he is old; death is looking him in the face. He has seen too much bloodshed to boast of the beauty of battle; he has seen too many ruined cities and disfigured corpses to sing of the glories of war. The old commander is concerned with the geography of the heart. Joshua knows that all choices have to be renewed, that people don't stay dedicated to a cause just by continuing to exist. As Israel Zangwill observed about the Jewish tradition: "We are not the chosen people, but the choosing people." Joshua asks his people to choose, and he declares before them his own choice to serve the Lord. Thus, Joshua wins the last and most important battle of his life when he leads his people to a victory of fidelity. They declare: "We too will serve the Lord, for he is our God."

Choosing to stay
The choice that Joshua offered his people is echoed in today's Gospel when Jesus offers his own followers the choice to stay with him or join the ranks of unbelievers. After hearing Jesus' teaching on the bread of life, many of the followers express their complete confusion. They find Jesus' language intolerable. Many of them do choose to leave him. Then, like Joshua to the twelve tribes, Jesus turns to the twelve apostles and gives them the choice to close the book on their shared past. But just as the twelve tribes told Joshua that they could not reject the Lord after all he had done for them, so Peter asks Jesus how could they turn to anyone else for the message of eternal life. So, the apostles exercise their freedom of choice by choosing to stay with Jesus.

Both Joshua and Jesus respect people's freedom of choice. They know that past choices can become old and exhausted, that they can die from being abandoned on the scrap heap of life. Past choices have to be kept alive by new commitment, because decisions in faith are never settled once and for all. The apostles do what we must all do: keep on choosing Jesus, stay with the one who has the message of eternal life. That is something that will always be outstanding on the agenda.

The kingdom: who's in, who's out

Door policy

The American comedian Groucho Marx was accepted as a member of the exclusive Friar's Club in Hollywood. Groucho however, expressed his disappointment that the club was not as exclusive as he first thought. His telegram to the committee read: "Please accept my resignation. I don't want to belong to any club that will accept me as a member."

According to popular lore about clubs, the more difficult a place is to get into, the more sought after it becomes. To test the door policy of fashionable London night-spots, *The Observer* magazine commissioned two men whose task was to get past the guardians who monitor the doors. The two men were dressed very differently. One man went as Mr Straight: he was dressed in a conventional grey suit, white shirt and silk tie. The other man went in the guise of Mr Swan: his multi-coloured outfit was covered by a red silk coat that would have embarrassed a cardinal. He had earrings to match.

Mr Straight didn't get past too many bouncers who guarded the doors. Most refused him entry with the ready excuse of "members only"; some were less diplomatic telling him, "You can't come in here dressed like that." Once when he protested, an attendant produced a hand mirror, held it up to him and asked: "Would *you* let yourself in?" Mr Straight did manage easy access to one club which had ballroom dancing for the over 40's. Inside he was offered free membership!

Mr Swan had an easier passage through the doors of the select clubs, although his clothes were no guarantee. One bouncer claimed: "We can sniff out phonies and weekend trendies a mile away. They don't really live the look." Mr Swan was sniffed out a few times but still managed to get past the heavies with his colourful outfit. He was not, however, judged a suitable prospect for ballroom dancing!

The door into the kingdom

In today's Gospel Luke tells us about the door policy of the kingdom of God and how there is no such thing as automatic membership. While Jesus is making his way to Jerusalem, someone asks him about the number of those who will be saved. Rather than speculate about the arithmetic of salvation, Jesus gives practical advice about the present time: "Try your best to enter by the narrow door, because, I tell you, many will try to enter and will not succeed." The door is not so wide that anyone can casually saunter through at any time; the door is narrow and individuals must strive now to enter it.

Nor will the door remain open indefinitely. When locking-up time comes and the master of the house has secured the door, those who missed their opportunity will not be admitted. The narrow door has now become the locked door. The image changes from tight space to time up. Those who wait until the door is shut try knocking, but the householder regards them as strangers. The latecomers try to remind the householder of common ties: they ate and drank with him, they listened to him teaching in their streets. But the Lord is not too impressed with superficial acquaintance: people who eat and drink in the same restaurants and bars, read the same papers, watch the same programmes, don't necessarily share the same commitments. Camp followers are not disciples.

The pain of being excluded from the kingdom is worsened when the latecomers see the kind of people who have been allowed in as members. There is not even the dubious consolation of knowing that at least so-and-so is also on the wrong side of the door. Members come from all over – "from east and west, from north and south" – and take their place at the feast in the kingdom of God. The prophecy of Isaiah that we heard in the first reading is seen to be fulfilled as people "from all the nations" enjoy the favour of the Lord. All sorts. The door policy of the kingdom keeps surprising people: there's no sure way of knowing who's in and who's out. In the kingdom of God there's no telling who is coming to dinner!

Fidelity to the word

The teaching of Jesus is clearly opposed to the kind of national or religious elitism that presumes it has an assured place in God's kingdom. As one who is treated as an outsider by his own people, Jesus has a natural allegiance to those who don't belong to the right crowd. Good roots are not enough; having the right address is not enough; having an impressive pedigree that goes back to Abraham is not enough. Borrowed fidelity does not impress Jesus. There is no substitute for a person's own decision for the kingdom of God.

Jesus describes the condition for entering the kingdom when he says: "My mother and my brothers are those who hear the word of God and keep it." (8:21) Fellowship in the kingdom is open to all peoples who hear the word of God and keep it. Whether we dress with the sobriety of Mr Straight or the extravagance of Mr Swan is unimportant for membership of the kingdom. The door policy is determined by fidelity to the word of God.

The course of suffering

Business as usual

Today's first reading opens with a dramatic accusation: the prophet Jeremiah accuses God of seducing him into becoming a prophet and deceiving him about the personal suffering his mission would involve. Throughout his prophetic ministry, from about 628 to about 580 B.C., Jeremiah appears the most plaintive and heartbroken of all the prophets. He is burdened by a ministry he does not want, and pained by the hostility of his own people, which he deeply resents. He is commissioned to tell the people of Judah and Jerusalem that their sins have earned them defeat and exile. He warns them that God's help is not automatic, that they might as well surrender to the invading Babylonian armies, because God will not help them.

Jeremiah's message is heard as treason; he is attacked by the crowds, imprisoned, tortured. His painful vocation isolates him from his family and friends; he becomes a laughing-stock around the streets of the city. Jeremiah is no robot; he is hurt and bewildered by how people respond to him. Many people just ignore him. He suffers so much that he tries early retirement, but it doesn't work because he cannot extinguish the fire burning in his heart. And in the midst of all his anguish and pain normal life goes on in the city. People continue their daily routines. Business is as usual. Reflecting on how suffering happens in the midst of the ordinary, the poet W.H. Auden noted how the Old Masters always depicted this in their paintings:

> About suffering they were never wrong,
> The Old Masters: how well they understood
> Its human position; how it takes place
> While someone else is eating or opening a window
>   or just walking dully along...
> They never forgot
> That even the dreadful martyrdom must run its course
> Anyhow in a corner, some untidy spot
> Where the dogs go on with their doggy life and the
>   torturer's horse
> Scratches its innocent behind on a tree.

The suffering of Jesus

Suffering happens while the sun shines, while others carry on as usual, while the traffic continues to flow. As Jeremiah spoke of the approaching

298

suffering of Jerusalem and his own troubled relationship with God, so Jesus in today's Gospel prepares his disciples for his approaching ordeal at Jerusalem. He speaks of it as necessary – not a necessity that lies in the nature of things, not a tragic fate, but the will of God made known through the prophecies. Like Jeremiah, Jesus has to face the stark truth that his relationship with God involves personal anguish and suffering and rejection. More than that, it will lead to a violent death.

Peter is frankly appalled at this prospect and tries to deflect Jesus from the path that lies ahead. After having declared Jesus to be the Christ, a title associated with victory and glory, Peter now denies that Jesus must suffer. Peter wants to banish suffering from the agenda; Jesus brings the subject to the forefront of the conversation.

To understand Jesus means to understand the cross. That is the essence of his teaching and that is why Peter is denounced so strongly. Peter is seen as a tempter; his ambitions and desires, Jesus says, belong to the realm of Satan. Peter wants Jesus to be immune from frustration, suffering and contempt. The Christ of his dreams is all glory and prestige, untouched by vulnerable humanity. It is a world away from the Christ that Jesus has to grow into, a future of suffering which he is about to enter.

Way of the cross

The way of the cross that Jesus outlines for himself is the way of renunciation his followers are called to tread. Jesus faced suffering which could be conquered only if it was accepted. He faced rejection which could be transformed only if he assented to it. If the suffering was to pass, it had to be endured: "For anyone who wants to save his life will lose it; but anyone who loses his life for my sake will find it."

The way of the cross which Jesus followed was one which passed through streets and markets, by houses and palaces, by windows and doors. While it happened people went about their business. Suffering must run the course of the familiar. As Christians we live in the assurance that our way of the cross does not go unnoticed. Jesus is our suffering companion; he proves to be our strength; his power is mighty in our weakness. If the cross is the price to be paid for love, then carrying it is love's proof in action. For Jesus, that is enough.

No respect for tradition

Tradition

The following exchange was overheard on the London Underground. "That's all very well, Bintock, but what you propose flies in the face of tradition." There is a pause before the reply. "Tradition can hardly settle the argument. After all, what you are pleased to call tradition is something that others see as a large pair of handcuffs. Who's to say which outlook is the right one?"

When it comes to the subject of tradition, people's attitudes can vary dramatically. Some people have an affectionate loyalty to traditional ways of doing things. They feel secure when they adapt their own values and behaviour to received wisdom, reassured by the knowledge that they are following in the footsteps of many others. As G.K. Chesterton remarked: "Tradition means giving votes to the most obscure of all classes, our ancestors. It is the democracy of the dead."

Other people feel fettered by tradition; they call for fresh approaches to fresh situations. For them, much of tradition is petrified opinion – a spent force that should be confined to the realm of once upon a time. They might consult tradition, but they do not feel obliged to stay within its confines. As W.S. Maughan observed: "Tradition is a guide and not a jailer."

Jesus and human tradition

In today's Gospel Jesus is accused of flouting sacred tradition. Religious officials from Jerusalem and local Pharisees want to know why Jesus permits his disciples to disregard the unwritten tradition of the elders. The problem is that the disciples do not wash their hands before they eat. The complaint is not that the disciples ignore good hygiene, but that they ignore the tradition of ceremonial washing. In doing this they are numbered among the unclean.

According to the written Law, ceremonial washing was required only of priests before they entered the sanctuary. By the time of Jesus, however, the ritual of hand-washing, before every meal and between each course, had been extended to include all pious Jews. This unwritten tradition of legal interpretation – the oral law – was regarded by the Pharisees to be as binding as the written Law. And they expect Jesus to share their religious outlook.

Jesus accuses his accusers of being hypocrites, quoting the prophet Isaiah to underline the point:

This people honours me only with lip-service,
while their hearts are far from me.
The worship they offer me is worthless,
the doctrines they teach are only human regulations.

In clinging to human tradition, they ignore the commandments of God. Jesus wants to free people from the weight of a stifling tradition that concentrates on approved performance. When religious performance is lacking in heart, it makes for worthless worship.

Jesus goes on to teach the crowd revolutionary doctrine which puts him at odds with his own religious tradition: nothing that a man eats can defile him, only what comes from his own heart. In this Jesus declares all foods clean and shifts the focus of moral attention to how people choose and what they actually do. For Jesus, eating with unwashed hands is imaginary defilement. So is eating unapproved food. Uncleanness is a matter of what proceeds from the human heart. It's not people's diet that interests Jesus, it's their heart condition.

Inward business
Jesus is interested in the stirrings of the human heart, the personal issues that preoccupy us and influence our choices and behaviour. The territory within, with all its complex emotions and desires, holds Jesus's attention. He knows that no external law can change people's hearts, even if it makes them socially conform. That is why, when he began his preaching, he invited everyone: "Set your *hearts* first on the kingdom of God." Jesus believes that when people's hearts are centred on God, they are emancipated from the litany of human regulations that would script their every move.

For many of his hearers, what Jesus said was bad news because it contradicted the tradition they honoured. We call it good news, Gospel, because it is a word that liberates us from a world of endless regulations. It also challenges us and invites us to live a religion of the heart. To have a heart for Jesus and his values: this will always be our real business as Christians.

A kingdom for the overlooked

Littleness and the kingdom

Once upon a time, so the story is told, there lived a king whose daughters were all beautiful, but the youngest was so beautiful that the sun itself was astonished whenever it shone on her face. Close by the king's castle lay a great dark forest, and under an old oak tree in the forest was a deep well; when the king's youngest daughter was bored she went into the forest to play with a golden ball.

One day when the princess was playing near the well, the golden ball rolled straight into the water. The well was so deep that the bottom could not be seen, and the princess started to cry and wail for her loss. Her cries attracted a big, ugly frog who asked her what she would give him if he got the ball back. The princess offered him her crown and her best dress, but our ugly hero had no longing to be the best-dressed frog in the kingdom!

"If you promise to love me," he said, "I will bring you your golden ball."

The princess agreed readily; since frogs were unimportant, she thought, you could promise them anything. When old splasher came back with the golden ball, the princess grabbed it and ran home leaving the frog and her promise behind her.

However, that evening when the king and all the courtiers were eating at table, there was a wet knock at the door. The princess ran to answer it but slammed it shut when she saw the caller. The king asked who it was and the princess was forced to tell the story of what had happened.

The king told her: "You should never despise those who have helped you in trouble. What you have promised, you must perform. Let him in." His daughter rose from the table and reluctantly let in old splasher who took the place of honour at the dinner table. The frog enjoyed what he ate, but the princess had a sudden loss of appetite.

After the feast, she took hold of the frog with two fingers, carried him upstairs, and put him in a corner. He challenged her to keep her promise: in sympathy he suggested that she kiss him on the nose while closing her eyes and thinking of England! Of course, then he was transformed into the most handsome prince she had ever set eyes on. He had been under a spell and could be released only by a little love. That was enough to transform him into someone who was recognisably human. The next day, needless to say, the couple left to inherit the kingdom that was awaiting them.

But, as one lady remarked when she heard the story: "That's all very well. In life you have to kiss a lot of frogs before you meet the handsome prince!"

A kingdom for the overlooked

In today's Gospel Jesus is at a meal in the house of one of the leading Pharisees. He has noticed an undignified scramble for the places of honour and is moved to comment on what he sees. When a guest arrives early at a feast to appoint himself a place of honour, his position is insecure because he runs the risk that a later guest will have more claim to his place. And when the host insists that he vacates the place, he will have to pass all the other places already occupied and take the lowest place. Jesus advises that his listeners take the lowest place at table – then the only risk they run is that of being exalted! Since it is the *host's* party, *he* should decide who sits where.

When Jesus addresses his host he advocates a more radical style: learning humility not so much by playing musical chairs at banquets, but by *associating* with the poor, the crippled, the lame, and the blind. The guest-list for Jesus' feast is a parable of the kingdom: God is the eccentric host whose delight is to feast those who are always overlooked in a society that scrambles for honour.

So the guest-list includes the old lady in the moth-eaten fur coat who carries her kingdom in plastic bags; the legion of the crippled who hobble where others hop; the blind who have to feel for the warmth of a fire they cannot see; the lonely who are never invited anywhere. These are the ones who are led to the seats of honour in the kingdom; the little people who cannot return the invitations and are hungry for the food and the company that table fellowship can bring. Jesus has a credo that hugs these people into importance.

In the upside-down world of the fairy-tale and the Gospel there is a wisdom of reversal: behind what appears to be ugliness there is beauty; behind what appears to be foolishness there is wisdom; behind the faces of the scarred and the broken there is great dignity. Jesus keeps God's preference for the little people at the forefront of his teaching. He has the kind of love that sees beyond appearances, the kind of love that pierces disguises, the kind of love that calls people out of imprisonment. *His love dignifies people*. He asks that our love does too. This week, then, watch out for the frogs!

What cannot hurt your neighbour

To tell or not to tell

What do you do when someone hurts or offends you? Do you keep the hurt to yourself and brood over your wounds? Or do you confront the person and give voice to your annoyance or anger? To tell or not to tell: that is the question. There is a poem by William Blake, "The Poison Tree", which imaginatively explores this problem:

> I was angry with my friend:
> I told my wrath, my wrath did end.
> I was angry with my foe:
> I told it not, my wrath did grow.
>
> And I water'd it in fears,
> Night and morning with my tears;
> And I sunned it with smiles,
> And with soft deceitful wiles.
>
> And it grew both day and night,
> till it bore an apple bright;
> And my foe beheld it shine,
> And he knew that it was mine.
>
> And into my garden stole
> When the night had veil'd the pole:
> In the morning glad I see
> My foe outstretch'd beneath the tree.

Having it out

In today's Gospel Matthew gives a setting for addressing issues and problems which arise in the life of the organised community of the local church. He is writing at a time when Jesus is present, not in the flesh, but in the spirit, wherever two or three are gathered in his name. The theme is the relationship of members of the church, "brothers" to one another, in an offence that violates the bond of brotherhood. Matthew writes this instruction in the setting of an address given by Jesus to his disciples.

The advice is straightforward: "If your brother does something wrong, go and have it out with him alone, between your two selves." The Gospel says that the offended party, not the offending one, should first seek reconciliation. It counsels personal intervention and honest confrontation.

It encourages members of the Christian community to straighten things out with each other privately, if that is at all possible. Christians are to deal with each other candidly and personally – no anonymous complaints to the authorities, no whisper campaigns. The purpose of confronting a brother who has done wrong is not to humiliate him, but to be reconciled with him. It is an honest attempt to avoid a poison tree springing up between two Christians.

If private reconciliation fails, another attempt must be made by invoking the help of one or two others, who are to try to settle the matter before it goes public. Only when this fails is the offended party to bring the matter to the attention of the whole community. If the wayward brother is still impenitent, he must be excluded from the life of the community. The decision of the local community will be the decision of God: as he inspires them in making the decision, so he will also honour their judgement.

Love: the one thing that cannot hurt your neighbour
All the practical advice in the Gospel centres on Christians taking responsibility for each other. Belonging to a community implies being involved in the life of its members. This is not a charter for the legion of the curious, but a procedure for a caring community to follow. It is a way of handling wrongdoing and hurt. Just as conflict is sure to happen in a community of sinners, so confrontation can sometimes be the only language of love. Like the story of the poison tree, the refusal to confront ends up in being the refusal to love.

Paul tells us in today's second reading: "Love is the one thing that cannot hurt your neighbour". If love faces the real, it cannot avoid facing conflict. Where silence would permit greater division in the community, love must do something. As Edmund Burke noted: "All that is necessary for the triumph of evil is that good men do nothing." And doing nothing in the face of wrongdoing and hurt is precisely what the Gospel opposes.

Today's Gospel is not easy to follow. So, we try to approach each other gingerly, hoping that our halting efforts at giving voice to our hurt will be accepted in the best spirit. It may not work, but it beats planting a fatal orchard with our anger.

A classless faith

Class

Barbara Cartland, a prolific writer of popular romances, came into remote contact with royal circles when her daughter Raine's stepdaughter became the Princess of Wales in 1981. When Miss Cartland was interviewed for the BBC radio programme *Today,* the woman interviewer asked her if she thought that class barriers had broken down in Britain. "Of course they have," replied Miss Cartland, "or I wouldn't be sitting here talking to someone like you."

That kind of snobbery can be dismissed as harmless stupidity or, depending on your point of view, can be interpreted as furthering the class division it claims has disappeared. We may smile at Miss Cartland, but she is not a minority of one. We know that prejudice forms part of our way of looking at each other and the world.

Each of us has inherited a mixed bag of beliefs and suspicions, some of which we have grown to discard, others we have adopted and made our own. The prejudices that serve to prop up our sense of superiority, while keeping others in diminishment, are particularly difficult to tear down. We can all decorate our insecurity by regarding as inferior those who are different from ourselves, for reasons of class or race or religion or whatever. But if our own sense of worth is maintained at the expense of other people's dignity, what value is it?

Faith and distinctions

In today's second reading, which comes from the letter of St James, we hear this simple advice: "My brothers, do not try to combine faith in Jesus Christ, our glorified Lord, with the making of distinctions between classes of people." The letter goes on to criticise the attitude which presumes that the well dressed man who enters the synagogue, with gold ring glinting its own message, naturally deserves more attention and care than the poor man who enters at the same time. If preference is going to be made, it should reflect the declared preference of God: he chose those who are poor according to the world, to be rich in faith and to be heirs of the kingdom he promises.

God's preference for those who are poor according to this world is seen clearly in today's Gospel. Jesus comes face to face with a deaf man who has a speech impediment. The man is doubly afflicted: he is a Gentile, hence regarded by orthodox Jews as unclean, and is also physically handicapped. Jesus takes him aside, away from the crowd, and cures his deafness and his stutter. Mark emphasises the response of the crowd, who publish their judgement that Jesus had done all things well. Thus the messianic prophecy of Isaiah heard in the first reading is seen to be fulfilled: the ears of the deaf are unsealed and the tongues of the dumb sing for joy.

Out of his infinite passion Jesus' love is available to everyone, without any presuppositions or any conditions. He is not disconcerted by the handicapped; neither is he prejudiced against those not of his own race or religion. His own uniqueness is not employed to lord it over others, but to be of service to them. In his presence no one has to conceal his handicap, no one has to remain isolated in a wordless world, no one has to be rejected because of his difference. Jesus' acceptance and love open up new possibilities; for him, nothing is settled. Prejudice, on the other hand, tries to settle everything.

Acceptance

Jesus knows that people shrink back under indifference, are wounded by prejudice, are hurt when they are rejected. Prejudice handicaps everyone it touches; it allows fear to dress up as social and religious propriety; it sneaks its way into our laws. It is a killer disease.

It is always good to remember that whoever we meet, God has first loved them. So let us be challenged by the words of wisdom:

> Our first task in approaching
> another people, another culture, another religion
> is to take off our shoes
> for the place we are approaching
> is holy.
> Else we may find ourselves
> treading on another's dream.
> More serious still, we may forget
> that God was there
> before our arrival.

Figuring things out

Nearness and distance

"Whatever you say, say nothing" was a piece of wisdom the Irish poet Seamus Heaney learned from his mother. But that advice doesn't make for writing poetry and the son had to shelve its claim on him. Heaney has reflected on his relationship with his father, a farmer close to the land, a quiet man who had reason to believe that language was a kind of betrayal. In his writing Heaney tries to figure out his father whose inwardness and reserve are a constant challenge to a son who wants to fathom him and get close to him. As he writes in his poem, *Follower:*

> I wanted to grow up and plough,
> To close one eye, stiffen my arm.
> All I ever did was follow
> In his broad shadow round the farm.
>
> I was a nuisance, tripping, falling,
> Yapping always. But today
> It is my father who keeps stumbling
> Behind me, and will not go away.

The son starts out trying to follow in his father's footsteps but he discovers later that their skills are different: the son's new produce is poems, not potatoes. There doesn't appear to be much common ground there; but even though their skills divide them, their roots keep them attached. Perhaps it is true to say that no matter how close people may be, everyone still has a lot of figuring out to do!

Figuring people out

In today's first reading the author of Wisdom reflects that it is hardly surprising that we have trouble figuring out the intentions of God when we have so much trouble figuring each other out. He warns: "It is hard enough for us to work out what is on earth, laborious to know what lies within our reach." There are times when those within our reach puzzle us, just as we puzzle them; there are times when we have to work at understanding our *own* intentions and behaviour because we are a puzzle to ourselves. If people can be compared to books, nobody can be understood after a first reading. And even though God has revealed himself through his Holy Spirit, nobody can claim to fully understand the mystery that is God. We still have much to figure out.

In the second reading there is a marvellous image of Paul, under house arrest in Rome, trying to figure out how to send a runaway slave back to his Christian master. Paul writes to Philemon who legally owns Onesimus as his slave. The slave ran away to Rome where he was converted by Paul. So Paul writes with care speaking of himself as an old man and the slave as "a child of mine...part of my own self." He expresses his hope that Philemon will receive Onesimus not as a slave, but as "a dear brother; especially dear to me." Paul pulls at the old heartstrings hoping that Philemon can see that he is not regaining a slave but receiving a brother in Christ. As a prisoner, Paul puts his love to work in the service of someone else in bondage.

In the Gospel there is plenty of figuring out to be done too. Jesus gives people notice that they have to work out for themselves if they are equal to the demands of discipleship. That means that first they have to figure out the cost of discipleship, then consider whether they have the resources to meet that cost.

To drive the point home, Jesus uses twin parables. Anyone intending to build a tower would *"first sit down and work out the cost"*. If he started without finishing, the sum of his achievement would be a monument to his own stupidity. Likewise, the king who discovers that his forces are outnumbered would *"first sit down and consider"* whether the opposing arithmetic is too heavy. If he wants to be a smart survivor he will practice his speeches on the wonders of peace! In both instances the advice is clear: take the time; sit down; look at the demands; figure out whether you can honestly meet them.

No casual followers

There is a simple, practical realism in Jesus' advice. He doesn't want people rushing headlong into instant commitment while ignoring the cost and their own capabilities. Discipleship involves having no security other than total commitment to Jesus.

Much of our lives involves figuring out what is within our reach and what we ourselves can realistically achieve. Jesus knows that his disciples must prefer following him to following in their fathers' footsteps. He calls them away from the primacy of the family because discipleship means a new and all-consuming loyalty. It means following in the "broad shadow" of a master who makes his way of love with a cross on his back. Nobody can do that casually.

Remembering to forgive

Nursing anger

Abraham Lincoln, sixteenth president of the United States, was elected to office on an antislavery ticket, an election that precipitated the Civil War. In 1863 Lincoln issued a proclamation freeing Southern slaves, and two years later masterminded the Thirteenth Amendment, prohibiting slavery anywhere in the United States. Lincoln was opposed to all forms of slavery, not least people becoming slaves of their own anger and resentment.

Lincoln's secretary of war, Edwin Stanton, had some trouble with a major general who accused him, in abusive terms, of favouritism. Stanton complained to Lincoln, who suggested that he write the officer a sharp letter. Stanton did so, and showed the strongly worded statement to the president, who applauded its powerful language. "What are you going to do with it?" he asked. Surprised at the question, Stanton said: "Send it, of course." Lincoln shook his head. "You don't want to send that letter," he said. "Put it in the stove. That's what I do when I've written a letter when I am angry. It's a good letter and you had a good time writing it and feel better. Now, burn it and write another."

Lincoln could have been following the advice in today's first reading, which underlines the futility of vengeance:

> If a man nurses anger against another,
> can he then demand compassion from the Lord?
> Showing no pity for a man like himself,
> can he then plead for his own sins?

Nursing anger or cherishing resentment is dangerous for our health, indeed fatal: it disables us and renders us defenceless when we look for our own sins to be forgiven.

Forgiveness without limit

In today's Gospel Matthew continues to deal with relations between Christians, focusing on the need for forgiveness between members of the community. Peter asks Jesus how often he should forgive his brother, then answers his own question by suggesting seven times. The Jewish tradition taught that God forgives three times and punishes on the fourth occasion; it was not believed that injured people could be more gracious than God, so forgiveness was limited to three times. According to that tradition Peter's measure is generous; but according to Jesus it is radically insufficient. In his reply Jesus reverses the old law of vengeance: "If Cain is to be avenged seven-fold, truly Lamech is to be avenged seventy and seven-fold." (Gen 4:24) Just as in the old days there was no limit to hatred and vengeance, so among Christians there is to be no limit to mercy and forgiveness.

The parable of the unforgiving official is told in order to underline the need for forgiveness. When a king calls his court officials to audit the accounts, one shows a deficiency of ten thousand talents, a colossal sum of money. The sum is deliberately extravagant, running into millions of pounds, to heighten the contrast with the few pounds owed to the official. When the king orders the sale of the debtor and his family into slavery, the official pleads for time. The king feels sorry for him and decides to remit the whole of the vast debt. The official, however, learns nothing from his experience, for he refuses to give a colleague time to pay a trifling debt; instead, he has him thrown into prison. When this heartless behaviour is reported to the king, the grant of full forgiveness is retracted and the unforgiving official is thrown to the torturers.

Remembering to forgive

Apart from anything else, the unforgiving official is condemned for loss of memory. Forgetfulness of our own sins leads to lack of compassion; remembering how our sins have gone unpunished by God should lead us to forgive others. Through forgetfulness of God's compassion, we can end up becoming cruel to each other. That is why at the beginning of each eucharist we are invited to be mindful of our own sins. Only when we do that can we pray the "Our Father": "forgive us our trespasses as we forgive those who trespass against us."

The purpose of calling our sins to mind is not to paralyse us, but to remind us that we all live in the gracious forgiveness of God. To forget that is theological suicide. Whoever we are, we remember our sins because we need to remember always to forgive.

The true identity of Jesus

Identification

The US film actor James Cagney is credited with having an extraordinary memory. His wife recalled an instance of it. "One day not long ago, we were getting into a car in New York, and he saw a man across the street. 'You see that fellow over there?' Jimmy said to me. 'He sat next to me in school. His name is Nathan Skidelsky.' 'Prove it,' I told him. 'Go and say hello.' So he did. And you know what? It *was* Nathan Skidelsky. The only problem was, he didn't remember who Jimmy Cagney was."

When people we know fail to recognise us, usually we are disappointed. We like people to get our name right, if only for the purpose of correct identification. Perhaps few of us would risk asking our friends, "Who do people say that I am?" Hearing reports of what people say about us or how they see us, however politely phrased, can dishearten us. Even alarm us. What if none of the answers match our own self-understanding?

When Jesus asks his disciples in today's Gospel, "Who do people say that I am?" the guesses all point to someone else, Elijah or John the Baptist or one of the prophets, figures celebrated for pointing forward to the Messiah. In contrast to what others think, Peter speaks on behalf of the disciples who have shared Jesus' life intimately: he identifies Jesus as the Christ. Jesus is not numbered among those pointing to the Messiah; he *is* the Messiah.

Jesus answers his own question

In response to Peter's confession Jesus swears the disciples to silence, as if he does not wish to be known publicly as the Messiah. The traditional understanding of the title portrayed a spectacular figure who would accomplish victory over Israel's oppressors by the use of military might, a conqueror who would never be touched by suffering or defeat. This understanding is a world away from Jesus' understanding of his own role. The secret of his true identity will be revealed in his passion. The cross will uncover the truth of who he really is.

Jesus speaks about himself through the figure of the Son of Man, who must suffer and be rejected and be put to death. Not only must he suffer, but experience comfortless suffering in being rejected. That rejection robs the suffering one of his dignity. He has to face forsakenness. He will not die of natural causes, but be put to death. And this experience of dereliction will be answered by God who will raise him up on the third day. Thus, whoever wants to understand Jesus must first look upon the figure of the suffering Son of Man.

That future of suffering is what Peter denies has to happen. He strongly objects to what Jesus has said. Peter wants his Messiah strong and victorious and invulnerable. But Jesus rejects the idea of a future free from suffering; he rejects Peter's longing for invulnerable leadership; he rejects the God of Peter's dreams. A God who is a stranger to suffering and rejection is the invention of Satan. God will permit himself, in his Son, to be wounded and rejected and slain. Jesus is determined to suffer for the sorrows of others: to understand that is to understand the uniqueness of his being.

The identity of Jesus' followers

When the passion of Jesus gets under way, Peter will deny his master: "I do not know the man." Only later will Peter fully understand the depth of meaning in what Jesus says. In the meantime, Jesus calls the crowd and the disciples to him and says: *"If* anyone wants to be a follower of mine..." Jesus compels no one, not even his disciples, to follow him on the road of suffering. If they do, if we do, denial of self is the first requisite. That is essential if we are to take our cross upon ourselves and share Christ's passion in the world.

The cross of Jesus was for Jesus alone. No one is expected to carry the burden that lay on him alone. Jesus invites us to take up our own crosses, the weight of suffering which comes our way when we follow in his footsteps.

The Son of Man has gone before us, and in following his way we find our community with God. As Jesus' true identity was revealed in the story of the Son of Man, so our true identity is uncovered when we become the followers of the Son of Man. In the language of the letter of St James, that happens when we put our faith to work. Our faith is tested in the real world, and reality comes to us often in the shape of a cross. In taking it up, in accepting its burden, we live up to our true name as Christians.

A Father and Two Sons

Hostility or hospitality

In today's Gospel two religious attitudes collide with each other. The conflict that Luke addresses is an important one: what is the correct religious attitude towards sinners? On the one hand there are the scribes and the Pharisees who complain that Jesus welcomes sinners and actually eats with them. They believe that religious people should separate themselves not only from sin but from sinners. They believe in segregation. Jesus, on the other hand, holds the opposite view: he believes in association. Rather than separating himself from sinners, Jesus welcomes them and eats with them. The scribes and Pharisees believe that hostility is the answer; Jesus believes that hospitality is the answer. Hence the collision.

In the Gospel of Luke Jesus sees his mission in terms of seeking out the company of sinners, moving into their lives: "For the Son of Man has come to seek and save the lost." (19:10) The Pharisees, whose name means the "separated ones", feel obliged to register their complaint about Jesus' pastoral strategy. While they come to complain to Jesus, the tax-collectors and sinners come to hear what Jesus has to say. These two opposing groups form Jesus' audience, and both are represented in the story that Jesus tells.

Two sons

The story is told of a father who has two sons and who loses them both. One son is lost in a far country, and the other is lost in the wilderness of his own hostility. One leaves home in the fond hope that he will experience happiness in the unfamiliar, only to discover it is found at the heart of the familiar. One stays at home but is such a stranger to the love and acceptance which surround him that he might as well be an alien in a foreign land. They are a mixed human family in which tenderness and selfishness and hostility vie with each other for possession.

The younger son yearns for a life different from that at home. He leaves home and soon discovers that his promised land is barren. He experiences failure, but his failure is not unimportant: through his failure he comes to himself. It appears that the younger son has gone on a fruitless journey to end up where he started; but if he ends up in the same place, *he* is different. At journey's end he is a man on new insight. As T.S. Eliot wrote:

> And the end of all our exploring
> Will be to arrive where we started
> And know the place for the first time.

The elder son does not leave home, but staying at home has not led him to hospitality. When he returns from the fields, with the sweat of the slave on his brow, he hears music and dancing. Rather than hurry in to join the party, he reacts with anger. Unlike his father, he does not have the generous instinct to rush to meet the younger brother. The elder brother refuses to move. He sees himself as a slave: "All these years I have slaved for you..." His own anger immobilises him. Now, it is he who is far from home. He is "the separated one" who cannot move to accept his brother and rejoice with him.

The father's attitude

The father loves both his sons and he lives in the hope that they will love and accept each other. The father's attitude reflects the generosity of Jesus' way of dealing with sinners. Jesus has both sons represented in his audience: the separated ones who, like the elder son, refuse to welcome their brother sinners; and the sinners who, like the younger son, hope to be accepted when they make for home. Jesus' appeal, like the father's appeal, is aimed at religious intolerance.

Like the elder son in the parable, the Pharisees and scribes are good and upright. They do their duty faithfully. They may be without sin. But if their sinlessness adds up to lovelessness, what virtue is in it? If their religious fidelity permits them to reject their brother, what purpose does it serve? They end up being enslaved by their own religious intolerance.

At the end of the parable Jesus does not say if the elder brother moves to accept his younger brother who was lost. The story is still being told today. The answer is in our own behaviour.

A Gospel for latecomers

Unlikely winners

Once upon a time in the kingdom of fairyland there lived a large section of people who seemed to have little going for them. They are the youngest sons, the natural late-comers in life, who arrive too late to inherit the property, who never have the first choice of anything, who are the last to inherit the genes. They are always compared to their discredit with their elder brothers, who are smarter, harder working, preferred by their parents, acknowledged by their peers, and who always look more likely to marry the princess and inherit the kingdom.

Yet at the heart of these stories there is the wisdom of reversal: the youngest son, the last to arrive and the most unlikely winner of anything, marries the princess and inherits the kingdom. This is never because of his own ingenuity or heavy work schedule; it is not because of any self-improvement course he has undergone; rather, it is because of the graciousness and generosity of others.

Children, whom Jesus recognised had a nose for the kingdom of God, are delighted with these stories of reversal. As adults we often feel the stories to be ridiculous, perhaps because they ridicule the conventional wisdom we cherish. This is the wisdom that teaches us: you get what you work for; if you want something, you must earn it; you get what you pay for; you are rewarded according to your efforts. We are threatened when our world of values is invaded by someone who turns them upside down, when our uncritical presumptions are questioned, when our precious wisdom slips on a banana skin. And yet we know well that the most important experience of life, being looked on in love by the other, is not something which we earn: it is something which depends on the mysterious preference and generosity of someone else.

The Gospel latecomers

The world of the Gospel is peopled with life's latecomers, who find themselves with some form of handicap. They are the physically crippled, the psychologically crippled, the spiritually crippled, the economically crippled. They are the prodigal sons, the outcasts, the overlooked, the ones people think they can safely ignore or shun. They are found in the midst of the Gospel because they are in the midst of life. Jesus has a clear prejudice in their favour, not least because he teaches us what we keep unlearning: that God's ways are not our ways, that he does not work from the arithmetic of the calculator but from the fullness of his own heart.

In today's Gospel Jesus gives us a marvellous insight into the wisdom of reversal which is at the heart of the kingdom. A landowner goes to the market place at dawn to hire casual labour to work in his vineyard. He arranges to pay them the average daily wage, one denarius. The landowner hires other labourers at nine in the morning, noon and mid-afternoon. About five o'clock, an hour before work ends at sunset, he hires the last group of workers. At six o'clock the fun starts: the first to be paid are the last to arrive, and they are given a full day's wage. Those who worked from dawn to sunset receive no more than those who put in only an hour's work in the cool of the evening. The landowner's generosity to the latecomers aggrieves the early starters, even though they are paid the agreed sum. So the landowner confronts them with the question: "Have I no right to do what I like with my own? Why be envious because I am generous?"

The generosity of God

If the parable originally referred to the Pharisees' complaint at Jesus' generous treatment of sinners, then it means that Jesus is treating sinners, the latecomers, with the same mercy as he has for those who have borne the burden of the Law. In Luke's Gospel the Pharisees' complaint is met with the parable of the prodigal son, in which the elder brother complains that he has not been treated according to his deserts. In both parables we are invited to consider the generosity of God, a generosity that makes other people furious.

Do we allow God the freedom to do things his way, or do we get furious when he diverts from our way of operating. We may think it only our right to sing "I did it my way", but what happens when we hear the Lord singing it? If we resent his freedom to show mercy to whom he pleases, not only do we repeat the grumble of the labourers in the parable, but we forget how we ourselves benefit from his mercy. As Shakespeare noted in *The Merchant of Venice:*

> Though justice be thy plea, consider this –
> That in the course of justice none of us
> Should see salvation; we do pray for mercy,
> And that same prayer doth teach us all to render
> The deeds of mercy.

Welcoming the little ones

Littleness

King Oscar II, monarch of Sweden and Norway at the turn of the century, enjoyed visiting schools to talk informally with the pupils. Calling on a village school one day, the king asked the pupils to name the greatest kings of Sweden. The answers were unanimous: Gustavus Vasa, Gustavus Adolphus, Charles XII. The teacher was embarrassed with the response, so she leaned over to one little boy and whispered something in his ear. "And King Oscar," proclaimed the child. "Really? And what has King Oscar done that is so remarkable?" asked the king. "I – I – I don't know," stammered the confused child. "That's all right, my boy," said the king. "Neither do I."

The king readily welcomed the child's remark, even agreed to its stuttering truth. Children have a way of expressing their own limited insights, unaided by the delicacies of language which can disguise adult thinking. Their complete dependence on grown-ups makes them frank about their needs. So much has to be done for them, so much has to be shared with them. Their attitude of trust is necessary for survival.

In today's Gospel Jesus brings the child to centre stage and instructs his disciples: "Anyone who welcomes one of these little children in my name, welcomes me; and anyone who welcomes me welcomes not me but the one who sent me." In this instance Jesus doesn't ask his disciples to *become* like children; he asks his disciples to *welcome* them. Were the disciples having a problem about welcoming littleness?

Powerlessness

You remember that in last week's Gospel Jesus spoke of himself through the figure of the Son of Man who had to suffer and be rejected and be put to death. Following that prediction of the passion, Jesus invited those who would follow him to take up their own crosses. In this week's Gospel Jesus is now travelling secretly through Galilee, taking time to instruct his disciples about how the Son of Man will be delivered into the hands of men and be put to death. The ministry in Galilee is now over; the road that leads to Jerusalem beckons. Jesus is seen to be anxious that his disciples understand the meaning of what lies ahead.

Mark tells us how the disciples respond to this second prediction of the passion: "They did not understand what he said and they were afraid to ask him." The disciples cannot comprehend the future of powerlessness that Jesus maps out for himself. They are afraid to ask him, perhaps because their worst suspicions will be confirmed. Perhaps Jesus does mean exactly what he says; perhaps he will face the coming terror without resorting to power tactics. The disciples cannot face that scenario, so they start their own discussion group about power and prestige.

When the group arrives in Capernaum, Jesus asks them what they have been arguing about on the way. It didn't take long for their seminar on power to grow into an argument about which of them was the greatest. To the question of Jesus, the disciples respond with the silence of shame. It is in that silence that Jesus takes a little child, sets him in front of them, puts his arms around the child, and challenges his disciples to accept the little one. When they can *welcome* that little child, they can welcome the real Jesus.

The way of Jesus

Jesus compares himself to the little child, the one who cannot resort to power tactics when threatened or maltreated. Jesus' protection is his Father; his trust is placed in the God who will ensure his protection. When suffering comes, Jesus refuses to abandon trust in the Father. That trust makes him vulnerable, like a little child, but unless the disciples can come to welcome that vulnerability they will never understand the way of Jesus.

Jesus offers a permanent challenge to his followers to welcome the powerless, to take to heart the weakest members of the community. He places himself in their company. Special hospitality should be offered to those from whom we can benefit the least. Their vulnerability is something that Jesus not only shares but values.

As he takes the road to Jerusalem, his own vulnerability will expose him to those who lie in wait. There will be people keen to explore his gentleness and put his endurance to the test. In drawing his own followers away from looking to power and prestige for models of discipleship, Jesus invites them to a new openness to the Father. No earthly power will save Jesus from death in Jerusalem; only his Father can save him from being left for dead. That is what the Father does. That is how the Father welcomes the trust of the little one.

Acting justly; acting smartly

To act justly

The place is Tekoa, a small town five miles from Bethlehem. The time is about 760 B.C. Something happens to a sheep-farmer called Amos. He receives a call from God to leave his flocks and become a prophet. Amos does not belong to any of the professional schools for prophets; his call comes directly from God. Being a prophet is not a career he could have chosen for himself or an interesting side-line to what he is doing: it becomes a full-time duty. As he says himself: "The lion roars: who is not afraid? Lord Yahweh has spoken: who will not prophesy?" (3:8)

Amos is sent to the northern kingdom of Israel, a society that is sharply and cruelly divided between the rich and the poor. Through the voice of Amos, the invisible God speaks to his people. The prophet is deeply unimpressed by the fancy liturgies and the solemn assemblies:

> Spare me the din of your chanting,
> let me hear none of your strumming on lyres,
> but let justice flow like water
> and uprightness like a never-failing stream. (5:23f)

Amos confronts the vast concrete problem of social injustice. In today's first reading he rails against those who can't wait until the religious festivals are over until they can get back to their real devotion of exploiting the poor and the needy. What is the point of impressive liturgies that feed the egoism of the rich and powerful while keeping the poor as the permanent victims of an unjust system? When liturgy becomes the ally of oppression, it becomes an affront to God. When the worship of God remains wholly uncritical of what is happening in an unjust society, it becomes privileged theatre signifying nothing. For the prophet Amos, the best liturgical music is when justice sounds through the land.

Amos does not try to seduce his listeners with sweet reasonableness; he never saw the inside of a school of diplomacy. He is a countryman who speaks frankly and critically. He feels passionately. Through him God lends his voice to the agony of the poor who are plundered. He screams in protest. Long after everyone else has settled for compromise, the prophet still mourns the loss of fidelity. He hurts from the injustice he sees. His God does not accept that oppression is inevitable or that injustice should be tolerated. That is why Amos calls the people back to wholeness of life and to solidarity as one people under God. They cannot enjoy the protection of God while living off the misery of poor people. Religion and greed cannot worship in the same pew.

To act smartly

The point is made by another country prophet who was born in the same region as Amos. A man who has the same frankness in speech, the same preference for the poor, and the same message: "You cannot be the slave both of God and of money." Jesus expresses his belief that people who cannot be trusted to deal with money can hardly be trusted with the genuine riches of the kingdom of God. The danger is that they will begin to twist their religious beliefs around their money-belts.

Jesus tells an unusual parable which appears to support dishonesty. A steward who manages his master's estates is accused of wasting his employer's goods; he is dismissed, but before he goes he must submit his final account. This gives the steward *time* to plan his future. He is about to join the ranks of the unemployed and he wonders how he will survive. He doesn't waste much time looking at digging and begging as job-creation schemes. Instead, he calls in all those who owe his master and deals with them one by one. A smart operator, he knows the value of secrecy. He gives them an offer they can't refuse by reducing their debts; by the time he is finished, a number of merchants owe him for his inventive arithmetic! Now, his job prospects look healthy; his future is looking good.

In a time of crisis the steward takes firm and immediate action to ensure his own future. He is praised not for his dishonesty, but for his resourcefulness in coping with an emergency with such speed. If a dishonest man can use his employer's money to ensure there will be people to welcome him when he's out of a job, how much more should honest people use their money in such a way that they will be welcomed into the kingdom of God. This is not to argue that people can buy themselves into the kingdom; it is to acknowledge that if the use of money is unrelated to the values of the kingdom then usually people get hurt. And the people who usually get hurt most are the poor.

Whenever God speaks to us, a reminder about the poor and the needy is never far away. Amos and Jesus both voice God's concern by reminders of social justice and personal responsibility. The worship of God has to influence the way we behave; our dealings with each other indicate our worthiness of the kingdom. It's all tied together. If money talks, it should talk in the accent of the kingdom.

"Late have I loved Thee"

In parables

One of the interesting points that emerges from the Gospel is how Jesus does so much of his teaching through storytelling. Paradoxically, Jesus communicates his most telling truths through the medium of fiction. He invites his hearers to use their imagination and follow him into the world of parable. The truth of Jesus' parables does not depend on whether the tales told actually happened – that is not their claim on the hearer; rather, their claim to truth depends on whether they catch something of the unseen reality of the kingdom, or whether they disclose unrecognised truths about people's commitment to God and their relationship with each other.

In the parable we are invited to enter a visual world of dinner parties, sheepfolds, vineyards, welcome households, threatening journeys; a world peopled by rich merchants, mugged travellers, callous judges, awkward neighbours, selfish hosts, good employers, searching housewives, broken families, warring kings, surprised guests, wise and foolish bridesmaids. The point of the parables is not that they make interesting illustrations; the stories tell us it is at the level of our eating, drinking, sleeping, forgiving, choosing, reaching out, journeying, noticing people, answering doors, offering hospitality, sharing bread and listening to midnight stories that our happiness and salvation are being worked out.

In Jesus' parables there is a marked absence of the supernatural: Jesus baptises the ordinary and tells us that it is in the theatre of the ordinary that the drama of the kingdom is lived out. By evoking everyday experience, the parables tells us that we are saved where we are. In the parables we are invited to make a judgement and to come to a decision; they invite us to pay attention, come alive and face things.

Promise and performance

All this can be seen in today's Gospel where Jesus confronts the chief priests and elders of the people. He confronts them with a story, a parable which criticises them for being "yes-men" whose easy promises are not matched by their performance. Fiction is used to face this problem of religious deception. The story is told of a man who has two sons and who asks them both to work in the vineyard. The first son refuses bluntly, "I will not go", but afterwards regrets his decision and changes his mind. The second son agrees politely and readily, "Certainly, sir", but his instant consent is not matched by his behaviour: he doesn't turn up. Jesus' question, "Which of them did the father's will?", only allows for one answer. Only one son *did* anything.

Jesus' own reply identifies the two sons. The son who refused but repented stands for the tax collectors and prostitutes who complied with God's requests set forth in the Baptist's preaching. The other son stands for the priests and scribes who maintain the outward appearance of piety but without any real devotion to the will of God. They did not trust the Baptist, even when they saw the testimony of the changed lives of the tax collectors and prostitutes. Their outward piety, unsupported by obedience to God, is criticised earlier in the Gospel, when Jesus says: "It is not those who say to me, 'Lord, Lord', who will enter the kingdom of heaven, but the person who does the will of my Father in heaven." (7:21)

"Late have I loved Thee"
The son whose word was 'no' but whose action became 'yes' is held out to us as the one who did his father's will. The story doesn't tell us why he changed his mind or what the change cost him, only that his generosity of spirit had the last word. In time he caught up with the best that was in him. He was late in doing his father's will, but not too late.

That son had a real counterpart in St Augustine, whose early life was a blunt refusal to follow the Gospel his mother had held out to him. In his *Confessions* he admits his sexual exploits – from the age of seventeen he had a mistress who bore him a son. The Gospels he regarded as fit only for simple minds; he hunted elsewhere for truth. In time – when he was thirty-two – he caught up with the best in himself and his 'no' turned into a committed 'yes'. The son who eventually said 'yes' reflected on his late decision when he wrote:

> "Late have I loved Thee, O Beauty so ancient and so new, late have I loved Thee!...Thou didst call and cry out and burst in upon my deafness; Thou didst shine forth and glow and drive away my blindness; Thou didst send forth Thy fragrance, and I drew in my breath, and now I pant for Thee; I have tasted, and now I hunger and thirst; Thou didst touch me, and I was inflamed with desire for Thy peace."

Christian tolerance

Being recognised

Few of us go through life without ever joining some kind of group or club. Some people take pride in their membership of a whole range of different groupings, from the local neighbour's association to international companies. For some people, the more select the group the better they feel. Victor Mature, the US film actor who specialised in rather leaden romantic roles, applied for membership in the exclusive Los Angeles Country Club. He was told. "We don't accept actors." "I'm no actor," Mature protested, "and I've sixty-four pictures to prove it." He may have been right, but he didn't get in.

Joining a particular group, religious or political or social, can enlarge our world and introduce us to new people and new possibilities. It can help us to move within a relatively secure network of relationships. That sense of belonging is important to our identity: membership is proof of how others accept and recognise how we see ourselves. Rejection is a clear signal of disapproval. As the clinical psychologist Professor Smail observed:

> In order satisfactorily to function, we depend, throughout our lives, on the presence of others who will accord us validity, identity and reality. You cannot *be* anything if you are not *recognised* as something; in this way your being becomes a dependent on the regard of somebody else.

Rivalry in ministry

In today's Gospel the disciples of Jesus refuse to recognise the authority of an exorcist who doesn't belong to their company. John appeals to Jesus: "Master, we saw a man who is not one of us casting out devils in your name; and because he was not one of us we tried to stop him." The exorcist has been successful in his ministry, and that success clearly worries the disciples.

Earlier in the chapter Mark has told us of a man who appealed to Jesus' disciples to free his son from a spirit of dumbness. This anxious father told Jesus: "I asked your disciples to cast it out and they were unable to." The disciples, who have been noted as unsuccessful exorcists, now see an outsider successfully exorcising in Jesus' name. They don't want this man to function as an exorcist, so they hope Jesus will refuse to *recognise* him. If this happens the man's whole identity will be suspect.

The disciples are obviously threatened by the outsider's success. Are they apprehensive about being displaced? Are they fearful of being supplanted? Do they see ministry in terms of rivalry? Seeing a man's success, the disciples seem to feel diminished, reduced, lessened as disciples. It's as if their own self-esteem will be reinforced if the outsider is rejected. But Jesus refuses to do this. Instead, he invites his fragile company to a larger vision of God's goodness; he commands his followers to leave the outsider in peace: "Anyone who is not against us is for us." Thus Jesus recognises and confirms the exorcist in his identity, and tells his followers that all who welcome *them* because they belong to Christ will not lose their reward.

Recognising the outsiders
The interesting thing to remember is that the disciples are themselves outsiders in their own society. In a world where they hope to be recognised and accepted in Jesus' name, Jesus asks them to extend the same favour to others. Why should the disciples hope for tolerance and hospitality while meeting with intolerance everyone not of their company? Jesus is not threatened by goodness outside his own chosen circle. If his passion is for the good of others, that passion will be served by *anyone* who does God's work. In that sense Jesus is indiscriminate when it comes to goodness – anyone will do.

Jesus' lesson is instructive for ourselves. The cause of Catholicism is not served by the rejection of other ways of Christian discipleship. The case for Christianity is not reinforced by those who claim that no real good can happen beyond the boundaries of faith. We can all take pride in the community to which we belong without denigrating the good work of those who are not "one of us".

Jesus calls on each of us to be tolerant. Christian tolerance is not weakness or a lazy acceptance of whatever movement happens to be in vogue. Christian tolerance is a reverence for the truth that is always larger than ourselves; it is recognition of the charity that flourishes beyond the reaches of our borders; it is a profound respect for the freedom of God to move in his chosen ways. It is a humility before the greatness of God. After all, if God risks hoping in us, why should we deny his hope in others?

When innocence becomes a crime

Fortune and misfortune

In today's Gospel Jesus tells a story of two men, a rich man and a poor man. The first detail we have concerns the rich man's wardrobe: he dresses in purple and fine linen, an outfit which was similar to that worn by the high priest. He feasts magnificently – not once a week, but every day – a figure of massive self-indulgence. You might wonder when he comes up for air in his obsessive commitment to eating. The rich man is wealthy not only in clothes and food; he is also rich in privilege and in the freedom he enjoys from the worry that besets the poor. You cannot imagine him praying, "Give us this day our daily bread". His privilege conceals from him his responsibilities; it blinds him to the man who lies at his own gate.

In contrast to the rich man's clothing, the poor man Lazarus is covered in sores. Lying at the gate of the house, Lazarus can see the traffic that is heading for the rich man's table. He does not expect to be invited to the table: experience has educated him to have humble hopes, and he wishes only for the scraps that fall from the rich man's table. In those days they used their hands rather than knives and forks to eat with, and in wealthy houses the diners cleaned their hands with bread which was then thrown to the dogs.

Remember the Gentile woman who came begging Jesus to help her daughter and how she said: "Even house-dogs can eat the scraps that fall from their master's table." (Mt 15:27) The scraps were regarded as dog-food. That is what Lazarus desires. Dog-food. All he gets is the attention of the half-savage dogs which hunted in packs for food. Meanwhile, he lies there waiting. You *can* imagine Lazarus praying: "Give us this day our daily bread". But he receives not a crumb.

Lazarus dies at the gate of the rich man. The unburied dead were believed to bring a curse on the land. There is no mention of a funeral or a burial for Lazarus. Later, "the rich man died and was buried." No doubt with a rented crowd of mourners. So ends the first scene.

Reversal

In the next scene we are in the other world and there is a reversal of fortunes. Lazarus now reclines in the place of honour at the heavenly banquet, and drinks the best liqueurs in the bosom of Abraham! He is feasted, cherished and happy. In contrast, the rich man is in agony, and the flames which surround him represent the destruction of everything he valued. His wardrobe is gone; his feasting is finished; his fate is fixed. The new agony of the rich man educates him; it awakens in him a compassion for his brothers and he hopes that Lazarus can return to earth and warn them. For the rich man, the flames have become a refining fire.

His regret and his new compassion are not enough, and no warning can be given to his brothers. Unlike the clever steward in last week's parable the rich man did not use his time and resourcefulness to ensure that he would be welcomed in the future. Abraham tells him that no ghostly apparition is going to save his brothers: they have the teachings of scripture and the poor at their gates. That is enough. Finally, then, we are brought back to earth, to the brothers who represent ourselves. Like them, we have the teachings of scripture and we have Lazarus at our gate. We also have someone who *did* rise from the dead. That is more than enough.

When innocence becomes a crime
Remember one of the images Jesus gave of the kingdom of God – the image of the grand dinner party. The people who were invited were too busy about their own affairs to bother coming, so the invitation went out to the poor, the crippled, the heavy of heart. The feast did not begin until all the guests had arrived. Contrast that with the image of the rich man's dinner-table, where the poor and the crippled had no place. It was not that he was rich, but that he was not rich enough to share his goods with those in need.

Christ, on the other hand, shared his riches with everyone. He did not argue that these gifts were like certain foods – to be consumed on the premises; rather, that they had to be shared to be enjoyed. That we are given the gift of compassion because someone, somewhere, is hurting. That we are given the gift of speech because someone, somewhere, is dying for the lack of a kind word. That we are given the gift of forgiveness because someone, somewhere, is cloistered in wrongdoing. None of these gifts is for hoarding. They were given freely; they are to be given freely.

Not to share them is a crime. Dorothee Soelle made the point well in her book, *Suffering:*

> When you look at human suffering concretely you destroy all innocence, all neutrality, every attempt to say, 'It wasn't I; there was nothing I could do; I didn't know.' In the face of suffering you are either with the victim or the executioner – there is no other option.

The rich man did nothing to Lazarus, but he was not innocent. There are times when our innocence is our crime.

The vineyard of the Lord

The Grapes of Wrath

In 1970 Alexander Solzhenitsyn, the Russian émigré writer, published a prose poem entitled "Lake Segden". All roads to this lake are barred, guards with swords and pistols protect it from intruders. The lake is surrounded by a silent wood where no one ventures; everyone has been frightened away. A secret lake in a secret forest. It is a beautiful place, where people could live in harmony with the elements and be inspired. But it cannot be. Away beyond the wood people sweat and heave, whilst all the roads leading to the lake are barred. Solzhenitsyn finishes the story: "Beloved, deserted lake. My native land..."

All imaginative writing, secular and sacred, uses symbols and imagery to describe the beauty and the pain of human experience. In biblical writing the portrayal of the chosen people as *the vineyard of the Lord* was a familiar prophetic image, and we have an example of that in today's first reading, Isaiah's "Song of the Vineyard":

> Let me sing to my friend
> the song of his love for the vineyard.
> My friend had a vineyard
> on a fertile hillside.
> He dug the soil, cleaned it of stones,
> and planted choice vines in it.

With all the care and cultivation he lavishes on his vineyard, the owner has a lively expectation of a good yield at harvest time; but all he receives for his labours are sour grapes. In his disappointment he turns the vineyard into a wasteland, knocking down its walls, leaving it unpruned, undug and overgrown. The vineyard, Isaiah explains, "is the House of Israel, and the men of Judah that chosen plant."

The evil tenants

In today's Gospel Matthew borrows some ideas from Isaiah's Song, but alters the central imagery: Israel is no longer the vineyard itself but tenant farmers working for their landlord. Features of the parable reflect conditions of life in rural Galilee: it was common for land to be owned by absentee landlords, who would collect their rent in kind from the tenant farmers at harvest time. The lengthy absence of the landlords alongside the harsh economic climate of the country often led to difficulties between landlord and tenant, sometimes leading to assaults on the agents sent to collect the rent.

In the parable the landlord plants a vineyard, leases it to tenants and entrusts them with the responsibility of caring for his estate and paying their dues. When vintage time comes the landlord sends his servant to collect what is due him. When they are treated with brutality the landlord sends a larger number – but they meet with the same fate. If desperate situations demand daring remedies, the landlord follows these two catastrophes by sending his son, hoping his tenants will respect him. The landlord's hope is misplaced: his son is thrown out of the vineyard and killed.

Matthew clearly uses the parable, addressed to the chief priests and the elders, as a summary of salvation history. The landlord's servants stand for the succession of prophets God has sent to Israel, only to see them treated with disdain and violence. The son is clearly a figure of Jesus himself, dragged out of Jerusalem to be murdered. Jesus is not just another of the prophets, but God's own Son. The punishment of leasing the vineyard to other tenants clearly indicates Matthew's thought that the kingdom of God will be granted to the Gentiles, who will be expected to deliver the produce.

Patience and judgement

The chief priests and elders react with hostility to the parable, but they cannot yet lay hands on Jesus without endangering their own position. In wanting to lay hands on Jesus, the leaders underline the truth of the parable; and it will only be a matter of time before they create the opportunity to enact its conclusion.

The parable speaks to us about the patience of God: when his servants are killed he sends more and more in the hope that people will turn from their evil ways. Even when these are killed, he still hopes that his beloved Son will make his people change their ways. Jesus is God's last appeal, his final challenge. Depending on our response to him, judgement is then made. If we are now the tenants, then we are subject to God's expectation of us and subject to his judgement of us. God looks to us for the fruits of faith and love and obedience; he expects that we will deliver forgiveness and mercy and justice. Today's parable has its own question addressed to each of us: are these the fruits we produce?

Jesus' teaching on divorce

Beginning together

Every great religion has sacred stories which account for the beginning of creation and the human race. The book of Genesis has two stories of creation, the second of which we hear in today's first reading. God fashions man of dust from the soil and then breathes into his nostrils a breath of life. God's breath is man's life. When God plants a garden in the midst of the wasteland, this garden becomes man's first address. He inhabits a beautiful place in Eden, but the wasteland still surrounds his domain.

The man God creates *is* the human race; he embodies in his person the whole of humanity. He is not one human being among many; he is the Human. To relieve man's aloneness, God begins work at creating a helper. Then there is the striking and comical image of God creating all the beasts and the birds which he brings to man to see if he will name any of them "helper". There is a long procession of candidates for the post: man gives names to them all, but none is named helper. After the interviews, man is still alone. Clearly, God has to think again.

So the Lord makes the man fall into a deep sleep and then takes something from him. What is taken is enclosed in flesh to become a new creature, a woman. The original man makes for two creatures: an individual man and an individual woman. When God brings the woman to the man, this time there is success as the man exclaims, "At last..." The writer adds: "That is why a man leaves his father and mother and joins himself to his wife, and they become one body." In marriage the two separate human beings become *one* body. Only marriage captures the original completion of the total human in one body.

The question of divorce

That original vision of unity and completion is what Jesus calls on in today's Gospel. Some Pharisees ask Jesus if it is against the Law for a man to divorce his wife. When Jesus asks his interrogators what Moses commanded, they reply that Moses permitted it. The Law allowed divorce to the male partner provided that he safeguarded the woman's interest by giving her a writ of dismissal, which freed her to marry again (Deut 24:1-4). What the Law did not settle was in what circumstances divorce was legal.

Divorce was man's prerogative. A woman could sue, asking the court to compel her husband to divorce her; but it was he who divorced her. There was little agreement about the grounds for divorce. The strict school of Shammai interpreted the only ground to be adultery; the lax school of Hillel allowed a man to divorce his wife for trivial causes – if she displeased him, "even if she spoiled a dish for him." Not surprisingly, divorce was common in the time of Jesus, and marriage offered little security for a woman who could be dismissed at her husband's whim. Jesus seeks to change all that.

In his answer to the Pharisees Jesus does not question the validity of the Law of Moses, but claims that it was a concession to human sinfulness. He recalls God's original plan for marriage, revealed in Genesis: that man and woman be united in an indissoluble bond. For Jesus, what God intended from the beginning is the norm for every marriage. And in attempting to restore marriage to a serious life-long commitment, Jesus' argument also protects the woman from being treated as a disposable possession of her husband.

The call of Jesus

In a world where marriage was taken lightly because divorce was managed easily, Jesus calls everyone to go back to the beginning to uncover the original plan of God. It is a call to return to the roots of marriage, an invitation for man and woman to see their commitment to each other in the light of God's seeing. This is not to punish people with idealism, but invite them to live in loyalty to God's original call.

Experience teaches us that things do go terribly wrong. People do make mistakes. Infidelities do happen. Hurt does appear on the agenda. Spouses do become victims and oppressors. Endless silences do happen. Marriages do collapse. There are legions of causalities to prove this, the walking wounded of broken marriages. The Church does try to make provision for human failure and inadequacy, even if the help seems to many to be slow in coming. Nevertheless, the Church must submit to the vision of Jesus, and that vision remains the norm. Because we believe that marriage is a sacrament, we refuse to see it as a casual experiment for adventurous people. In recalling Genesis, Jesus invites all of us to catch up with our beginning.

Not a spirit of timidity

Accusing God

The year is 1965. The place is a synagogue in Russia. The Jewish writer Elie Wiesel, who survived Auschwitz concentration camp as a boy, is attending the service. His eyes are fixed on the old rabbi who is praying and sighing as though in a trance. An ancient, bewildering sadness seems to come from the old man; he appears to be living elsewhere, resigned to all that has happened. Wiesel has a mad thought that the rabbi will shake himself, pound the pulpit, and cry out his pain, his rage, his truth. In his heart he addresses the rabbi:

> Do something, say something, free yourself tonight and you will enter our people's legend; let the hushed reality buried inside you for so many years explode; speak out, say what oppresses you – one cry, just one, will be enough to bring down the walls that encircle and crush you. My eyes pleaded with him, prodded him. In vain. For him it was too late. He had suffered too much, endured too many ordeals for too many years. He no longer had the strength to imagine himself free.

So nothing happened. Nothing interrupted the rhythm of the solemn service. Wiesel was hoping that the old rabbi would find a voice to express suffering, that he would name the anguish that fidelity to God can bring. Suffering can deaden boldness of spirit; but it can also give the sufferer a liberating madness to become God's accuser. And Judaism, which Pope John Paul II has called "our elder brother in faith", has given us a tradition of boldness in dealing with God. It is the boldness of faith which dares to scream at God.

Not a spirit of timidity

Six hundred years before the coming of Christ the prophet Habbakuk screamed at God. As we heard in the first reading, the prophet asks God how long he is going to ignore the cries of his battered people. He accuses God of simply looking on while tyranny and violence flourish. The people suffocate under oppression and under the silence of God. But if God is silent, his prophet thunders as he goes into battle with God. *Because he believes, the prophet is angry.* His cry is not a scream of despair but a cry that is rooted in faith in God. He believes God will *do* something and his faith is proved right. The psalmist put it well when he wrote: "Men's anger will serve to praise you; its survivors will surround you in joy." (Ps 76:10)

That prophetic boldness is something which St Paul demonstrated in his own life – not least when he faced the early opposition from the Jerusalem church. He encourages Timothy to be not only a guardian of the faith he has received but also a minister of boldness. Be a bold guardian! Timothy was Paul's companion for some seventeen years and Paul knew that his close friend was by nature timid and reserved, and also suffered from frequent ailments. Paul tells him that God's gift of ministry is not a spirit of timidity but the Spirit of power and love. As a prisoner himself, Paul asks Timothy to bear the hardships which fidelity to the Gospel brings in its wake. Like the prophet Habbakuk, Paul's boldness of spirit is rooted in his faith in God and is not silenced by suffering.

A bold faith

In the Gospel the apostles ask Jesus to increase their faith and Jesus replies by illustrating the power of faith as small as a mustard seed. That faith is strong enough to uproot the mulberry and plant it in the sea. Transplanting trees into the ocean would certainly be regarded as bold, although Jesus himself never bothered with such eccentric demonstrations. He put his faith to work on behalf of the afflicted who came to him for help and healing. However, Jesus' point still stands: a faith that is rooted in God is capable of a boldness that is awesome.

Jesus' own boldness in dealing with God led the authorities to accuse him of blasphemy and eventually to plot his death. His familiarity with God made him bold – bold enough to call God "Father" and encourage his followers to do the same. In the end, Jesus' deeply rooted faith in God enabled him to see through suffering. Jesus was bold enough to face the cross. He was also bold enough to accuse God of forsaking him.

Sometimes boldness shocks people and upsets them: they would prefer to hang back and suffer in silence. Boldness with God always looks a risky business – not least because God always has the last word! But what if we believed in a God who really *encouraged* boldness? A God who did not get nervous at people screaming at him and coaxing him towards justice? That is the God of the prophet Habbakuk and the apostle Paul. That is the God and Father of our Lord Jesus Christ. That is our God.

We believe in a God who gives us a spirit not of timidity but of boldness, a God for whom we can do wonders while doing only our duty. He is our Father, and it is never too late to argue with him.

Dressing for the party

Invitation to the wedding

In today's Gospel we have two parables from Matthew: the parable of the wedding feast and the parable of the wedding garment. Both are such symbolic stories – allegories – that they only make sense when we see what they stand for; as straightforward stories they make little sense by themselves. A king invites guests to the wedding feast of his son. The king is the figure of God; the great feast was a popular Jewish image for the joy of the life to come – as we heard from today's first reading, "On this mountain, the Lord of hosts will prepare for all people a banquet of rich food, a banquet of fine wines". The image of God in the tradition and in the parable speaks of a generous host who knows how to throw a good party.

When the wedding feast is prepared, the king sends his servants to inform those already invited that the feast is now ready. The servants stand for the prophets of Israel; the invited guests who refuse to come stand for the chosen people of Israel. The king sends out a second group of servants to plead with his guests to honour the invitation; these servants represent the first apostles and their mission to Israel. The original invitation speaks of God's gracious call to his chosen people; the second invitation underlines the patience of God – even when "everything is ready" he still hopes there will be a change of heart.

As Matthew saw it, the consequences of the refusal were terrible. The armies sent by the king are a figure of the Roman armies which besieged and captured Jerusalem in AD 70, demolishing the Temple and burning the city. Finally, the extension of the invitation to the highways and byways represents the carrying of the Gospel to the Gentiles, after Christ has been rejected by the Jewish people.

Dressing for the party

Matthew's story is so overlaid with symbols that it is easy to forget the central image of God as a gracious host who hopes that everyone will come to his banquet. That central image is at the heart of Matthew's story, but it could easily be lost amid the contrary symbols, where roast oxen get cold while a military expedition burns the city. And after that, when the king sees that among the bad and good picked up from the streets there is one without proper attire for a wedding, he has him bound hand and foot and thrown into outer darkness. All this makes it difficult to hold on to the original image of a generous host who knows how to throw a party!

The conclusion to Matthew's parable of the wedding feast is another parable, the story of the wedding garment. It is similar to a parable of Rabban Johanan ben Zakkai, who was teaching about the same times as Matthew was writing. In this parable a king invited his servants to a feast, without saying what time it would take place. The wise prepared themselves at once and waited at the palace gates, for they believed that a palace could prepare a feast very quickly. The foolish went off to their work, for they believed the preparations would leave them plenty of time. Suddenly the king announced that everything was ready. The wise ones came into the royal presence as they were, dressed in clean clothes – the acceptable wedding garment. The foolish ones arrived as they were, in their dirty work clothes. The king welcomed those who were properly dressed, and commanded the others to stand and look on at the joy they had lost.

Matthew's version has been overlaid with symbol: the outside of the hall is described as outer darkness, where men will weep and gnash their teeth; that represents the hall of life in the age to come, and outside it is hell. The wedding garment, the condition for entering the feast, is readiness, that is, conversion. At the final judgement, for the good and the bad, only those who are clothed in goodness will be invited to the banquet of life.

Proper wardrobe
For ourselves, we hold precious the image of God who calls the good and the bad to the banquet of life. The expectation is that we will prepare ourselves now by being dressed appropriately for the occasion. Perhaps the best description of the proper wardrobe for a Christian is given to us by the apostle Paul. If we wear the clothes he describes we will never be thrown out of any banquet.

> You are God's chosen race, his saints; he loves you and you should be clothed in sincere compassion, in kindness and humility, gentleness and patience... Over all these clothes, to keep them together and complete them, put on love. And may the peace of Christ reign in your hearts. (Col.3:12-15)

Discipleship and detachment

Eager and reluctant

In today's Gospel Mark paints a vivid scene of a rich man meeting Jesus on the road to Jerusalem. The aristocrat is eager, impetuous and effusive. The prophet from Nazareth is calm and practical as he meets the seeker's enthusiasm with the challenge of the kingdom. When the rich man throws himself at the feet of Jesus and addresses him as "Good Master", Jesus declines the flattery and tells his suppliant that God alone is good. When the man asks Jesus what he must do to inherit eternal life, Jesus gives him the standard rabbinical answer – keep the commandments. However, this man has sincerely tried to keep the Law all his life; clearly, that observance is not enough. It is his dissatisfaction with mere observance that has led him running to Jesus.

Jesus looks on the rich man with love; he wants this blameless enthusiast to become one of his disciples. So, the challenge is made: "There is one thing you lack. Go and sell everything you own and give the money to the poor, and you will have treasure in heaven, then come, follow me." The cost of Christian discipleship is heavy for this prospective disciple: he must renounce his security and the prestige his wealth brings him; when he sells everything he owns, he must not give the money to his family or friends, but to the poor. If he does this he will have treasure in heaven. That treasure will be his new security.

But that new security is not enough for the rich man. What is treasure in heaven beside the tangible security of his own possessions? Where before he fell on his knees before the person of Jesus, now his face falls at the words of Jesus. He says nothing. The cost of discipleship is too much. He turns and goes away, sad and disappointed, to return to the wealth that holds him from being a disciple of Jesus.

Riches and the kingdom

The sorrowful departure of the would-be disciple that Jesus loved is one of the most touching scenes in the Gospel. He is too attached to what he has to become attached to what Jesus asks. When he goes, and we hear no more of him again, Jesus turns round to tell his disciples how hard it is for those who have riches to enter the kingdom of God.

The disciples are astonished at what Jesus says, mainly because they accepted the traditional Jewish morality which taught that wealth was a sign of God's favour. But Jesus insists on his new teaching: it is hard for anyone to enter the kingdom, but it is easier for a camel to pass through the tiny eye of a needle than for a rich man to enter the kingdom. That vivid picture of the impossible increases the disciples' astonishment. The question now becomes: who can be saved? The answer is that nobody can achieve that on the basis of human effort, for salvation is due solely to the power of God. Everything is possible for God.

Detachment

The story of Jesus' encounter with the rich man and Jesus' teaching on wealth are issued as a challenge to us today. We live in a society which measures success in terms of economic growth and security, a society which rewards the rich with more riches. Nothing succeeds like excess. The danger is that our own values can centre on power, profit and property. If we are what we are devoted to, our real identity is revealed by what we worship. We can all become the devoted disciples of consumerism, powered by desires that will never be satisfied.

The Gospel asks us to pause and reflect about this matter, to look at ourselves critically in the light of Jesus' values. If our identity is locked into our possessions, who are we when our possessions are taken from us? We are afraid that if we have nothing, we are nothing. Like the rich man in today's Gospel, attachment to our possessions can soon lead to our being possessed by our attachments. When this happens, we are no longer free to accept the invitation of Jesus. Attachment to material goods can steal our freedom to choose.

Jesus wants us to enjoy an inner independence, so that who we are is not dependent on what we have. His disciples are identified by their *relationship* with him and by their *relationship* with their neighbour. Detachment from possessions frees the disciple to pay attention to others, and Jesus says that in doing that the disciple will have a whole host of "brothers, sisters, mothers, children and land." When the rich man left Jesus he returned to his possessions; if he had become a disciple he would have inherited a new family. This man without a name ended up the poorer.

Showing gratitude

The risk of helping

The English writer Somerset Maughan had a problem. He had earned a good sum of money from his Spanish royalties but the law forbade him to take any of the money out of the country. Maughan decided to use the money to pay for a luxury holiday. He chose one of the best hotels and dined extravagantly every evening. Nothing was too costly. When he felt satisfied that he had spent most of the money that was due to him, he told the manager that he would be leaving the following day. He asked for the bill.

Instead of going off to get the bill, the manager stood where he was and beamed at his distinguished guest. Maughan was confused. The manager said to him: "It has been an honour having you in our hotel. You have brought much publicity to us while you have been here. We would like to show our gratitude. Therefore, there is no bill."

When we don't expect it, gratitude can be very confusing! When we do expect it and it isn't shown, we are often left feeling bewildered and disappointed. There is a great deal of awkwardness surrounding gratitude. We know from experience that doing some people a favour is to risk losing their friendship. Mark Twain put it bluntly when he wrote: "If you pick up a starving dog and make him prosperous, he will not bite you. That is the principal difference between a dog and a man." Why bother getting hurt by doing some people favours? Why do some people treat you as a leper after you have helped them? This is the issue faced in today's readings.

Grateful lepers

The leper we hear about in the first reading is Naaman, a pagan commander of the Syrian army who has already led military incursions into Israel. His wife had an Israelite slave who had been taken captive, and this girl told Naaman about the prophet Elisha. Naaman was desperate for a cure and made another expedition into Israel, not to capture slaves but to be cured of his leprosy. When Elisha heard he was coming, he sent a message to the Syrian commander to bathe seven times in the Jordan river. Naaman was furious, but eventually his friends persuaded him to follow the advice of the prophet. He did and was cured.

Rather than return to Syria, the commander sought out the prophet to show his gratitude and offer him a reward. Elisha declined the reward but agreed that Naaman should take back some earth to build a shrine to the one true God. Naaman not only rejoiced in the gift of healing he had received but also recognised the giver. He praised God and thanked the prophet. So it is that the God of Israel heals the outsider and the pagan.

It is worth noting that Luke is the only writer in the New Testament to mention Naaman (4:27) and he sees this story as a good example of God's reach to those outside Israel. Remember that Luke is writing to the Gentiles and he has a particular interest in presenting God's call to all peoples. So, when Luke tells the story of the ten lepers, it isn't surprising that the only one who shows gratitude is a foreigner, the Samaritan. Like Naaman, it is the outsider who shows his faith in God and his gratitude to God's servant.

All ten lepers experience healing. One turns on his tracks and begins a charismatic shout in praise of God and makes Jesus his new destination. When the Samaritan returns to thank Jesus, the absence of the other nine leaves Jesus hurt and puzzled. He asks, "Were not all ten made clean?" It's as if Jesus is beginning to doubt whether all ten could have been healed since the response is so shabby. He checks his arithmetic. The ingratitude of the nine makes him wonder. What makes people that way? Why do the nine who are healed now treat Jesus as the leper and stay away from him? Why is saying thank you such a problem?

A faith which thanks

Probably the nine lepers were appreciative of what Jesus had done; we don't know, however, why they never bothered to *show* their gratitude to Jesus. We can only look to ourselves to ask why we are often reluctant to say thank you. Sometimes it is because we resent the fact that we needed help in the first place; sometimes we are suspicious of good Samaritans and wonder about their motives. Whatever the reason for our own ingratitude, we know that it diminishes us and those who help us. Ingratitude makes the bill for helping people hard to pick up.

Eucharist means "thanks". When we gather here each Sunday we come to eucharist God in the midst of the assembly. We do what Naaman and the Samaritan leper did: we give praise to God and give thanks for his chosen ones who have graced us with their help. We do not want our thanks chained up inside us; we do not want our gratitude a prisoner that cannot go free. If God's news cannot be chained up, we know that our response to it can. Let our thanks find expression in this eucharist, and perhaps we could all surprise someone this week with a note that is long over-due and which says thanks.

Caesar and God

The question of taxes

When he went hunting, Louis XIV never wore gloves, even in the coldest weather. One day two French peasants paused from their work in the fields to watch the king ride past in the hunt. One voiced his surprise that the king took no precaution against the cold. "Why, his hands must be freezing," he said. The other replied: "Why should they be freezing? He always has his hands in our pockets."

In today's Gospel the issue is about Caesar's right to have his hand in Jewish pockets. Two groups come to confront Jesus with the question; they are members of the Pharisees' sect and the Herodians. The Pharisees resented paying taxes to a foreign king as an infringement of the divine right of God. The Herodians, on the other hand, were supporters of Herod the Great and his family, so favouring collaboration with the Romans and paying taxes to Caesar. These two groups were unnatural associates. If, as Shakespeare noted, "Misery acquaints a man with strange bed-fellows", the same could be said of hatred. The Pharisees and the Herodians are united in their common desire to eliminate Jesus.

Matthew has already developed the story of conflict between Jesus and the religious authorities, who now appear committed to bringing about the downfall of the prophet from Nazareth. Fearing for their own reputation, which has already suffered in open debate with Jesus, they now try to entrap him. Jesus has already shown that he is not intimidated by the religious authorities into a necessary agreement with their practices; they now test him to see if Caesar's imposed rule has intimidated him into agreeing to pay the annual poll tax.

The question

The delegation tries to lay the ground for the charge of treason: if Jesus denies the need to pay tax to Caesar, he could be charged with treason before the Roman governor, Pontius Pilate. Failing that, if Jesus answers affirmatively, he will alienate the majority of his fellow countrymen. Either way, it appears that Jesus has to lose.

As a preface to their question, the spies flatter Jesus by addressing him as "Master" and profess their admiration for his impartial teaching of the ways of God. Only then do they ask the question – whether it is lawful for God's people to pay tribute to Caesar – a question which they have loaded in favour of a negative reply. The tax they refer to is the annual poll tax of one denarius, which was payable to the imperial exchequer by everyone in the land, from the age of puberty to the age of sixty-five. When the tax was first introduced it was the cause of riots and bloodshed. As an annual reminder of Israel's subjugation to Rome, it still caused grievance among the people.

Matthew mentions that Jesus is aware of his questioners' malice. He asks to be shown the money for the tax. They hand him a denarius, the silver coin which bore the image and the inscription of the emperor Tiberius. The fact that Jesus' questioners can produce the Roman coin might suggest that they recognise the rule of Caesar: many pious Jews refused to use the denarius because it violated the Mosaic prohibition against images.

The reply

In his reply Jesus does not answer the original question, but makes an announcement which seems engagingly vague: "Give back to Caesar what belongs to Caesar – and to God what belongs to God." It is tempting to interpret the reply as a teaching on temporal and religious obligations, and argue that Jesus is acknowledging the need to pay taxes to Caesar, while stressing one's primary duty to God: one must pay tribute to Caesar and God, in recognition of one's dual citizenship.

Jesus, however, does not specify the things that belong to Caesar, for Caesar does not possess anything *independently* of God; he does not need to specify the things that belong to God, since everything does. Jesus is hardly arguing to two independent spheres of power and obligation, that of Caesar and that of God, with parallel sets of obligation. Since God has dominion over the whole of creation, *Caesar's relative power is subservient to the ultimate power of God.*

All authority and power have to be evaluated in the light of God's plan. Jesus' questioners could hardly have marvelled at his reply if the only thing he did was to avoid a question by a debating trick. In his reply Jesus gives a teaching: it is for the people to evaluate whether in demanding tribute, Caesar is reflecting the things of God. This evaluation continues in every political community. The political arena is not a territory protected from religious evaluation and criticism. If Caesar is subservient to God, then his laws are open to Christian evaluation. In the world of politics nothing is sacred.

Power and service

Favours

On the 1st July 69 AD Titus Flavius Vespasian was proclaimed Roman emperor by the legions under his command. As emperor he worked hard to improve the conditions of the Roman people, but he had a reputation for meanness. One day a favourite servant approached Vespasian to ask a favour, for a stewardship for a man he claimed was his brother. The emperor told him to wait and asked the candidate for the stewardship to come to him for a private interview. "How much commission have you paid my servant?" he inquired. The applicant mentioned a sum of money. "You may pay that directly to me," said Vespasian and granted him the post. Later the servant referred to the matter, and Vespasian told him: "You'd better go and find yourself another brother. The one you mistook for yours turned out to be mine."

The emperor's servant was trying to do himself a favour by arranging a privileged post for his invented brother. In today's Gospel two real brothers try to do themselves a favour by asking Jesus to ensure their privileged seating arrangements when Jesus is in glory. The favour they want from Jesus is favouritism. They want to sit above the salt, one at Jesus' right hand and the other at his left. While they don't specify which of them should sit at Jesus' right – no doubt that problem would have emerged later – they imagine themselves in a cosy triumvirate of their own devising.

Not long ago the disciples had argued among themselves which of them was the greatest. They had come to no conclusion – perhaps because nobody was voting for anyone else! Given that power vacuum, James and John want to fill the vacuum by asking Jesus to ensure their supremacy. If he does that, the only outstanding issue on the agenda will be which of *them* is the greater.

The authority of service

Jesus tells the two brothers that they don't know what they are asking. He has already spoken about how he will be handed over to the religious authorities, who will condemn him to death and hand him over to the pagans, who will mock him and scourge him and put him to death. The two disciples mention nothing of all this. Their request is to share Jesus' power *when he comes into glory,* so timing their appointment to begin when the suffering is done. Jesus brings the conversation back to what happens before the glory.

Jesus' kingdom is not about who wears the crown, but who bears the cross. So he asks the power-brokers: "Can you drink the cup that I must drink, or be baptised with the baptism with which I must be baptised?" They boast that they can. Jesus tells them that they will have a share in his sufferings, but it isn't for him to assign who sits where in the kingdom. The message is clear: there is no shortcut to God's favour.

Not surprisingly, there is trouble when the other ten disciples hear how the two brothers have tried to set up a junta. So, to avoid more conflict, Jesus reflects on his own image of religious authority. The model for religious authority must not be the pagan rulers: they lord it over others and make their authority felt. Jesus' command to his followers is unambiguous: "This must not happen among you." Before anything else is said, his followers must not imitate those whose standard of greatness is how much power and control they have over people. That has nothing to do with the Gospel.

A service industry

Jesus' image of authority is the one who is servant of all. If there is primacy in his community, it is a primacy of service. Jesus' image of "greatness is service" is not some advertising gimmick, more ingenious than accurate. It addresses real problems. We all know people whose image of service is indistinguishable from fascism, whose insecurity makes them lord it over others, to make sure that their authority is keenly felt. As someone who fled when people wanted him as their king, Jesus is suspicious of people who need to arrange their own enthronement.

Jesus does himself what he asks others to do: to serve, not to be served; to give love freely, not to exact everyone's worship; to reach out to those in need, not to wait for adoring approval. Christian discipleship is a service industry in which there should be no unemployment. There is work for everyone. And as we become more aware of the giftedness of *all* God's people, we see many new ministries arising in the Church. This should continue, until all Christians feel that their service is not only called for, it is actually wanted in the Church. When that happens, we shall be a serving people.

Praying with nerve

Reflection

His name is Bruce MacDonald. He has never married and is earnestly looking for a wife. At sixty-one years of age he protests that he is not a confirmed bachelor but a prospective husband. In a television interview he admitted that time was running out and that he was suffering from writer's cramp with all the petitions he had submitted to lonely hearts advertisements. From the interview it became clear that our hero had developed through the years a dry sense of humour. He said that nobody seems to want the serious attention of a sixty-one year old whose declared pastime is playing the bagpipes!

In an effort to speed his chances of success, Mr MacDonald has taken to going on "Singles Weekends". These adventures have not been easy because he prefers darts to discos, and although some people like darts, few women saw themselves bonded until death to a bagpiper. His success so far has been the exchange of addresses with promises to keep in contact. Nobody ever has. Everyone has lives to pick up again and the farewells are always polite and have a touch of the eternal about them. Still, Mr MacDonald lives in the belief that his persistence will be rewarded and Cupid will hit the target before too long.

When people are persistent but seem to have little chance, we wonder why they bother. Persistence is often regarded in our society not as a virtue but as a vice: "He's got a nerve asking again when he's been refused time and time again." Some people refuse to take no for an answer and hope that their persistence will pay off in the long run. Sometimes it does.

Having nerve

In today's first reading we have a dramatic example of an endurance test. After their freedom from bondage in Egypt, the Israelites are having a tough time dealing with the wilderness and fighting off attacks from nomadic tribesmen. Moses sends Joshua off to engage the enemy and goes to the top of the hill to pray. As long as he keeps his arms raised, the Israelites do well; but when his arms fall, his army seems to follow suit. Even if his companions cheat a little by propping him up, Moses stays with his prayer until the enemy is defeated. His perseverance spells the first military victory for Israel.

In the Gospel the victory is less dramatic but the widow's perseverance wins the day. According to the tradition of Israel a judge was expected to be impartial except to three groups of people – the widow, the orphan, and the stranger. Because these people lived in the absence of familiar love and support, they were vulnerable in a society where influence and money talked. A judge was expected to be partial to them and champion their cause to ensure their rights. The religious law stated: "if you ill-treat them in any way and they make any appeal to me for help, I shall certainly hear their appeal" (Ex 20:22).

When we meet the judge and the widow in the parable we meet them at a crisis point, when both of them are maimed. We have no case history for the widow but we do for the judge. He is a man who is influenced neither by religious principle nor by public opinion. Both justice and compassion are absent from his dealings with the widow. She has no influential friends to bring pressure on the judge and she has no money to bribe him: all she has is the justice of her cause and her own persistence.

The justice of her cause, however, is clearly not enough. She has nerve and she exercises it relentlessly on the judge. He refuses her "for a long time" but she refuses for even longer to take him seriously! It becomes a war of nerves and eventually it's *his nerves* that give in: he grants her justice for the sake of his own health. She puts him on the sick-list and he can imagine himself being worried to death. In fact the widow does the judge an enormous favour: she exhausts him into justice. Her persistence pays off in the end.

Persistence

In telling the parable, Jesus is not comparing God to the unjust judge and suggesting that he answers prayers only to avoid being bothered further. Rather, Jesus *contrasts* God with the judge arguing that if an unjust man can come to justice eventually, how much more will God answer his chosen ones "when he delays to help them". Strange expression that. Usually we say "rush to help". But God has his own time and his *delay* in judgement can give people *more time to repent*.

Jesus encourages us to be persistent in our prayer and never lose heart. In an age where we have become accustomed to instant coffee and instant results, we are impatient with what appears to be endless delays. But the values we cherish are not instantly available: values like peace and justice take time to establish. The danger is that we give up too quickly, that we rest our case too easily. We have to be persistent; *we have to invest our time in our beliefs*. If a sixty-one year old bagpiper can still search for a wife, we can still search for justice until the unjust are worried to death.

Strangers and ourselves

Not one of us

We all like the comfort that comes from belonging, the sense of being attached to particular people and particular places. That sense of belonging gives shape to our identity and provides security in which to grow. Outside our small familiar world there are worlds of strangers, people whom we notice or ignore, depending on our likes and fears and prejudices. Strangers are people we don't know, outsiders defined by their difference and by the fact that they are "not one of us". Often we fear what we don't understand and distrust those whose background or race or belief is different from our own. The question is always one of association or segregation. Do we travel on what we share or do we make a god of how we differ?

In today's first reading we hear how the people of Israel were expected to treat the stranger: "You must not molest the stranger or oppress him, for you lived as strangers in the land of Egypt." The Israelites had themselves been poor and strangers, and just as God had taken pity of them so they were to take pity on outsiders. They were commanded: "If a stranger lives with you in your land, do not molest him. You must count him as one of your own country men and love him as yourself – for you were strangers in the land of Egypt. I am Yahweh your God." (Lev 19:33-34)

The Israelites were commanded *to love the strangers as they loved themselves.* The reason for this was no further than their own experience: they were to look into their own heart and remember the time when they were the outsiders, when they were out of their element. Loving the stranger was something that had to be done because that was what God did: "It is he who sees justice done for the widow and the orphan, who loves the stranger and gives him food and clothing. Love the stranger then, for you were strangers in the land of Egypt." (Deut 10:18)

Hospitality

The stranger ceased feeling estranged when he was offered hospitality. Not surprisingly, hospitality came to be regarded as one of the primary virtues. Especially for a nomadic people, hospitality could be a matter of life and death: travellers depended for their survival on the hospitality of strangers. The stranger, the wayfarer, the outsider, the shadow figure – anyone outside his home territory or natural space – was regarded as someone deserving special care. If the host was an enemy of the stranger, the act of hospitality was seen as a sign of reconciliation. When accepted, the guest was sacred and given the full protection of the host. In response, the guest honoured the customs of the house.

In the tradition of Israel the simple questions which we ask to unmask the stranger (Who are you? Where do you come from? Why are you here?) were reserved for the time *after* hospitality had been offered and accepted, and the guest had bathed and rested and been fed. The guest was allowed to wear the mask of the stranger until he had experienced the courtesies of hospitality. In that atmosphere he then revealed himself. That tradition can be seen in the ancient Welsh greeting:

> Hail guest, we ask not what thou art:
> If friend, we greet thee, hand and heart;
> If stranger, such no longer be;
> If foe, our love shall conquer thee.

The love that conquers

In the Gospel Jesus speaks of the conquering power of love when he asks his followers, "You must love your neighbour as yourself." As the Israelites were asked to love the stranger as themselves, so Christians are asked to love their neighbours. The ultimate offer of hospitality is the offer of love. Often the real stranger is not the person we don't know but the person we don't want to know, the person we refuse to love. That person could be a neighbour or a member of our own family. We can all have strangers in our own house, still waiting to be welcomed and loved.

We are often scared to take people in because we are afraid of being taken in ourselves. We don't want to be duped, taken for a ride. Hospitality, like everything else, has a price. Jesus knew that when he opened up his heart to receive people: after a while the reception room begins to look like an emergency ward. People make demands on you; they bleed you. But remaining secure behind our locked doors has its own penalty: people die from being unvisited, people die behind locked doors and locked hearts, from caring only for themselves. We all need strangers and neighbours to test the quality of our mercy. When we respond, we have the assurance that we minister to Christ: "I was a stranger and you welcomed me." Christ still comes to us not only in the forms of bread and wine but in the form of the stranger seeking welcome. That is Gospel.

Lamentation

Finding a language for suffering

When we think there's something wrong with someone we know, we usually ask, "What's the matter with you today?" That question provides the opportunity for the other person to express in language what, if anything, is wrong. But there are some people whose suffering is so extreme that they cannot speak. We have seen pictures of people on television whose families have been killed, whose homes have been destroyed, who have been left isolated in their suffering. They sit on the ground, head in hands, preoccupied with their own pain and loss. Their suffering has left them numb and mute. Before that extreme suffering, we feel helpless; it seems senseless to say anything at all.

The first step towards overcoming this suffering is to find a language that leads the sufferer out of silence, a language for pain and fear and loss. One of the great teachings of the biblical tradition is that people should express their suffering in lamentation, not repress it in brooding silence. Remaining silent is remaining hopeless, for there is no belief in the possibility of change.

It is not surprising, therefore, that there are so many prayers of lamentation throughout the history of God's people. Lamentations are cries from the heart, shouts of suffering, groans of anguish, screams for help. They are written on a bed of pain, but they express the hope that things will change, that God will listen. Lamentation is the voice of suffering:

> Have mercy on me, Lord, I have no strength...
> I am exhausted with my groaning;
> every night I drench my pillow with tears;
> I bedew my bed with weeping.
> My eyes waste away with grief;
> I have grown old surrounded by my foes. (Ps.6)

The shout of a blind man

The expression of suffering is intended to be more than just self-expression; it is made out of the hope that things can change. Lamentation, therefore, is not pessimistic; it refuses to remain powerless and passive, so it expresses its longing for change. The prayer of lamentation makes a bridge between silent endurance and change. And that can be seen vividly portrayed in today's Gospel.

Jesus is leaving Jericho with his disciples and a large crowd, probably pilgrims travelling to the holy city for Passover. When the blind beggar

Bartimaeus hears that Jesus is so near, he shouts his prayer of lamentation: "Son of David, Jesus, have pity on me." Some of those following Jesus resent this disturbance, so they tell this one-man-uproar to keep quiet. No permission to scream; no permission to find a language for suffering. They represent the school of thought which is content to leave the afflicted to suffer in silence, no doubt in the belief that this is a religious response to suffering.

Without the capacity to communicate his suffering, the blind man will continue to inhabit his world of darkness. He knows that *if there is going to be change, he must communicate his loss to Jesus.* So he screams his lamentation. It stops Jesus in his tracks and he tells the crowd to minister to this blind man by calling him over. The crowd changes its tune: "Courage," they say. "Get up; he is calling you." Jesus asks the question of questions: "What do you want me to do for you?" When the blind man finds a language for his loss, Jesus heals him and compliments him for a faith that saved him. Saved by faith, he uses his new sight to follow Jesus along the road.

Praying lamentation

The healing in the Gospel takes place as a result of the prayer of lamentation. That prayer expresses the pain *and* the faith of Bartimaeus; he believed in a God who pays attention. Why bother screaming if you believe that no one is there to pay attention? Bartimaeus focused on Jesus, ignoring all other advice. He gave his unmixed attention to Jesus. And Jesus returned the compliment.

If we have been brought up to believe that the religious response to suffering should be silence and passivity, then we will find the prayer of lamentation a subversive act. But the loss of that prayer is the loss of a language for our suffering, the loss of a faith that desires to speak honestly to God. When Jesus reaches the end of his road, he will use the prayer of lamentation in Gethsemane. There, on the ground, he will find a language for his own pain and loss and fear. The Good News is that the Father hears that prayer of Jesus. Lamenting is not a useless exercise; it is a prayer that reaches the heart of God.

Praying with honesty

No respecter of the privileged

Before the great spiritual leader Mahatma Gandhi led India in its struggle for independence, he practised law in South Africa. He became keenly aware of the injustice there and he managed to persuade the Indian community to offer passive resistance to the government's policy of discrimination. He had no official political status; his power was based on his immense moral and spiritual authority. One incident which impressed itself on his mind was when he was obliged to step into the gutter so that a group of white passers-by would not be contaminated. Reflecting on the experience afterwards he wrote:

> It has always been a mystery to me how men feel themselves honoured by the humiliation of their fellow beings.

Gandhi made the remark not in anger but in surprise. When he returned to his native India he abandoned the practice of the law to practise *satyagraha* – the non-violent force that is born of truth and love. Gandhi saw truth as having a power of its own and, although he was imprisoned four times for resisting British Colonial rule, he never doubted the rightness of his cause. The little figure in white lived to see power transferred back to 400 million people, one fifth of the earth's population.

In the language of the first reading, Gandhi believed in a God who was no respecter of the privileged to the detriment of the poor. His persistence in his cause for justice is a powerful illustration of the truth we heard proclaimed: "The humble man's prayer pierces the clouds, until it arrives he is inconsolable, nor will he desist until the Most High takes notice of him."

The Pharisee and the tax-collector

In the Gospel Jesus addresses people who pride themselves on their virtue while despising everyone else. They honour themselves by humiliating others. His listeners are in for a shock when he tells them the parable of two men who go to the Temple to pray. One was a good man, the other a real crook. One led a decent religious life, the other was mixed up in corruption – tax collectors worked for the Roman occupying power and made sure they collected high taxes so that they could get a good cut. The good and the bad go to pray, but only one of them actually prays.

The Pharisee addresses his prayer "to himself". There is no doubt who is in the lead role and his prayer sounds like the annual report of current assets. He blesses God that he is not like so many others, although he seems unsure about who exactly he is. He compares himself to the tax-collector whom he treats as a doormat to walk over. He fasts twice a week and gives ten per cent of his earnings to the poor. That is certainly good. If every Christian did that, the complexity of the world would change! But for all his giving, the Pharisee never gives himself. His real self is secret.

The tax-collector stands far off in the shadows. He has no annual accounts to boast of: his percentage is stolen from his own people, including the poor. He tells the simple truth about himself: "God, be merciful to me, a sinner." He doesn't beat about the bush but beats his breast instead. He knows the truth about who he really is, and he throws himself entirely on God's mercy. He has nothing to offer God but his own wrongdoing and brokenness. They are his. He doesn't go outside himself but recognises *his* truth and hopes that God's mercy can take care of it. He owns his own sin. His real self is no secret.

Beloved sinners

Jesus now comments on the story he has told, "But I tell you..." Remember who his listeners are – those who honour themselves by despising others. What Jesus now says will come as a shock to their whole religious system. He declares that the tax-collector goes home justified while the Pharisee does not. The tax-collector gets much more than he asked for: he prayed for *mercy* but is now *justified.* In the judgement of Jesus everything is turned upside down. The tax-collector's prayer "pierced the clouds". The Pharisee's prayer reached its destination: himself.

In the Gospel Jesus is described as the friend of tax-collectors and sinners. Jesus does not put their sinfulness on hold, but enlarges their world by calling them away from sinfulness into the freedom of God's mercy. Long before Gandhi was mystified by how people feel honoured by the humiliation of their fellow beings, Jesus was mystified too. For him, sinners were not just sinners, they were beloved sinners. They deserved more than the violence which keeps them oppressed in their wrongdoing, the violence which rubbishes them and writes them off.

If we come to pray and realise that our religion has a heavy investment in despising other people then we will just go home again as we came. "God, be merciful to us, sinners" is the whole truth and nothing but the truth. Anything else is for the mercy of God.

Fake leadership

Different loyalties

Sometimes when we listen to the Gospel being read we can hear a voice of frustration speaking to us. That voice can be heard in today's Gospel. The evangelist Matthew is torn between his respect for the Law and his criticism of the Law as interpreted by the scribes and the Pharisees. Matthew himself was probably a scribe before he became a convert to Christianity. As a Jewish Christian, he has different, but not opposing, loyalties: he wants to be faithful to the Law of Moses, but at the same time he has a new allegiance to the person of Jesus, the new lawgiver. He is addressing a large urban church, probably at Antioch in Syria, towards the end of the first century. And he tries to respect the two major groups that dominate his church – the Jewish Christians and the Gentile Christians.

Around the year 85 A.D. Christians were excluded from the synagogues. Christians believe, as Matthew is keen to show, that Jesus is the messiah revealed in Hebrew scriptures, the teacher, and the lawgiver of the Church. The evangelist presents the teaching of Jesus as the new Law, and the Christian Church of Jews and Gentiles as the new Israel. By the time Matthew is writing his Gospel, he knows that official Judaism has rejected Jesus. The unbelief and hostility of Judaism has opened up the Gospel to the Gentiles; but Matthew still has to face the hostility of those who oppose Christian belief. In that atmosphere of hostility he writes his Gospel, reflecting the conflict between Christians and Jews in his own city.

The scribes and the Pharisees

The atmosphere of hostility towards the religious leaders of Judaism is evident in today's Gospel. The scribes and Pharisees are presented as bad examples of religious leadership, not to be followed by leaders of the Christian community. Jesus is presented as engaging in violent caricature, arousing the crowds to condemn the scribes and Pharisees. It is a tense and angry scene in which Jesus makes sweeping generalisations: "Everything they do is done to attract attention..." No exceptions admitted. When people are angry there is little point in looking for precise accuracy or neat distinctions: whole groups are written off indiscriminately, real people are pegged as stereotypes. All this happens in the frustration of conflict.

Obviously, there were many scribes and Pharisees who were upright and extremely holy men. But angry caricature takes no account of that truth, and we have to be careful not to dismiss them out of hand. Matthew is warning against attitudes and practices which are not peculiar to any religious group. The scribes and Pharisees happen to serve as useful examples – especially since at the time of writing they represent the religious leadership opposed to Matthew's church and the style of leadership Matthew is opposed to *within* his church.

Religious leadership

In his criticism of religious leadership Matthew argues that the requirements of the Law as laid down by the scribes are a burden which people cannot bear. Not only are the burdens imposed too heavy, but religious leaders absolve themselves from all responsibility of removing them. This criticism is echoed in the Acts of the Apostles when Peter opposes certain members of the Pharisees' party who have become Christians: "It would only provoke God's anger now, surely, if you imposed on the disciples the very burden that neither we nor our ancestors were strong enough to support?" (15:10) Faith in Jesus should bring people a new freedom which many had not experienced in Judaism.

Religious leaders are also criticised for craving attention and expecting to be treated with deference by the rank and file members. Honorific titles are criticised, principally because they introduce distinctions which obscure a most important truth: that all disciples have only one Father, therefore they are brothers and sisters.

All of Matthew's argument reflects his concern about what is happening in his own church. He is clearly opposed to Christian leaders arrogating to themselves titles that divide the family of the Church into a hierarchy. To do that is to imitate the mistakes of the scribes and the Pharisees. If religious leaders want to strive for any title, it should be that of "servant". Real religious leadership is humble work in the service of the Gospel. The true style of any Christian leader must reflect the style of Christ, the servant of God. Matthew is unambiguous about Christian leadership: if it is not humble service, it is fake.

Why Charlie Chaplin got it right

Love, pity and humanity

On Christmas Day 1977, the world's most celebrated and controversial comedian died. A genius of the silent films, Charlie Chaplin left behind him miles of film featuring the pathetic and lovable little tramp. He also wrote a brilliant autobiography, detailing his life of trials, triumphs and disappointments. At the time of his birth, his mother was a singer on the variety stage; a year later, his parents separated and his mother was left to support the two children. Everything went reasonably well until his mother's voice grew progressively worse through laryngitis. Engagements fell to nothing; their savings soon vanished; his mother's belongings were sold to supplement a tiny income from her dressmaking.

Chaplin recalled that they lived in a world of cheerless twilight, but that the love they shared sustained them. He wrote: "I remember an evening in our own room in the basement of Oakley Street. I lay in bed recovering from a fever. Mother and I were alone. It was late afternoon, and she sat with her back to the window reading, acting and explaining the New Testament and Christ's love and pity for the poor and for little children. She read into the dusk, stopping only to light the lamp, then told of the faith Jesus inspired in the sick. She described Jesus and his arrest and his calm dignity before Pontius Pilate. And in his last dying agony crying out: 'My God, why hast thou forsaken me?'

"Mother had me so carried away that I wanted to die that very night to meet Jesus. But Mother was not so enthusiastic. 'Jesus wants you to live first and fulfil your destiny here,' she said. In that dark room in the basement of Oakley Street, Mother illuminated to me the kindliest light this world has ever known, which has endowed literature and the theatre with their greatest and richest themes: love, pity and humanity."

That's what it's all about

Charlie Chaplin summed up Jesus' life in terms of the kindliest light in the world, one which showed love, pity and humanity. We all have our own way of summing up the importance of Jesus, and in the process we say as much about our own values as we do about the person of Jesus. That practice of summing up what really counts is one we all engage in. And in today's Gospel we see how Jesus is invited to give his summary of the essence of the Law.

The practice of focusing the mind by summarising the Law was a popular tradition among rabbis and their pupils. Perhaps the most famous example in Jewish tradition is the student who asked to be taught the essence of the Law while he stood on one leg. His teacher, Hillel, replied: "What you hate for yourself, do not to your neighbour. This is the whole Law, the rest is commentary; go and learn."

Jesus gathers up the traditional wisdom of Israel in one statement. The first part of his statement quotes the creed of Judaism, to love the one God who is Lord with your whole person and everything in your power. This creed was contained inside a tiny case called the *mezuzah*, which was fixed to the doorpost of every Jewish house and to the door of every room inside. No pious Jew could disagree with this part of Jesus' summary. But alongside this, Jesus places another scriptural passage, to love your neighbour as yourself. For Jesus, it is a *combination* of these separated texts that makes for the essence of the Law. And it is that combination that has given Christianity its basic commandment for life.

The challenge to love
In his reply to the scribe Jesus makes it clear that you cannot compose summaries of the Law while forgetting love of neighbour. The scribe is pleased with Jesus' reply and adds his own point, that the love of God and neighbour is far more important than any ritual worship. In supporting the scribe's addition, Jesus places the demands of liturgy far below the demands of active love. This we see clearly developed in the parable of the Good Samaritan, where the priest and the levite hurry past the demand for love to attend to the demand for liturgy. As Jesus *combines* love of God and love of neighbour, so these religious officials *disconnect* them.

Jesus' summary of the Law is not an academic pastime, it is a personal challenge to love God wholeheartedly and have tender regard for our neighbour in actively promoting his good, just as we should want to do in our own case. That is not only Jesus' digest of the Law, it is also the Gospel portrait of Jesus. That is why Charlie Chaplin's concise summing up of Jesus is right. The man whose pants were too baggy, whose coat was too tight, whose hat was too small, whose shoes were too big summed up Jesus with Gospel accuracy: "Love, pity and compassion." All the rest is commentary.

Zacchaeus

Overlooking sin

We all have our own images of God. Sometimes people imagine God as the great accountant who keeps exact records of everyone's wrongdoing. This God preserves the details of our failings on computer; nothing escapes his attention, nothing is overlooked by him. Given what he sees, he regards his handiwork in creation with omnipotent disapproval, and he waits for the last day when he can confront us with the punishing record of our sin. This depiction of God is a world away from the image of God presented in today's first reading, which comes from the book of Wisdom:

> You are merciful to all, because you can do all things
> and overlook men's sins so that they can repent.
> You love all that exists...
> You spare all things because all things are yours,
> Lord, lover of life...

In this radical understanding God is celebrated as the great lover of life who abhors nothing he has made and who conserves his own creation in a spirit of mercy. Out of this commitment to showing mercy God deals with sinners: he "overlooks men's sins so that they can repent". The sequence is important: first, God overlooks sin; after that, repentance is expected. That sequence underlines the difference between the way God forgives and the way we forgive: we demand repentance first, then we overlook the wrong. Unlike us, God is a professional artist at forgiving. His alertness to sin does not mean that he stays with it, transfixed by human wrongdoing; he overlooks it, hoping that this generosity of spirit will lead sinners to repentance.

The chief tax-collector

That attitude to sinners is evident in today's Gospel, when we see how Jesus treats Zacchaeus. Jesus was passing through Jericho on his way to Jerusalem. Jericho was a wealthy city, an important customs centre on the trade route between Jerusalem and the East. It was the ideal spot for an ambitious tax-collector. Zacchaeus as chief tax-collector would seem to have more than distinguished himself in exploiting others for his own purposes. Although his occupation made him very rich, it would have made him an obvious target for the hatred of his fellow Jews. Tax-collectors were put in the same company as thieves, murderers and prostitutes. And because they were in the employment of the Romans, they were regarded as traitors by their own people.

Confined to his own small circle of friends, Zacchaeus would have had a lonely and isolated life; his riches gave him a loveless privilege. But he has heard of the prophet from Nazareth and his reputation for dealing with sinners and outcasts. Perhaps Zacchaeus had heard that Jesus had a former tax-collector, Levi, who had started his apostleship by organising a feast for Jesus and his fellow tax-collectors (5:27-32). Zacchaeus wants to see Jesus; the Gospel does not say that he wants to meet Jesus. The tax-collector is too small to see over the crowd, so he climbs a sycamore tree. From there, he could overlook Jesus as he passed by.

Jesus' attitude to sinners
Jesus, however, does not pass by the tree; he notices the little man up a tree. Jesus initiates the contact and calls Zacchaeus by name. He does not shout condemnation at Zacchaeus, which might only have served to drive him farther up the tree. Jesus does not exact repentance from him; rather, he overlooks the sins of Zacchaeus and invites him down from his lonely perch. "Hurry, because I must stay at your house today."

Zacchaeus is delighted to welcome Jesus to his house. The crowd, on the other hand, are enraged. But Jesus is more interested in the outcast than the outraged. The crowd is transfixed by the sins Zacchaeus has committed; Jesus sees beyond the sins to the person that Zacchaeus can become. And Jesus' generous attitude to the tax-collector has good results: Zacchaeus does make public amends for his wrongdoing.

Jesus does not demand repentance from Zacchaeus before eating with him. The sequence is important: Jesus overlooks the wrongdoing of Zacchaeus in the hope that he will repent. Because of Jesus' attitude to sinners in welcoming them and eating with them, Jesus gives them the opportunity for repentance *in an atmosphere of acceptance.* That is why Zacchaeus comes down from the tree to face Jesus. That is why we will all come down from our lonely perches to face the one who loves us and wants us to repent. The story continues to be told.

357

Oil Crisis

Wisdom

Herbert Hoover served as President of the United States from 1929 until 1933, and was in office during the Great Depression. His encouragement of big business led to a handful of companies, including Standard Oil, controlling a large proportion of the country's wealth. The Wall Street crash in October 1929 indicated the failure of this policy, and the subsequent depression revealed Hoover's lack of political foresight. He believed the setback was only temporary, and he declared at the height of the collapse that "the fundamental business of the country...is on a sound and prosperous basis". Not surprisingly, he was decisively beaten in the 1932 presidential election. Years later, speaking with the voice of experience, Hoover reflected:

> Wisdom consists not so much in knowing what to do in the ultimate as in knowing what to do next.

Wisdom is the theme of two of the readings today. In the first reading wisdom is personified as a mysterious woman who is never far from those who look for her. Lady Wisdom is near, she lingers at people's gates and doors, she waits to be consulted on all manner of things, she walks the streets looking for those who are worthy of her. She is portrayed not as a rare and elusive being but as a resource within everyone's reach. Like common sense. She is invisible to those who don't expect to find wisdom at the heart of experience.

Oil crisis

When it comes to wisdom, many people shy away from the subject in the belief that it is the proper concern of philosophers or poets. But if wisdom is about knowing what to do next, it clearly concerns all of us. And the parable of the ten bridesmaids and their oil lamps confirms this view. The Gospel story about a small oil crisis in the Middle East tells us of five bridesmaids who are accounted foolish precisely because they weren't prepared for what happened next.

In the story it would seem that the bride awaits the arrival of the bridegroom at her own home. Her friends, acting as bridesmaids, are to meet the bridegroom when he comes with his friends, then join in escorting the couple back to the bridegroom's house, where the wedding-feast will be celebrated. But, as happens at many weddings, there is a hitch; and, as happens at few of our weddings, it is the bridegroom who is late. All ten bridesmaids have lamps and all the lamps have oil. Five of the bridesmaids, however, have no reserve supply of oil. They are unprepared for any delay.

When the bridegroom fails to make his expected appearance, the bridesmaids, weary with waiting, doze off to sleep. At midnight a cry goes up to announce the arrival, and the foolish bridesmaids appeal to the wise for oil from their reserve stock. But the wise need the oil they have to make the lighted escort for the couple. So, the wedding procession, minus five bridesmaids, goes into the feast and the door is shut. When the foolish bridesmaids arrive later, they are refused admission. They were not ready when it mattered; they were not prepared with lamps burning brightly when the bridegroom appeared.

Being ready

The wisdom of the five wise bridesmaids consisted in doing what was expected of them, in being prepared for the arrival of the bridegroom. Their wisdom wasn't extraordinary, but eminently practical. In the language of Herbert Hoover's maxim: their wisdom consisted not so much in knowing what to do in the ultimate as in knowing what to do next.

The message of the Gospel is simple: if we do what we have to do conscientiously, we have no reason to fear the unexpected coming of Christ. There is a blessing in doing the ordinary with sensitivity, in doing the sane and sensible thing, in acting with common sense and prudence. The fourteenth century mystic Meister Eckhat summed it up perfectly when he said: "Wisdom consists in doing the next thing you have to do, doing it with your whole heart, and finding delight in doing it."

All this reflection about wisdom can be seen in one simple well-known story. A holy old monk was sweeping up the fallen leaves in the monastery garden when a visitor asked him: "What would you do, brother, if you knew you were to die in ten minutes." The old monk replied: "I'd carry on sweeping."

The mighty widow

Prosecution

Hugo Black, US politician and Supreme Court justice, was attending the funeral of a dignitary whom he had heartily disliked and whose funeral he would have happily avoided had it not been expected of him. The service began with the invocation of God's blessing on the deceased, then the priest thanked God for gracing the deceased with so many gifts throughout his distinguished life. While this was happening, another judge, arriving late, tiptoed into his place next to Justice Black and whispered, "How far has the service got?" Black whispered back, "They have just opened for the defence."

The dignitaries in today's Gospel need more than a defence counsel, for Jesus is putting his case for the prosecution. The scribes were expert lawyers, who interpreted and applied the written Law through a complicated system of traditions. They were respected teachers, both in the schools and in the courts, and had become accustomed to the honour shown them by the ordinary people. Many of them were devoted and selfless scholars, anxious to save people from transgressing the Law; others were ambitious for their own advancement, anxious only for their vanity to be satisfied. It is the latter group that Jesus confronts in today's Gospel. He reverses the roles: the lawyers become the accused.

Jesus makes a series of charges against the scribes. He criticises their habit of wearing distinctive dress, which marks them as different from others and is calculated to win people's deference. He criticises their habit of taking the places of honour at religious and civil functions. He criticises their habit of long-winded prayers, made not to God but to their immediate audience. Finally, he denounces their practice of exploiting helpless widows by living off their savings. Jesus says that religious leaders who behave like this will face a more severe sentence than the sinners they readily condemn.

The mighty widow

In contrast to the counterfeit piety of the scribes, Jesus honours true pity in the generosity of the poor widow. The pious frauds who abused their religious status by devouring the property of widows could take a lesson from a woman who had no status in religion or society, a poor widow.

The scene is set in the Temple area. Around the walls of the court of women there were thirteen collecting boxes, known from their shape as trumpets. They were set up for people's contributions towards the costs of the sacrifices and running expenses of the Temple. Many rich people put in large sums of money – some, no doubt, trumpeting the size of their contribution. A poor widow puts in two of the smallest coins on circulation. In the arithmetic of the kingdom the widow's offering is worth more than all the other contributions. Whereas the others give from their surplus, she gives everything.

The two small coins make up the total of her resources. She could have kept one. She doesn't. Her reckless generosity cannot be bettered. *For Jesus, true generosity is measured not by what people give but by what they have left after they give.* The poor widow leaves herself with nothing. She cannot give more, for she has nothing more to give. In Jesus' estimation she is a mighty widow.

Real pity

The story of the widow's generosity is well placed at this stage in Mark's Gospel. The poor widow typifies what Jesus will do himself – give everything as an offering to God. When Jesus is finished giving, their will be nothing left for him to give. He gives his all. That is the reality of his piety.

Jesus hopes that his own disciples will takes their cue from that example of real piety, not from the scribes hungry for status and honour. He hopes that we, his followers, will be equally generous with our own resources. Those resources are not always measured in money. We are called on to give of our time, our talent, our understanding. We are asked to give not just from our abundance but from our substance. That kind of giving always hurts, because we feel all spent after it. Like the widow, we might feel that we have nothing more to give; but it's that kind of giving that counts with Jesus.

Every day demands are made on us. We are called on to be generous with our love, our forgiveness, our patience, our resources. And the Good News is that when we do that out of love, Jesus will be our constant support. No matter who the prosecuting counsel turns out to be when our case comes up, Jesus will be leading for the defence.

Questioning Sadducees

The Sadducees

In the course of his public ministry Jesus faces a variety of groups and individuals critical of his beliefs and values. In today's Gospel Jesus is approached by some Sadducees who question him about the resurrection. It is worthwhile recalling how influential the Sadducees were in the political and religious life of Judaism. They formed a select party, drawing their members mainly from the well-to-do class, the higher officials, wealthy merchants, landowners and priests. They originated as a party in the second century B.C. during the time of the Maccabean priest-kings, when the nation was divided over its attitude to foreign culture and influence. The Sadducees were tolerant of Greek culture and ideas, and it was from their party that the statesmen and diplomats were chosen.

Politically, at the time of Jesus, the Sadducees accepted Roman rule and customs in exchange for retaining their power and influence over the Temple and the Supreme Council. They were adept at political compromise and many of their opponents regarded them as political collaborators and traitors. Caiaphas, like other high priests, was a committed Sadducee. In Jesus' time the party enjoyed security under Roman patronage and, not surprisingly, advocated political coexistence. They openly opposed the aggressive nationalism of the Zealots and any activity that endangered the stability of their political base.

The worldly influence of the Sadducees led them to be religiously conservative. Unlike the Pharisees, they accepted as scripture only the written Law of Moses and rejected the authority of oral tradition. As wealthy aristocrats, they did not look to a liberating messiah; neither did they believe in the resurrection of the dead. Belief in angels and spirits was regarded by them as a dangerous novelty. Instead of the resurrection, the Sadducees believed that all men, good and bad, went to the shadowy world of Sheol after their death. That convenient belief left them to enjoy the present, without any worry about the afterlife.

The question of the Sadducees

In today's Gospel the Sadducees pit their fundamentalist interpretation of the Law against what they regard as an unorthodox innovation, belief in the resurrection. They attempt to ridicule the resurrection of the dead by recalling the Mosaic Law on levirate marriage. This law stated that if a man dies and has no son, and, therefore, no legal heir, his brother must marry the widow so that the "first son whom she bears shall succeed to the name of his brother who is dead" (Deut 25:5). In this way the continuity of the family line was guaranteed. The Sadducees develop an example to the point of absurdity in instancing seven brothers each of whom marries the same woman, but each of whom dies childless. None of the brothers has proved husband in terms of producing an heir: in that case, whose wife would the woman be in the resurrection?

In his reply Jesus makes it clear that there is no comparison between human life, shared by all, and the resurrection, shared by those who are children of God. Jesus makes the distinction between two ages and two peoples: the people of this age who live a life peculiar to this time, and the just who are resurrected from the dead into a new age. Jesus does not speak of the resurrection of all people, but resurrection from the dead of those people who "are accounted worthy" to share the new age. As children of God, they cannot die again; therefore, marriage does not apply to them. There will be no need to propagate the human race or to ensure legal succession; therefore, the question of the Sadducees is irrelevant. Since the resurrected are all sons and daughters, their relationship is as members of the same family. And it doesn't make heavenly sense to talk about marrying one's sister.

God of the living
Jesus appeals to the scripture that the Sadducees do accept: Moses called God the God of Abraham, of Isaac and of Jacob. If the Lord is God of the living, then he will continue to be so to those who have died. Relationship with God does not end in death: to God all people are alive.

Jesus' argument with the Sadducees may seem too remote and abstruse to our modern ears. However, religious arguments are rarely simple to understand but sometimes they are worth staying with. Through his argument Jesus reveals something of his own image of God – a God who keeps his promise to his faithful ones even when they die. Jesus does more than argue that case; the time comes when he himself *becomes* the argument. He undergoes death, and he experiences the glory of resurrection when God refuses to let death have the last word. The risen Jesus is the ultimate argument against the Sadducees.

A matter of talent

Risk

In today's Gospel we are introduced to a man who entrusts his property to his servants while he is abroad. He is an enterprising employer, who hopes that his own flair and daring in business matters will be reflected in his servants' attitude to this new challenge. He doesn't instruct them what to do with the talents; he trusts them to use their own initiative and imagination in this economic venture. As in all stories and jokes with three characters, our attention is focused on number three: the third servant is portrayed as the one who refuses to involve himself in the spirit of the enterprise. He believes that the safest way to handle his talent is to bury it and return it intact to his master.

Jesus is seen to be making a point against the scribes and the Pharisees. Their chief aim was to keep the Law which they had been given exactly as it was – not to change it, not to develop it, not to alter it in any way. In their own phrase their mission was "to build a fence around the Law." It's as if they wanted to put the Law into a state of perpetual coma or paralysis – that way they would avoid the risk of its walking the streets, where it would have to change and grow according to the conditions it met. Better to keep the Law in an oxygen tent, under continuous surveillance, and keep it alive on hot air.

Like the man with the one talent, the Pharisees are seen to have an investment in keeping things exactly as they were, and it is for that stale attitude that Jesus condemns them. In this parable Jesus tells us that there can be no religion without risk, no religion without adventure, no religion without enterprise. Willingness to dare is an essential part of our faith.

Attitudes to God

The parable speaks to us about God. Through the story we are invited to imagine a God who bestows gifts on all of us – and so we are gifted. He is a God who gives talents to all of us – and so we are talented. What matters is not what people's talents are, but how they are used in the service of the kingdom. The parable imagines God as a gambler, one who is forever taking risks in entrusting us with his gifts. He has no guarantee on his return, but that is the risk. He dares us to share a common enterprise; he trusts us to do it in our own way, knowing that if it succeeds *both his will and ours will be done.*

The parable also explores different attitudes to God. The first two servants have a completely different attitude to their master than the third. They know that their master is expecting them to share his business attitude for the sake of possible advantage. They know that he expects them to travel on his trust and share his go-for-broke style. The third servant shares none of this, regarding his master as a fierce, exacting man. He is afraid of his master, so he plays out his own fearful attitude by becoming an undertaker to the talent he has received. Instead of rejoicing in his talent, he organises a quiet funeral service. To lose nothing, he risks nothing. And, not surprisingly, nothing comes of it.

The defence of the third servant is interesting. He focuses on the reputed meanness of the master, not on his own proven lack of enterprise. He takes the problem away from where it is – with himself – and places the problem where it is not – with his master. He portrays the master as harsh; there is no admission that his own creativity leans towards the cemetery. He ends up burying part of himself. And we should only bury what is dead.

Our own faith

We can ask ourselves how we imagine God, and how the way we see him influences our attitudes and behaviour. Is God an exacting master who demands that we return to him exactly what we have been given? Is he a gambler and an adventurer, who lives in the fond hope that we will live in the spirit of his trust?

Is our life of faith a life of fear? The American cartoonist Ashleigh Brilliant has a cartoon with two luminous eyes, rounded in terror, peering from the dark enclosure of a stone vault. Underneath, the caption reads: "If you're careful enough, nothing bad or good will ever happen to you." That can never be a portrait of Christian faith. Our faith begins with God. God risked his own Son, the talent of his life. He takes a risk with us every day. It seems only fair that we should return the favour and take a risk with God.

Apocalypse

Vision of the future

The leader of a certain Indian tribe was dying. For many generations his people had been encamped at the base of a large mountain. The chief summoned his three sons and said: "I am dying; before my death I must choose one of you to succeed me as the head of our tribe. I have the same task for each of you. I want you to climb our holy mountain and bring me back something beautiful. The one whose gift is the most outstanding will be the one who will succeed me."

The following morning the sons set out on their search, each taking a different path to the top of the holy mountain. After several days the three sons returned. The first brought his father a flower which grew near the summit of the mountain; it was extremely rare and beautiful. The second son brought his father a valuable stone, round and colourful, which had been polished by rain and sandy winds. When the third son approached his father, everyone saw that his hands were empty.

The empty-handed son said to his father: "I have brought back nothing to show you, father. As I stood on the top of the holy mountain, I saw that on the other side was a beautiful land filled with green pastures. In the middle of these pastures there is a crystal lake. And I have a vision of where our tribe could go for a better life. I was so overwhelmed with what I saw and by what I could see that I could not bring anything back." And the father replied: "You shall be our tribe's new leader, for you have brought back the most precious thing of all – the gift of a vision for a better future."

Apocalypse

In the pages of the Bible there are many stories of great figures who, as they see their death approaching, gather their children or followers to give a final testament. Before Jacob died, he called his twelve sons to give an appropriate blessing to each one. The dying Moses encouraged his people to be strong and stand firm, then appointed his successor to lead the twelve tribes. Before King David ended his days, he addressed the officials of Israel and passed authority to his son Solomon. In the same way Jesus, before he died, gathered his disciples and delivered his final teaching on the future age, instructing them how to live in the midst of political and cosmic upheavals. Part of Jesus' final testament is what we hear in today's Gospel.

It's helpful to remember that Saint Mark is writing at a time when there is widespread oppression and persecution of the Christian community in Rome. No doubt Jesus' followers are wondering if the end is near, uncertain in their suffering how things are going to turn out. Nobody knows the details of the last pages of history, but there is a form of writing that imagines the end time: it is called apocalyptic. To give his readers hope, Mark gives them Jesus' vision of the future.

The vision of the future doesn't look very appealing at first reading. The bad news is delivered first of all. Jesus imagines a time of terror and trouble and persecution. People will be betrayed and handed over to the authorities. There will be wars and earthquakes and famines. Jesus says, "These things must happen." Then there will be cosmic upheavals: "the sun will be darkened, the moon will lose its brightness, the stars will come falling from heaven". After this catalogue of disaster there is the good news. Jesus looks beyond the time of distress to the final time, when the Son of Man will gather the scattered people of God to himself. Jesus sees beyond suffering and persecution to a future of peace with God.

Attending to the present

After the cosmic fireworks, Jesus imagines a peace beyond suffering. This vision of peace is important for Mark's persecuted community: they need more than a fireworks' display to see them through their own historical apocalypse. If their hope is not to be exhausted by force of circumstances, they need help to imagine a far side to pain and suffering. Mark gives their hope help in sharing Jesus' vision. For that is the purpose of all apocalyptic writing: to fund the hope of those who suffer in the present.

In the meantime, we have to depend on the promise of Jesus: "Heaven and earth will pass away, but my words will not pass away." No one, not even the Son, knows when all this will take place. The only sure thing we can hold to is the word of Jesus.

We live in an age of uncertainty; the future never looks wholly secure. In a nuclear age the word of Jesus holds out a vision that takes us beyond our worst imaginings. There is a place beyond the mountains of arms and weapons. This vision doesn't free us from the duty to strive for peace, but it does free us from the blasphemy of believing that a nuclear holocaust will be the last word in the human story. There is only one final word: Jesus. That word has to be enough for us.

A faith that faces disaster

A catalogue of disaster

In today's Gospel reading, Luke gives us the collected sayings of Jesus on the subject of the future. They make for grim listening. Jesus hears a group from the Fine Art Society discussing the beauties of the Temple buildings. They point out the details of the fine architecture; they dwell on the visual splendour of the decorations. But their seminar on aesthetics gives rise to a thundering reply from Jesus which speaks of total destruction for Jerusalem and disaster for the rest of the world. There doesn't seem much prospect for the Fine Art Society in Jerusalem in a future where there will be nothing left standing to admire. However, one thing is left standing. When Titus destroyed the city and the Temple in A.D.70 he ordered that a wall should be left standing for the Jews to wail at. The wall is still there.

In his catalogue of disaster Jesus first warns his listeners against the deceivers. These are the people who pose as saviours and claim to know the ultimate secret – when the world will end. In an age of anxiety it is easy to win followers from those who are overcome by a sense of defeat. But Jesus educates his hearers to avoid leaders who will manipulate their fear. Real saviours don't do that; they know too much about fear themselves.

It's more difficult to follow Jesus' advice not to be frightened by wars and nations fighting each other. In our modern nuclear climate it's hard not to be afraid that we will be mushroomed into oblivion by the idiocy of a leader who wants to make his point with nuclear finality. In the time of Jesus battles and wars were limited by the weapons available. Today they are not. There is no such thing as nuclear finesse.

Jesus goes on to mention earthquakes, plagues and famines. These are still regular features of human suffering. The Richter scale cannot measure human loss; for all the advances of medicine we are still afflicted by incurable diseases on a large scale. And even though we do have enough food to feed the world we are still confronted with famine. We know that these disasters *do* mean the end for millions of people, even though they do not signify the end of the world.

When comfort seems finished

Jesus adds that his followers will be persecuted for their beliefs. He never suggests that following him will be a bloodless affair; but he sees in suffering an opportunity for the courage of witness. Our whole community of faith lives in awe of the men and women who value their faith over their life, who refuse to change their commitment to the Gospel for the sake of their own survival. They live the truth not only of the words of Jesus but the pattern of his life.

Finally on his list, Jesus mentions betrayal. He warns his followers against the naive optimism that supposes that families will understand them and support them in their life of faith. When some people adopt Christianity, they are orphaned by their families. Many converts feel betrayed by their families who sever all ties with them. Jesus acknowledges the truth that *faith makes its own suffering,* one which can be particularly painful when it involves those whose love was never in doubt.

At the end of this catalogue of disaster you might wonder where to turn for comfort. It seems to mark the time when comfort is ended, when misfortune has become part of the air we breathe. But if Jesus is taking his own advice he is not manipulating our fear. He is trying to make faith face the reality of suffering in the world; he faces the question of living as a religious person in a world where so much seems to make nonsense of God. Jesus has the faith that does not turn its back on the suffering and evil in the world. His is not a faith that refuses to pay attention to the difficult questions.

A faith which endures
When he wanted to portray the blindness of our own society to the questions that confront us, a poet used the image:

> We picnic at the edge of the precipice
> With our backs to the abyss

Jesus asks us to face the abyss with faith.

Many good people lose their faith when they see the evil and suffering in the world. They cannot look into the eyes of a starving child and still praise God. They cannot witness the pointless suffering of so many and still believe in a God who cares. They cannot see that these questions are answered by the argument of "freedom of choice" when so many people in the world have no choice. No one chooses to die from famine; no one elects to be blown up by a bomb that has gone astray.

There are no ready answers to these questions. *Because they are our questions too.* There are times when all our faith can do is to endure. That is what Jesus says in today's Gospel. He has no quick answers; he calls on his followers to endure in spite of the horror and the suffering. If we had the answers our faith wouldn't have to endure. Because the questions are still with us, we pray for an enduring faith.

A community of mercy

The hidden Jesus

In today's Gospel Matthew gives us an apocalyptic vision of the last judgement, when all the nations – without distinction between Jew and Gentile, without discrimination between priest and people – are assembled before the king. It would be a pity to limit the value of the passage to a last judgement scene, because what it offers is a picture of the kind of community where Jesus sees himself to be recognised, the kind of community where Jesus sees himself to be at home.

The presence of Jesus is hidden among the poor and the vulnerable: where their needs are recognised, Jesus is acknowledged. When the hungry are fed, when those who thirst are offered drink, when strangers are offered hospitality, when the naked are covered in dignity, when the sick are seen to, when prisoners are visited, Jesus himself is touched by mercy. Their vulnerability is his vulnerability; he is present where human need is greatest.

According to this vision, if an alien came from outer space and asked us where our Jesus lived, we might have to take him to strange sanctuaries: refugee camps, back alleys, hospitals, prisons, and tell him that Jesus is to be found somewhere in these places. And tell him, too, that the blessed of God are to be found there, feeding, welcoming, clothing, visiting, paying attention.

Human graciousness

In Matthew's vision we have a list of human needs and appropriate responses by a caring community. None of the needs is specifically religious: they are human needs as wide as the human heart. To those ordinary human needs there is the response of the kingdom. That response is an authentically human one, and, therefore, a profoundly religious one; it is honoured by the title "blessed of my Father".

The blessed are praised for the simplest actions – and they are all actions not attitudes – to those who experience simple human needs. There are no records of great heroism, no stories of conquest, no great trials or sufferings, no marvellous triumphs over disaster, no feats of imaginative daring. The requirements are simple and don't go beyond the capacity of any human being. There is no training required, no academic qualifications necessary. The actions are the simple response of those who pay attention to what happens in the world of the familiar and who move to answer the needs which confront them.

370

For Jesus, what happens in the world of the familiar has an eternity of importance about it: little acts of kindness have eternal significance; human graciousness and charity are ground enough for welcome into the fullness of the kingdom.

A community of mercy
Those who are blessed are not conscious of having done any special service to Jesus: "When did we see *you*...? They have responded with mercy to those in need, without any great thought beyond that response. In the mission discourse in chapter 10 Jesus declared that any kind of service done to his apostles would be rewarded as done to him, and indeed to God: "He who receives you receives me, and he who receives me receives the one who sent me...Whoever gives a cup of cold water to one of these little ones because he is my disciple, I tell you he shall not lose his reward." In today's Gospel that thought is extended to embrace "one of the least of these brothers of mine."

The thought now is that Jesus looks upon every kindness done to a person in need, however lowly, as a kindness done to himself. Those who are cursed bring the doom upon themselves because they failed to respond to simple human needs. They are not accused of violent crimes, or offences on a grand scale – any more that the blessed were praised for heroic virtue; rather, they are accused because they failed to act on the human need they saw before them.

The shared problem of the blessed and the cursed is: "When did we see you?" That may be our question too, for all we see is the legion of those in need. But the Gospel asks us to *interpret* what we see. The Gospel challenges us to see the broken body of Christ in the brokenness and the woundedness of those we see around us. Christ still suffers in the hungry, the thirsty, the stranger, the naked, the sick, the imprisoned. To pay attention to them is to pay attention to the broken body of Christ. And to do that is to be welcomed as blessed of God, because it is to live as a community of mercy.

The interview

Interview technique

The story is told of a man who travelled to London to attend an interview for an important post in the security services. When he arrived at the appointed place he found five other applicants in the waiting room, all discussing their prospects. There was no secretary on duty. A sign on the wall stated that applicants were to knock and enter the interview room at fifteen minute intervals, beginning at eleven o'clock. They were to leave the interview room by another door, so that the nature of the questioning could be kept secret.

The applicants discussed the strange arrangement; they reflected on what questions might be asked; they wondered what qualities would be needed for the post. At eleven o'clock one of them, who said he had been the first to arrive, went to the door of the interview room, knocked and entered. The remaining five men continued to discuss various matters among themselves. So, the time passed.

At a quarter past twelve the last man to arrive rose from his chair, walked over to the door of the interview room, knocked and entered. When he stepped into the room he was confused by what he saw. Behind the large oak table that dominated the room sat his interviewers: they were the same five men who had been in the waiting room. The interview was already over.

Interrogation

In today's Gospel Jesus is interrogated by the Roman governor, Pontius Pilate, the man directly responsible to the emperor for keeping the Roman rule in Judaea. For the occupying power, Jewish festivals were regarded as potential emergencies: at the time of Passover, therefore, Pilate came with his garrison to Jerusalem, where he kept his security forces on alert in case of a riot or national uprising. Jesus has been handed over to Pilate by the Jewish authorities. It is Passover time. Pilate offers to hand Jesus back, arguing that Jewish law can dispose of the case. The authorities refuse, so Pilate questions Jesus about the charge made against him: "Are you the king of the Jews?"

Jesus replies to Pilate with his own question: "Do you ask this of your own accord, or have others spoken to you about it?" You wonder who is interviewing whom. If the governor is interrogating his prisoner, the prisoner has his own agenda for interviewing the governor. Jesus calls Pilate to face the truth of the question he has asked, but Pilate is beyond troubling about the consequences of his own questions. Instead, he defends himself by saying that he is not a Jew and that Jesus' own people have handed him over. However, Pilate is curious about what Jesus has done to engender such fierce hostility.

Jesus refuses to satisfy Pilate's curiosity but points out that his kingship is not in the realm of political struggle; his claim to be king, therefore, can hardly affect national security. Jesus' kingship is in the realm of witnessing to the truth – something that the Roman procurator is having great trouble doing. Pilate has already found Jesus innocent; if he acts on that truth then he will free Jesus. Pilate may be *sincere* in his concern for Jesus' safety, but he is not *serious* about the truth he has discovered. Jesus is innocent. That truth is not a force that is going to influence Pilate's real behaviour. He fails the interview, therefore, because he cannot meet the basic condition of witnessing to the truth.

Witnessing to Jesus

As the passion gets under way, Jesus has to witness to his own truth. He remains stubborn in his trust of the Father, in spite of the catcalls of his accusers and the silence of his absent friends. He may wonder where all the witnesses to truth have gone and why they are so few in number when the authorities come out in force. He may wonder why you end up being pushed around so much for the sake of the kingdom. He may have his own questions about the worth of it all. He may doubt if the pain will ever go away.

To crown it all, Pilate ensures that Jesus has his title above his cross: "Jesus of Nazareth, King of the Jews". Is that comic relief? Is that protest? Is that the nearest Pilate will ever get to witnessing to the truth? Who knows?

What we do know is that Jesus' unfailing witness to the truth marks his true kingship. As his subjects, we will be judged on how we have witnessed to his truth, his love, his way. For a place in his kingdom we will be questioned on our own attitudes and behaviour. We don't have to wait for the last judgement to find out the questions we will be asked. When it comes to places in his kingdom, the interviews are already taking place. Here and now. When our time comes for judgement, we shouldn't be surprised by the familiar faces.

The king and the criminal

"We are your own flesh and blood"

Kings are a rare breed. There used to be legions of them around the world occupying thrones of various importance, and the history that most of us learned at school was the story of the rise and fall of royal households. There are few kings left; now you could fit them all into a telephone box. Most nations have become disenchanted with royalty and wonder why people need to be reigned over. Other nations are protective of their monarchy, arguing that even though their royals do not exercise real power they serve a useful function as the focus of the nation's unity.

In 1950 King Farouk of Egypt told a group of reporters that soon enough there would be only five kings left in the world: the king of hearts, the king of spades, the king of diamonds, the king of clubs, and the king of England.

The fate of kings is behind our first reading today. King David has come a long way from tending sheep and playing on his harp. He was a shepherd from Bethlehem before he was called to the court of Saul: his job was to play the kind of music that would entice the king out of his fits of depression. He proved more than a musician; he killed the giant Goliath and distinguished himself in battle. King Saul, however, became nervous at David's success and popularity and threw a javelin in his direction twice. He was a rotten shot. The harpist was forced to flee and started his own guerilla movement in the Judean hills, where he remained a fugitive until the death of Saul.

When Saul died, David was promoted from being a criminal to being the king of Judah, the strongest of the tribes in the south. David had his eye on the northern tribes and their territory, and after seven years he was accepted as the king of Israel. As we heard from the first reading, when David travels north to make the agreement with the tribes, their leaders remind him: "We are your own flesh and blood." With the kinship established, kingship is conferred. So, David is anointed king of Israel.

A kingdom not of this world

When Luke comes to tell the story of Jesus he is careful to present Jesus in kinship with a particular people and their history. Jesus is born into a tradition. So, Gabriel announces to Mary: "The Lord God will give him the throne of his ancestor David; he will rule over the House of Jacob forever and his kingdom will have no end." When Jesus is born, the birth takes place in "the town of David called Bethlehem." Jesus is of royal lineage, but he will refuse to occupy any throne.

At the beginning of his public life Jesus is tempted in the desert. One of the temptations is to exercise power and authority over the kingdoms of this world. Rather than establish a kingdom that is not of this world, Jesus is tempted to govern existing kingdoms. But that is not his way. He resists the authority of domination, the power that exalts itself and exults in itself. His route is along the path of powerlessness. And he tells his followers:

> Among the pagans it is the kings who lord it over them, and those who have authority over them are given the title Benefactor. With you this must not happen. (Lk 22:25f)

Jesus also educates his followers to have a healthy suspicion of the religious authority of his day. Those who spent their time inventing new burdens for people and investing in handcuffs were not to be imitated. He warns against the kind of authority that refuses to busy itself in lightening the heavy burdens that people carry. The kind of authority that will not lift a finger to help is alien to the values of Jesus.

The authority of holiness

The authority of Jesus is the authority of his unique holiness. No one on earth conferred that authority on him and no one could take it away. People kept asking "Where did he get all this?" Or they demanded to know "By what authority do you do these things?" Jesus' authority came from his Father, who endowed him with the Spirit and with power. He needed no other investiture.

His kingdom is one that looks out for people who are ignored in every other kingdom: the poor and the broken and the wounded. This is especially true in Luke's Gospel that we have heard throughout this liturgical year. It is fitting then that Jesus should end up between two criminals, between the kind of people he sought out in his ministry to tell the good news that they had a kingdom for their repentance.

Throughout his ministry Jesus shared his forgiveness; he dies breathing it. He dies as he lived, reaching out to the distressed on either side of him. In the midst of his own agony he still has time for others. The crown he wears is of thorns; the throne he has is the cross; his royal banner is a scribbled sign that he is the King of the Jews. That is the Gospel image of royalty: the king and the criminal who go *together* into paradise. This is the king we celebrate and whose values we are pledged to live. May his kingdom come.

FEAST DAYS

The old who wait on the Lord

Memory

As young Walter leans on the door-bell of his grandfather's house he waits impatiently for the old man to open the door. It's his grandfather's eightieth birthday and he has brought him a carefully chosen present. Eventually he hears the familiar shuffle coming to the door, and after the locks are unfastened the door is inched open. He hugs the old man and solemnly makes his presentation. His grandfather unwraps the packaging slowly to reveal a large photograph album.

"Thought you could do with that," Walter says "to keep all those old photos you have lying around the place."

"Thanks son," says grandfather. "That's the trouble with old age. Trying to put all your memories in order. Don't know where to start. You'd better come and help me."

Memory is the way we all bring time to mind, and of course the thing about the past is that the longer we live there's more of it! As the French playwright Anouilh observed: "When you're forty, half of you belongs to the past – and when you're seventy, nearly all of you."

When we grow old there is a tendency to be long on memory and short on expectation. There's not much time left for us, and the time there is might not appear all that appealing. Our hopes can become as wrinkled as our faces. So we can look to the security of a familiar past with familiar faces and places. We can get out the photograph albums and page through lost times, and be content to remember how it was in the good old days.

Expectation

In today's Gospel we meet an old prophet and an old prophetess in Simeon and Anna. As old people they are connected with the past and with memory; Luke presents them as *anawim* – the devout remnant of those who stayed faithful to the ancient promises of God. Listen to the words of the prophet Isaiah and try to catch the promise Simeon and Anna were waiting to see fulfilled:

> The Lord has revealed his holy arm
> in the sight of the Gentiles
> and all the ends of the earth
> will see the salvation that comes from God.

I shall give you as a light to the Gentiles
that you may bring salvation to the ends of the earth.
Then the glory of the Lord will be revealed
and all flesh will see the salvation of our God.

Simeon and Anna long to see the fulfilment of those promises. They are an unusual couple of old people because their total concern is for the future. They don't live backwards, but forwards. Something yet to happen dominates their life. They are alive with expectation and hope, waiting for the one who will be the consolation of their own people and the light for the Gentiles. They are an old couple who are totally open: they hunger for God's presence, and wait for the day when they can see it themselves.

Their waiting is not in vain. As Luke says, the parents come with the child Jesus to the temple. They are a good Jewish family which keeps the Law which obliged them to consecrate to God the first male that opened the womb. However, after the tribe of Levi was consecrated to God, the parents of the child were released from that demand: instead they were required only to pay a small "ransom" to the priest to buy back the child.

So, in today's Gospel we have the meeting between youth and old age; between the young parents and the old venerables; between hope and fulfilment. Old Simeon takes the child into his arms, he gathers it to himself and hymns the poetry of the Nunc Dimittis: "Now, Master, you can let your servant go in peace, just as you promised....."

The hopes of Simeon are fulfilled, for he sees in Jesus the promised salvation of God. And Anna, whose timing is exquisite, since "she came by just at that moment", praises God for what has happened. In the person of Jesus, all the ancient promises are fulfilled.

The challenge

When Jesus was taken to the temple in Jerusalem the temple accepted him as a child; but when he became a man the temple said "No" to the person he had become and the values he stood for. Today we are not being presented with a child who is a bundle of cuddle that no one can resist. We are presented with the one whom we all can resist and do.

And that is the challenge of each eucharist: we can take Jesus to ourselves, we can share in his life, and pledge ourselves anew to his Gospel. No matter what age we are, we are presented with the same challenge: can we take the Lord into our lives, say yes to who he is, and the person he wants us to be? When we can say yes to that, then we too can go our way in peace.

The witness of unreserved love

Persecution and Peter

In the year 43 A.D. four legions of the Roman imperial army landed on the coast of Kent to begin their task of turning Britain into a Roman province. After they had advanced on London, and before they had crossed the river Thames, the legions received an important visitor in the shape of Claudius, their new emperor. Claudius was no soldier, but he had been raised to the throne by the imperial bodyguard and he was anxious to show his support for the army. But even above the army, there was one man who had helped Claudius to the throne – his Jewish friend, Herod Agrippa. Claudius had just rewarded Agrippa by granting him the territory of his grandfather, Herod the Great. And while the new emperor of Rome was overseeing his soldiers in the capture of London, the new king in Palestine, Herod Agrippa, was overseeing his soldiers in the persecution of certain leading Christians in Jerusalem.

As we hear from today's first reading, King Herod beheaded the apostle James. Remember how it was that James together with his brother John and Simon Peter made up the group of three that was closest to Jesus during his lifetime. When Herod saw that the execution pleased most of his subjects, his next target became Peter, who was thrown into prison to await trial and execution. The Jerusalem church must have been very discouraged: with James executed and Peter imprisoned, the prospects for the future hardly looked promising. So they all gathered to pray for Peter and, no doubt, for the future of the Church.

Luke tells us that their prayers were answered in a very dramatic way. The night before Peter's condemnation he received a visitor in the shape of an angel. Peter, who seems to have made a habit of sleeping through crises, was awakened and led through the prison gates to freedom. He thought he was still dreaming, so the angel had to stay with him for the length of the street until he woke up! When he did, Peter came to see that the power of God was stronger than the power of King Herod.

Persecution and Paul

About two years before Peter's imprisonment, the church in Jerusalem was visited by a new convert, Paul of Tarsus. Paul had been an accomplished persecutor of the followers of Jesus and was feared for his fanatical commitment to his cause. But he had experienced a conversion in which Christ had spoken to him in a vision appointing him as his chosen instrument to the Gentiles. Paul went to Jerusalem to tell his experience to the apostles, but he stayed in the city for only fifteen days. Luke tells us why: When Paul arrived "he tried to join the disciples, but they were afraid of him; they could not believe he really was a disciple." (Acts 9:26)

Nonetheless Paul started to preach in the city, but he so angered the Greek-speaking Jews that they sought to kill him. It is worth noting that this was the same group that had stoned Stephen to death, the same group that had placed Stephen's clothes at the feet of Saul the persecutor. Now the persecutor had become the persecuted. To save his life, members of the Jerusalem church took him to the port of Caesarea and shipped him back to Tarsus where he came from. And as Luke tells us: "The churches throughout Judaea, Galilee and Samaria were now left in peace."

Throughout his ministry Paul always claimed that he was in truth an apostle of Jesus, on an equal footing with the Twelve. Most of his letters open with his defensive claim: "From Paul...an apostle who does not owe his authority to men or his appointment to any human being but who has been appointed by Jesus Christ..." (Gal.1:1,2) Perhaps more than any imprisonment or lashing, Paul's real pain arose from his awareness that he would never be accepted without reservation in his lifetime. He always had to struggle to prove himself an authentic apostle, not a spy planted by his former employers. Perhaps that agony was his cross.

Love without reserve

Peter had denied Jesus three times, but he had returned as a rock to strengthen and lead the Christian community. Paul had persecuted Christ, but he had changed his ways to become the energetic apostle who pushed the reaches of the Gospel far beyond the confines of Judaea and Samaria. Both men had fallen; both men had risen again to new heights. Peter was Jesus' choice to head the Christian community and be its source of unity; Paul was Jesus' choice to take his message to the Gentiles.

Both apostles were martyred in Rome under the persecution of the emperor Nero. In their final witness there is nothing doubtful about their love; in the end they are equal in love. Both of them had a love without reserve.

That is why we honour both of them without reserve. In honouring Peter and Paul we also celebrate the ancient foundation of the Church in Rome, which was to become the mother of all the Christian churches. The Church in Rome had these two great apostles and martyrs at its beginning, a fact the community regarded as a unique privilege. In their foundation they had a double dimension: apostolic leadership and evangelical energy, both marks of the Church today. That is why in the Roman canon of the Mass the first two apostles who are mentioned are not Peter and Andrew, but Peter and Paul. Paul does get his unreserved recognition in the very canon of the Mass! And today we celebrate them. Together. In one breath.

Discipleship: two outstanding witnesses

Introduction

One night in the middle of July in the year 64 A.D. a fire started in Rome. The fire spread rapidly and burnt for a week. By the time it was stopped it had destroyed half the imperial city. There was little doubt in people's minds that the emperor Nero was responsible, and in response to the public outcry Nero set up a commission which quickly found that a new religious minority was responsible for the arson: the Christians. There started a series of terrible persecutions. To be a Christian was to be an outlaw; to profess the name of Jesus was to incur the penalty of death. Two leading outlaws were executed under Nero's persecution, two men we celebrate today as Saint Peter and Saint Paul.

Peter, the leader

All four Gospels were written after the death of Peter and they all acknowledge the special role he enjoyed during the life of Jesus. In the earliest Gospel, Mark, Peter is the first to be called by Jesus. Although Jesus is from Nazareth in Galilee he centres his early mission in the town of Capernaum, beside the lake. And the address of his first mission centre is the house of Peter, the same house where he cures Peter's mother-in-law. Peter's boat serves as Jesus' earliest pulpit. Even Peter's name is given to him by Jesus.

All the Gospels see Peter as the spokesman for the apostolic group. He is portrayed as the most vivid character who acts on behalf of the others. He is not a cardboard figure who can do no wrong: he is a man aware of his own sinfulness but keenly aware too of the power of God at work in Jesus.

In today's Gospel we have Matthew's version of Peter's famous confession of Jesus. The Church is seen to be built on Peter's confession: *he is the one who is enabled by God to say who Jesus is.* The Gospel acknowledges that not only does Peter confess Jesus, he also denies Jesus. But the importance is that he can do both and *still be a rock.* He can use his failure as a source of strength for others. After the resurrection we see that because of his love for Christ Peter can be chief pastor to the people of Christ.

It is Peter who heads the movement of the early church after Pentecost. Even though there is opposition to some of his ideas, he is acknowledged as the chosen leader and the centre of unity. Both his authority and his love are confirmed in his greatest act of witness when he dies as a martyr for the sake of Christ.

Paul, the pilgrim

Unlike Peter, Paul never met Jesus of Nazareth. Paul never had the experience of seeing Jesus, hearing him preach, witnessing his great deeds. Instead, Paul was dedicated to the elimination of Jesus' followers. As he admits himself, he was so bent on suppressing the Jesus movement that he would pursue Christians into foreign cities to track them down. He was an accomplished fanatic.

His physical appearance is described in the *Acts of Paul,* which was written about a hundred years after his death: "a little man. His legs were crooked, but his bearing was noble. His eyebrows grew close together and he had a big nose. A man who breathed friendliness." Whether friendliness was all that Paul breathed is doubtful! After his conversion he brought the same dynamism to the spread of the Christian message as he had brought to its suppression. Paul was driven to share the exciting truth of the Gospel: that in his death Christ had gained freedom for all people.

However, Paul's Gospel vision brought him into conflict with many people. He seemed to have a charism for causing a riot wherever he went. His first attempt at preaching in Jerusalem made him a target of assassination and the local church had to get him out fast. Luke tells us in the Acts that after Paul was shipped back to Tarsus: "The churches throughout Judea, Galilee and Samaria were now left in peace" (9:31). Apparently you could have Paul or you could have peace, but it wasn't easy to have both!

Paul was an intellectual as well as a man of action; he personally thought through great questions of faith and communicated the Gospel with passion and intelligence. He came into conflict with religious authority even to opposing Peter "face to face"; but he never questioned Peter's authority to lead the whole community. In the end he and Peter gave the ultimate witness to Christ in dying for his name.

Conclusion

In celebrating Peter and Paul we bless God for gracing them for their mission in the life of the Church. Today the Church still needs their different gifts and their shared commitment. Christians throughout the world still need a Petrine figure to unite the different factions in the community and be a source of unity and strength. Christians still need apostles like Paul, people on fire with the love of Christ who can reach out to all people with a faith that is energetic.

Neither Peter nor Paul put a torch to Nero's city of Rome. But they did light a fire that has not gone out. For that we praise God.

A dangerous woman

Theotokos

If you walk into any Catholic church anywhere, usually you don't have to hunt to find some shrine or altar erected in honour of Mary, the mother of God. To many non-Catholic people, Catholics used to be identified popularly as the ones who ate fish on Fridays and had missals bulging with litanies and devotions to our Lady. Catholics were different, somehow. You could watch them taking to the streets in May in glittering processions, carrying statues, banners, candles, rosaries, hymn sheets – all dressed in their Sunday best and singing hymns to the Queen of heaven, the ocean star. And apart from the decked-out altar-boys, they all looked as if they were having a good time.

Honouring Mary, however, had a late start in the life of the Church. In the first four centuries there was no devotion to our Lady and little reflection on her place in sacred history. At that time the pressing question was the true identity of Jesus, and the Church was fully absorbed in finding an answer to the complex questions surrounding the humanity and divinity of Jesus. This was a matter that concerned not only bishops and theologians but everyone: whole cities were divided over the answers. There was confusion, bickering, battles, persecutions. Everyone was involved. One venerable Father of the Church complained that he couldn't go to the public baths without the attendants asking him if he really thought Jesus was divine.

Only after the divinity of Christ was proclaimed in the early councils of the Church did attention then turn to Mary. The Council of Ephesus in 431 devoted much attention to the subject of how the Son of God was given birth to *humanly.* It was then that the Church gave Mary one of the oldest titles: Mary was *theotokos,* which literally means God-bearing. To affirm that the Son the God had a human birth, the Fathers proclaimed that Mary was *theotokos:* she bore him in her womb and gave birth to him like any mother. But it wasn't until Vatican II, in 1964, that a council of the Church referred to Mary as "Mother of God".

The Assumption

Until the middle of the sixth century there were no feasts in the Church to celebrate and honour Mary. She was commemorated alongside the saints and martyrs. The Eastern Church, however, had plenty of Marian feasts – celebrating her Conception, her Birth, her Presentation in the Temple, and the Annunciation. But their most important Marian feast was the Assumption. This feast and all the other Marian celebrations were adopted by the Roman church and included in the western Catholic Church.

The belief in the Assumption had its origin in the popular faith of the people. Christians could not believe that Mary's body underwent decay after being separated from her soul at death; they could not imagine that her body would disintegrate after the unique role she played in sacred history. The faithful came to believe that Mary was bodily assumed into heaven, thus guaranteeing that she was present with God, body *and* soul.

Although it was only proclaimed as dogma in 1950, the Assumption had been taught in the Church for centuries as a truth that emerged from the faith of the people. It also points to what we believe God will do for us. We believe that our whole person, body and soul, will be raised to a new existence in the peace of God. This is what the dogmatic definition tells us as it expresses the hope "that faith in the bodily assumption of Mary into heaven may make our faith in our resurrection both stronger and more active."

A dangerous woman

Mary's importance is not limited to giving us hope about the afterlife; she gives every Christian hope in the growing struggle of everyday life. In today's Gospel Luke portrays her as the one who glorifies God because "the Almighty has done great things for me." She is a woman of the people whose song delights in God's choice of her, whose spirit soars because God has not overlooked this lowly handmaid. But she is also a dangerous woman because she is the one who voices the subversive hope of the poor and the little ones:

> He has pulled down princes from their thrones
> and exalted the lowly.
> The hungry he has filled with good things,
> the rich sent empty away.

For many poor people, the song of Mary expresses their own hope in the liberating power of God. For them Mary is not alive in statues and pictures but in the real and powerful change that can be brought about in the world *when God's preferences and God's choices are taken seriously.* She is the mother of all who are oppressed and overlooked and scorned. She was the little one, the lowly servant, made great by the choice of God. That same choice is extended to all the lowly. Mary voices God's opposition to tyranny, his determination to pull down the powers that brutalise their subjects. In that, Mary is no passive silent woman. It is hardly surprising, therefore, that it is the poor who look to her most for help. It is they we see on our television screens who carry her statue with great dignity as they process in circles outside palaces and prisons and army headquarters.

Clearly they believe something that we have come to forget.

Mary: disciple and prophet

The first disciple

All Christians are indebted to St Luke for his Gospel portrait of Mary, the mother of Jesus. It is an unfinished portrait, but the simplicity of its lines has appealed to generations of believers who have honoured Mary as the chosen woman of God. We can all echo Elizabeth's blessing in today's Gospel: "Of all women you are the most blessed, and blessed is the fruit of your womb." We honour Mary as the woman who put her whole self at the service of God's plan, who consented to let God's Spirit take hold of her, so that the Son of God could take flesh in our midst.

Luke's portrait of Mary shows her as a young Jewish maiden who is surprised and afraid of what God is asking of her. But she does not allow her fear to form her response; she agrees to let God's proposal form her into a young mother. God announces his choice of Mary; she, in her turn, announces her choice of God. Two choices meet; two choices find fulfilment in each other.

In the meeting of those two choices Luke presents Mary as the great woman disciple. For the adult Jesus, the description of the true disciple is the one who hears the word of God and keeps it. Long before the adult Jesus appears on the scene, Luke shows how Mary is seen to fulfil the requirements of the true disciple: she hears the word of God and she responds by letting that word happen in her life. Mary is the first true disciple in Luke's Gospel.

The Assumption

Luke does not mention the death of Mary in his writings. The New Testament says nothing about the Assumption of Mary. It was not until the sixth century, when Mary become a symbol of faith and hope for all believers, that devout Christians began to celebrate feasts of Mary. They also began to speculate about her death. They were already persuaded of her unique holiness and place in God's plan, and they began describing her death as an extraordinary event, one that befitted such an extraordinary person.

Just as devout Jews envisioned the death of Moses as a graceful event in which angels carried his body to God, so Christians began describing the death of Mary as her return to God. What the New Testament could not supply, an imaginative faith readily provided. So, images abounded of Mary being carried to heaven and crowned Queen of Heaven. Artists and poets vied with each other in expressing images of the heavenly scenes. So, the paintings which adorn so many art galleries around the world:

legions of chubby angels conveying Mary on a celestial flight; saintly choirs celebrating her arrival with Mozart motets; baroque coronation scenes so grand that even the Trinity can only look on in wonder. We may smile at these adventures in faith, but they were inspired by a love of Mary which insisted that nothing on earth or in heaven could overstate the importance of the mother of the Son of the most high God.

The dogma of the Assumption, proclaimed in 1950 by Pope Pius XII, has its origins in the popular faith of the Christian community. The definition does not decide whether Mary died or not before being taken to heaven: it states that Mary enjoys eternal life with her Son, a goal that we all hope to attain eventually. As Paul states in today's second reading: "...all men will be brought to life in Christ; but all of them in the proper order: Christ as the first-fruits and then, after the coming of Christ, those who belong to him." The Church states that Mary, who belongs to Christ in a special way, already enjoys the fullness of new life.

Mary, the radical woman
We may understand the Assumption of Mary in the images of today's first reading: "a woman, clothed with the sun, standing on the moon, and with twelve stars on her head for a crown." However we imagine Mary's Assumption, we always return to the simple portrait of her in the pages of the Gospel, where she is neither an earthbound star nor a heavenly queen. In Luke's Magnificat Mary is the lowly handmaid who rejoices in the loving look of God her saviour and blesses him for the great things he accomplishes in her.

In the Magnificat we see Mary as the radical woman. She is the woman who hungers for a new justice on earth, one that reflects the justice of God. The God who did not overlook her is the God who dethrones the mighty and exalts the lowly. In this dispensation the hungry are filled with good things, the rich sent empty away. Mary voices a contrary wisdom. She voices a radical protest against what we all take for granted: that the mighty will always prevail over the weak, that the well-fed nations will thrive while others starve to death, that the politically strong will always occupy the thrones of power.

Such is the woman we celebrate today. Such are her profound hopes. So, in turn, ours should be.

The foolishness of God

Ave crux, unica spes

He was a Roman statesman, an orator, a philosopher, a man of letters. His name was Marcus Tullius Cicero. In the year 63 B.C. he stood up in the Roman Forum to argue that the very idea of crucifixion was barbaric and should be banned from the minds of civilised people. This is what he said:

> If we are to be threatened with death, then we want to die in freedom; let the very name of the cross be banished from the body and life of Roman citizens, and from their thoughts, eyes and ears.

Cicero argued that the practice of crucifixion cast doubt on the Roman claim to civilisation. Twenty years later, a year after the assassination of Caesar, Cicero was executed by his own countryman while fleeing from Rome.

One hundred years after Cicero's declaration about the barbarity of crucifixion, another public figure addressed himself to the question. He was a Roman citizen, a man of letters, a great public speaker. His name was Paul. This is what he said:

> Where are the philosophers? And where are the debaters of this age? While the Jews demand miracles and the Greeks look for wisdom, we are preaching a crucified Christ. God's folly is wiser than human wisdom, and God's weakness is stronger than any human strength. (1 Cor.1:20-25)

For Cicero, the crucifixion of a Roman citizen was a sure sign of barbarity; for Paul, the crucifixion of a Palestinian Jew was the essence of his message of hope. It was a sign of supreme love; a sign of the folly of love; a sign of the lengths love will go to. That love enabled Paul to face his own execution in Rome in the year 67 A.D.

The cross as a sign of hope is a paradox. It is like the writing we can read on tombs in old graveyards: *Ave crux, unica spes* – Hail cross, our only hope. That is a good summary of the Christian faith: in the cross of Jesus, our hope has dawned.

The folly of God

Death and hope seem unsuitable companions. We say, "Where there's life there's hope." As long as we live we're able to hope and open ourselves to the future. Our hope gives shape and direction to our lives; it gives us a reason for getting up in the morning. But we know that when we hope we become vulnerable. Hoping is always a risk because it looks to what is not here. To avoid the pain of disappointment some people give up

hoping. They follow the sad advice: expect nothing and you will never be disappointed. But those who live without hope become bitter and cynical. To lose hope is to die in the midst of life.

Like the people of Israel in today's first reading: they stop hoping in God because of the pain that goes with their new freedom. They want freedom without wilderness; they want liberation without suffering. God sends a plague of serpents and the people get stung. Sometimes we get smart only after we get stung! Moses makes an image of the brazen serpent so that those who looked on it might be saved. Another paradox: the serpent as saviour.

The brazen serpent makes sense: the one sent to bring the people to their senses is the one that becomes a sign of their new liberation. The serpent as saviour is understood fully only in the Gospel. The God who sent the serpents later sends his beloved Son – one who would not sting the people into freedom but who would be stung to death himself. In Jesus it is God himself who is stung; it is the crucified God who pays the price for freedom. And the price is paid by Jesus himself.

The folly of the cross

That is the folly of the cross; that is the weakness of God. Jesus does what so many want to avoid: he suffers so that others might be free. He is willing to be rejected, to be deprived of the dignity of suffering. To suffer *and* be rejected signify the cross. In Jesus, God does not despise a broken humanity but takes it on himself. He reveals God by making himself vulnerable. He takes on his back what we all want to avoid: responsibility for our sins, our hate, our violence, our bigotry.

He is nailed to the cross. He does not die a natural death; he is put to death. In all this, he does not despise what is human. As Paul says, Jesus does not cling to his equality with God, but becomes a servant. He enters the deprivation of humanity and the forsakenness of death. And God raises him and gives him a name which is higher than all names. In the resurrection, hope is born again.

That is why we hope. Hope is born out of realism; it is born out of love. Christian hope is born out of the death of Jesus. That is why Cicero was wrong and Paul was right: in the cross there can be new life, there can be triumph. And that is why we celebrate today.

Jesus' crowd

Ordinary folk

In 1906 Keir Hardie, who started his working life as a coal miner, became the first parliamentary leader of the British Labour party. On Hardie's first day at the House of Commons, the policeman at the gate took one look at the former miner, dressed in his working clothes and wearing a cloth cap, and asked suspiciously, "Are you working here?"

"Yes," replied Hardie.

"On the roof?" asked the policeman.

"No," said the new MP. "On the floor."

People have their own peculiar image of what an MP should look like in the House of Commons, just as people have their peculiar image of what a saint should look like in the House of God. Ordinary folk people both places; perhaps the comparison stops there! In St John's vision of the heavenly court, which we heard in the first reading, the arithmetic and universality of God's elect make up a hopeful scene: "I saw a huge number, impossible to count, of people from every nation, race, tribe and language".

The heavenly court is an international assembly of ordinary people who have been faithful to God, real people whose struggle through crisis and frustration comes to a merciful end in the peace of God's house. God's house is not an exclusive club for pious cronies who would fail an interview for the human race; God's house is truly every nation and race and language who live in the light of God. Even members of parliament.

Jesus' folk

In today's Gospel Matthew gives us a summary of Jesus' teaching, in the beatitudes. To the inner circle of his chosen followers and the great crowds that have come from many parts Jesus recognises as blessed a wide range of people, from the poor in spirit to those persecuted for their faith. This is not a belated recognition of the dead, but a joyful recognition of the living people of God.

Those who are absolutely destitute, those who have no access to influence and power, those not represented in any parliament are the ones dear to God. Whoever depends wholly on the favour of God is already a saint in his kingdom. The gentle folk are not overlooked; on the contrary, they shall inherit the earth. Those who mourn, who grieve for their sins, who are moved by the affliction of others will surely know comfort. The people in our community who hunger and thirst for what is right, who refuse to live by bread alone will find satisfaction to their hearts' content in the kingdom.

The people who show mercy, who don't hoard hurt as if it were gold, can be sure that they will be greeted with mercy in return. If anyone will have the privilege of looking on the face of God, it will be the pure in heart, those whose commitment is undivided and whose loyalty is sure. Those who actively promote peace are recognised as God's children, for they are like their heavenly Father, the bringer of peace. Finally, those who suffer persecution in the cause of what is right are assured of their place in the kingdom.

All these people are Jesus' folk. These are the people who have enlivened the history of the Church with their quiet witness, the people whose lives are unheralded and whose names are unknown. But Jesus knows their name – they are his people, the saints. And they are among us today.

Celebrating our own folk

Today's feast of All Saints invites us to celebrate our own folk, to take pride in the saints who have preceded us and those who grace our community. To celebrate with pride is not to be triumphalistic; we can admit the horror stories while still being proud of the numberless people who have remained stubbornly open to God's Spirit.

We rejoice in the saints we have known and know: their name is legion. We bless God for those who attend to the hungry, the orphans, the aged, the lepers, the outcasts, the overlooked. We thank God for those who have outsmiled the jibes and taunts of oppressors, for those whose whispered prayers have enriched the holiness of us all, for those who struggle honestly against ending up selfish and unloving. We express our gratitude for those whose lives are welcomed as good news by the poor, for those who confront religious pretence, for those who keep on forgiving with an energy that is worthy of God.

For all these people, among us still, we give thanks. And if you feel thanked in the process, don't feel confused. You're lucky to be part of the same crowd.

The sanctified brethren

Sanctified brethren

Lake Wobegon is a quiet town, the seat of Mist County in Minnesota, U.S.A. It doesn't actually appear on any map because it's an imaginary place, the centre of a marvellous portrait of small-town American life in *Lake Wobegon Days* by Garrison Keillor. We follow the fortunes of a skinny kid who is raised in this strait-laced town where the first car and the first radio were greeted with stubborn scepticism by the townsfolk. Our hero is fascinated by the Catholic Church with all its saints and processions and colour; he belongs to a small sect that meets in his uncle Al's bare living room where they sit on folding chairs and wait for the Spirit to move them. He says:

> In a town where everyone was either Lutheran or Catholic, we were neither one. We were Sanctified Brethren, a sect so tiny that nobody but us and God knew about it, so when kids asked what I was, I just said Protestant. It was too much to explain, like having six toes. You would rather keep your shoes on.

Today we celebrate the feast of the Sanctified Brethren – not a small sect in an imaginary town, but a great many men, women and children, the faithful in Christ Jesus. When St Paul wrote his first letter to the Christian community in Corinth, he began: "Paul called by the will of God to be an apostle, to you who have been sanctified in Christ Jesus and called to be saints." To the Christians at Ephesus, he wrote: "Paul an apostle of Christ Jesus by the will of God, to all the saints who are at Ephesus." In his great Epistle to the Romans he spoke the same language: "To all God's beloved who are in Rome, called to be saints."

Saints alive

Paul is not writing letters to the dead. He is addressing the living, those who have committed themselves to following the way of Christ in the world. For Paul, those who live that life are sanctified brethren, they are saints. That is the life all of us have pledged ourselves to following. And when we celebrate the feast of All Saints, we are not celebrating aliens from another planet; we are celebrating our own folks, everyone whose life is a witness to the love of Christ.

In today's Gospel we have Jesus' charter for his kingdom, the beatitudes, a list of qualities which characterise the sanctified brethren. When we listen to them we can all put faces to the virtues. We remember these people and we know them. The people whose simplicity and littleness

shine like a light in a world of darkness. The gentle folk whose energetic non-violence will never win medals. Those who cry and mourn their loss because they have tasted the presence of love. The ones who hunger for what is right and who stay hungry until what is right becomes a reality. Those who scandalise us with their mercy because they exclude no one from its embrace.

The people who have an undivided heart, whose loyalty to God is never in question. Those who not only look for peace but do everything in their power to make peace and build a kingdom among the ruins. The faithful who are not fairweather Christians but who suffer persecution for the sake of the kingdom, and who still manage to smile at their persecutors. Those who are snarled at for their beliefs and who meet abuse with a blessing, who sing a song of the Lord for their captors.

These people are among us. They are the same as the saints that Paul addressed, the faithful of Jesus Christ. They are real people whose stories may never be told and whose goodness may never be celebrated. We celebrate them today and we bless them in the name of the Lord.

Past and present
The kingdom of God is not peopled by cardboard cut-outs or robots programmed to perform as their designer planned. The kingdom is peopled by those who have gone before us and those among us who live Gospel lives. Goodness is not limited to any age of history: neither the past nor the present has a monopoly on saints. We belong to a community that has a history of goodness and fidelity to the Gospel. We are related to those who went before us, those who linked their belief to those who went before them. We are part of that chain of holiness.

We belong to the sanctified brethren. You might feel uncomfortable with that – like having six toes. But it is not something to be explained but to be rejoiced in. We are a small part of a marvellous company of believers who struggle into holiness.

And we are not abandoned to our own devices; we have our ancestors in faith who are blessed in heaven. In John's vision he sees "a huge number, impossible to count, of people from every nation, race, tribe and language". Among them are counted people who know us and love us. There will even be some from Lake Wobegon, from the places that no one has heard of. The sanctified brethren, today we salute them.

Joy eternal

Loss and return

There is a sacred story from the Jewish tradition which tells of a certain rabbi and his wife who had two sons to whom they were extremely devoted. One Sabbath morning while the rabbi was teaching the Law in the synagogue, both boys were struck by a sudden illness and died. Their mother laid them out on a bed and covered them with a white sheet. When the rabbi came home for his meal and asked where the children were, his wife made some excuse and waited until the rabbi had eaten.

She did not answer her husband's question but instead asked one of him. "I am placed in a difficulty," she said, "because some time ago a person entrusted to my care some possessions of great value which he now wants me to give back. I am unsure of what to do. Am I obliged to return these great valuables to him?"

"That you should need to put this question surprises me," the rabbi replied. "There can be no doubt about what you must do. How can you hesitate to restore to everyone what is his own?"

His wife then rose from the table and asked the rabbi to follow her. She led him to the room where the two bodies lay and pulled back the sheet. "My sons, my sons," groaned the father in pain. "The Lord gave and the Lord has taken away," said his wife through her tears. "Blessed be the name of the Lord. You have always taught me to restore without reluctance what has been lent to us for our happiness. We have to return our two sons to the God of all mercies."

Those who have returned home

Just as Mary was forced to give up her only Son, just as she had to return to God the Father the great gift of life he gave to her in Jesus his Son, so we must learn to return to God those who have died. Today we celebrate their sacred memory, today we remember them as the faithful departed. They are not just the faithful departed from us, they are the faithful returned to God. Our faith calls on us not only to lament our loss but to celebrate their gain. And to pray for their eternal peace.

Like the Jewish woman in the story, we are consoled by our faith in difficult times. Of course, faith does not banish our sense of loss, but it affirms the great truth that all life is a gift from God. Who we are is what we have been given. Our faith also educates the hope we share that we will return to the source of life, the God of all beginnings. Death is not a door into the dark, it is a dark door into the light. Those we have loved and all the faithful departed have passed through that door, and during this Mass

we pray for their eternal peace and joy.

Sometimes non-believers say that we are deceiving ourselves by hoping in heaven. But we can say with St Paul: "Hope is not deceptive, because the love of God has been poured into our hearts by the Holy Spirit which has been given us." Our hope is not wishful thinking but is grounded in the love of God within us. Only in that love can we hope; without it, we are helpless.

The love of God within us urges us to believe, urges us to hope; it directs us to the very source of our being. In a peculiar sense our faith and our hope will be fully realised only in death. Only in death can we face the love that called us by name and calls us to return.

Joy eternal

Today we hold holy the memory of all the faithful who have been called to return to God. We bless God for the many ways they have enriched our families, our communities, our life of faith. We pray that as we remember their names before God, they will remember us. The faith and love that bound us together with them in life still binds us in their new life.

We pray that their prayers will support our own hope as we continue our journey in faith. Our journey is the road that will take us to eternal joy. As St Alphonsus Liguori wrote:

> This earth is for us a battlefield
> where we have to fight and conquer
> in order to be saved.
> But when we reach heaven
> our state is changed.
> There will be no more toil, but rest;
> no more fear, but security;
> no more sadness or weariness,
> but gladness
> and Joy Eternal.

The charity that goes beyond death

Iron Annie

The priest was working as a chaplain in a New York hospital. One of the patients, an old lady who was dying, never received any visitors. She told the chaplain to stop bothering her with his visits: "Look, son, I don't need professional mourners. You've got to do your duty, but don't do it on me. There's plenty of people to exercise yourself on – go to them and leave me alone."

The nurses and doctors were more than kind to her, but they met with a rebuff that was not as delicately phrased as the one the chaplain received. They all felt hurt and helpless. All the other patients in the ward received regular visitors, but "Iron Annie" as she was called liked to boast to the others that she needed no one. She had played hide-and-seek with God whom she claimed had lost interest in the game long ago. She would go out as she had lived, neither looked for nor remembered.

The chaplain continued to stop by her bed; she continued to swear at him for his "cussedness". He explained that he was Scottish, but that offered no historical insight. Three weeks passed. At 2.20 a.m. the chaplain woke to the sound of the phone ringing. The nurse apologised for the lateness of the hour, but Iron Annie wanted to know why he never wore a kilt and would he care to explain? She added that the explanation would be too late in the morning.

The hospital was only a few minutes walk from the rectory and when the chaplain arrived at the bedside, Iron Annie greeted him with a well-rehearsed curse. They both laughed in relief. Under cover of darkness, they talked of kilts and Scottish cussedness, of night wards and rectories and loneliness. Iron Annie unloaded an old grief that had been part of her baggage for too long. The two exchanged blessings and said no more. There was nothing more to say. The divine game of hide-and-seek had ended with a find. Iron Annie died just after eight o'clock that morning.

Two nurses came to the funeral; they made up the congregation. Neither of them was asked to come; they came to show their respect and because they believed that no one should make their final departure alone. Their simple gesture of kindness gave the funeral an enormous dignity: as they cared for the living, so they cared for the dead. The chaplain and the nurses lived an ancient truth: it is good to remember the dead and to pray for them.

Hope is not deceptive

The Church has always taught that our charity should not be limited to the living. Charity and prayer have the power to cross the last boundary – death itself – and when we celebrate the feast of All Souls we pray for the dead and keep their memory alive. Today's feast is keeping a pledge not to forget. Not to forget those who have gone before us, those who await completion, those who can still be touched by the charity that finds its voice in prayer.

Unless we are very young, probably all of us have experienced the death of someone we loved. No matter how prepared we are for the death of those we love, their death is always a numbing experience. Because we love people, we miss them when they die. And we can feel disabled inside for a long time. We can feel abandoned like the two disciples on the road to Emmaus. In the death of Jesus they feel orphaned. They leave Jerusalem, the place where everything went wrong, and try to put it behind them.

They are joined in their journey by a stranger who invites them to share their story. In telling their story they tell themselves: both had hoped that Jesus would be the Messiah, but now that he is dead their hopes are dead too. They are two people whose hope is all behind them. They have nothing to look forward to, nothing to live for. They are ex-followers of a dead prophet with nowhere to go but away from Jerusalem.

Then the stranger tells his story. That suffering and death have their own place in the plan of God; that they can lead to the glory of the kingdom. The two disciples ask him: "Stay with us, for it is almost evening and the day is now far spent." He goes in to stay with them. The stranger gives himself away by giving himself away in the breaking of the bread. They realise that Jesus is risen. And when they realise that, *they* are changed. They are now disciples of the risen Lord. They have a future again. They have a story to tell. Their hope had not been deceptive after all. Christ has conquered death itself, and in him our hope is reborn.

Hope extended to the dead

We believe that Jesus is Lord. We believe that he is Lord not only of the living but of the dead. That is our faith, which gives substance to our hope. Our hope is not deceptive and it is extended to all who have died and who await the day of their fulfilment when they see God face to face.

We gather to pray for all the dead who need our prayer. We pray for those we have known and we pray for those we never knew. Our charity and our prayers embrace all those who have died lonely deaths in the absence of love and support. They are part of our ministry of prayer. When we die we will be encouraged by the charity of the Christian community which will remember us in prayer. We keep that tradition of charity alive today when we pray for the dead.

"You are God's building"

Visible Christianity

One of the first trials any group or movement has to face early in its life is its critics. Among other things, at least it's a sign of being taken seriously. In the second century A.D. Christianity was under attack from Greek and Roman thinkers who argued that it was a godless religion which engaged in barbaric practices. These attacks gave rise to a group of people known as apologists, those who defended Christianity against these charges. One of the earliest of these defenders was a Greek philosopher, Aristides, who addressed his apology to the Roman emperor Hadrian. These are his words:

> Christians love one another. They never fail to help widows; they save orphans from those who would hurt them. If a man has something, he gives freely to the man who has nothing. If they see a stranger, Christians take him home and are happy, as though he were a real brother...If they hear that one of them is in jail, or persecuted for professing the name of their redeemer, they all give him what he needs...This is really a new kind of person. There is something divine in them.

That is the defence of the Christians by a man who was not a Christian himself, but who argued that the good of the Christian community was evident for all to see. As a working description of Christians today it might seem more promising than actual. We all know from experience that the visible community of believers has its fair share of the crooked and the cracked. Most of us are invisible Christians most of the time whose Christianity appears at intervals; but we are committed to letting our Christianity become more visible so that something of the divine may show through.

"You are God's building"

About seventy years before the philosopher from Athens wrote his defence of the Christian faith, Paul wrote to the Christian community at Corinth, in the south of Greece. He had stayed there for about eighteen months working as a tent-maker and preaching the message of Jesus in the public squares and in houses. By the time Paul left, he had established a thriving Christian community in a city that was renowned both for its culture and its squalor. When he writes to them later, Paul encourages the community he has left behind to see themselves as God's building. They are God's holy temple, and as such they are a sacred people.

The Greek word for church is *ekklesia,* which does not mean a building but an assembly called together, a community of those who believe. We are part of the universal Church, the people who profess their belief in the Lordship of Jesus. As a community of believers, we are united in faith under the leadership of the Pope and the bishops, the successors of Peter and the apostles. We all recognise that we have Christ for our foundation.

We belong to the same Church as the community of believers at Corinth. Like them we are invited to see ourselves as God's building – not a building of bricks and mortar, but a building of flesh and blood, a community of faith and charity. When a building is dedicated it stays dedicated just by being there. But we are a dedicated Church not because we can point to our dedicated buildings, but because we can point to a dedicated community. We do not dedicate a thing; we dedicate our freedom in the service of the Gospel.

And we know that we do not stay dedicated just by existing. Our dedication can become old and tired; we can become disenchanted with the Church; we can feel that we no longer belong or want to belong. We can stop taking responsibility for seeing ourselves as the Church, as God's building, and instead see the Church as *that crowd* who make life difficult for everyone else. There are times when all of us become tired of it all.

A Church dedicated to renewal

That is why we need to renew our dedication. We stay dedicated not just by existing, but by struggling to grow up in the faith and taking responsibility for our own crowd. Warts and all. There are times when we need the faith and love of the community to support us in our weakness and failure; there are times when we can help others grow because something of the divine shows through our genuine efforts to help people without humiliating them, to care for them without imposing ourselves on them.

The Church still needs to be defended without being whitewashed. In his autobiography, *Blessings in Disguise,* the English actor Alec Guinness speaks with love about the Church he joined many years ago:

> She has books to read aloud, pictures to show, consolations to offer, strength to give and some marvellous people, from all ages, to hold up for the world's admiration; not many in high places, perhaps, but thousands in the market square, hospital ward, back pew, desert and jungle.

These are the people who make up the Church. We are privileged to be numbered among them, and for that, we give thanks today.

GOSPEL INDEX

Index of Gospel Passages

Index of Gospel Passages